THE PENGUIN CLASSICS

FOUNDER EDITOR (1944–64): E. V. RIEU

Editor: Betty Radice

ARISTOTLE was born at Stageira, in the dominion of the kings of Macedonia, in 384 B.C. For twenty years he studied at Athens in the Academy of Plato, on whose death in 347 he left, and some time later became tutor of the young Alexander the Great. When Alexander succeeded to the throne of Macedonia in 336, Aristotle returned to Athens and established his own school and research institute, the Lyceum, to which his vast erudition attracted a large number of scholars. After Alexander's death in 323, anti-Macedonian feeling drove Aristotle out of Athens, and he fled to Chalcis in Euboea, where he died in 322. His writings, which were of extraordinary range, profoundly affected the whole course of ancient and medieval philosophy, and they are still eagerly studied and debated by philosophers today. Very many of them have survived, and among the most famous are the *Ethics* (also in Penguin Classics) and the *Politics*.

THOMAS ALAN SINCLAIR was Professor of Greek at the Queen's University of Belfast for twenty-seven years before his death in 1961. He was also Dean of the Faculty of Theology and, for eleven years, Secretary of the Academic Council. Prior to his Belfast appointment, he held posts at Southampton University and Birkbeck College, London, and was a Fellow of St John's College, Cambridge, from which he had graduated. He published a number of books; the most widely known, his *History of Greek Political Thought*, has been translated into several languages.

TREVOR J. SAUNDERS was born in Wiltshire in 1934, and was educated at Chippenham Grammar School, University College London, and Emmanuel College, Cambridge. He has taught at the Universities of London and Hull, and is now Professor of Greek at the University of Newcastle upon Tyne; he has been Visiting Member of the Institute for Advanced Study, Princeton. His main interest is in Greek philosophy, especially political, social and legal theory, on which he has published numerous works, including a translation of Plato's *Laws* in Penguin Classics. His recreations include railway history and the cinema.

ARISTOTLE
THE POLITICS

———— ✳ ————

TRANSLATED BY T. A. SINCLAIR,
REVISED AND RE-PRESENTED BY
TREVOR J. SAUNDERS

PENGUIN BOOKS

Penguin Books Ltd, Harmondsworth, Middlesex, England
Penguin Books, 40 West 23rd Street, New York, New York 10010, U.S.A.
Penguin Books Australia Ltd, Ringwood, Victoria, Australia
Penguin Books Canada Ltd, 2801 John Street, Markham, Ontario, Canada L3R 1B4
Penguin Books (N.Z.) Ltd, 182–190 Wairau Road, Auckland 10, New Zealand

—

The translation by T. A. Sinclair first published 1962
Revised edition 1981
Reprinted 1982, 1983, 1984

—

Made and printed in Great Britain by
Richard Clay (The Chaucer Press) Ltd,
Bungay, Suffolk
Set in Linotype Baskerville

TO THE MEMORY OF

T. A. SINCLAIR

Last Easter I read the greater part of the *Politics*: last month I read the whole of it . . . It is an amazing book. It seems to me to show a Shakespearian understanding of human beings and their ways, together with a sublime good sense.

Henry Jackson, letter to J. A. Platt, 16 August 1900

CONTENTS

THE POLITICS

CONTENTS

CONTENTS

CONTENTS

CONTENTS

TRANSLATOR'S INTRODUCTION
BY T. A. SINCLAIR

ARISTOTLE'S LIFE AND WORKS

ARISTOTLE was born in 384 B.C. at Stageira in Chalcidice
which was part of the dominion of the kings of Macedon. He
was the son of a physician who attended the family of King
Amyntas. Later the throne was occupied by Philip, who spent
his life augmenting the power and territory of Macedon and
making it dominant among Greek states, whereas prior to his
reign it had lain somewhat on the fringe. At the age of about
seventeen Aristotle went to Athens and became a student in
the famous Academy of Plato. Here he studied mathematics,
ethics and politics, and we do not know what else besides. He
remained there, a teacher but still a learner, for twenty years.
At this period he must have written those works which Plutarch called Platonic, dialogues on ethical and political subjects, which were much admired in antiquity for their style
but which are now lost. After the death of Plato in 346 he left
the Academy, possibly disappointed that he had not been
chosen to succeed him as head. In any case it was quite time
that he left. The Academy offered little scope for his rapidly
extending intellectual interests. With a few companions he
crossed the Aegean Sea to Asia Minor and settled at Assos
in the Troad. Here he continued his scientific studies, especially in marine biology. It is doubtful whether he wrote anything at this period, but the experience had a profound
effect on his general outlook on the physical world and his
view of man's place in it. Man was an animal, but he was
the only animal that could be described as 'political', capable
of, and designed by nature for, life in a *polis*. It was at this
period of his life also that he married his first wife; she too was
a Macedonian. In 343 he returned to his native land whither
he had been invited to teach King Philip's young son, the
future Alexander the Great. He did this for about two years,
but what he taught him and what effect either had upon
the other remain obscure. We know very little about the next

four or five years but by 336 B.C. he was in Athens with his family.

Politically much had happened at Athens during his ten years' absence. The eloquence of Demosthenes had not been sufficient to stir up effective resistance to the increasing encroachment of Aristotle's own King Philip. After winning the battle of Chaeronea in 338 Philip had grouped most of the Greek states into a kind of federation firmly under the control of Macedon. Preparations were set afoot for an invasion of Asia, but Philip was assassinated in 336 and it was Alexander who led the expedition. At Athens opinion about Philip had long been divided. Macedonian supporters were fairly numerous among the wealthier upper classes and among these Aristotle had friends; he also had the useful backing of the Macedonian Antipater whom Alexander left in charge. So he had no difficulty in realizing his ambition of establishing at Athens a philosophical school of his own. He was a foreigner, not a citizen, and so could not legally own property there; but arrangements were made for a lease, and his school, the Lyceum, with its adjoining Walk (*Peripatos*), was successfully launched. Thus the most important and productive period of Aristotle's life, that of his second sojourn at Athens, coincides with the period when Alexander was conquering the Eastern world – a fact which no one could guess from reading his works. The news of Alexander's death in 323 was a signal for a revival of anti-Macedonian feeling at Athens, and Aristotle judged it prudent to retire to Euboea, where he died in the following year at the age of about sixty-two.

At the Lyceum, Aristotle had a staff of lecturers to assist him. These included the botanist Theophrastus, author of *Characters*, a man whose learning must have been as diversified as that of Aristotle. Perhaps, like the Regents in Scottish Universities in the eighteenth century, the staff were expected to teach a variety of subjects, theoretical and practical, and their surviving writings are a reflection of what they taught. But the distinction between *theōrētikē* and *praktikē* was not at all the same as between theory and practice. They were two separate branches of knowledge, not two different ways of dealing with knowledge. The former, regarded as truly philosophical and truly scientific, was based on *theōria*, observation *plus* contemplation. This branch included theology, metaphysics, astronomy, mathematics, biology, botany, meteorology; and on these subjects Aristotle lectured and wrote extensively. To the practical branch belong the works entitled *Ethics*, *Politics*, *Rhetoric*, and *Poetics*. Of course these subjects, no less than the 'scientific' group, must be based on collecting and studying the available data. But the data, arising as they do out of human endeavour, are of a different and less stable kind. Moreover these sciences have a practical aim and the students were expected to become in some measure practitioners. In *Ethics* and *Politics*, for example, it does not suffice to learn what things are; they must find out also what can be done about them.

ARISTOTLE'S 'POLITICS' IN THE PAST

There was a story current in antiquity that after Aristotle's death his unpublished works (that is most of the Aristotle that we have) were hidden in a cellar in Scepsis in the Troad and remained there unknown till the first century B.C. The story is probably untrue but there is no doubt that his *Politics* was not much studied during that time. Polybius, who was well read in Plato and would have had good reason to read the *Politics*, shows no real acquaintance with it. Cicero too, who *might* have read the *Politics* if the story is true that the manuscript reached Rome in Sulla's time, seems not to have done so. But Cicero knew Aristotle's earlier and published works, the now lost dialogues, including 'four books about justice'. Besides, teaching at the Lyceum continued to deal with *Politica* after the death of Aristotle, and the works of the Peripatetics Theophrastus and Dicaearchus were well known. Thus in various ways the political philosophy of the Lyceum may have been familiar to the men learned among Romans. Still, there is no denying the fact that both for Greeks and Romans the fame of Plato's *Republic* quite outshone that of Aristotle's *Politics* during classical antiquity. The same is true of Aristotle's work in general; it was little read in the days of the Roman Empire. Some of it (but not the *Politics*) became known in the West through the Latin translations of Boethius in the sixth century A.D. In the East, translations were made into Syriac and thence into Arabic. Some of these Arabic translations eventually found their way to Europe by way of Spain, where they were closely studied by learned Jews, and Latin translations were made from the Arabic before the twelfth century. But again the *Politics* was not included. The influence of the *Ethics* and the *Politics* does not begin to appear in Western Christendom till the thirteenth century; and that beginning was due to three members of the Dominican Order – William of Moerbeke (in Flanders), Albert of Cologne, and, most of all, St Thomas of Aquino.

William of Moerbeke knew Greek sufficiently well to make a literal translation into Latin for the use of Albert and Thomas. His versions of the *Ethics* and the *Politics* are extant, barely intelligible but interesting as exercises in translation. St Thomas made constant use of them, and everything that he wrote touching upon politics, rulers, and states was strongly influenced by the *Politics*. The state itself was for him, as for Aristotle, something in accordance with nature, something good in itself and needed by man in order to fulfil his nature. St Augustine had seen in the state the institutions and laws of the Roman Empire, certainly not good in themselves, but necessary as a curb on man's sinful nature; and this view was not abandoned when the Empire broke up. St Thomas in discarding it does not, of course, accept Aristotle's view of the state in its entirety. He may agree with the philosopher about property and about usury and the need to control education; but to be a good citizen in a good society, to be well-endowed with property, virtue, and ability – this ideal could not be made to fit the contemporary outlook merely by the addition of religion. The good life must needs now be a Christian life and a preparation for Eternity. St Thomas reproduces much of the six-fold classification of constitutions which Aristotle sometimes used and sometimes ignored; but he really had little use for it. He found (as we find) that Aristotle has no clear-cut answer to give to the question 'which is the best form of constitution?' But he found plenty of warrant in the *Politics* for saying that the rule of one outstandingly good man, backed by just laws, is most desirable, if only it can be attained. Besides, here he was on familiar ground. For centuries monarchical rule of one kind or another had occupied the central position in political thought; the contrast between the good king and the bad tyrant had been part of the stock-in-trade since classical antiquity; obedience and disobedience, legal status and legal rights, these were the topics; and above all how to build up what they called a 'Mirror of Princes' for the monarch to copy. We must not forget that the *Policraticus* of John of Salisbury (A.D. 1159) was just as much a precursor of St Thomas's *De regimine principum* as was the *Politics* of Aristotle, which John had not read.

In the domination exercised by Aristotelian philosophy over scholastic thought in the later Middle Ages, the *Politics* had little part to play; its influence and prestige were very great but of a very different kind and in a different field. Dante, for example, in his *De Monarchia* (1311) differed utterly from St Thomas, but his work is just as much permeated by the thought and language (latinized) of the *Politics*. Even farther removed politically from St Thomas is Marsilius of Padua (*Defensor pacis*, 1324), yet here too the influence of the *Politics* is unmistakable. After the more general revival of classical learning in the fifteenth century, Plato and Cicero were more favoured than Aristotle by the majority of readers, but the *Politics*, which was first printed in 1498 (Aldine press), continued to be part of the essential background of political philosophers such as Machiavelli, Jean Bodin, or Richard Hooker. In the seventeenth century Thomas Hobbes poured scorn on the Aristotle of the Schoolmen, but his own *Leviathan* testifies to his reading of the *Politics*. In the eighteenth century a superficial acquaintance with the *Ethics* and the *Politics* could be taken for granted among educated Europeans. But it was not until the next century, and the publication in 1832 by the Prussian Academy of the great Berlin *Corpus* of his works that the study of Aristotle *as a Greek author* was really taken seriously. The *Politics* shared in this, and soon began to profit greatly from the industry and application of German scholarship. Political philosophy in its turn derived benefit from the translations and interpretations of nineteenth-century classical scholars and was enabled to see its own ancient antecedents in truer perspective. In the twentieth century this work continued unabated but political philosophy itself began to lose interest for academic philosophers. On the other hand there was a growing interest in the newer disciplines of anthropology and sociology, and the comparative study of political institutions. Where in all this does the *Politics* of Aristotle now stand?

ARISTOTLE'S 'POLITICS' TODAY

The *Politics* of Aristotle is still read as a textbook of political science in universities. It may be asked why this is so, why it has not been discarded, since all that is of value in it must surely have been absorbed and taken over by subsequent writers on the subject. Euclid was used as a textbook of geometry till well into the twentieth century, but his discoveries have been embodied in better textbooks for schools. For mathematicians the interest of Euclid is largely antiquarian; he is a part of the history of mathematics. Nor is Aristotle's biology any longer taught. Why is his *Politics* worth studying today for its own sake?

Broadly speaking the reasons are first, that the problems posed by ethical and political philosophy are not of a kind that can be solved once and for all and handed on to posterity as so much accomplished; and second, that the problems are still the same problems at bottom, however much appearances and circumstances may have altered in twenty-three centuries. How can men live together? The world has grown smaller and men are more than ever forced to live together. The problem is larger, more acute, and more complicated than it was when ancient philosophers first looked at it. How in particular can top-dog and under-dog be made to live together? Is it enough to say 'Give the top-dog arms and the under-dog enough to eat'? Or should there be only one class of dog? Then the under-dogs abolish the top-dogs, only to find themselves burdened with a new set. How perennial are the problems of government and how little they have changed are indeed all too clear. Recent events, the expansion of civilization, the spread of technological advances, and the growth of political power in all parts of the world have emphasized this. Western Europe no longer holds its former dominance either culturally or politically; but the *Politics* is not simply part of our Western heritage nor is it tied to the European political concepts which it helped to form. Just as it transcended the city-state era in which and for which it was written, so it has transcended both the imperialism and the nation-states of the nineteenth century. The nascent or half-formed states of Africa and Asia will recognize some of their own problems in Aristotle's *Politics*, just as the seeker after

18

norms of behaviour will learn from his *Ethics*. Neither will find, nor expect to find, ready-made answers to his questions, but it is always illuminating to see another mind, sometimes penetrating, sometimes obtuse, working on problems that are fundamentally similar to one's own, however different in time, setting, and local conditions.

Works written about the science of politics may be said very roughly to fall into two classes, one of which may be called prescriptive, the other descriptive. The one seeks to make a pattern of an ideal state and, in varying degrees according to the taste of the author, to lay plans for the realization of that pattern. The other examines the data of politics, looks at constitutions as they exist now or have existed in the past, and seeks to draw conclusions about the way they are likely to develop. It does not aim at describing an ideal state or at determining what kind of constitution is best. Both types of study have, actually or potentially, a practical use, the prescriptive with a blue-print for the future, the other analysing and comparing. Both may also move in the domain of pure theory, the one deducing from a set of principles what human behaviour in society ought to be, the other evolving principles of human behaviour from the ways in which men do in fact behave. This does not mean that a descriptive writer suspends value-judgement altogether; he can hardly avoid appraising, by some standard or other, the work of the consitutions which form the data of his subject.

The *Politics* of Aristotle belongs to both these classes and moves in and out of them. It is the only work of an ancient author of which that could be said. All through antiquity (and in more modern times too) the utopian method of study predominated. Long before Plato or Aristotle, the Greeks for good practical reasons had been asking themselves 'What is the best form of consitution?' And after Plato the fame of the *Republic* and the *Laws* kept much of political thought fastened to the same topics. In later antiquity discussions of the ideal state took the form of discussions about the perfect ruler, the ideal king. The search for the ideal state and the best constitution are of course the very heart of Aristotle's *Politics*; he had inherited the topic from his predecessors and is constantly commenting on and drawing from Plato. But he also had the analytical approach; it was part of his scientific cast of mind. And it is this that gives the *Politics* part of its special interest today, when the prescriptive method, from Plato to Marx, is out of fashion.

It is difficult to be a thoroughly detached observer even of the data of the physical sciences, virtually impossible when it comes to the study of man. Among the ancients only Thucydides came near to it. He observed and analysed human behaviour as manifested by nations at war, and nothing of that has changed since he wrote; but he was not a political theorist and nothing could have been farther from his mind than constructing a form of constitution. Yet even in the pages of Thucydides it is not difficult to see in broad outline what kind of policy he would prefer and would regard as best for Athens. All the more then when we come to Aristotle; his views about what is best are constantly to the fore and not always consistent. He draws a distinction between the ideally best, and the best in the circumstances or the best for a particular people; but his own ethical standards and political preferences stand out clearly at all times, even in those parts where the methods of descriptive analysis and comparison are extensively employed. Hence although we may reasonably say that Aristotle carried over from his biological studies to his political an analytical mind and a zeal for classifying and understanding all the data of his subject, we cannot claim that his observation is detached and unprejudiced. Nor of course must we fall into the common error of making such a claim for ourselves.

Again, Aristotle had more understanding than most ancient writers of the connection between politics and economics. Just because the links between these two are nowadays so complex, it may be useful to study observations that are based on a much simpler form of society, however barren they may seem in themselves. The acquisition and use of wealth, the land and its produce, labour, money, commerce, and exchange – such topics as these are perpetually interesting and much of the first book of the *Politics* is devoted to them. Aristotle proceeds from a discussion of household management (*oikonomia*), regarding that as state-management on a smaller scale; goods, money, labour, and exchange play a big part in both. All that he has to say on these matters is strongly coloured by two obsessions, first, his prejudices against trade and against coined money and second, his reluctance to be without a labour-force which was either the absolute property of the employer (slave-labour) or so economically dependent on him as to make their free status positively worthless. In his thinking about these matters Aristotle was saddled with a piece of theory which because of its quasi-scientific appearance had been resting as an incubus on much of Greek thought for a century or more; the notion that whatever is good is according to nature. The *polis* itself was for Aristotle obviously good; it was made by man, but by man acting according to his own nature. But commerce and labour were not so easy. In the matter of trade Aristotle decided that exchange and barter of surplus goods were natural but that the use of coined money as a medium of exchange was contrary to nature, as was also usury. To own property was natural and indeed most meritorious, so long as the property was land. But in accordance with the principle 'Nothing too much' (to which the average Greek paid no more than lip-service) Aristotle lays it down that unnecessary accumulation cannot be allowed. What he has to say about money-making, about the responsibilities of wealth and the possibility of private ownership co-existing with public use of property, has a particular interest today, since the habits, methods, and ethics of money-making have become subjects of interest and importance for a much larger section of the population than formerly. As regards slavery he was in a dilemma; slaves were both a form of property and a source of labour. He was aware that previous thinkers had shown that the enslavement of human beings, especially Greek by Greek, was contrary to nature. But he was sure that slaves were indispensable in creating the conditions for the life of culture which was the aim of the *polis*. He could not therefore reject slavery, but he must endeavour to prove that after all it is not contrary to nature and that the slave though a human being is designed by nature to be as a beast of burden. Needless to say the attempt breaks down (see Book I, Chapter v *ad fin.*), as he himself must have been aware. Yet the arguments which he used were still in use among the defenders of slavery in the nineteenth century; the difference between black and white races gave them just that outward manifestation of nature's supposed intention that Aristotle had looked for in vain (Book I, Chapter v).

Surprise is sometimes expressed that Aristotle continued to write about and to prescribe for the city-state, unaware that its era of independence had come to an end with the Macedonian conquest. But there is really no occasion for surprise; contemporaries cannot be expected to foresee the effects of events. Besides, the city-state was destined to remain the standard form of living for the majority of the Greek-speaking world for centuries yet to come. It is true that the cities had lost their absolute autonomy and notably their military power, so that they could not henceforth oppose the wishes of the Syrian, Macedonian, or other monarchs within whose territory they lay. But even in the time of the Roman Empire city-state life still went on; and if they had no real independence of action, there were still varying degrees of independence and certain privileges to be won.

But there *are* surprising things about Aristotle in his *Politics*. His attitude to slavery, to which reference has just been made, seems strange in one who must have read Euripides; and we do not know whether to ascribe it to callousness or to obtuseness. But he had other blind-spots; we can grant that he could not foresee the effects of the Macedonian domination and of Alexander's conquests. But was it necessary to omit all reference to them as if they were irrelevant to his subject? No one would ever guess from reading the *Politics* that Aristotle himself was a Macedonian or that a Macedonian king was then conquering the world. He has much to say about monarchy, but in spite of one or two casual references to Macedon we cannot see that either the country or its king was of the slightest interest to him, or that they presented, as they undoubtedly did, features worth mentioning. He makes a casual and unimportant reference to the murder of Philip in 336, but otherwise the latest identifiable event is the loss of Spartan military supremacy at the battle of Leuctra in 371. So one must conclude that the silence about modern times was deliberate. All the same it seems strange in a manual intended for practical use.

Aristotle was a subject of the king of Macedon. His status at Athens, while he lived there, was that of *metoikos*, resident alien. As we have seen, he had powerful friends there and his position was an easy one. But he was not a citizen, and the privileges of citizenship were to him a matter of supreme importance. Yet never at any time in his life had he the satisfaction of being a land-owning citizen of a Greek *polis*. Perhaps that is just the reason for his ceaseless insistence on citizenship (see especially Book III). As he realized the advantages of being a citizen, so too, one would think, he must have been fully alive to the disadvantages of not being one. His own position as a resident alien was tolerable enough, but what, in theory or in practice, would be the position of all the other non-citizens, permanent residents trying to earn their living? The number of persons in this category, neither slaves nor citizens but paid employees, might, in any form of constitution which Aristotle would tolerate, be fairly numerous, and it is surprising that he has little to say about them except that they are a possible source of discontent and a danger to the established order. Modern parallels in different parts of the world will occur to a discerning reader of the *Politics*; non-participation in the *politeia*, to use a phrase of Aristotle's, is a real problem. Aristotle hardly sees it as such, beyond making a plea for moderation (beginning of Book V). Nor did he see any connection between these and that other depressed class, the slaves; their legal status was different, and that was an end of the matter. In spite of their similar economic positions it was hardly even suspected that there could be common interests between slaves and free men.

The comparative study of political institutions in different countries is frequently made a part of the normal course of study in modern political science; and the fact that it began with Aristotle is an added reason for continuing to read him. He is known to have written, probably with the aid of collaborators, historical and descriptive accounts of 158 city constitutions. One of these, the Athenian, has survived largely intact on a series of papyrus-rolls discovered in Egypt in 1891. Aristotle refers to this collection in the concluding passage of his *Ethics* as being part of the material which he will use in his *Politics* (see Preface to Book I). He needs in particular to have examples to hand of the actual working of constitutions and to note the changes to which the different types are liable (see especially Book V). He also wishes to make comparisons with, and criticisms of, constitutions which only existed on paper, and for this he had in his library not only the *Republic* and the *Laws* of Plato but the work of other predecessors, most of them unknown now except for what he tells us (mostly in Book II). Thus he uses both actual and imagined states for comparative purposes. Between one source of comparison and another he casts his net pretty wide. Chiefly of course he is concerned with the typically Hellenic product, the city-state, including the non-Hellenic but very interesting Carthage. But not all Greeks lived in city-states, and there are frequent references to the fact that many peoples lived a much less centripetal life in communities of a varying degree of cohesion. (See Aristotle's own note on *ethnos,* Book II, Chapter ii). He knows monarchy well and describes many types of it but he shows no particular interest in the Macedonian type. Indeed his interest in monarchy is generaly either antiquarian or theoretical.

There is a tendency when reading Aristotle's *Politics* to interpret what he says about the city-state in terms of the modern nation-state. This is natural and in part appropriate, since independent sovereignty was the mark of, and the claim made by, the ancient *polis,* no less than the modern state. But in the history of political thought the notion of a state is not a constant in the way that the notion of triangle is a constant in the history of geometry. Wherever and whenever we read about the theory of the state we are reading about a conception of it current in the author's time or else created by him. About the ancient Greek state two salient points (apart from its size) need to be emphasized which at first sight appear to contradict each other; on the one hand its unity and solidarity, on the other its limited membership. Even in a democracy there would be numerous adult males who would be non-citizens or slaves; they would form no part of the *polis.* The city is made up of its members, its citizens, enrolled as such in accordance with the rules of the constitution. Much of what they do in their daily lives arises directly out of the fact of their membership. Not only the duties of administration, of military service, and of the courts of law, but equally games, religion, festivals, recreation, even eating and drinking, are often closely connected with membership of the state. In short the state embraced a much smaller proportion of the population but a much larger share in the daily lives of each. The extent to which these facts are true of any one state in history varies greatly, but for Aristotle as for Plato they are not only true but right.

Aristotle calls the state the supreme form of human association, not the only one. He recognizes the existence of others, but except for the household or family he has little to say about them separately; he is mainly concerned with organs of government within the different kinds of constitution. But when Aristotle calls man 'a political animal' he has in mind all aspects of life in humane society, all that contributes to 'the good life'. The smaller social units within the larger *koinōnia* of the state have an important part to play here, and one wishes that Aristotle had gone into greater detail. But it is legitimate to take the general principles governing the larger associations as applicable also to the smaller. We need not always be thinking of the modern nation-state as a single whole when we are reading about ancient *politeia*. There is an immense variety of the lesser units in any modern state. Some of these are closely connected with the constitution, others entirely separate from it; but all contribute in some measure to the life of the citizens and Aristotle would have regarded them as part of the *politeia*. The nineteenth century saw religious organizations becoming separated from the constitution, the twentieth has seen medicine, education, and even sport drawn into it. But all these bodies, great or small, and subordinate bodies under them, are associations of human kind, and much of what Aristotle has to say about the supreme form of association has application also to the lesser.

Like the ancient lawgivers the founders of a club or society, local or national, have to build a framework within which the members will together pursue the objects of their common purpose. A constitution has to be drawn up and rules agreed upon; the constitution will generally be what some ancient writers called a mixed one, the committee being an oligarchic element, the annual general meeting a democratic one. Clearly therefore the manner prescribed for elections to committees is a matter of supreme importance to all members, as Aristotle saw. But how rigid should this framework be? Can it be made to last for ever? Aristotle advises that a constitution should be of such a kind that the majority of its members will wish it to remain in being. But that is certainly no guarantee of permanence. Thus the questions raised in the *Politics* are not always those which concern the state and its rulers; they may be such as affect our daily lives and our social activities.

For Aristotle, as for Plato, the subject of political philosophy, or *politikē*, embraced the whole of human behaviour, the conduct of the individual equally with the behaviour of the group. Ethics was, therefore, a part of politics; we might also say that politics was a part of ethics. It was the aim of

25

political philosophy to establish standards of social behaviour. Aristotle is thinking of both aspects of the matter when he writes near the beginning of his *Ethics*: 'Our account of this science will be adequate if it achieves such clarity as the subject-matter allows; for the same degree of precision is not to be expected in all discussions, any more than in all the products of handicraft. Instances of morally fine and just conduct – which is what politics investigates – involve so much difference and variety that they are widely believed to be such only by convention and not by nature. Instances of goods involve a similar kind of variety, for the reason that they often have hurtful consequences. People have been destroyed before now by their money, and others by their courage. Therefore in discussing subjects, and arguing from evidence, conditioned in this way, we must be satisfied with a broad outline of the truth.... Since in every case a man judges rightly what he understands, and of this only is a good critic, it follows that while in a special field the good critic is a specialist, the good critic in general is the man with a general education. That is why a young man is not a fit person to attend lectures on political science, because he is not versed in the practical business of life from which politics draws its premisses and subject matter.'[1]

Alongside the strong ethical bias in political philosophy went a sense of the need for fixing standards. An ethical code had to be embodied in a code of law, and this code of law in turn described the whole framework of the social and political system and the moral standards under which the citizens were to live, and for which the Greek word was *politeia*, usually translated by 'Constitution'. Inevitably therefore young citizens had to learn these laws; only thus could they learn to live either the life of a citizen or the life of an individual following accepted standards of right and wrong. Thus when we say that a young Athenian was educated in the *laws* of his country, we do not mean legal education, but moral and social.

There is a short passage at the end of the *Ethics* which some editors omit as being properly part of the *Politics*. At

1. *The Ethics of Aristotle: The Nicomachean Ethics*, translated by J. A. K. Thomson, revised with notes and appendices by Hugh Tredennick, introduction and bibliography by Jonathan Barnes (Penguin Classics, Harmondsworth 1976), Book 1, Chapter iii.

any rate it clearly makes a transition from one to the other and refers to some at any rate of the books of Aristotle's *Politics* as we have them. We will therefore translate this passage[1] as a preliminary to Book I, remembering, however, that we do not know that Aristotle so intended.

*

The text used is that of O. Immisch (Teubner). It has been translated in its entirely, including those passages which were bracketed by Immisch; but his bracketings and insertions of isolated words have been respected. His use of marks of parenthesus has not always been followed. The printing of some parts of the text as footnotes is due to the translator; it follows a principle now well established in Penguin translations and of proved assistance to the reader. The *Politics* has often before been translated into English, but the only version which has been at all times beside the present translator is that of one of his early teachers, H. Rackham (Loeb Library). It will be evident that the present translation is of an entirely different character. It aims at offering to English readers the *Politics* as a whole. In an attempt to convey something of the complexity of meaning attaching to certain Greek terms different English words have been used to translate them. At the same time the reader's attention is often called to these important terms in the passages (printed in italics) which are at intervals inserted in the text. It is hoped that these will help the reader to follow the drift of Aristotle's discourse, but he should remember, first, that these are no substitute for a commentary on the text, and second that the translator's interpretation of Aristotle's meaning may not always command acceptance. He has attempted to make the *Politics* readable; he could not be expected to make it all easy.

Notes by the Reviser

1. The above introduction is reproduced unchanged from the first edition, except that a few references have been recast and the long quotation from the *Nicomachean Ethics* has been supplied in the version published in the Penguin Classics in 1976.

1. It is not included in Thomson's translation of the *Ethics*.

2. This revision of the *Politics* has been carried out on the basis of the most readily available and widely used text: *Aristotelis Politica*, ed. W. D. Ross (Oxford Classical Text, 1957). I have departed from it on only a few occasions, which are indicated in footnotes.

3. In my own introduction I discuss the principles and aims of the revision, with some reference to Sinclair's final paragraph above.

T.J.S.

REVISER'S INTRODUCTION
BY T. J. SAUNDERS

A MODERN REPORT ON THE 'POLITICS'

Let us suppose that Aristotle is alive today, and has submitted his *Politics* to a publisher. The publisher's reader, a man of few words and incisive judgement, reports as follows:

Author: Aristotle   *Title*:   The Politics

Theme and Content. Survey and analysis of ancient Greek political theory and practice; concludes with recommendations of an 'ideal' state. Shows intimate knowledge of the whole field. Firmly based on historical detail. Full of revealing information and shrewd critical comment. Philosophical standpoint unfashionable, but none the worse for that. Sheer intellectual quality very high.

Presentation and Arrangement. Not so much a book, more like a series of loosely related monographs. Sequence of topics ostensibly systematic, in fact meandering; relation of one part to another often obscure. By contrast, argument of the individual sections, taken simply on their own, lucid and coherent (though sometimes over-compressed).

Assessment. Important work; likely to be controversial and influential.

Markets. Classics; political history and theory; constitutional studies; law.

Recommendation. Accept, subject to revision of presentation.

How then did such a remarkable work come to be written? To answer this question we have to turn detective; and we have few clues apart from the internal evidence of the text itself.

TEACHING AND RESEARCH IN THE LYCEUM

The *Politics* dates from roughly the last dozen years of Aristotle's life, from 335 till 323, when he was in Athens engaged in teaching and research in the Lyceum. It is written in a highly distinctive style: it is plain and simple and stripped for action; it has the spare charm of economy; its only rhetoric is the absence of rhetoric; but it sports occasional anecdotes, poetical quotations, pithy maxims and wry jests. It has also what are perhaps the faults of its very merits: it can be bafflingly cryptic and elliptical. But in general it is a perfect vehicle for its special purpose, philosophy; and therein lies its beauty.[1]

In structure and organization, as the publisher's reader noted, the text is often puzzling: Aristotle is apt to announce, with some austere flourish, what seems to be a systematic programme of inquiry, which he carries out in part; then he digresses; then he resumes the programme in a different form, and from a different point of view; in the course of discussion he makes promises he does not fulfil, and then tells us the inquiry is complete – and thereupon announces a fresh programme on a fresh topic. All his advanced work[2] is more or less like this; but the *Politics* is disorderly to a degree.

The most common explanation of this state of affairs is not simply that Aristotle was an untidy genius, but that the texts we have are the notes he used when he gave lectures or conducted seminars in the Lyceum. We may reasonably conjecture that he lectured frequently on the same topic, and that the semi-organized state of the text has come about because of his fresh starts, second thoughts, insertions, deletions, and retreading of old ground with different interests or questions or

---

1. Compare Richard Robinson's splendid description of his personal reaction to Aristotle's style (*Aristotle's Politics, Books III and IV*, Oxford, 1962, pp. xxvii–xxx). He remarks *inter alia*: '... unlike most people, I really enjoy it ... Aristotle's style is ... dense, tightlipped and sketchy.... His style is beautiful.'

2. On the other categories of Aristotle's works, see page 32 footnote 3 and page 34, footnote 2.

answers in mind – and all this over a period of several years, and under the constant stimulus of suggestions and objections from an ever-changing body of pupils. At some point, we may suppose, either he himself or an editor arranged all his material on political and social questions in a roughly intelligible order, in which condition, under the title *Ta Politika*, 'The Politics', it has survived.

But if we suppose that the text was meant *only* as lecture-notes, we must face the difficulty that it does not really consist of 'notes' at all. It amounts to something appreciably more elaborate than mere ungrammatical and unsyntactical jottings designed only to 'trigger' a train of thought in a speaker skilled at ad-libbing. Grammar and syntax are usually perfect, the argument is presented in logical and carefully connected steps, and the choice and order of words exhibit a certain minimum attention to literary grace. It may be of course that Aristotle was *not* good at ad-libbing, and needed a continuous discourse to read out. Yet the text will hardly suit that purpose either: it is too close-knit, too tightly argued, to be taken in at a hearing; it has rather the character of plainly stated raw material, inviting leisurely reflection. What we seem to have, then, is something intermediate between mere notes and a fully elaborated discourse; and the clarity and consistency of thought and uniformity of style discourage the alternative hypothesis that we have inherited notes taken in class by Aristotle's students, which they subsequently wrote up.[1]

The suggestion that the text represents notes made by Aristotle for use in teaching is therefore plausible, but not utterly free of difficulty. The best solution is perhaps to suppose that he disliked ad-libbing from notes, but was happy enough to enlarge impromptu on the relatively full texts that have come down to us. But whether he so used them or whether he did not, he surely intended them to serve another and ultimately more important purpose. He was an encyclopedist and a polymath; his Lyceum was a research institute; it possessed a library and a collection of objects (e.g. maps) useful both for

1. R. Weil briefly and judiciously assesses the character of Aristotle's writings in *Aristote et l'histoire: essai sur la 'Politique'* (Paris, 1960), pp. 52–6; cf. Newman II, pp. xxxv–xxxix (see page 478 below for full reference).

teaching and for research.[1] Many passages in his works conclude with a formula such as 'it is now clear that ...', or 'now that we have settled these points,' which show that he believes that a problem has been isolated, investigated, discussed and at least partly or provisionally solved. It looks as if we have the records of completed research, which were deposited in the library for consultation and for possible correction or amplification in the light of further inquiry. Those who subsequently turned to them found not disjointed notes, but material sufficiently *fully* written to be intelligible on deliberate and reflective reading, yet sufficiently *succinctly* written to be copied without undue labour; and it would be open to the insertion of passages of revision, amendment or addition. In short, Aristotle's works demand *readers*.[2]

It is unlikely, though not impossible, that these specialized treatises were meant for readers outside the Lyceum; but some few do seem to have found their way to a limited public.[3] The story, if it be true, of their vicissitudes after Aristotle's death is quite amazing, and clearly there were many opportunities for them to be lost, damaged or disorganized.[4] It was not until the middle of the first century B.C. that they were edited and published, by Andronicus of Rhodes; all our texts derive ultimately from his edition.

1. See H. Jackson's entertaining account of the equipment of Aristotle's lecture-room, 'Aristotle's lecture-room and lectures', *Journal of Philology*, 35 (1920), pp. 191–200. For an exhaustive discussion of the Lyceum's status and organization, see J. P. Lynch, *Aristotle's School: A Study of a Greek Educational Institution* (Berkeley, 1972).

2. Cf. J. L. Stocks, 'The composition of Aristotle's *Politics*', *Classical Quarterly*, 21 (1927), pp. 177–87, esp. p. 180: 'The architectonic seems to me to point rather to the library than to the lecture room', and I. Düring, 'Notes on the history of the transmission of Aristotle's writings', *Symbolae Philologicae Gotoburgenses*, 56. 3, 1958: '... an oral tradition in written form.'

3. For an account of Aristotle's 'exoteric' or non-specialized works, which were written in a more finished style and for a wider circulation, see e.g. G. E. R. Lloyd, *Aristotle: The Growth and Structure of His Thought* (Cambridge, 1968), pp. 9–13.

4. Most accounts of Aristotle's life and works rehearse the intriguing details.

THE CONTENTS AND STRUCTURE OF THE 'POLITICS'

What exactly, then, has come down to us? It is obvious that we do not have a work which has been systematically organized and finally polished for publication by the author, but 'a number of originally independent essays, which are not completely worked up into a whole'.[1] Unfortunately, it is often by no means clear exactly where the 'independent essays' begin and end; but here is at any rate a conspectus of the contents:

Book I: Origins and nature of the household and the state as associations; the economics of the household, with special reference to the role of slaves; history and analysis of the modes of acquiring property.

Book II: Review of ideal states, both projected and existing.

Book III: Classification of constitutions according to varying conceptions prevailing within them of the 'just' distribution of political power; more specifically, since political power is the prerogative of *citizens*, a review of various answers to the question, 'Who ought to be a citizen?'

Book IV: Survey of the main types of constitution, of their suitability to various kinds of citizen-bodies, and of the chief departments of state (deliberative, executive and judicial).

Books V and VI: Analysis of the causes of instability and permanence in the various constitutions.

Books VII and VIII: The construction of the ideal state (site, population, etc.), with special reference to education and the arts.

Comparison of this summary with the detailed chapter-by-chapter table of contents reveals that while it is possible to isolate the broad theme of a book, the sequence of topics is not fully systematic. In part, this must be because politics is not a discipline with precise boundaries, and it is fairly easy to move from one topic to another by a loose association of ideas. Some

1. W. D. Ross, *Aristotle* (5th ed., Oxford, 1949), p. 15 (The divisions into books and chapters are not Aristotle's, though they are mostly neat enough and no doubt often occur at what he himself would have regarded as the 'natural breaks'.)

individual chapters seem almost haphazardly placed (e.g. VI viii), while groups of others obviously cohere, e.g. IV xiv–xvi:

    xiv The Deliberative Element in the Constitution.
    xv The Executive Element in the Constitution.
    xvi The Judicial Element in the Constitution.

On the larger scale too, there are some curious and striking features, e.g.
(a) Why are Books VII and VIII, the description of Aristotle's ideal state, clearly so very incomplete?
(b) Why are VII and VIII so widely separated from the discussion of other ideal states in II?
(c) Why, in spite of some words at the end of III suggesting that VII should follow immediately, do IV–VI intervene?
(d) Why are IV–VI, in particular, so unusually 'realistic' and 'empirical', replete as they are with historical evidence?

There are countless other oddities of structure and detail that for many years fuelled a very vigorous controversy about the composition of the work. Some editors simply printed VII and VIII immediately after III, and put IV–VI last, on the grounds that the order of the books had become muddled in transmission. Jaeger treated II–III and VII–VIII as an *early* version; VII and VIII he regarded as Platonic in tone and detail,[1] and as dating from the 340s, when Aristotle was still working under Plato's inspiration; IV–VI dated from the very last period of Aristotle's career, when he had moved away from Platonic idealism, and was far more interested in the systematic collection and analysis of the facts of Greek political life, being now able to draw on the material in at least some of the 158 'Constitutions' assembled and described by members of the Lyceum.[2] By contrast, von Arnim saw VII and VIII

1. For the Platonic reminiscences in these books, see also E. Barker, *Greek Political Theory, Plato and His Predecessors* (London, 1918), pp. 380–82; 5th ed. (1960), pp. 443–4.
2. These 'Constitutions', and other collections of facts on a wide variety of topics, are the ancient forerunners of our modern surveys based on systematic fieldwork and/or questionnaires. Aristotle's conclusions about Greek politics are sometimes so familiar that they seem true to the point of triteness; yet given the state of communications in the ancient world, and the paucity of reliable records, the ability to base even obvious conclusions, let alone

(prefaced by II) as noticeably *un*-Platonic, and as reflecting Aristotle's own mature views of his latest period, when he had departed furthest from Platonic doctrine.[1]

We need not linger over these and similar theories, some of which are of pixilating complexity. They depend largely on arbitrary assumptions about the order in which the subject-matter of the *Politics* ought logically to be arranged, and on controversial hypotheses about Aristotle's gradual self-liberation from Platonic influence. I touch on them only because a modern reader of the *Politics* should be aware that he is reading something of a medley, a work not fully formed but in gestation; in particular, he should be alert to the possibility that books and chapters may be in a sequence not intended by Aristotle, and that they may date from different stages of his career. The controversies about these matters have in fact proved largely inconclusive, and today most people are content to take the *Politics* on its own terms and accept it for what it is: a series of topics examined and re-examined from a single and fundamentally consistent standpoint.[2] Seen in this light, the variations of treatment and discrepancies of approach are utterly natural; and they are witnesses not only to the fluidity and versatility of Aristotle's philosophical methods, but to the rich complexity of Greek political ideas and practice.

---

unobvious ones, on a survey of the relevant facts is in itself a tremendous achievement. (Not that Aristotle himself, in all probability, wrote more than a few of the 'Constitutions'; presumably most were compiled by persons we should today call 'research assistants' or 'research students', who could cut their scholarly teeth in this manner, much as a modern research student writes his dissertation. Perhaps Aristotle laid down a certain standard pattern of presentation and supervised the day-to-day work; certainly he exploited the results: see 'Preface to Book I'.)

1. For full references to the work of Jaeger and von Arnim, see the Select Bibliographies.

2. See C. J. Rowe's sensible judgement: 'We may need the genetic method to explain the peculiarities of the form of the *Politics*; but in the end it will not, I think, seriously affect our interpretation of its contents' ('Aims and methods in Aristotle's *Politics*', *Classical Quarterly*, 27 (1977), pp. 159–172 (171)).

ARISTOTLE'S PHILOSOPHICAL ASSUMPTIONS

In short, the *Politics* is a work whose strength lies in its parts: it is a banquet whose courses, nourishing and succulent though they be, may have come up from the kitchen in the wrong order. Moreover, to a palate unaccustomed to Aristotle's cuisine, the dishes taste a little strange; and there seems to be a certain powerful ingredient that gives them all a distinct tang.

This ingredient can be isolated by a comparison, admittedly a fairly rugged one and subject to all sorts of qualifications, between Aristotle's characteristic approach to any problem and that of Plato. Throughout his works Plato exhibits a kind of cosmic pessimism: he believed that not only moral concepts but all objects in the whole of existence had a perfect supra-sensible counterpart, which he called a Form or Idea. An individual just act, for instance, is just only in so far as it partakes of Justice, absolute and perfect Justice with a real and independent existence, which, the individual just act merely 'imitates' and 'falls short of'. Similarly a bed, in this imperfect and approximate world, is not really a perfect bed, or a triangle a perfect triangle: they 'fall short of' Bedness and Triangularity, perfect examples to which individual beds and triangles only approximate. Plato's political works are therefore penetrated by the sad conviction that moral and political conduct is always in some sense second-rate; the ruler should no doubt strive to produce the best possible conduct and institutions in his state, but perfection will elude him always.

Aristotle, by contrast, is a cosmic optimist. Things are always *moving towards* their full completeness: the acorn is not destined to become an oak tree that inevitably falls short of Oaktreeness; it is destined to grow into an adult and fully formed oak tree, which is its 'end' or 'purpose'; it is here, in the final and complete stage of the natural process, that perfection is to be found; and the form of the oak tree resides *in* the oak tree, it is not something 'out there' and unattainable. Aristotle's 'teleology' (Greek *telos*, 'end', 'purpose') flavours all his work, and is that 'powerful ingredient' of the *Politics*: everywhere he asks of any custom, law, practice, office, or constitution, 'what it is *for*?'. The 'end' of man is to live 'well' or 'happily'; the state arises naturally as assisting and working towards that end; and the various institutions of the state should be judged by the standard of how far they assist the state to achieve its purpose.[1]

Further, the 'end', happiness, pursued by man is in accordance with his nature; it is not something random.[2] Aristotle concedes, of course, that men can attain some measure of happiness even when they fail to live fully in accordance with their nature; but it would be only *in so far as* they live thus that they would be happy. In other words, the kind of life needed for perfect happiness is something fixed and given, being somehow dictated by men's very nature. In part, men have an inbuilt tendency to live such a life: by natural impulse they group themselves in family, village and state, spontaneous natural creations which facilitate the exchange of goods and services men's nature needs if they are to live the good life. Hence Aristotle's celebrated description of man as a *politikon zōon*, 'an animal that [naturally] lives in a state, *polis*'. Beyond that point, however, the conditions of the good life have to be found out – partly empirically, partly by the philosopher's reflections on the facts of man's social and political experiences.[3] The crucial point is that for Aristotle those conditions, though at present unclear to us, are in principle discoverable, as matters of *fact*; hence political disputes are likewise about questions of fact, and are as much open to definitive solutions as (say) problems in mathematics.[4]

The *Politics* is then best seen as a mixture of reported fact and teleological assessment, the overall aim being to discover how men may attain the 'good life', or at least one of the many possible approximations. Sometimes analysis is para-

1. On Aristotle's teleological assumptions, see J. Hintikka, 'Some conceptual presuppositions of Greek political theory', *Scandinavian Political Studies*, 2 (1967), pp. 11–25.

2. The concept of nature in Aristotle's political thought is discussd by G. Boas, 'A basic conflict in Aristotle's philosophy', *American Journal of Philology*, 64 (1943), pp. 172–93.

3. See e.g. Aristotle's recognition in the first paragraph of III xii of the need for political philosophy, and cf. E. F. Miller, 'Primary questions in political inquiry', *Review of Politics*, 39 (1977), pp. 298–331.

4. Though Aristotle would admit that the nature of the subject-matter of political solutions prevents their being expressed with the same degree of precision and rigour.

mount, sometimes raw factual material; but throughout, to maintain a firm grasp on Aristotle's 'natural teleology' as his basic technique of analysis is the best way of thinking oneself into his head.

WHY READ THE 'POLITICS'?

But why trouble to think oneself back into Aristotle's head? A sceptic might argue as follows : 'Aristotle's world has vanished, and his comments on it can be of antiquarian interest only. We live in a unique twentieth century, which has its own unique and pressing problems, of which the ancients had not an inkling. Conversely, we ourselves are conceptually so locked into our own culture that to understand a society of the past is probably beyond us, in principle. The study of history is therefore a time-consuming fad we had better give up. Henry Ford was right: "History is bunk." '[1]

My riposte to such radical gloom would be simple and short. To expect to discover in history a series of edifying lessons that can be read off and applied to modern circumstances in some straightforward manner is of course naïve; but that is not the point. The study of history is part of man's awareness of himself and the nature and place of his society in the world at large; it is valuable not so much because he can find in the past rough parallels to the present, but because he can find societies and events and ideas that are sharply *different* from those he encounters from day to day. Just as the arts – painting, sculpture, theatre, film, literature – are powerful and influential because they afford us alternative models to consider, so too history allows us to examine other societies, other critical approaches to life, which we may compare and contrast with our own, and so understand and take the measure of our own more securely. The society that loses its grip on the past is in danger, for it produces men who know nothing but the present, and who are not aware that life has been, and could be, different from what it is. Such men

1. Some of these large issues are discussed by E. M. Wood and N. Wood, *Class Ideology and Ancient Political Theory: Socrates, Plato and Aristotle in Social Context* (Oxford, 1978), pp. 5–12. See also J. H. Plumb, *The Death of the Past* (London, 1969).

bear tyranny easily; for they have nothing with which to compare it.[1]

Aristotle in his political work offers for our contemplation a society in some ways similar to, yet very different from, our own; and he offers us an analysis of it based on the startling assumption that the right, the expedient and the natural are the same thing, and that human happiness resides in conformity to some naturally given pattern. To jolt oneself by study of that society and that analysis is an education.

THE REVISED TRANSLATION

Principles of Revision

Some such conviction as this has guided the revising of the translation: at every stage I have tried to enable the reader to immerse himself in the world of the ancient Greeks and to observe it through Aristotle's eyes.

T. A. Sinclair's translation of 1962 was a brilliant success. It was nicely readable and readily intelligible, and won the *Politics* a very large new readership. In this revision I have followed the principle of economy of intervention, and I have tried to retain those special merits of Sinclair's work, so that it remains substantially and recognizably his. My innovations are chiefly two:

1. To bring the actual translation – particularly in the more closely argued passages – into greater conformity with Aristotle's text, by retaining its full complement of detail, qualifications, ellipse, rough edges and awkward nuances which Sinclair ironed out in the interests of readability and swift comprehension. In particular, I have sought to modify

---

1. Cf. the treatment of the past in George Orwell's *1984* (Penguin edition), esp. pp. 198–200, and the Appendix, 'On the Principles of Newspeak', *ad init.*: 'The purpose of Newspeak was not only to provide a medium of expression for the world-view and mental habits proper to the devotees of Ingsoc, but to make all other modes of thought impossible. It was intended that when Newspeak had been adopted ... a heretical thought ... should be literally unthinkable, at least so far as thought is dependent on words.'

Sinclair's freedom of translation of key terms[1] by what I describe as 'flexible consistency' of rendering (see further below).

2. An abundance of aids to the reader, notably this introduction, prefatory comments to each chapter, footnotes to provide cross-references and to clarify points of detail, bibliographies, and two glossaries of key terms.

In short, the apparatus of this edition will, I hope, help to bring the reader face to face with Greek society and with one of its most knowledgeable and trenchant critics.

Detailed notes now follow on both 1 and 2.

Translation of Key Terms

To describe and analyse political ideas and institutions Aristotle employs a fairly large, but by no means huge, set of key terms, which recur over and over again throughout the work, in different combinations and relationships appropriate to the particular topic or problem in hand. Many of these terms demand, according to context and subject-matter, a range of English words to translate them (particularly when they are used in special or technical senses). Now as soon as the translator adopts several English words for one Greek word, he may indeed accurately render his author's meaning, but he will conceal the structure of his thought, as embedded in a particular culture; hence the reader needs to be told which single Greek term it is that lies behind the range of English terms. On the other hand, always to use the same English word for the same Greek word denies the Greek author flexibility of usage, and in any case leads to distinctly weird English.[2]

1. See the last paragraph of his introduction: 'In an attempt to convey something of the complexity of meaning attaching to certain Greek terms different English words have been used to translate them.' That indeed does great service, and makes for idiomatic translation; there are problems, as I explain. Sinclair drew attention to key terms in his italic comments inserted at intervals in the text, but not extensively or systematically; thus my own more elaborate way of coping with the problem builds on a good foundation laid down by Sinclair himself.

2. On this central dilemma of a translator, see further my article, 'The Penguinification of Plato', *Greece and Rome*, 22 (1975), pp. 19–28, esp. p. 27.

Since Aristotle uses language with more than usual pre-cision, it seemed to me essential to make some attempt to reproduce the terminological structure of his argument. I have therefore:

(a) restricted as far as possible the range of English equivalents for a given Greek key term, so as to achieve a certain 'flexible consistency';

(b) inserted, in the italicized prefaces and in the footnotes, frequent transliterations of these terms, with comment on their meaning in the passage in question;

(c) provided a Greek–English and an English–Greek glossary, which will give the reader a fair chance of finding out the range of English words used for a Greek term, and of dis-covering which Greek word lies behind a given English one.[1]

The purpose of this rather lavish provision of aids to the reader is simply to enable him to think in Greek and Aris-totelian terms. Once he moves away from the translation to the various aids, he will constantly bump into Aristotle's con-cepts in their original dress, or rather in the borrowed cloth-ing of English transliteration. It is increasingly common to find Greek literature and culture discussed with frequent refer-ence to transliterated Greek words, and I hope the glossaries will strengthen this healthy trend, as well as encourage the increasing interest now being taken in learning Greek.

Refractory Terms

A number of the key terms have no natural equivalent in English, and at the cost of a certain strangeness I have allowed some traditional renderings to survive. I discuss a few only, by way of example:

(a) *Aretē* I have nearly always translated by the time-honoured 'virtue'. The renderings 'efficiency' and 'excellence' have gained ground in recent years, but on the whole it

1. I have also tried to translate with some degree of consistency a number of rarer or less important words; but they are not in-cluded in the glossaries, which clearly need to be of manageable size. The potential ramifications are endless, and if not strictly controlled rapidly generate glossaries of Himalayan bulk. Further notes on the scope and use of the glossaries will be found as a preface to them (p. 489).

seemed preferable to stick to what is familiar; and Aristotle is after all usually dealing with a *moral* quality of human beings, a notion which is still best conveyed by 'virtue'. Moreover, in Greek, things too have virtues, which suits English usage: whereas a tool may have 'the virtue of adaptability', to say it has 'the goodness of adaptability' sounds wrong.

(b) *Gnōrimoi*, 'notables', a certain social group. One just has to get used to this Greek term for the well-off upper classes.

(c) *Politikos*, 'statesman'. There simply is no English term for 'a *politēs* (citizen) active in running the affairs of the *politeia* (constitution) of his *polis* (state)'. A 'statesman' nowadays is of course a superior kind of politician, usually full of years and honour; but in spite of that I stick to 'statesman', not only for its familiarity as an equivalent but because it offers a desirable verbal link with 'state' (*polis*). 'Politician' has quite unsuitable associations, notably of professionalism.

These and other awkwardnesses inherent in any translation simply have to be tolerated, or (better) actually welcomed as a fairly painless means of encountering the sheer Greekness of the text.

Italicized Prefaces to Chapters

In a work like the *Politics*, the reader needs specific comment related to each chapter, rather than a long general introduction.[1] The purpose of my italicized prefaces is to elucidate, and to offer succinct comment on, the theme and purpose of the argument. I have tried to bring out the strength and value of Aristotle's discussion, but I have not hesitated to criticize too; and I stress that my intention is to stimulate discussion rather than to exhaust it. I have adopted and adapted, and sometimes relocated, a good deal of Sinclair's much briefer material. The prefaces also contain references to background reading not only in the *Politics* itself but in Aristotle and Plato in general, and in other authors both ancient and modern.

1. There is an abundance of comprehensive accounts of Aristotle's political thought which could usefully supplement the two brief introductions in this volume: see the Select Bibliographies.

Numerical References

Throughout, references to passages of Aristotle, including the *Politics*, are made by book and chapter, and/or by line. Book and chapter numbers are printed in Roman numerals, book numbers in *capitals*, chapter numbers in *lower case*. Line numbers are shown above the title of each chapter, and in italic type at the start of each paragraph; they follow the standard method of making exact references to Aristotle's Greek text, by page, column and line of I. Bekker's edition (*Aristotelis Opera*, Berlin, 1831): for instance, *Politics* 1294b21 refers to page 1294, column b, line 21.

The titling of the chapters and their division into paragraphs are of course mine, not Aristotle's.

Footnotes

Sinclair followed the now abandoned practice of printing as footnotes those portions of the text he supposed Aristotle himself would have presented as footnotes had he known the convention. I have restored such passages to their proper place in the text, and all footnotes are mine.

Historical events and persons I commonly identify with the utmost brevity; in any case, we know about some of them little or nothing apart from what the text tells us. Full discussions may be found in the commentaries, and in R. Weil, *Aristote et l'histoire: essai sur la 'Politique'* (Paris, 1960).

Bibliographies

The bibliographies are selective, but still probably full enough for all categories of readers except the most specialist of scholars. They concentrate on the *Politics*, and contain little explicitly on the other works of Aristotle.

Table of Contents and Index of Names

The index covers proper names only, the longer entries being subdivided by topic. Its use in conjunction with the 103 chapter titles in the table of contents will fairly rapidly lead the reader to the particular subjects in which he happens to be interested. For the convenience of readers who are studying a single book or some other limited part of the text, the table of contents for each book is repeated before its opening chapter.

All dates are B.C. unless otherwise indicated.

ACKNOWLEDGEMENTS

Professor T. A. Sinclair and I had met once or twice in the late 1950s, and we had formed the pleasant habit of exchanging offprints on our common interest, Greek political theory. In 1962, shortly after his death, a copy of his newly published Penguin translation of the *Politics* was presented to me by his family, 'in memory of T.A.S.'. I am most grateful to Mrs S. Sinclair for assenting to the suggestion of the Editor of the series, Mrs Betty Radice, that I should revise and re-present her husband's work. It has been both a pleasure and an honour to do so.

Richard Sorabji and Christopher Rowe each read in draft a large proportion of the revision, and I benefited enormously from their informed and penetrating comments. My colleagues John Lazenby and Jeremy Paterson cheerfully allowed me to tap their brains on questions of ancient history. George Benfield read the entire revision and improved it at many points. Scrutiny of the proofs was entrusted to the vigilant eye of my wife, Teresa. For all this invaluable help I express my most cordial thanks. My special gratitude goes to Betty Radice for much friendly guidance and patient encouragement over a period far longer than either of us anticipated.

Newcastle upon Tyne   T.J.S.
1974–9

THE POLITICS

BOOK I

PREFACE TO BOOK I
(Nicomachean Ethics 1181b12–23)*

THE LINK BETWEEN THE 'NICOMACHEAN
ETHICS' AND THE 'POLITICS'

Since, then, the question of legislation has been left unexamined by previous thinkers,[1] presumably we had better investigate it more closely for ourselves, together with
the question of constitutions generally, so that our philosophy of human conduct may be as complete as possible.
So let us first try to review any valid statements (about
particular points) that have been made by our predecessors; and then to consider, in the light of our collected
examples of constitutions,[2] what influences are conservative and what are destructive of a state; and which have
these effects upon each different kind of constitution;
and for what reasons some states are well governed, while
in others the contrary is the case. For after examining
these questions we shall perhaps see more comprehens-

* Translation and notes by Hugh Tredennick, extracted from his
revised edition of the *The Ethics of Aristotle* (Penguin Classics,
1976), p. 342.

1. This concluding passage was obviously written to connect the
Ethics to the *Politics*; but written by whom? Opinions have been
sharply divided. The implication that Plato had nothing of importance to say about education by legislation, or about types of
constitution and their changes, seems perverse and is in fact inconsistent with the actual procedure in the *Politics*, where Plato's
views are nearly always traceable as underlying A.'s thought, and
often explicitly criticized or rejected. At the same time the fact
that the outlined programme does not correspond very accurately
with the actual treatment may tell for no less than against authenticity, because an 'editor' might have been expected to produce a
neater and more convincing link. The problem can only be stated
here: it does not yet seem to have been solved.

2. According to tradition A. wrote 158 such *Constitutions*, of
which the *Constitution of Athens* is the only survivor.

ively what kind of constitution is the best, and what is the best organization for each kind, and the best system of laws and customs for it to use. Let us, then, begin our account.

I i

(1252a1–23)

THE STATE AS AN ASSOCIATION

Aristotle's purposes in this chapter are (a) to assert that the 'state', by which he means specifically the Greek polis *or 'city-state', is an association distinct in kind from other associations, and (b) to discourage facile parallels between a 'statesman'* (politikos, *i.e. a citizen,* politēs, *of a* polis *in his capacity as ruler or office-bearer) and the 'rulers' of, for example, a household or a monarchy. His reasons for combating such parallels are not stated here, but emerge subsequently (e.g. in I vii); the crucial point is that the statesman rules over 'equals', i.e. persons of the same status as himself. Aristotle is quite uninformative – curt, indeed – in his dismissal of his unnamed targets. If he is thinking of anyone in particular, it is probably Plato and perhaps Socrates too (see e.g. Plato,* Politicus *258e ff. and Xenophon,* Memoirs of Socrates *III, iv 12); but obviously the views he attacks could be held by any unreflective or non-philosophic person who had not carried out the necessary analysis of the* polis *and its parts. For Aristotle's method, as he himself states and as becomes clear in later chapters, is essentially analytical: he believes that the peculiar character and purpose of the state as an association can be discovered only by examining the character and purpose of its 'parts' (households, social classes, etc.). The inspiration of this method is twofold: (a) the fundamental teleological assumption, revealed in his first sentence, that the state does have a particular function or aim; (b) the methodological assumption that the mode of analysis he employs in several other works – conspicuously in his biological writings, in which he examines the functions of an animal's parts as contributing to the functions of the animal as a whole – is a guide,*

*when applied analogously, to discovering the function
and aim of the state; in short, he sees some sort of functional parallel between a living thing and a polis (see I ii
and IV iv, second section). Both assumptions are large
and disputable; but to Aristotle's synoptic mind they are
irresistibly attractive.*

1252a1 Observation tells us that every state is an association, and that every association is formed with a
view to some good purpose. I say 'good', because in all
their actions all men do in fact aim at what they think
good. Clearly then, as all associations aim at some good,
that association which is the most sovereign among them
all and embraces all others will aim highest, i.e. at the
most sovereign of all goods. This is the association which
we call the state, the association which is 'political'.[1]

1252a7 It is an error to suppose, as some do, that the
roles of a statesman,[2] of a king, of a household-manager
and of a master of slaves are the same, on the ground
that they differ not in kind but only in point of numbers
of persons – that a master of slaves, for example, has to
do with a few people, a household-manager with more,
and a statesman or king with more still, as if there were
no differences between a large household and a small state.
They also reckon that when one person is in personal
control over the rest he has the role of a king, whereas
when he takes his turn at ruling and at being ruled
according to the principles of the science concerned, he
is a statesman.[3] But these assertions are false.

1252a17 This will be quite evident if we examine the

1. *Hē koinōnia politikē*: 'the association that takes the form of a
polis (state)'.
2. *Politikos*, 'statesman', in the sense explained in the introduction to this chapter.
3. The formulation is adequate as far as it goes; but Aristotle's
point is that a king and a statesman differ sharply in *kind*: a
king is set apart in some fundamental respect from his subjects,
while a statesman is the *equal* of his; cf. I vii and xii.

matter according to our established method.[4] We have to analyse other composite things till they can be subdivided no further; let us in the same way examine the component parts of the state and we shall see better how these too differ from each other, and whether we can acquire any systematic[5] knowledge about the several roles mentioned.[6]

I ii

(1252a24–1253a39)

THE STATE EXISTS BY NATURE

This long chapter is an admirable illustration of Aristotle's analytical and genetic method, and contains many rich and suggestive ideas. By imaginative reconstruction rather than by factual history (cf. Plato, Laws III) he traces the formation (a) of the 'pairs' of husband/wife and master/slave, (b) of the household from the 'pairs', (c) of the village from a coalescence of households, and (d) of the state from a coalescence of villages. The 'nature' of a thing, he claims, is not its first but its final condition; just as an individual man is the natural end of the process of human coming-to-be, so too the state is the natural end and culmination of the other and earlier associations, which were themselves natural; the state therefore exists by nature. It provides all men's needs (material, social, religious, etc.), and offers them the fulfilment not only of living but of living 'well', in accordance with those virtues that are peculiarly human. The state is thus 'all-providing', which is 'best', which is characteristic of natural ends. (Aristotle's discussion and

4. The analytical method described in the introduction to this chapter.
5. *Technikos.*
6. Of statesman, household-manager, etc.

definition of 'nature' in Physics *II i would be useful background reading.)*

The repeated emphasis Aristotle places on the state's being 'natural' suggests that the chapter has also the polemical purpose of refuting those who believed that the state was an 'artificial' or a 'conventional' creation. Such argument was a special form of the general controversy of the fifth and fourth centuries about the relative status and merits of nomos, *law,* and phusis, *nature (see Newman's discussion, I 24 ff.). Aristotle does not name his opponents, and it is doubtful whether he has any particular persons in mind.*

Two further points are worth noting: (a) Aristotle regards human society as inevitably and naturally hierarchical; he assumes as self-evident that the male's abilities are superior to the female's, and the master's to the slave's (not that slave and female are on that account to be treated alike: see n. 4), and that Greeks are superior to non-Greeks. 'Who rules whom?' and 'With what justification?' are questions at the centre of his political theory, and his defence of slavery in subsequent chapters is all of a piece with this general approach. (b) Like most Greek writers, he delights in appealing to the poets, and to the popular ideas they express, in order to justify his position. He believes that in subjects such as political and ethical theory, in which precise demonstration is impossible, one should welcome support from the experience of mankind.

The Two 'Pairs'

1252a24 We shall, I think, in this as in other subjects, get the best view of the matter if we look at the natural growth of things from the beginning. The first point is that those which are incapable of existing without each other must be united as a pair. For example, (a) the union of male and female is essential for reproduction; and this is not a matter of *choice,* but is due to the *natural* urge, which exists in the other animals too and in plants, to propagate one's kind.[1] Equally essential is (b) the combination of the natural ruler and ruled, for the purpose of preservation. For the element that can use its intelligence to look ahead is by nature ruler and by nature master, while that which has the bodily strength to do the actual work is by nature a slave, one of those who are ruled. Thus there is a common interest uniting master and slave.

Formation of the Household

1252a34 Nature, then, has distinguished between female and slave: she recognizes different functions and lavishly provides different tools, not an all-purpose tool like the Delphic knife;[2] for every instrument will be made best if it serves not many purposes but one. But non-Greeks assign to female and slave exactly the same status. This is because they have nothing which is by nature fitted to rule; their association[3] consists of a male slave and a female slave.[4] So, as the poets say, 'It is proper that Greeks should rule non-Greeks',[5] the implication being that non-Greek and slave are by nature identical.

1252b9 Thus it was out of the association formed by

1. Male and female are 'incapable of existing without each other' not as individuals but as members of a species, over a period of many generations. Note the contrast between instinctive *nature* (*phusis*) and rational and purposive *choice* (*prohairesis*); on the latter, see *Nicomachean Ethics* III ii.
2. Evidently a knife capable of more than one mode of cutting, and not perfectly adapted to any one of them.
3. I.e of marriage.
4. Somewhat confusingly, Aristotle uses 'slave' both in a literal and in a metaphorical sense. In non-Greek societies a woman and a slave are 'in the same position' in that their *de facto* rulers (husband and master respectively) have not the wisdom and the rationality nature demands in a 'natural' ruler: authority is exercised by persons who are in point of fitness for rule *no better than* slaves. The 'slave' husband makes a 'slave' of his *wife*.
5. Euripides, *Iphigeneia in Aulis* 1400.

men with these two, women and slaves, that a household was first formed; and the poet Hesiod was right when he wrote, 'Get first a house and a wife and an ox to draw the plough.'[6] (The ox is the poor man's slave.) This association of persons, established according to nature for the satisfaction of daily needs, is the household, the members of which Charondas calls 'bread-fellows', and Epimenides the Cretan 'stable-companions'.[7]

Formation of the Village

1252b15 The next stage is the village, the first association of a number of houses for the satisfaction of something *more* than daily needs. It comes into being through the processes of nature in the fullest sense, as offshoots[8] of a household are set up by sons and grandsons. The members of such a village are therefore called by some 'homogalactic'.[9] This is why states were at first ruled by kings, as are foreign nations to this day: they were formed from constituents which were themselves under kingly rule. For every household is ruled by its senior member, as by a king, and the offshoots too, because of their blood relationship, are ruled in the same way. This kind of rule is mentioned in Homer:[10] 'Each man has power of law[11] over children and wives.' He is referring to scattered settlements, which were common in primitive times. For this reason the gods too are said to be governed by a king – namely because men themselves were originally ruled by kings and some are so still. Just as men

6. *Works and Days* 415.

7. Charondas was a lawgiver of Catana, in Sicily, probably of the sixth century; Aristotle refers to him several times. Epimenides was a Cretan seer and wonder-worker of about 600.

8. *Apoikia*: 'settlement', 'colony', 'extension'.

9. I.e. 'sucklings of the same milk'.

10. *Odyssey* IX, 114–5.

11. *Themisteuei*, 'lays down *themis*' ('ordinance', 'customary law', a term in early Greek social and legal thought).

imagine gods in human shape, so they imagine their way of life to be like that of men.

Formation of the State

1252b27 The final association, formed of several villages, is the state. For all practical purposes the process is now complete; self-sufficiency[12] has been reached, and while the state came about as a means of securing life itself, it continues in being to secure the *good* life. Therefore every state exists by nature, as the earlier associations too were natural. This association is the end of those others, and nature is itself an end; for whatever is the end-product of the coming into existence of any object, that is what we call its nature – of a man, for instance, or a horse or a household. Moreover the aim and the end is perfection; and self-sufficiency is both end and perfection.[13]

The State and the Individual

1253a1 It follows that the state belongs to the class of objects which exist by nature, and that man is by nature a political animal.[14] Any one who by his nature and not simply by ill-luck has no state is either too bad or too good, either subhuman or superhuman – he is like the war-mad man condemned in Homer's words[15] as 'having

12. *Autarkeia*, 'political and/or economic independence'. Aristotle's use of the word here is however somewhat wider than this, and embraces opportunities to live the 'good' life according to the human virtues.

13. Aristotle makes succinct use of his teleological technicalities: the 'aim' ('that for the-sake-of-which', *to hou heneka*) is the 'final cause', the 'end' or purpose towards which a process of development is directed and in which it culminates.

14. *Politikon zōon*, 'who lives/whose nature is to live, in a *polis* (state)'; cf. *Nicomachean Ethics*, I vii *ad fin.*

15. *Iliad* IX, 63.

no family, no law,[16] no home'; for he who is such[17] by nature is mad on war: he is a non-cooperator like an isolated piece in a game of draughts.

1253a7 But obviously man is a political animal[14] in a sense in which a bee is not, or any other gregarious animal.[18] Nature, as we say, does nothing without some purpose; and she has endowed man alone among the animals with the power of speech. Speech is something different from voice, which is possessed by other animals also and used by them to express pain or pleasure; for their nature does indeed enable them not only to feel[19] pleasure and pain but to communicate these feelings to each other. Speech, on the other hand serves to indicate what is useful and what is harmful, and so also what is just and what is unjust. For the real difference between man and other animals is that humans alone have perception[19] of good and evil, just and unjust, etc. It is the sharing of a common view in *these* matters that makes a household and a state.

1253a18 Furthermore, the state has priority over the household and over any individual among us. For the whole must be prior to the part. Separate hand or foot from the whole body, and they will no longer be hand or foot except in name, as one might speak of a 'hand' or 'foot' sculptured in stone. That will be the condition of the spoilt[20] hand, which no longer has the capacity and the function which define it. So, though we may say they have the same names, we cannot say that they are, in

16. *Athemistos*: see n. 11.

17. I.e. without a state. It is such a person's *pugnacity* that Aristotle seems to regard as marking him out as in some sense non-human; cf. *Nicomachean Ethics* 1177b9.

18. A slightly comic sentence; but obviously it is the notion of the state as an *association* that Aristotle has in mind. On this sentence see R. G. Mulgan, 'Aristotle's doctrine that man is a political animal', *Hermes*, 102 (1974), pp. 438–45, and cf. Aristotle, *History of Animals* 487b33–488a13.

19. *Aisthēsis*.

20. Literally 'destroyed', 'ruined' (by the dismemberment apparently envisaged in the preceding sentence).

that condition,[21] the same things. It is clear then that the state is both natural and prior to the individual. For if an individual is not fully self-sufficient after separation, he will stand in the same relationship to the whole as the parts in the other case do.[22] Whatever is incapable of participating in the association which we call the state, a dumb animal for example, and equally whatever is perfectly self-sufficient and has no need to (e.g. a god), is not a part of the state at all.

1253a29 Among all men, then, there is a natural impulse towards this kind of association; and the first man to construct a state deserves credit for conferring very great benefits. For as man is the best of all animals when he has reached his full development, so he is worst of all when divorced from law and justice. Injustice armed is hardest to deal with; and though man is born with weapons which he can use in the service of practical wisdom and virtue, it is all too easy for him to use them for the opposite purposes. Hence man without virtue is the most savage, the most unrighteous, and the worst in regard to sexual licence and gluttony. The virtue of justice is a feature of a state; for justice is the arrangement of the political association,[23] and a sense of justice decides what is just.[24]

21. Of not having a function and a capacity.
22. E.g. limbs (individuals : state :: limbs : body).
23. *Politikēs koinōnias taxis*, 'the framework or organization of the association that takes the form of a *polis* (state)'.
24. In this paragraph *dikaiosunē*, the 'virtue' or 'sense' of justice, seems to be distinguished from *dikē*, 'justice', the concrete expression or embodiment of that virtue or sense in a legal and administrative system. 'What is just' (*dikaion*) evidently means particular and individual just relationships arrived at or (in courts) re-established by the application of *dikaiosunē* through the medium of the system of justice, or just system, *dikē*.

I iii

(1253b1–23)

THE HOUSEHOLD AND ITS SLAVES

Aristotle now focuses attention on the household and its economic arrangements, and turns first to consider slaves. Slavery was an integral part of the economy of ancient Greece; and since Aristotle thinks of life in the Greek state as being the 'natural' and 'best' life for man, he is immediately faced with the crucial task of showing that at least some slavery is 'natural'. Although for the most part slavery was simply taken for granted, there was, as he candidly admits, some opposition from those who held it to be against nature, because based on force (cf. I vi). Again, it is not clear that Aristotle has identifiable opponents in mind. Certainly there seems to have been some controversy about slavery, of which echoes may be found also in Plato, Laws 776 ff.; Newman I 139 ff. discusses the evidence. In this short chapter, then, Aristotle girds his loins for a defence of slavery as a 'natural' institution.

1253b1 Now that I have explained what the component parts of a state are, and since every state consists of households, it is essential to begin with household-management. This topic can be subdivided so as to correspond to the parts of which a complete household is made up, namely, the free and the slaves; but our method[1] requires us to examine everything when it has been reduced to its smallest parts, and the smallest division of a household into parts gives three pairs – master and slave, husband and wife, father and children. And so we must ask ourselves what each one of these three relationships is, and what sort of thing it ought to be. The word 'mastership' is used to describe the first, and we may use 'matrimonial' (in the case of the union of man and woman) and 'pater-

1. See I i.

nal' to describe the other two, as there is no more specific term for either.[2] We may accept these three; but we find that there is a fourth element, which some people regard as covering the whole of household-management, others as its most important part; and our task is to consider its position. I refer to what is called 'the acquisition of wealth'.

1253b14 First let us discuss master and slave, in order to see (a) how they bear on the provision of essential services, (b) whether we can find a better way towards understanding this topic than if we started from the suppositions usually made. For example, some people suppose that being a master requires a certain kind of knowledge, and that this is the same knowledge as is required to manage a household or to be a statesman or a king – an error which we discussed at the beginning.[1] Others say that it is contrary to nature to rule as master over slave, because the distinction between slave and free is one of convention only, and in nature there is no difference, so that this form of rule is based on force and is therefore not just.

I iv

(1253b23–1254a17)

THE SLAVE AS A TOOL

In this notorious chapter Aristotle describes, from his own teleological standpoint, the position of the slave in

2. *Despotikē* ('of a master'), with some such noun as *archē* ('rule') to be supplied here and (in the plural, *archai*) after 'three' in the next sentence. In the case of 'matrimonial' (*gamikē*, 'to do with marriages'), and 'paternal' (*teknopoiētikē*, 'procreative'), Aristotle gropes for words. He lacks an adjective for a husband's authority over his wife and for *all* their relationships in general, including the sexual, and for the relationship (mainly of authority) of both parents to their children, not only of the father (for which he *could* have used *patrikē*); cf. I xii. For once, a Greek did not 'have a word for it'.

*his day. According to him, the slave is a 'live tool' used
by the master for purposes of 'life' and 'action', not of
production. He is of course thinking of the household,
which is not primarily productive; but even so it looks
as if his bias in favour of a 'gentlemanly' life has tempted
him into thinking of a slave as invariably in personal
attendance on his master. In fact, many slaves were used
in productive labour in factories and mines and on farms.*

*In the third paragraph of the chapter, the argument
seems to be: (a) a piece of property is described in the
same terms as a part; (b) a part 'belongs to another
tout court' (i.e. to the whole); (c) slaves are pieces of
property; so (d) slaves 'belong to others tout court' (i.e.
to their masters) – whereas masters, not being pieces of
property, are master 'of' their slaves but do not 'belong
to them tout court'.*

*Is Aristotle suggesting that the slave 'belongs tout
court' to his master in the sense of being dependent on
him as a member of a 'pair', or perhaps in the way an
individual is 'part' of the state (I ii)? If so, the naturalness
of the 'belonging' is in a sense established. But the implications of the argument are none too lucid, and evidently it is in Chapters v–vii that the main arguments
for the naturalness of slavery are presented.*

1253b23 Now property is part of a household, and the
acquisition of property part of household-management;
for neither life itself nor the good life is possible without
a certain minimum supply of the necessities. Again, in
any special skill the availability of the proper tools will
be essential for the performance of the task; and the
household-manager must have his likewise. Tools may be
animate as well as inanimate; for instance, a ship's
captain uses a lifeless rudder, but a living man for
watch; for a servant is, from the point of view of his craft,
categorized as one of its tools. So any piece of property
can be regarded as a tool enabling a man to live, and his
property is an assemblage of such tools; a slave is a sort

of living piece of property; and like any other servant is a tool in charge of other tools. For suppose that every tool we had could perform its task, either at our bidding or itself perceiving the need, and if – like the statues made by Daedalus or the tripods of Hephaestus, of which the poet says that 'self-moved they enter the assembly of the gods'[1] – shuttles in a loom could fly to and fro and a plucker[2] play a lyre all self-moved, then master-craftsmen would have no need of servants nor masters of slaves.

1254a1 Tools in the ordinary sense are productive tools, whereas a piece of property is meant for action.[3] I mean, for example, a shuttle produces something other than its own use, a bed or a garment does not. Moreover, since production and action differ in kind and both require tools, the difference between their tools too must be of the same kind. Now life is action and not production; therefore the slave, a servant, is one of the tools that minister to action.

1254a9 A piece of property is spoken of in the same way as a part is; for a part is not only part of something but belongs to it *tout court*; and so too does a piece of property. So a slave is not only his master's slave but belongs to him *tout court*, while the master is his slave's master but does not belong to him. These considerations will have shown what the nature and functions of the slave are: any human being that by nature belongs not to himself but to another is by nature a slave; and a human being belongs to another whenever, in spite of being a *man*, he is a piece of property, i.e. a tool having a separate existence[4] and meant for action.[3]

---

1. Homer, *Iliad* XVIII, 376: Hephaestus' statues were fitted with wheels. Daedalus' statues were so lifelike that they were thought to move.

2. A 'plucker' was the instrument with which the strings of the lyre were played by the performer.

3. *Praktikon*, 'with which to do something'.

4. I.e. separate from its possessor (unlike the hand in I ii, which loses its power when severed from its owner).

I v

SLAVERY AS PART OF A UNIVERSAL NATURAL PATTERN

The purpose of this chapter is to argue that at least some slavery must be natural, because the relationship of master and slave conforms to a broad pattern found universally in nature in the widest sense: better/worse, male/female, man/beast, mind/body, rational/irrational, ruler/ruled. *Such a pattern makes obvious sense to Aristotle, who justifies it teleologically by its beneficial results: to be ruled is to the slave's advantage, and is to that extent just. In the final paragraph some admitted exceptions to the pattern do not make him doubt its essential validity: presumably he finds it sufficient for the purposes of his argument that nature achieves her ends only 'for the most part' (as he often concedes in other contexts).*

Aristotle's view that slavery is expedient both for master and for slave has attracted a great deal of criticism, much of it obvious and justified. Is there anything to be said in its favour? It clearly relies on the assumption that most masters are rational and most slaves are not; or rather, that men fall readily into two classes, rational and irrational, and that the former should rule the latter. With large qualifications, it is at least arguable that such rule ought to be enforced, and is in fact enforced, in society at large. One does not have to defend the particular institutional form of such rule that Aristotle seeks to justify (ancient slavery). If (and it is a big if) we grant his asumptions, the master/slave relationship does indeed seem analogous in some respects to certain other relationships which are presumably desirable (e.g. mind over body, man over beast). But this is of course to defend not slavery as such, but only in so far as it embodies the rule of rational over irrational. In so far as it does not, even Aristotle would hesitate to defend it, as his next chapter makes clear.

I conclude with two points that are forgotten easily and often: (a) The fact that slavery is a dirty word nowadays should not trick us into believing that ancient Greek slavery was invariably harsh and therefore not *'expedient' for slaves: much depended on the masters' attitudes, which in the nature of the case varied widely. (b) The distinction between slave and free was much sharper in point of legal and political status than in social life and economics, where there was some overlap between the poorer free men and the better-off slaves.*

1254a17 But whether anyone does in fact by nature answer to this description, and whether or not it is a just and a better thing for one man to be a slave to another, or whether all slavery is contrary to nature – these are the questions which must be considered next. Neither theoretical discussion nor empirical observation presents any difficulty. That one should command and another obey is both necessary and expedient. Indeed some things are so divided right from birth, some to rule, some to be ruled. There are many different forms of this ruler–ruled relationship, and the quality of the rule depends primarily on the quality of the subjects, rule over man being better than rule over animals; for that which is produced by better men is a better piece of work; and the ruler–ruled relationship is itself a product created by the men involved in it.

1254a28 For wherever there is a combination of elements, continuous or discontinuous,[1] and a common unity is the result, in all such cases the ruler–ruled relationship appears. It appears notably in living creatures as a consequence of their whole nature (and it can exist

---

1. E.g. mind and body form a continuous combination (an individual living being); master and slave form a *dis*continuous combination.

also where there is no life, as dominance in a musical scale,[2] but that is hardly relevant here). The living creature consists in the first place of mind and body, and of these the former is ruler by nature, the latter ruled. Now we must always look for nature's own norm in things whose condition is according to nature, and not base our observations on degenerate forms. We must therefore in this connexion consider the man who is in good condition mentally and physically, one in whom the rule of mind over body is conspicuous – because the bad and unnatural condition of a permanently or temporarily depraved person will often give the impression that his body is ruling over his soul.

1254b2 However that may be, it is, as I say, within living creatures that we first find it possible to see both the rule of a master and that of a statesman.[3] The rule of soul over body is like a master's rule, while the rule of intelligence over desire is like a statesman's or a king's.[4] In these relationships it is clear that it is both natural and expedient for the body to be ruled by the soul, and for the emotional part of our natures to be ruled by the mind, the part which possesses reason. The reverse, or even parity, would be fatal all round. This is also true as between man and the other animals; for tame animals are by nature better than wild, and it is better for them all to be ruled by men, because it secures their safety. Again, as between male and female the former is by nature superior and ruler, the latter inferior and subject. And this must hold good of mankind in general.

1254b16 Therefore whenever there is the same wide discrepancy between human beings as there is between soul and body or between man and beast, then those

2. A clipped reference to the special position of the note *mesē* in the scale: see [Aristotle], *Problems* 920a19–23, b7–15, 922a22–7.
3. See I i.
4. That is, I take it, mind *commands* body, but intelligence has to *persuade* desire.

whose condition is such that their function is the use of their bodies and nothing better can be expected of them, those, I say, are slaves by nature. It is better for them, just as in the cases mentioned, to be ruled thus.[5] For the 'slave by nature' is he that can and therefore does belong to another, and he that participates in reason so far as to recognize[6] it but not so as to possess it (whereas the other[7] animals obey not reason but emotions). The use made of slaves hardly differs at all from that of tame animals: they both help with their bodies to supply our essential needs. It is then part of nature's intention to make the bodies of free men to differ from those of slaves, the latter strong enough to be used for necessary tasks, the former erect and useless for that kind of work, but well suited for the life of a citizen of a state[8], a life which is in turn divided between the requirements of war and peace.

1254b32 But the opposite often occurs: people who have the right kind of bodily physique for free men, but not the soul, others who have the right soul but not the body. This much is clear: suppose that there were men whose bodily physique showed the same superiority as is shown by the statues of gods, then all would agree that the rest of mankind would deserve to be their slaves. And if this is true in relation to physical superiority, the distinction would be even more justly made in respect of superiority of soul; but it is much more difficult to see beauty of soul than it is to see beauty of body. It is clear then that by nature some are free, others slaves, and that for these it is both just and expedient that they should serve as slaves.

5. I.e. by a master.
6. *Aisthanesthai*, cf. *aisthēsis*, I ii, n. 19.
7. I.e. other than man.
8. *Politikos bios*, 'the *polit*ical life, life as a member of a *polis*'.

I vi

(1255a3–b15)

THE RELATION BETWEEN LEGAL AND NATURAL SLAVERY

Aristotle has to face the fact that the generalizations of the last chapter do not hold good universally: some slavery comes about not by nature but by human force, as when men perfectly fitted for mastership become slaves through capture in war. He reports that this 'legal' slavery had both defenders and attackers, and in the second paragraph briefly explores some confused reasoning which he suggests led to the difference of opinion. In the remainder of the chapter he argues that the defenders, in not making the right to enslave in war absolute and justified in all circumstances, in effect presuppose that some men are 'natural' masters and some 'natural' slaves – which is precisely his own position. At the end of the chapter it becomes clear that his sympathies are not with the defenders of the doctrine that 'might is right'.

The argument of the opaque second paragraph is in my view as follows. Aristotle suggests that the reason for the difference of opinion about the justice of forcible enslavement of captives in war arises from false conclusions from the following propositions: (a) that virtue (moral 'superiority') with resources is well equipped to use force; (b) that a victor in war uses force and conquers because of some 'superiority' or goodness' (in something); (c) [the 'overlap'] that the 'superiority' in (b) is that in (a).

One side, noting (rightly) that moral superiority and superiority of force are different, so that forcible enslavement in war is not always just, concludes (wrongly) that it is always unjust, and that to talk of justice in such connections is a nonsense (cf. I iii, end). The other side, wrongly accepting the identification, or invariable linking, of the two 'superiorities', argues that forcible enslave-

ment in war is always *just, i.e. that justice* is *the 'rule of the stronger'. Since the 'overlap' does not invariably exist (superiority of force may or may not go with moral superiority, according to circumstances), neither the arguments that assume their invariable identity nor those assuming their invariable lack of identity can be cogent against Aristotle's own view that the justification of slavery lies in the moral superiority of the master (i.e. that forcible enslavement is just, presumably, if and only if imposed by the morally superior). The Greek, however, is teasingly vague, and admits various interpretations; and Ross's text alone has* ἄνοια *('nonsense') in 1255a17 (the MSS have* εὔνοια, *'good will'). A full new critical interpretation of the paragraph is very much needed.*

1255a3 On the other hand it is not hard to see that those who take opposing views are also right up to a point. The expressions 'state of slavery' and 'slave' have a double connotation: there exists also a *legal* slave and state of slavery.[1] The law in question is a kind of convention, which provides that all that is conquered in war is termed the property of the conquerors. Against this right[2] many of those versed in law bring a charge analogous to that of 'illegality' brought against an orator:[3] they hold it to be indefensible that a man who has been overpowered by the violence and superior might of another should become his property. Others see no harm in this; and both views are held by experts.

1255a12 The reason for this difference of opinion, and for the overlap in the arguments used, lies in the fact that in a way it is virtue, when it acquires resources, that is best able actually to use force; and in the fact that anything which conquers does so because it excels in some

1. I.e. as well as a 'natural' slavery.
2. *Dikaion*.
3. In the Athenian Assembly a charge 'of illegality' (*paranomōn*) could be brought against a proposer of a law which contravened existing law.

good. It seems therefore that force is not without virtue, and that the only dispute is about what is just. Consequently some think that 'just' in this connection is a nonsense, others that it means precisely this, that 'the stronger shall rule'.[4] But when these propositions[5] are disentangled, the other arguments[6] have no validity or power to show that the superior in virtue ought not to rule and be master.

1255a21 Some take a firm stand (as they conceive it) on 'justice' in the sense of 'law', and claim that enslavement in war is just, simply as being legal; but they simultaneously deny it, since it is quite possible that undertaking the war may have been unjust in the first place. Also one cannot use the term 'slave' properly of one who is undeserving of being a slave; otherwise we should find among slaves and descendants of slaves even men of the noblest birth, should any of them be captured and sold. For this reason they will not apply the term slave to such people but use it only for non-Greeks.[7] But in so doing they are really seeking to define the slave by nature, which was our starting point; for one has to admit that there are some who are slaves everywhere, others who are slaves nowhere. And the same is true of noble birth: nobles regard themselves as of noble birth not only among their own people but everywhere, and they allow nobility of birth of non-Greeks to be valid only in non-Greek lands. This involves making two grades of free status and noble birth, one absolute, the other conditional. (In a play by Theodectes,[8] Helen is made to say, 'Who would think it proper to call me a slave, who am sprung of divine lineage on both sides?') But in introducing this point they are really basing the distinction between

4. Cf. Thrasymachus' arguments in Plato, *Republic* I.
5 (a) 'virtue, when ... force'; (b) 'anything which ... good'.
6. Those outlined in the first paragraph of the chapter?
7. Cf. Plato, *Republic* 469bc.
8. A tragic poet of the mid fourth century. The quotation is fr. 3 in A. Nauck, *Tragicorum Graecorum Fragmenta* (2nd ed., Leipzig, 1889), p. 802.

slave and free, noble-born and base-born, upon virtue
and vice. For they maintain that as man is born of man,
and beast of beast, so good is born of good. But frequently,
though this may be nature's intention, she is unable to
realize it.

1255b4 It is clear then that there is justification for the
difference of opinion: while it is not invariably true that
slaves are slaves by nature and others free, yet this distinction does in some cases actually prevail – cases where
it is expedient for the one to be master, the other to be
the slave. Whereas the one must be ruled, the other should
exercise the rule for which he is fitted by nature, thus
being the master. For, if the work of being a master is
badly done, that is contrary to the interest of both parties;
for the part and the whole, the soul and the body, have
identical interests; and the slave is in a sense a part of his
master, a living but separate part of his body.[9] For this
reason there is an interest in common and a feeling of
friendship between master and slave, wherever they are
by nature fitted for this relationship; but not when the
relationship arises out of the use of force and by the law
which we have been discussing.

I vii

(*1255b16–40*)

THE NATURE OF RULE OVER SLAVES

*This chapter is a good example of the fluidity of Aris-
totle's thought, and of some difficulties in his view of
slavery. First he again distinguishes mastership from other
forms of rule, and then suggests that the essence of being
a master lies in being a certain sort of person (i.e. rational,
wise, etc.), not in having knowledge of how to use slaves.
This curious point seems to be made because, as he
notices, some fairly humble knowledge, which we are*

9. Cf. I iv.

*tempted to call a 'master's' knowledge, may be possessed
and exercised by those who are not masters, e.g. overseers (who might be slaves themselves): how then can
it be the essence of mastership? On the other hand it is
difficult to see how one can be a master simply by being
of a certain character, without having an active relationship, presumably of command, with one's slaves. Aristotle
could perhaps have distinguished between (a) the knowledge, characteristic of and peculiar to a master, of the
'ends' of a slave's work, in some wide context, and (b) the
technical knowledge, possessed by overseers also, of the
work itself. But he does not do this, and seems to feel
in something of a dilemma. In this chapter we hear him
'thinking off the top of his head'.*

1255b16 From all this it is clear that there is a difference
between the rule of master over slave and the rule of a
statesman.[1] All forms of rule are not the same though
some say that they are.[1] Rule over naturally free men is
different from rule over natural slaves; rule in a household is monarchical, since every house has one ruler; the
rule of a statesman is rule over free and equal persons.
1255b20 A man is not called master in virtue of what
he knows but simply in virtue of the kind of person he
is; similarly with slave and free. Still, there *could* be such
a thing as a master's knowledge or a slave's knowledge.
The latter kind may be illustrated by the lessons given
by a certain man in Syracuse who, for a fee, trained
house-boys in their ordinary duties; and this kind of
instruction might well be extended to include cookery
and other forms of domestic service. For the tasks of the
various slaves differ, some being more essential, some
more highly valued (as the proverb has it 'slave before
slave, master before master').[2]

1. See I i.
2. A line of Philemon (fourth–third century), a poet of the
New Comedy (fr. 54 in T. Kock, *Comicorum Atticorum Fragmenta*, Leipzig, 1880–88, II i).

1255b30 All such fields of knowledge are the business of slaves, whereas a master's knowledge consists in knowing how to put his slaves to *use*; for it is not in his acquiring of slaves but in his use of them that he is master. But the use of slaves is not a form of knowledge that has any great importance or dignity, since it consists in knowing how to direct slaves to do the tasks which they ought to know how to do. Hence those masters whose means are sufficient to exempt them from the bother employ an overseer to take on this duty,[3] while they devote themselves to statecraft or philosophy. The knowledge of how to *acquire* slaves is different from both these,[4] the just method of acquisition, for instance, being a kind of military or hunting skill.[5]

So much may suffice to define master and slave.

I viii

(*1256a1–b39*)

THE NATURAL METHOD OF ACQUIRING GOODS

The main point of this chapter is simple enough: that the acquisition of goods/wealth (chrēmatistikē) is 'part' of household management in that the manager must have available a supply of certain necessary articles (food, money, etc.) which have to be acquired from somewhere by some means. True to his principles of natural teleology, Aristotle attempts to delimit a 'natural' mode of goods-acquisition (in the widest sense of 'goods'), by arguing from a comparison between (a) the way animals gain the 'goods' (food) provided by nature, by taking it directly

3. *Timē*.

4. The knowledge appropriate to a slave and the knowledge appropriate to his master as user.

5. A reflection evidently suggested by the preceding chapter (presumably with a tacit restriction that those enslaved by the 'just' method of acquisition must be 'natural' slaves: see also I viii and VII xiv, end).

*and by natural instinct from the environment, and (b)
certain modes of acquisition open to men (hunting, fishing, farming, etc.), by which they too take what nature
'gives'. The methods of (b) he suggests, being similar to
those of (a), are natural.*

*The argument is suggestive, and has the merit of point-
ing up a certain parallelism of behaviour as between
human and other animal life. Aristotle believes that each
species is eternal; inevitably and naturally, then, the
members of each must and do have some inner cause or
drive which ensures they get enough to live on, or the
species would not survive; and each animal species seems
to live off some other animal and/or vegetable species.
On the other hand, an opponent could make various
objections. They will centre on: (1) Have men and animals the same nature? If not, is it legitimate to infer
anything at all from (a) and (b), however formally similar
they may be as patterns of behaviour? (2) The difficulty
of deciding what behaviour is 'natural'. For example,
animals sometimes kill and eat their young. Is this practice 'natural', or a perversion of nature? If natural, should
human beings also kill and eat each other? (3) Even if one
could decide what human behaviour is 'natural', ought
this necessarily to be adopted as an ethical or social
norm? The chapter is in fact full of large assumptions
and inferences both expressed and unexpressed; and
again, as in I ii, his own account of the criteria for what
is natural (Physics, II i) would be informative background
reading.*

*One may note also: (a) Aristotle's inclusion of piracy
among the 'direct' modes of acquisition – in this he
simply reflects the fact that the ancient world took it
more or less for granted; (b) the near-equation of men
'fitted to be ruled' with animals: both are 'for' use by men
fit to rule, and slave-raiding against such inferior people
is evidently therefore 'natural'; (c) his disapproval of the
pursuit of unlimited wealth, on the grounds that only a
limited amount is necessary for the 'good' life.*

I viii

*In this set of four chapters on economics (viii–xi), and
the related discussion of* Nicomachean Ethics V v, *Karl
Marx found important anticipations of his own ideas;
for references, see Select Bibliographies.*

1256a1 Let us then, since the slave has proved to be
part of property, go on to consider property and the
acquisition of goods in general, still following our usual
method.[1] The first question to be asked might be this:
Is the acquisition of goods the same as household-
management, or a part of it, or subsidiary to it? And if
it is subsidiary, is it so in the same way as shuttle-making
is subsidiary to weaving, or as bronze-founding is to the
making of statues? For these two are not subsidiary in
the same way: the one provides instruments, the other
the material, that is, the substance out of which a product
is made, as wool for the weaver, bronze for the sculptor.
Now it is obvious that household-management is not the
same as the acquisition of goods, because it is the task
of the one to provide, the other to use; for what other
activity than managing the house is going to make use of
what is in the house? But whether acquisition of wealth
is *part* of household-management or a different kind of
activity altogether – that is a debatable question, if, that is
to say, it is the acquirer's task to see from what sources
goods and property may be derived. For there are many
varieties of property and riches, so that a first question
might be whether farming, and in general the provision
and superintendence of the food supply, are parts of the
acquisition of goods, or whether they are a different kind
of thing.
1256a19 But again, there are many different kinds of
food, and that means many different ways of life, both of
animals and humans; for as there is no life without food,
differences of food produce among animals different kinds
of life. Some animals live in herds and others scattered
about, whichever helps them to find food, some of them

1. See I i.

being carnivorous, some frugivorous, others eating anything. So, in order to make it easier for them to get these nutriments, nature has given them different ways of life. Again, since animals do not all like the same food but have different tastes according to their nature, so the ways of living of carnivorous and frugivorous animals themselves differ according to their different kinds. Similarly among human beings there are many varieties of life: first there are the nomads, who do least work, for nutriment from domestic animals is obtained with a minimum of toil and a maximum of ease; but when the animals have to move to fresh pastures, the human beings have to go with them, tilling as it were a living soil. Others live from hunting in all its variety, some being simply raiders, others fishermen who live near a lake, a marsh, a river, or a fish-bearing area of the sea; others live off birds and wild animals. The third and largest class lives off the earth and its cultivated crops.

1256a40 These then are the main ways of living by natural productive labour – ways which do not depend for a food-supply on exchange or trade. They are the nomadic, the agricultural, the piratical, fishing, and hunting. Some men live happily enough by combining them, making up for the deficiencies of one by adding a second at the point where the other fails to be self-sufficient; such combinations are nomadism with piracy, agriculture with hunting, and so on. They simply live the life that their needs compel them to.

1256b7 Such a mode of acquisition is clearly given by nature herself to all her creatures, both at the time of their birth and when they are fully grown. For some animals produce at the very beginning of procreation sufficient food to last their offspring until such time as these are able to get it for themselves; for example those which produce their young as grubs or eggs. Those which produce live offspring carry in themselves sufficient food for some time – the natural substance which we call milk. So obviously, by parity of reasoning, we must believe that animals are provided for at a later stage too – that plants exist for their sake, and that the other animals exist for the sake of man, tame ones for the use he can make of them as well as for the food they provide; and as for wild animals, most though not all can be used for food or are useful in other ways: clothing and instruments can be made out of them.

1256b20 If then nature makes nothing without some end in view, nothing to no purpose, it must be that nature has made all of them for the sake of man. This means that it is according to nature that even the art of war, since hunting is a part of it, should in a sense be a way of acquiring property; and that it must be used both against wild beasts and against such men as are by nature intended to be ruled over but refuse; for that is the kind of warfare which is by nature just.

1256b26   One form then of property-getting is, in accordance with nature, a part of household-management, in that either the goods must be there to start with, or this technique of property-getting must see that they are provided; goods, that is, which may be stored up, as being necessary for providing a livelihood, or useful to household or state as associations. And it looks as if wealth in the true sense consists of property such as this. For the amount of property of this kind which would give self-sufficiency for a good life is not limitless, although Solon in one of his poems said, 'No bound is set on riches for men.'[2] But there *is* a limit, as in the other skills; for none of them have any tools which are unlimited in size or number, and wealth is a collection of tools for use in the administration of a household or a state. It is clear therefore that there is a certain natural kind of property-getting practised by those in charge of a household or a state; and why this is so is also clear.

2. Fr. 13, line 71 in J. H. Edmonds, *Elegy and Iambus I* (London and New York, Loeb edition, 1931).

I ix

(1256b40–1258a18)

NATURAL AND UNNATURAL METHODS
OF ACQUIRING GOODS

Aristotle now proceeds to develop the distinction he has already mentioned briefly in I viii, between natural and unnatural methods of acquiring goods, chrēmatistikē. *In these two chapters he distinguishes:*

(1) The acquisition of goods (food, etc.) directly from the environment, by hunting, etc. Mutatis mutandis, *this method is common to animals and men, and is 'natural'* chrēmatistikē.

(2) Exchange, of goods for goods or for money. This too is natural: it adjusts inequalities due to nature in the distribution of goods, and is not pursued beyond the satisfaction of needs.

(3) Trade, strongly characterized by the use of money and a desire to pursue monetary gain beyond the satisfaction of needs. This is unnatural.

Of these, (2) and (3) are both chrēmatistikē, *'the acquisition of goods', in a general sense; but the word is also in this chapter used several times of (3) in a stronger and unfavourable sense: 'money-making'. Only (2), exchange* (metablētikē *or* allagē), *is naturally part of household-management, for (3), trade* (kapēlikē), *goes beyond what is necessary for the maintenance and self-sufficiency of a community, and is thus not natural.*

Aristotle's imaginative and plausible historical explanations of barter and of the invention of money, and his psychological speculations about the desire for unlimited acquisition, have impressive range and subtlety. Perhaps the sharpest reasoning of this chapter occurs in his comparison between money-making and other skills. A doctor recognizes no limit to the 'end' (health) of his craft: he would hardly wish to restrict the 'amount'

*of health he produces by his 'tools' (drugs, instruments,
etc.). But 'money-making' too is a skill, with an unlimited
end, money, and money is also its 'tool' or means. Ends
and means are therefore formally identical, and (unlike
in other skills) the ends do not tend to limit the means;
so means too, as a result of the skill of 'money-making',
chrēmatistikē, become unlimited. The unfortunate result
is that household-managers, who have the same means,
goods and money, as traders ('money-makers'), with which
to achieve their ends, i.e. of the household, suppose that
their means too, i.e. as well as those of traders, ought to
be unlimited. This, Aristotle claims, is a mistake, for the
manager's 'means' are for 'living', for which limited and
modest means (in the other sense of this word) suffice.
All this is nicely observed and cleverly argued in the
terminology of Aristotle's teleology, and his exposition
is an intricate combination of logic, imagination, psychology and common sense.*

1256b40 But there is another kind of property-getting
to which the term 'acquisition of goods'[1] is generally and
justly applied; and it is due to this that there is thought
to be no limit to wealth or property. Because it closely
resembles that form of acquisition of goods which we
have just been discussing,[2] many suppose that the two
are one and the same. But they are not the same, though
admittedly they are not very different; one is natural,
the other is not. This second kind develops from the
exercise of a certain kind of skill won by some experience.
1257a5 Let us begin our discussion thus: Every piece
of property has a double use; both uses are uses of the
thing itself, but they are not similar uses; for one is the
proper use of the article in question, the other is not. For
example a shoe may be used either to put on your foot
or to offer in exchange. Both are uses of the shoe; for

1. *Chrēmatistikē*, 'the acquisition of goods' in the unfavourable
sense (type (3) in the introduction to this chapter).
2. The 'natural' kind, described in the last paragraph of I viii.

even he that gives a shoe to someone who requires a shoe, and receives in exchange coins or food, is making use of the shoe as a shoe, but not the use proper to it, for a shoe is not expressly made for purposes of exchange. The same is the case with other pieces of property: the technique of exchange can be applied to all of them, and has its origin in a state of affairs often to be found in nature, namely, men having too much of this and not enough of that. (It was essential that the exchange should be carried on far enough to satisfy the needs of the parties. So clearly trade is not a natural way of getting goods.)[3] The technique of exchange was obviously not a practice of the earliest form of association, the household; it only came in with the large forms. Members of a single household shared all the belongings of that house, but members of different households shared many of the belongings of other houses also. Mutual need of the different goods made it essential to contribute one's share, and it is on this basis that many of the non-Greek peoples still proceed, i.e. by exchange: they exchange one class of useful goods for another – for example they take and give wine for corn and so on. But they do not carry the process any farther than this.

1257a28 Such a technique of exchange is not contrary to nature and is not a form of money-making;[1] for it keeps to its original purpose: to re-establish nature's own equilibrium of self-sufficiency. All the same it was out of it that money-making[1] arose, predictably enough – for as soon as the import of necessities and the export of surplus goods began to facilitate the satisfaction of needs beyond national frontiers, men inevitably resorted to the used of coined money. Not all the things that we naturally need are easily carried; and so for purposes of exchange men entered into an agreement to give to each other and accept from each other some commodity, itself useful for the business of living and also easily handled, such as

3. Because it carries exchange beyond the extent necessary to adjust natural inequalities in the distribution of goods.

iron, silver, and the like. The amounts were at first determined by size and weight, but eventually the pieces of metal were stamped. This did away with the necessity of measuring, since the stamp was put on as an indication of the amount.

1257a41 Once a currency was provided, development was rapid and what started as a necessary exchange became *trade*, the other mode of acquiring goods. At first it was probably quite a simple affair, but then it became more systematic[4] as men become more experienced at discovering where and how the greatest profits might be made out of the exchanges. That is why the technique of acquiring goods is held to be concerned primarily with coin, and to have the function of enabling one to see where a great deal of money may be procured (the technique does after all produce wealth *in the form of* money); and wealth is often regarded as being a large quantity of coin because coin is what the techniques of acquiring goods and of trading are concerned with.[5]

1257b10 Sometimes on the other hand coinage is regarded as so much convention[6] and artificial trumpery having no root in nature, since, if those who employ a currency system choose to alter it, the coins cease to have their value and can no longer be used to procure the necessities of life. And it will often happen that a man with wealth in the form of coined money will not have enough to eat; and what a ridiculous kind of wealth is that which even in abundance will not save you from dying with hunger! It is like the story told of Midas:[7] because of the inordinate greed of his prayer everything that was set before him was turned to gold. Hence men

4. *Technikos*; cf. 'skill' at end of first paragraph.

5. In shops, etc.: see end of next paragraph.

6. An etymological point: 'coinage' = *nomisma*; 'convention' = *nomos*.

7. A legendary King of Phrygia, notorious for extreme wealth. He prayed to the god Dionysus that everything he touched should turn to gold: the prayer was granted, and naturally he found he could not eat.

seek to define a different sense of wealth and of the acquisition of goods, and are right to do so, for there *is* a difference: on the one hand wealth and the acquisition of goods in accordance with nature, and belonging to household-management; on the other hand the kind that is associated with trade, which is not productive of goods in the full sense but only through their exchange. And it is thought to be concerned with coinage, because coinage both limits the exchange and is the unit of measurement by which it is performed; and there is indeed[8] no limit to the amount of riches to be got from this mode of acquiring goods.[1]

1257b25 The art of healing aims at producing unlimited health, and every other skill aims at its own end without limit, wishing to secure that to the highest possible degree; on the other hand the *means* towards the end are not unlimited, the end itself setting the limit in each case. But for this kind[1] of acquisition of goods the end provides no limit, because the end is wealth in that form, i.e. the possession of goods. The kind which is household-management, on the other hand, does have a limit, since it is not the function of household-management to acquire goods.[9] So, while it seems that there must be a limit to every form of wealth, in practice we find that the opposite occurs: all those engaged in acquiring goods go on increasing their coin without limit, because the two modes of acquisition of goods are so similar. For they overlap in that both are concerned with the same thing, property; but in their use of it they are dissimilar: in one case the end is sheer increase, in the other something different. Some people therefore imagine that increase is the function of household-management, and never cease to believe that their store of coined money ought to be either hoarded, or increased without limit.

8. See the quotation from Solon in I viii.

9. Not, at any rate, without limit. See the first paragraph of I viii and the first two of I x: the function of household-management is to *use* goods (and use sets limits to their acquisition).

1257b40 The reason why some people get this notion into their heads may be that they are eager for life but not for the good life; so, desire for life being unlimited, they desire also an unlimited amount of what enables it to go on. Others again, while aiming at the good life, seek what is conducive to the pleasure of the body. So, as this too appears to depend on the possession of property, their whole activity centres on business, and the second mode of acquiring goods[1] owes its existence to this. For where enjoyment consists in excess, men look for that skill which produces the excess that is enjoyed. And if they cannot procure it through money-making,[1] they try to get it by some other means, using all their faculties for this purpose, which is contrary to nature: courage, for example, is to produce confidence, not goods; nor yet is it the job of military leadership and medicine to produce goods, but victory and health. But these people turn all skills into skills of acquiring goods, as though that were the end and everything had to serve that end.

1258a14 We have now discussed the acquisition of goods, both the unnecessary kind of acquisition,[1] what it is and why we do in fact make use of it, and the necessary, which differs from the other in being concerned with household-management and food in a way that accords with nature, and also in being limited as opposed to unlimited.

I x

(*1258a19–1258b8*)

THE PROPER LIMITS OF HOUSEHOLD-MANAGEMENT; THE UNNATURALNESS OF MONEY-LENDING

In recapitulating the last two chapters, Aristotle first argues, more explicitly than hitherto, that the duty of the household-manager is to use and distribute goods, not to acquire them. He then adds a point of major importance: that the acquisition of goods (chrēmatistikē) *from the charging of interest* (tokos) *is the most 'unnatural' of all modes of business. In effect, he now subdivides the third method of acquiring goods (see introduction to I ix) into: (a) trade, the exchange of goods for money and money for goods, with a desire to make a profit; (b) making a profit from dealing in money alone, i.e. by charging interest. Both methods are 'unnatural', but (a) retains some features of genuine exchange since actual commodities do enter into the transactions, and at least the money is used for its proper purpose, exchange, even if there is a desire for profit. Method (a) is therefore less contrary to nature than (b).*

No doubt money-lending was, as Aristotle says, disliked; but it is noticeable that his own objections to it here are not directly social and humanitarian or even economic: rather, they are ideological and metaphysical. However, if the state is (as he believes) natural, and money-lending unnatural, then the latter will presumably hinder the well-being of the former. To this extent, his objections to money-lending do indeed rest on social grounds.

1258a19 The answer also is clear to the question raised at the beginning,[1] namely whether or not acquiring goods is the business of the household-manager and statesman.[2] The answer is perhaps that wealth should be at hand for his use from the start. Just as statesmanship has no need to make men, who are the material which nature provides and which statesmanship takes and uses, so nature can be expected to provide food, whether from land or sea or from some other source, and it is on this basis that the manager can perform his duty of distributing these supplies. So weaving is not the art of producing wool but of using it, though it is also the art of knowing good yarns from bad and the suitable from the unsuitable.

1258a27 If, on the other hand, we do allow that acquir-

1. I viii *ad init.*   2. See I i.

ing goods is a part of management, why, it may well be asked, is not the art of medicine also a part? After all, the members of a household need to be healthy quite as much as to keep alive or meet their daily needs. The answer is that up to a point it *is* the business of manager or ruler to see to health, but only up to a point; beyond that it is the doctor's business. So in the matter of goods: to some extent these *are* the concern of the manager, but beyond that they belong to the subsidiary skill. But best it is, as has been just said, that goods should be provided at the outset by nature. For it is a function of nature to provide food for whatever is brought to birth, since that from which it is born has a surplus which provides food in every case. We conclude therefore that the form of acquisition of goods that depends on crop and animal husbandry is for all men in accordance with nature.

1258a38 The acquisition of goods is then, as we have said, of two kinds; one, which is necessary and approved of, is to do with household-management; the other, which is to do with trade and depends on exchange, is justly regarded with disapproval, since it arises not from nature but from men's gaining from each other. Very much disliked also is the practice of charging interest; and the dislike is fully justified, for the gain arises out of currency itself, not as a product of that for which currency was provided. Currency was intended to be a means of exchange, whereas interest represents an increase in the currency itself. Hence its name,[3] for each animal produces its like, and interest is currency born of currency. And so of all types of business this is the most contrary to nature

3. *Tokos* ('offspring').

(1258b9–1259a36)

SOME PRACTICAL CONSIDERATIONS, ESPECIALLY ON THE CREATION OF MONOPOLY

This somewhat miscellaneous chapter starts promisingly by stressing practice as opposed to theory; but the first three paragraphs give us only a résumé of the useful and profitable ways of acquiring goods (chrēmatistikē), classified in a manner broadly similar to that adopted in the preceding three chapters, but differing in certain respects. Aristotle rightly stresses the usefulness of describing practical details, but clearly his heart is not in them, and he soon announces, after some swift generalizations in the third paragraph, that other writers may be consulted. He then draws attention to scattered reports of successful methods of acquiring goods, and with the instinct of an encyclopedist suggests they should be collected. He gives us two entertaining examples of the creation of monopolies, and no doubt feels a certain satisfaction at Thales' triumphant demonstration that philosophers are far from the financial idiots they are often taken to be. He concludes with the claim that such information about methods is useful to statesmen.

1258b9 Now that we have discussed adequately the theory,[1] we ought to speak also about practice. In matters like this, theoretical speculation is free, but practical experience is tied fast to circumstances and needs. Some useful branches of the technique of acquiring wealth will now be mentioned. One may have experience in: (1) *Stock-rearing*, in which one needs to know what kinds are most profitable and where and how, e.g. how to acquire horses, cattle, sheep and other animals similarly;

1. Of the acquisition of goods.

and further one must know by experience which of these are most profitable as compared with the rest, and which kinds in which areas, since some do better here, others there. (2) *Tillage*, of fields sown with crops and fields planted for fruit. (3) *Bee-keeping*, and rearing such birds and fishes as can contribute to supplies. Those are the three main branches of the first and most appropriate way of acquiring wealth.

1258b21 Of the other method, that of exchange, the main branch is (1) *commerce*, subdivided into (a) shipping, (b) carrying goods, (c) offering them for sale. In all these there are wide differences according to whether one looks for a high return or for security. Then (2) *money-lending*, and (3) *working for pay*, whether (a) as a skilled mechanic, or (b) as an unskilled worker useful only in manual labour. Somewhere between these two main categories of acquisition of goods we might put a third, since it has elements in it both of nature and of exchange: I refer to what is got out of the earth itself or from uncultivated but useful things growing out of the earth – such occupations as timber-working, and mining of every description. This latter can be extensively subdivided, for the substances mined from the earth are of many types.

1258b33 About each of these methods I have still[2] spoken only in a general way; and however useful a detailed account might be for those likely to be engaged in such occupations, it would be irksome to spend much time on them. Those occupations which require most skill are those in which there is the smallest element of chance, the most mechanical are those which cause most deterioration to the bodies of the workers, the most slavish those in which most use is made of the body, and the most ignoble those in which there is least need to exercise virtue too. Moreover, people have written books on these topics. Charetides of Paros and Apollodorus of

2. I.e. the foregoing details, though abundant, are nevertheless so incomplete as to be mere summaries.

Lemnos have manuals on agriculture, both crops and fruits, and others on other subjects, so that anyone who is interested may study them in those writers' works.

1259a3 It would be advisable to make a collection of all those scattered reports of methods by which men have succeeded in making money. It would certainly be very useful for those who think money-making[3] important. For instance, Thales of Miletus used a money-spinning device which, though it was ascribed to his prowess as a philosopher, is in principle open to anybody. The story is as follows: people had been saying reproachfully to him that philosophy was useless, as it had left him a poor man. But he, deducing from his knowledge of the stars that there would be a good crop of olives, while it was still winter and he had a little money to spare, used it to pay deposits on all the oil-presses in Miletus and Chios, thus securing their hire. This cost him only a small sum, as there were no other bidders. Then the time of the olive-harvest came, and as there was a sudden and simultaneous demand for oil-presses he hired them out at any price he liked to ask. He made a lot of money, and so demonstrated that it is easy for philosophers to become rich, if they want to; but that is not their object in life. Such is the story of how Thales gave proof of his cleverness; but, as we have said, the principle can be applied generally: the way to make money is to get, if you can, a monopoly for yourself. Hence we find states also employing this method when they are short of money: they secure themselves a monopoly.

1259a23 There was a man in Sicily, too, who used a sum of money that had been deposited with him to buy up all the iron from the foundries; then, when the merchants arrived from their shops, he used to be the only seller; and without raising the price unduly he turned his fifty talents into a hundred and fifty. When the ruler Dionysius heard of this he told the man that he regarded such

3. *Chrēmatistikē* in sense (3) in the introduction to I ix.

ways of raising money as detrimental to his own interests
and that he must therefore depart from Syracuse at once,
though he might take his money with him. Thales' notion
and this man's are the same: both managed to create
a monopoly for themselves. All this knowledge is useful
for statesmen too; for many states are in greater need of
business and the income it brings than a household is.
Hence we find that some of those who direct the affairs
of a state actually make this their sole concern.

I xii

(*1259a37–1259b17*)

BRIEF ANALYSIS OF THE AUTHORITY
OF HUSBAND AND FATHER

*Aristotle now reverts to the three relationships he had
enumerated at the beginning of I iii: master/slave, hus-
band/wife, parent/child. (I iii–vii had discussed the first;
viii–xi was devoted to* chrēmatistikē *in its various senses.)
The burden of this chapter is to suggest that a husband
is to his wife as a statesman-ruler is to his fellow-citizens,
and that a father is to his child as a king to his subjects.
It is, as he uneasily recognizes, a point against the first
parallel that citizens usually rule turn and turn about
(cf. III vi). The chapter is rather sketchy and contains
a number of unargued assumptions (e.g. that the male
is by nature more fitted to rule than the female); it is
perhaps best taken rapidly as an introduction to the next,
which is the last in Book I.*

1259a37   There are, as we saw,[1] three parts of household-
management, one being the rule of a master, which has
already been dealt with, next the rule of a father, and a

---

1. Cf. I iii *ad init. Despotikē* = 'rule of a master' (over slaves);
patrikē = 'rule of a father', 'paternal'; *gamikē* = 'to do with
marriages', 'matrimonial'.

third which arises out of the marriage relationship. This is included because rule is exercised over wife and children – over both of them as free persons, but in other respects differently: over a wife, rule is as by a statesman; over children, as by a king. For the male is more fitted to rule than the female, unless conditions are quite contrary to nature; and the elder and fully grown is more fitted than the younger and undeveloped. It is true that in most cases of rule by statesmen[2] there is an interchange of the role of ruler and ruled, which aims to preserve natural equality and non-differentiation; nevertheless, so long as one is ruling and the other is being ruled, the ruler seeks to mark distinctions in outward dignity, in style of address, and in honours paid. (Witness what Amasis said about his foot-basin.)[3] As between male and female this kind of relationship is permanent. Rule over children is royal, for the begetter is ruler by virtue both of affection and of age, and this type of rule is royal. Homer therefore was right in calling Zeus 'father of gods and men',[4] as he was king over them all. For a king ought to have a natural superiority, but to be no different in birth; and this is just the condition of elder in relation to younger and of father to son.

I xiii

(1259b18–1260b24)

MORALITY AND EFFICIENCY IN THE HOUSEHOLD

The three relationships internal to the household (master/slave, husband/wife, parent/child) are for

2. *Politikē archē*, in the particular sense of citizens ruling over fellow-citizens; cf. I i, v, vii.

3. Herodotus (II 172) relates how King Amasis of Egypt (sixth century), being reproached for his humble origins, had a foot-basin refashioned into a statue of a god, which the Egyptians then worshipped – the moral being that it is what one is *now* that matters.

4. *Iliad* I, 144.

*Aristotle, as a moralist, of greater importance than econo-
mics. It is clearly essential that all members of the household should possess fitness for the performance of their
various functions; and this fitness is described by the very
general term* aretē, *'virtue'. This can include physical
strength or technical skill; but the burden of this chapter
is to distinguish between these qualities and* moral *virtue,
which Aristotle regards as equally part of fitness for a
task. Moral virtue is in fact not merely a spiritual or
mental state: it is related to activity and function. And
since a slave has no function but to serve his master, the
virtue of a slave need reach no more than a minimal level
required to enable him to perform his tasks. Moral virtue
also requires the faculty of reasoning, which is possessed
by the master rather than the slave; the master must therefore impart to his slaves, by instruction and habituation,
such moral virtue as he judges necessary. Free craftsmen,
by the nature of their occupation, approximate to slaves.
Much modern sentiment would of course distinguish between technical efficiency and moral virtue in a quite
different spirit, and wish to say that a man of humble
occupation may nevertheless be very 'virtuous' indeed.
Aristotle would find this difficult, since his notion of
moral virtue is conditioned by his assumption that it is
for particular purposes – which in the case of slaves are
lowly and limited.*

*The chapter is particularly rich in suggestion, and in
his comparative treatment of the moral virtues and capacities of men, women, children and slaves Aristotle
diverges from Plato in several interesting and thoughtful
ways, which have been discussed by Fortenbaugh (in the
third collection of essays in the Select Bibliographies).*

*The discussion of households in Book I has been
largely concerned with property and its acquisition, and
with slaves. Personal family relationships are analysed in
this chapter to the extent that Aristotle treats the male
head of household as the source of virtue in his wife and
children (and slaves), but he does not go into practical*

*detail, and in the last two paragraphs he postpones
further discussion until later (though something is said of
marriage relationships in VII xvi). The final sentence announces a transition to the topic of Book II, ideal states.*

1259b18 It is clear then that in household-management
the people are of greater importance than the inanimate
property, and their virtue[1] of more account than that of
the property which we call their wealth; and also that the
free men are of more account than slaves. About slaves
the first question to be asked is whether in addition to
their virtue as tools and servants they have another and
more valuable one. Can they possess restraint, courage, justice, and every other condition of that kind, or have they in
fact nothing but the serviceable quality of their persons?
1259b26 The question may be answered in either of
two ways, but both present a difficulty. If we say that
slaves have these virtues, how then will they differ from
free men? If we say that they have not, the position is
anomalous, since they are human beings and share in
reason. Roughly the same question can be put in relation
to wife and child. Have not these also virtues? Ought a
woman to be 'restrained', 'brave', and 'just', and is a child
sometimes 'intemperate', sometimes 'restrained', or not?
1259b32 All these questions might be regarded as parts
of our wider inquiry into the natural ruler and ruled, and
in particular whether or not the virtue of the one is the
same as the virtue of the other. For if the highest excellence is required of both, why should one rule unqualifiedly, and the other unqualifiedly obey? (A distinction
of more or less will not do here; the difference between
ruling and obeying is one of kind, and quantitative
difference is simply not that at all.) If on the other hand
the one is to have virtues, and the other not, we have a
surprising state of affairs. For if he that rules is not to be
restrained and just, how shall he rule well? And if the
ruled lacks these virtues, how shall he *be* ruled well? For

1. *Aretē.*

if he is intemperate and feckless, he will perform none of his duties. Thus it becomes clear that both ruler and ruled must have a share in virtue, but that there are differences in virtue in each case, as there are also among those who by nature rule. An immediate indication of this is afforded by the soul, where we find natural ruler and natural subject, whose virtues we regard as different – one being that of the rational element, the other of the non-rational. It is therefore clear that the same feature will be found in the other cases too, so that most instances of ruling and being ruled are natural. For rule of free over slave, male over female, man over boy, are all different, because, while parts of the soul are present in each case, the distribution is different. Thus the deliberative faculty in the soul is not present at all in a slave; in a female it is present but ineffective, in a child present but undeveloped.

1260a14 We should therefore take it that the same conditions inevitably prevail in regard to the moral virtues also, namely that all must participate in them but not all in the same way, but only as may be required by each for his proper function. The ruler then must have moral virtue in its entirety; for his function is in its fullest sense that of a master-craftsman, and reason is a master-craftsman.[2] And the other members must have such amount as is appropriate to each. So it is evident that each of the classes spoken of must have moral virtue, and that restraint is *not* the same in a man as in a woman, nor justice or courage either, as Socrates thought;[3] the one is the courage of a ruler, the other the courage of a servant, and likewise with the other virtues.

2. *Architektōn*, 'chief maker', 'master builder'. This rather curious remark seems to mean that a slave has moral virtue only in so far as he is required by his master to have it to fulfil his function, with little or no intellectual appreciation of its nature and reasons. But his master has ethical virtue in its entirety, a full intellectual and rational understanding of it, and of why and how far his slave must possess it to perform his tasks well.

3. I.e. *wrongly* thought that in some sense they *were* the same (Xenophon, *Symposium* II, 9; Plato, *Republic* 452e ff., *Meno* 71e ff.).

1260a24 If we look at the matter case by case it will become clearer. For those who talk in generalities and say that virtue is 'a good condition of the soul', or that it is 'right conduct' or the like, delude themselves. Better than those who look for definitions in that manner are those who, like Gorgias,[4] *enumerate* the different virtues. For instance, the poet[5] singles out 'silence' as 'bringing credit to a woman'; but that is not so for a man. This is the method of assessment that we should always follow. Take the child: he is not yet fully developed, so we cannot speak of his virtue as belonging to him in relation to himself; it exists only in relation to the progress of his development towards adulthood, and to whoever is his guide. So too with slave and master: we laid it down that a slave is useful for necessary tasks, so the amount of virtue required will not be very great, but only enough to ensure that he does not neglect his work through intemperance or fecklessness.

1260a36 If this is true, one will naturally ask whether skilled workers too will not need virtue to keep them from the intemperance which often interferes with their work. But the parallel is far from exact, because the slave shares his master's life, whereas the craftsman lives away from his employer and participates in virtue in the same measure as he participates in slavery;[6] for the skilled mechanic is in a restricted sense in a condition of slavery. There is also this difference, that the slave is one of a group that are slaves by nature, which cannot be said of a shoemaker or other skilled worker. It is clear therefore that it is the master who ought to be the cause of such virtue in his slave, not the man who instructs the slave

4. As reported at the beginning of Plato's *Meno*. Gorgias was a 'sophist' of the fifth century.

5. Sophocles, *Ajax* 293.

6. Aristotle expresses himself rather mysteriously, but he probably means that the craftsman, though legally free, is 'slavish' because of his occupation, and like the slave attains moral virtue only in so far as he is controlled and instructed by a master/employer.

in his tasks. Hence they are wrong who would deny all reason to slaves and say that a master has nothing to do but issue orders;[7] suggestion and advice are even more appropriately given to slaves than to children.

1260b8 So much then for our discussion of these matters. As for man and wife, children and father, and the virtue that appertains to each and their intercourse one with another, what is right in that connection and what is not, and the proper pursuit of the good therein and the avoidance of the bad – all such matters it will be necessary to discuss in connection with the constitutions. For these relationships are part of the household, and every household is part of a state; and the virtue of the part ought to be examined in relation to the virtue of the whole. This means that both children and women must be educated with an eye to the constitution – at least if it is true that it makes a difference to the soundness of a state that its children should be sound, and its women too. And it must make a difference; for women make up half the adult free population, and from children come those who will participate in the constitution.

1260b20 So now that we have finished with these matters, and decided to discuss the rest in another place, we will regard the present topic as concluded, and make a fresh beginning. And let our first topic be those who have pronounced an opinion on the best constitution.

7. Presumably a reference to Plato, *Laws* 777e.

BOOK II

II i

(1260b27–1261a9)

INTRODUCTION TO IDEAL STATES:
HOW FAR SHOULD SHARING GO?

The final sentence of Book I stated the main topic of Book II, a consideration of ideal states. The book contains also an account of some actual *states which Aristotle considers to be good.*

This essay in the comparative study of political institutions has a long tradition behind it. From the very earliest stages of Greek thought as we know it there was sustained controversy about what constituted good and bad government (see for instance Hesiod, Works and Days, *and Herodotus III 80 ff.). But the debate was for the most part piecemeal and partisan; and although Aristotle has his prejudices, and axes to grind, his approach is by Greek standards systematic and detached. Like most of his extant work, it is also rather donnish in tone – and indeed in the opening paragraph of this chapter he seems to feel the need to apologize for a certain academic 'pernicketiness'.*

Aristotle starts from the point he had made at the beginning of Book I, that the state is an association. Now an association implies sharing of some kind; so the fundamental question seems to be, how far should sharing go in a state? This question prompts him to think of some of the most radical and celebrated proposals for shared life and property, those of Plato's Republic.

1260b27 We have undertaken to discuss that form of association which is the state,[1] and to ask which of all such associations would be best if we were in a position to

1. *Koinōnia politikē*; see I i *init.*

live exactly as we would like. So we must look at the other constitutions too, for example those that are in use in states that have the reputation of being governed by good laws, or any others that have been sketched by writers and appear to be good. Our purpose is partly to see what in them is right and useful and what is not; but we also wish to make it clear that if we keep looking for something different from what we find there, we do not do so out of a desire to be clever: we have embarked on this investigation simply because in fact none of these existing constitutions[2] is satisfactory.

1260b36 We must begin at the natural starting point of this inquiry. In a state, either all the citizens share all things, or they share none, or they share some but not others. It is clearly impossible that they should have no share in anything; at the very least, a constitution being a form of association, they must share in the territory, the single territory of a single state, of which single state the citizens are sharers.[3] The question then becomes twofold: if a city is to be run well, is it better that all the citizens should share in all things capable of being shared, or only in some of them and not in others? It is certainly quite possible for citizens to go shares with each other in children, in wives, and in pieces of property, as in the *Republic* of Plato. For in that work Socrates says that children, wives, and property ought to be held in common.[4] We ask, therefore, is it better to do as we now do, or should we adopt the law proposed in the *Republic*?

2. Whether written or actual, presumably.
3. The argument depends partly on the obvious verbal connection between *koinōnia* ('association') and *koinōnein/koinōnos* ('to share'/'sharer').
4. *Republic* 427c ff. 'Held in common' = *koina*.

II ii

(1261a10–1261b15)

EXTREME UNITY IN PLATO'S 'REPUBLIC'

Plato's proposal in the Republic *that wives should be held in common is now attacked by Aristotle for a number of connected reasons. His fundamental objection in this chapter is that the* purpose *of the proposal, i.e. to help make the state as much of a 'unity' as possible, is in itself misguided: diversity of membership and functions, he argues, is essential.*

Aristotle is often a puzzlingly unsympathetic and even obtuse critic of Plato, and the present chapter is a good example of his apparently rather perverse approach. (a) He ignores the fact that the community of wives in the Republic *is not meant to be practised by the whole state, but only by the two upper classes (the 'Guardians'), for special and particular reasons (eugenics, and to remove temptations of selfishness and rivalry from their path). (b) He misrepresents the kind of unity Plato advocated, which was not the literal unity of number or function, but of opinion and sentiment and moral standards – the agreement by all members of the state that certain political practices, social institutions and aesthetic standards were good, and others bad. Diversity of function (as between different occupations, and between ruler and ruled) was recognized and provided for as much by Plato as by Aristotle. Much of the criticism in this chapter therefore pushes at an open door.*

But Aristotle's relationship to Plato is a rich and complex topic, and it should be stressed that on the justice of his criticisms of Plato's philosophy, and of the political theory in particular, more than one opinion is possible. For references to discussions (especially Morrow's and Bornemann's), see the Select Bibliographies.

1261a10 The proposal that wives should be held in common presents many difficulties of which these three are the chief: (a) Socrates' arguments clearly fail to justify the *purpose* for which he claims such legislation is necessary; (b) further, the end which he says the state should have is, in the form described in that dialogue, unworkable;[1] yet (c) it is nowhere laid down in what other sense it is to be understood. I am referring to the assumption made by Socrates, 'It is best that the whole state should be as much of a unity as possible.'[2] But obviously a state which becomes progressively more and more of a unity will cease to be a state at all. Plurality of numbers is natural in a state; and the farther it moves away from plurality towards unity, the less a state it becomes and the more a household, and the household in turn an individual. (We would all agree that the household is more of a unity than the state and the individual than the household.) So, even if it were possible to make such a unification, it ought not be be done; it will destroy the state.

1261a22 The state consists not merely of a plurality of men, but of different *kinds* of men; you cannot make a state out of men who are all alike. Consider in this connection the difference between a state and an alliance: the purpose of an alliance is military assistance, and its usefulness depends on the amount of that assistance, not on any differentiation in kind; the greater the weight, the greater the pull. (This sort of difference can be observed as between a state and a nation, when the people are not scattered in villages, but are like the Arcadians.) On the other hand, constituents which must form a single unity differ in kind. Hence, as I have already stated in my *Ethics*,[3] it is reciprocal equivalence that keeps a state in being. This principle is essential even among citizens

1. Perhaps a reference to *Republic* 472–3.
2. *Republic* 422e ff., 462a ff.
3. *Nicomachean Ethics*, V v. 'Reciprocal equivalence', *to ison to antipeponthos*, the principle of mutually supporting *diversity* of function, whereby (to take a simple example) a shoemaker provides

who are free and equal; for they cannot all hold office simultaneously, but must do so for a year at a time or for some other appointed period. This does in fact ensure that all rule, just as much as if shoemakers and carpenters were to change places with each other instead of always keeping to the same kind of work.

1261a38 On this analogy, of course, it is better that those in charge of the political association[4] should, if it is possible, not change places but always be the same people. But where that is not possible, since they are all by nature equal, and where it is at the same time just that all should share in the benefit (or burden) of ruling, then the principles (a) that equals should yield place in turn, and (b) that out of office they should all be similar, at least approximate to that practice.[5] Some rule while others are ruled, and by doing this by turns it is just as if they became different persons every time. There is similar differentiation among those ruling, for they hold now one office, now another.

1261b6 It is clear from all this that the state is not a natural unity in the sense that some people think, and that what has been alleged to be the greatest good in states does in fact make for their dissolution; whereas that which is the 'good' of a thing makes for its preservation. And here is another indication that excessive striving for unification is a bad thing in a state: a household is a more self-sufficient thing than the individual, the state than the household; and the moment the association comes to comprise enough people to be self-sufficient,

---

shoes for a baker, who provides bread in return. Here, however, Aristotle uses the term in a wider and more political sense, to summarize the 'services' ruler and ruled render to each other by the proper performance of the duties of each role.

4. *Politikē koinōnia*, i.e. the state: see I i.

5. I.e. that those in charge should always be the same. The sentence is cloudily written, and not improved by Ross's punctuation, which seems to me plainly wrong: I replace the full stop in 1261b2 by a comma.

effectively we have a state. Since, then, a greater degree of self-sufficiency is to be preferred to a lesser, the lesser degree of unity is to be preferred to the greater.[6]

II iii

(1261b16–1262a24)

EXTREME UNITY IS IMPRACTICABLE

This chapter contains a number of related practical criticisms of Plato's proposals for community of wives and children. Aristotle's central point is, as far as it goes, perfectly fair: the scheme of the Republic *would dilute strong emotional, sexual and family ties to a point at which no one would feel any attachment to or responsibility for anything or anyone; and such a state of affairs, besides being hardly 'unity', is harmful.*

Has Aristotle missed the point? Or has he, at least, been unwilling to make Plato's assumptions? Plato was as conscious as Aristotle was of the weakness and selfishness of mankind; yet he apparently judged there to be no reason in principle why men and women should not all regard other members of their community with the same degree of affection that they now lavish on their own wives or husbands exclusively, nor why the same should not apply to attitudes to children and property. What Aristotle does is to bring some sensible and powerful practical objections, and claim that Plato's proposal is simply not 'on'. Very probably; but Plato thinks the effort worth making. Two connected points seem fair: (a) Plato may be, and probably is, unrealistic or even misguided in his aims; but in the absence of experiment, utopian ideals can hardly be invalidated by even the

6. That is to say self-sufficiency, which is desirable, is incompatible with unity: the individual (a unity) is least self-sufficient, whereas the state is most self-sufficient, though least a unity. If it *were* made a unity, its self-sufficiency would vanish.

*strongest doubts about their practicability. (b) Aristotle
seems to assume that to divide affection among several
persons is necessarily to dilute it, as if one had a sort of
finite 'fund' of affection that has (as it were) to be shared
round – that if I have (say) four brothers I must regard
each with only half the affection I would lavish on each
of two. But to regard all men as brothers has been the aim
of more than one religion (to say nothing of secular movements), and a certain success seems possible. In the long
run it may be achieved by education and habituation;
meanwhile, Plato's utopianism no doubt needs to be
balanced by Aristotle's sober scepticism.*

1261b16 Again, even if it is best to have maximum unity
within the association, the suggested criteria of its achievement do not seem cogent. Socrates thinks[1] that if all
unanimously say 'mine' and 'not mine', this is an indication of the state's complete unity. But the word 'all' is
used in two senses: 'all separately' and 'all together'. Used
in the former sense this might better bring about what
Socrates wants; for each man will always refer to the same
boy as his son, the same woman as his wife, and will
speak in the same way of his possessions and whatever
else comes within his purview. But that is not at all how
people will speak who hold wives and children in common. They may do so all together, but not each separately; and the same with regard to possessions. Thus there
is a clear fallacy in the use of the word 'all'; for words
such as 'all' and 'both', and 'odd' and 'even', owing to
their double senses, lead to highly disputable conclusions
even[2] in reasoning. So, while in one sense[3] of the word it
may be an admirable state of affairs where 'all' say the
same thing, it is nevertheless impossible; whereas in the

1. *Republic* 462c.
2. I.e. even where terms are used with more than ordinary care.
3. I.e. 'all separately': each object held in common would be
called 'his own' by each person individually in the usual strong
and private sense of 'own'.

other sense[4] it is not conducive to a feeling of solidarity.

1261b32 There is further harm in the doctrine: the greater the number of owners, the less the respect for common property. People are much more careful of their personal possessions than of those owned communally; they exercise care over common property only in so far as they are personally affected. Other reasons apart, the thought that someone else is looking after it tends to make them careless of it. (This is rather like what happens in domestic service: a greater number of servants sometimes does less work than a smaller.) Each citizen acquires a thousand sons, but these are not one man's sons; any one of them is equally the son of any person, and as a result will be equally neglected by everyone.

1262a1 Moreover, when a man uses 'my' in this way with reference to a fellow-citizen, he is speaking only as a small fraction of a large number. In saying 'my son' or 'X's son' is 'doing well' or 'not doing well', he is referring to each one of a thousand fathers (or whatever the number of the citizens may be), and even then with some dubiety, since it is uncertain whether any particular citizen is in fact the father of a son, and of one that has survived. Is not our ordinary use of the word 'my', in states as they are now, better than this use of it by two thousand or ten thousand individuals, all with reference to the same thing? In the ordinary way one man calls his own son the same person whom another calls his own brother, and whom a third calls cousin, or some other term of blood-relationship or of connection by marriage, his own in the first place, or of his own relatives; and yet another speaks of him as a member of his brotherhood[5] or tribe. Anybody would rather be a cousin who really was someone's own *personal* cousin, than a son in the manner described.

4. I.e. 'all together': each object held in common would be called 'his own' by each person, but in the weak sense of 'own', as being possessed by many others also.

5. *Phratria*, a formally organized kinship-group.

1262a14 Again, one could not prevent people from making assumptions about their own brothers, sons, fathers, or mothers. For the likenesses which exist between parents and their offspring would inevitably be regarded as sure signs of connection. And this is what actually occurs, according to reports of certain writers of travels round the world, who tell us that some of the peoples of Upper Libya have community of wives, but they can always tell whose children are whose by their resemblances. And there are some females, both human and non-human (like mares and cows), which have a remarkable natural power of producing offspring resembling their sires, like the one they called the 'just mare' of Pharsalus.[6]

II iv

(1262a25–1262b37)

FURTHER OBJECTIONS TO COMMUNITY OF WIVES AND CHILDREN

At the end of the last chapter Aristotle had pointed out that recognition of identity on grounds of likeness would inevitably frustrate Plato's intention to abolish private family ties among his Guardians. He now describes some awkward consequences of their not recognizing each other: i.e. the removal of certain inhibitions on undesirable conduct, and of certain incentives to desirable conduct. The final paragraph is a complaint that this confusion about identity will be accentuated by the transfer of certain children from one class to another.

Aristotle makes no mention of certain elaborate safeguards that Plato prescribed (e.g. 457–61), and some of his objections seem rather captious. But in general he has a sharp eye for the practical difficulties of Plato's

6. 'Just', because in producing offspring like the stallion she gave 'good value'. Pharsalus was a city of Thessaly.

scheme; and his criticism is the more telling in that he presents the drawbacks not merely as serious in themselves, from anyone's point of view, but as actually militating against the very ideals of amity and unity of which Socrates makes so much.

1262a25 Here are some further evil consequences which could hardly be avoided by those who set up such a form of association: assault, homicide, both intentional and unintentional, feuds and slander. All these are unholy if they are committed against father or mother or other close relatives, just as they are when committed against non-relatives. Yet such things are even more likely to happen when people are not aware of any relationship than when they are aware. And when they do happen, those who know the relationship can at least make the expiations which religious custom demands; the others cannot.

1262a32 It is equally curious that Plato,[1] while making sons shared by all, wishes to prohibit sexual intercourse between lovers, but not love itself, nor its most unseemly manifestations, as between brothers or between father and son,[2] where the mere unindulged passion is itself unseemly. And why prohibit sexual intercourse that is otherwise unobjectionable, merely on the grounds of the excessively powerful pleasure it gives,[1] and yet believe that it makes no difference if intercourse takes place between brothers, or father and son?

1262a40 Again, community of wives and children is prescribed for the Guardian class. It would seem to be far more useful if applied to the agricultural class. For where wives and children are held in common there is less affection, and a lack of strong affection among the ruled is necessary in the interests of obedience and absence of revolt.

1. *Republic* 403a ff.
2. I.e. where these persons were ignorant of each other's identity.

1262b3 So, taken all round, the results of putting such laws as these in practice would inevitably be directly opposed to the results which correct legislation ought to bring about, and moreover to those that Socrates regards as the reason for ordering matters in this way for children and wives. For we believe that the existence of affectionate feelings in states is a very great boon to them: it is a safeguard against faction. And Socrates is emphatic in his praise of unity in the state, which (as it seems, and as he himself says) is one of the products of affection. In another of Plato's dialogues, one which treats of love, we read[3] that Aristophanes said that lovers because of the warmth of their affection are eager to grow into each other and become one instead of two. In such an event one or other must perish, if not both. But in a state in which there exists such a mode of association[4] the feelings of affection will inevitably be watery, father hardly ever saying 'my son', or son 'my father'. Just as a small amount of sweetening dissolved in a large amount of water does not reveal its presence to the taste, so the feelings of relationship implied in these terms become nothing; and in a state organized like this[5] there is virtually nothing to oblige fathers to care for their sons, or sons for their fathers, or brothers for each other. There are two impulses which more than all others cause human beings to cherish and feel affection for each other: 'this is my own', and 'this is a delight'. Among people organized in this manner[5] no one would be able to say either.

1262b24 One further point, about the suggested transfer of children at birth from the farmers or skilled

---

3. *Symposium* 191a and 192de.
4. I.e. one like the *Republic*'s, which, by making wives and children common, aims at *excessive* unity, as in the *Symposium*.
5. Literally, 'in this sort of *politeia*' and 'people whose *politeia* is run in this manner' (*politeuomenoi*). *Politeia* is used here in a wide general sense of 'politico-social structure'. The reference is of course to the *Republic*.

workers to the Guardians, and also the transfer in the opposite direction:[6] there is the greatest confusion as to how such transfers shall take place. Those who hand over and transfer the children must be aware which children they are, and to whom they are being handed over. And such transfers would add greatly to the already mentioned risks – assault, homicide, love affairs; for those handed over to the other citizens will no longer use the terms brother, son, father, mother, of the Guardians, nor will those transferred to the Guardians so speak of the other citizens, so as to take precautions against any such act because of their kinship.

That concludes our discussion of community of wives and children.

II v

(1262b37–1264b25

THE OWNERSHIP OF PROPERTY

In this long chapter Aristotle discusses ownership of property and the right to its produce, first in very general terms and with wider reference than to Plato's Republic. Of the various possibilities, Aristotle recommends, broadly, private ownership combined with common use, and an ungrudging distribution of produce. 'Ungrudging' is important: Aristotle sees much merit in the spontaneous distribution of goods by customs of generosity, as against enforced distribution by regulation. This suppression of the virtue of generosity is one of several disadvantages he pinpoints in the community of property recommended by Plato for the Guardians in the Republic. *In particular, the economic and constitutional position of the rest of Plato's state is, he complains, left in obscurity; but so far as they can be ascertained, he thinks they are inimical to the unity Plato wishes to achieve.*

6. Republic 415b ff.

The justice of Aristotle's criticisms of the Republic *in this chapter provides further matter for debate (see bibliography). 'Practical men' of Aristotle's astuteness never find it difficult to punch holes in utopian schemes; yet here again, has Aristotle entered into the spirit of what he criticizes? At the end of the chapter, for instance, he claims that Plato deprived the Guardians of 'happiness' (eudaimonia), apparently quite unaware that Plato himself had in fact taken trouble to meet this objection. Aristotle may simply have read the* Republic *with insufficient care; on the other hand, he has made it perfectly plain that his assumptions are quite different from Plato's. That is, whereas Plato believed that if the Guardians fulfilled the role he allots them they would be happy, Aristotle just cannot see how men and women deprived of the normal and 'natural' satisfactions (private property, etc., see 1263a40 ff.) can possibly be anything but miserable; and that therefore the whole state cannot be happy either.*

There are very many other points of interest in this chapter, for example (i) the working out of the implications of extreme unification for the accepted virtues, (ii) the shrewd observations on the psychological effects of common ownership, and (iii) the deft adducing of examples of actual practice in Greek states.

1262b37 Connected with the foregoing is the question of property. What arrangements should be made about it, if people are going to operate the best possible constitution? Should it be held in common or not? This question may well be considered in isolation from the legislation about children and wives. A possible answer is that while *they* should belong to individuals, as is the universal practice, it would be better that either property or its use should be communal. In the latter case the plots of land are in private hands and its produce pooled for common use (as is done by some foreign nations); in the former, the land is communally held and communally worked but its produce is distributed according to individual requirements. This is a form of communal ownership which is said to exist among certain non-Greek peoples. There is also the alternative that *both* the land *and* its produce be owned communally.

1263a8 As to its cultivation, a different system will run more smoothly, i.e. if the land is worked by others, because, if they themselves work for their own benefit, there will be greater ill-feeling about the ownership. For if the work done and the benefit accrued are equal, well and good; but if not, there will inevitably be ill-feeling between those who get a good income without doing much work and those who work harder but get no corresponding extra benefit. To live together and share in any human concern is hard enough to achieve at the best of times, and such a state of affairs makes it doubly hard. The same kind of trouble is evident when a number of people club together for the purpose of travel. How often have we not seen such partnerships break down over quarrels arising out of trivial and unimportant matters! In the household also we get most annoyed with those servants whom we employ to perform the ordinary routine tasks.

1263a21 These then are some of the difficulties inherent in the common ownership of property. Far better is the present system – provided that it has the added attraction of being a matter of habit and of being controlled by sound laws. If so, it will have the advantages of both systems, both the communal and the private. For, while property should up to a point be held in common, the general principle should be that of private ownership. Responsibilty for looking after property, if distributed over many individuals, will not lead to mutual recriminations; on the contrary, with every man busy with his own, there will be increased effort all round. 'All things in common among friends' the saying goes, and it is the personal virtue of individuals that ensure their common use.

1263a30 And such an arrangement is by no means impossible: it exists, even if only in outline, in some states already, and in well-run ones particularly, where to a certain degree it is in actual operation and could be extended. Each man has his own possessions, part of which he makes available for his friends' use, part he uses in common with others. For example, in Sparta they use each others' slaves practically as if they were their own, and horses and dogs too; and if they need food on a journey, they get it in the country as they go. Clearly then it is better for property to remain in private hands; but we should make the use of it communal. It is a particular duty of a lawgiver to see that citizens are disposed to do this.

1263a40 Moreover there is an immense amount of pleasure to be derived from the sense of private ownership. It is surely no accident that every man has affection[1] for himself: nature meant this to be so. Selfishness is condemned, and justly, but selfishness is not simply to be fond of oneself, but to be *excessively* fond. So excessive fondness for money is condemned, though nearly every man is fond of everything of that kind. And a further point is that there is very great pleasure in helping and doing favours to friends and strangers and associates; and this happens when people have property of their own.

1263b7 None of these advantages is secured by those who seek excessive unification of the state.[2] And, what is more, they are openly throwing away the practice of two virtues – self-restraint with regard to women (for it is a fine practice to keep off another's wife through restraint), and liberality with regard to property. The abolition of private property will mean that no man will be seen to be liberal and no man will ever do any act of liberality; for it is in the use of articles of property that liberality is practised

1263b15 Such legislation might well on first hearing

---

1. 'Affection', 'fond' etc. = *philia*, *philein* etc.; 'selfishness' = *philauton* ('lover of self'); 'friends' = *philoi*.
2. I.e. by the abolition of private ownership.

sound attractive and humane;[3] it would seem to promise exceptionally warm affection of everyone for everyone, and to have a particular attraction for those who blame the prevalent evils of constitutions entirely on the absence of communal ownership of possessions.[4] I refer especially to charges and countercharges of broken contracts, trials for false witness, and sucking up to wealthy owners. But none of these things is due to the absence of communal ownership; they arise out of the depravity of human character. In fact we find more disputes arising between those who own and share property in common than we do among separate holders of possessions, even though, as we can see, the number of those who quarrel over partnerships is small as compared with the great multitude of private owners.[5] Again, it would be only fair to count not merely the evils of which sharing would rid us but also the advantages of which it would deprive us. Such a count shows that to live in the way suggested would be really impossible.

1263b29 The cause of Socrates' fallacy lies in his incorrect principle. Certainly there must be some unity in a state, as in a household, but not an absolutely total unity. There comes a point where the state, if it does not cease to be a state altogether, will certainly come close to that and be a worse one; it is as if one were to reduce concord to unison or rhythm to a single beat. As we have said before,[6] a state is a plurality, which must depend on education to bring about its common unity. It is strange that Plato, whose intention it was to introduce an education which he believed would impart a sound character to the state, should think that he could obtain good results

3. *Philanthrōpos.*
4. *Republic* 464c ff.
5. I.e. there are so few common owners that their quarrels, when measured against the sheer numbers of private owners, are rare. When measured against the numbers of *common* owners, the quarrels would be seen to be frequent.
6. II ii.

by such methods, which are no substitute for the training of the habits and of the intellect,[7] or for using the laws to that end. For example, at Sparta and in Crete the legislator effected a sharing of goods by means of the common meals.

1264a1 We must not forget another point that ought to be considered: simply the immense period of time during which this form of organization has remained undiscovered, as it surely would not have remained if it were really good. Pretty well all possible forms of organization have now been discovered, though no complete collection of them has been made, and many are known but are not practised. The force of our arguments would become clearer if we could see such a constitution being put together in practice: it will prove impossible to construct it without keeping its parts separate, dividing it either into messing-groups, or into brotherhoods and tribes. Consequently, new legislation will have boiled down to this, that the Guardians should not engage in agriculture – which is exactly the rule which the Lacedaemonians are now trying to introduce.

1264a11 But what of the arrangements of the constitution as a whole, and how do they affect participant members? In the absence of any positive statement by Socrates it is very hard to say. Certainly the bulk of the other citizens will make up almost the entire population of the state; but no decision was taken as to whether the farming class are to have communal or individual private possession, whether of property or of wives and children. Suppose that they too are to have all these in common, what will there then be to distinguish them from the Guardians? And what good will it do them to submit to their rule, or what inducement will there be to accept it? (Perhaps recourse might be had to some such device as the Cretans use, who allow to their slaves all privileges except those of training in gymnasia and possessing weapons.)

7. Literally 'philosophy', in a broad and non-technical sense.

1264a22 If on the other hand we assume that they arrange such things[8] exactly as in other states, how will they associate at all? The inevitable result would be two states within one,[9] and these in some degree in opposition to each other. For on the one side he puts the Guardians, like a garrison, on the other the farmers, craftsmen and the rest, as citizens.[10] This can only lead to disputes and litigation and all the other evils that he speaks of as arising in other states.[4] And yet Socrates says[11] that, thanks to education, there will be no need for a large number of regulations such as those governing the wardenship of the city and the market, and the like, and this while giving that education only to the Guardians. Again, he makes the farmers owners of their property but requires them to pay rent; but in that position they are likely to be much more troublesome and bumptious than the helots, serfs and slaves in some places nowadays.

1264a36 In any case no final decision was reached as to whether there is the same[12] necessity for such arrangements, nor yet about closely related questions, such as the type of constitution they will live under, and the nature of their[13] education and laws. This is not easy to discover; and yet the quality of these people will make all the difference to the maintenance of the association of the Guardians. But if he means to make wives shared and property privately owned, who will look after the house, as men tend the fields? And what if both the wives and the property of the farmers are held in common? To argue from an analogy with wild animals and say that male and female ought to engage in the same occupations is futile: animals have no household-management to do.

1264b6 Risky too is Socrates' way of appointing the

8. I.e. families and property, on a private basis.
9. *Republic* 422e.
10. I.e., apparently, like the citizens of an occupied state.
11. *Republic* 425d.
12. I.e. as among the Guardians.
13. The farmers', etc.

rulers: they are to be always the same people. This is a sure source of faction, even among those of no standing – to say nothing of those he calls warlike and spirited.[14] But clearly it is unavoidable that the same persons should always rule; for that divine 'golden' element in the soul does not vary in its incidence but is present always in the same people. It is, according to his own statement,[15] immediately at birth that the admixture takes place, of gold in some cases, of silver in others, and, for those who are going to be farmers or skilled workers, of bronze and iron.

1264b15 Again, though he denies to the Guardians even happiness,[16] he maintains that it is the duty of a lawgiver to make the whole city happy. But it is impossible for the whole to be happy, unless the majority, if not actually all, or at any rate some, parts possess happiness. For happiness is a very different thing from evenness: two odd numbers added together make an even number, but two unhappy sections cannot add up to a happy state. And if the Guardians are not happy, who will be? Certainly not the skilled workers and the general run of mechanics.

These are some, but by no means the most serious, of the drawbacks inherent in the kind of constitution described by Socrates.

II vi

(*1264b26–1266a30*)

CRITICISMS OF PLATO'S 'LAWS'

Aristotle devotes this single chapter to the Laws, *the last and longest of Plato's works, in which he depicts in considerable detail a* practical *utopia, second-best to that*

---

14. I.e. the Auxiliary Guardians, who have military and administrative functions.
15. *Republic* 415a ff.
16. Republic 419a ff., 465e ff., 519b ff.

of the Republic. *It is by no means certain that the version of the* Laws *Aristotle consulted coincided with the* Laws *as we have it today: certainly he ignores large parts of it, and sometimes seems unaware of certain passages that would go some way towards meeting his criticisms. The main speaker in the* Laws *is an elderly 'Athenian Stranger'; Aristotle, however, apparently thinks, though he does not quite say this, that it is 'Socrates', a celebrated slip presumably induced by reading many other Platonic dialogues, in which Socrates is indeed usually the central character. (Or is it an ironic joke, the ponderous lecturing of the Stranger being a poor replacement for the scintillating conversation of Socrates? Compare Aristotle's wry remark that 'the greater part of it (the* Laws) *is ... laws'.)*

But 'Socrates' is not the only eyebrow-raising feature of this chapter. As in the case of the Republic, *Aristotle's criticisms seem, at least at first sight, notably out of sympathy with Plato; yet in his own sketch of the ideal state in Books VII and VIII he pays Plato the compliment of adopting many of the institutions of the* Laws *(see Barker, cited on page 34 above). It is perhaps fairer to say that in accordance with his philosophical method of trying to sift what is of value in the ideas of others (see for example his procedure in* Nicomachean Ethics *VII i and ii), he subjects Plato's views to critical examination rather than rejects them root and branch. (The justice of his criticisms of the* Laws *is a tangled and contentious subject, and here I can only refer to the discussions of Bornemann and Morrow to be found in the Select Bibliographies.)*

Aristotle is chiefly interested in the economic and constitutional arrangements of the Laws. *In discussing the latter he refers to the use of the word* politeia, *'constitution', to describe a particular type, as it were a 'constitutional constitution'. In order to avoid confusion, the Greek term itself, transliterated as 'polity', is generally used to translate* politeia *in this restricted sense. It was*

*generally accepted in the fourth century that 'polity' was
a good thing, because it did not denote anything extreme;
all else was a matter of debate. In Book IV Aristotle describes his own particular brand of middle-class, middle-
of-the-road polity. He is not in this chapter rejecting the
notion of polity: he merely argues that as conceived in
the* Laws *it fails to do what Plato wanted it to do – be
a good second-best to the ideal state of the* Republic.

1264b26 The case of Plato's *Laws,* which was written
later, is somewhat similar; it would therefore be advisable to glance also at the constitution there depicted. We
have seen that in the *Republic* Socrates came to definite
conclusions only about very few matters – (a) arrangements necessary for the common possession of wives and
children, (b) property, and (c) the general organization
of the constitution, the bulk of the inhabitants being
divided into two parts, a farming class and a defensive
fighting class, while out of the fighters a third group is
formed which deliberates and is in sovereign charge of
the state.[1] But there are many things which Socrates left
undetermined: are farmers and skilled workers to have
a share in some office, or in none? Are they too to possess
arms and join the rest in fighting, or not? He certainly
thinks women ought to join in fighting and receive the
same education as the Guardians;[2] but for the rest he has
filled up his account with extraneous matter, and with a
description of the style of education which the Guardians
are to receive.

1265a1 Turning then to the *Laws,* we find that the
greater part of it is in fact 'laws', and he has said very
little about the constitution, which in spite of his wish
to make it more generally acceptable[3] to actual states, he
gradually brings back round again to the earlier one.
For, apart from the sharing of wives and property, he

1. *Republic* 373e ff., 412d ff.
2. *Republic* 451d ff.
3. *Koinoteros,* 'more common'.

constructs the two constitutions on very much the same pattern: the same kind of education, the same life of freedom from essential tasks, and the same arrangements for common meals – except that in the *Laws* women also are to have common meals, and the number of those bearing arms is 5,000, not 1,000.[4]

1265a10 Now all the Socratic dialogues are marked by a certain exaggeration and brilliance, by originality, and by an urge to investigate; but they can hardly be expected to be always right. For example, these 5,000 citizens just mentioned – we must not forget that it will require the territory of a Babylon or some other huge country to support so many men in idleness, to say nothing of further numbers, many times as great, of women and servants who would be attached to them. We can in our speculations postulate any ideal conditions we like, but they should at least be within the limits of possibility.

1265a18 It is further stated that in framing the laws a legislator ought to have regard both to the territory and to the population;[5] but surely we should add that he ought to take note of the neighbouring territories too. This is obvious if the state is to live the life of a state and not that of a hermit; for in that case it must provide itself with such arms for warfare as are serviceable not merely internally but also against the territories beyond its borders. And if one rejects such a life,[6] both for individuals and for the state at large,[7] the need is just as great to be formidable to enemies, both on their invasion and on their retreat.

1265a28 Then there is the amount of property to be

4. *Laws* 781, 737e; *Republic* 423a.
5. *Laws* 704 ff., 735a ff., 747d, 842c–e, 848a ff. and various other passages deal with these topics. Plato is not in fact inattentive to foreign affairs: see 737d, 758c, 949e ff.; cf. Jaeger (in Select Bibliographies) 288 ff.
6. I.e. of contact with the outside world, from which Plato's state in the *Laws* was largely insulated.
7. *Koinos*: literally, 'the common life of the state'.

possessed: this ought to be looked at to see whether there is not room for some clarification of the proposals. He says that a man ought to have enough to live on 'moderately'.[8] There are two objections to this: he uses 'live moderately' as if it meant the same as 'live the good life', which is a far more comprehensive expression; also it is quite possible to live a moderate life and yet be miserable. I suggest that a better formula would be 'moderate *and* liberal'; for taken separately, the one style leads to luxury, the other to too hard a life. And these are the only desirable dispositions that bear on the use of possessions: a man cannot use his possessions gently or bravely, but he can use them moderately and liberally. These then must be the dispositions that affect one's use of possessions.

1265a38 Furthermore, there is no point in equalizing property, if we do nothing to regulate the number of citizens, but allow births to go on unhindered in the belief that, as appears to happen in present-day states, the population would be kept sufficiently constant, however high the birth-rate, merely by the number of child-less couples. But in this state the balance would need to be maintained much more accurately.[9] At present, with the practice of dividing the stock of possessions among all the children, however numerous, nobody is in actual want. Under the arrangement proposed the property becomes indivisible and all excess children have to go without, whether there be few or many of them. Indeed it may well be thought that we ought to limit the production of children more than the stock of possessions, ensuring that no more than a certain number are born. In fixing this number regard should be had to chance factors such as the non-survival of some infants and the childlessness of some couples. To leave the number of births unrestricted, as is done in most states, inevitably causes poverty among the citizens, and poverty produces

8. *Laws* 737c–d.
9. Plato discusses these matters at *Laws* 740b–741a.

faction and crime. Pheidon of Corinth, one of the earliest of the lawgivers, held that the number of houses and the number of citizens should be kept equal, even if to begin with they all had estates of varying magnitude. In the *Laws* it is the other way round.

1265b16 Our own view as to how these matters would be best regulated will have to be stated later.[10] Here we add a further deficiency in the *Laws*. It concerns the rulers and how they are to differ from the ruled. He merely says[11] that the warp is made of different wool from the weft, and that is what the relation between ruler and ruled ought to be.

1265b21 Again, when he allows a man's total possessions to be increased up to five times a basic amount,[12] why should there not be a stated limit up to which *landed* property may be increased? Consider also his separation of one homestead into two:[13] I doubt if it is advantageous for household-management. He was for giving two separate homesteads to each man; but it is awkward to run two houses.

1265b26 The whole set-up is intended to be neither democracy nor oligarchy but midway between the two – what is called 'polity', because it consists of those who bear arms. If he is framing his constitution on these lines because such constitutions are far more acceptable[3] to states than any other type, we may perhaps approve his proposal. But we cannot do so if he means it to be second-best to the primary constitution. For in that case one might well prefer the Lacedaemonian, or some other constitution with a more aristocratic basis. There are indeed some who say that the best constitution is one

10. VII v, x, xvi.

11. *Laws* 734e–735a.

12. *Laws* 744e. Plato actually speaks of 'four times', but Aristotle is probably accurate. See T. J. Saunders, 'The property classes and the value of the κλῆρος in Plato's *Laws*', *Eranos,* LIX (1961), pp. 29–39.

13. *Laws* 745c ff., 775e ff.; but compare Aristotle's own proposal in VII x.

composed of a mixure of all types, and who therefore praise the Lacedaemonian. Some of these say that it is made up out of oligarchy, monarchy, and democracy: its kingship is monarchy, the authority of its Elders is oligarchy, and yet it is also run democratically through the authority exercised by the Ephors, who come from the people. Others say that the Ephorate is a tyranny, and that the democratic element is to be found in the common meals and the other features of daily life. But in the *Laws* it is stated that the best constitution ought to be composed of democracy and tyranny;[14] yet surely one would regard these two either as not constitutions at all, or as the worst of all. There is therefore a better case for including a large number of constitutions, because that makes a mixed constitution better.

1265a5 Next, we find that the constitution of the *Laws* proves to have nothing monarchical about it at all, only oligarchy and democracy with a bias towards oligarchy. This is shown in the method of appointment of office-bearers.[15] The practice of selection by lot from a number chosen by election is common both to oligarchy and democracy; but to impose upon the richer citizens, and upon them only, the obligation to be members of the Assembly,[16] to vote for office-bearers and do any other duty that falls upon a citizen – that is oligarchical. So also is the attempt to secure that a majority of the office-holders should come from among the wealthy, and that the highest offices should be filled by those from the highest property-classes.[17] Oligarchical also is the manner of election which he proposes for members of the Council.[18] It is true that all have to take part in the election;

14. See *Laws* 693e ff., 701e and esp. 756e.
15. *Laws* 751–68 is the chief discussion.
16. *Laws* 704a.
17. E.g. *Laws* 763de.
18. *Laws* 756b–e. The procedure is complex: see G. R. Morrow, *Plato's Cretan City* (Princeton, 1960), p. 166 ff. (In 1266a17 I read τούς , not τοῖς : see my note in *Liverpool Classical Monthly*, 3 [1978], pp. 179–80.)

but they have to elect first some from the highest property-class, then an equal number from the second class, then from the third class; there was, however, to be no obligation on everyone to elect members from the third class or the fourth class, and only the first two classes were to be obliged to elect from the fourth class. And from these nominees he says that from each property-class an equal number is to be appointed to the Council. The result will be that those who elect from the highest property-classes will be more numerous and of better quality, because some of the common people, not being obliged to vote, will refrain from doing so.

1266a22 These considerations show that such a constitution ought not to be compounded out of monarchy and democracy; and this conclusion will be strengthened by what will be said hereafter when we come round to consider this kind of constitution.[19] And with regard to elections of officials too, this idea of electing from the elected is a dangerous one.[20] For if a number of persons, not necessarily a large number, are resolved to stand firmly by each other, the elections will always go according to their wishes. So much for the constitution of the *Laws*.

II vii

(1266a31–1267b21)

THE CONSTITUTION OF PHALEAS

Aristotle now turns to a number of other 'ideal' constitutions, and deals first with that of the egalitarian Phaleas, of whom nothing is known apart from what we learn of him here. The tenor of Aristotle's criticism is that Phaleas' central proposal, for equality of property for all, is imprecise and simplistic: Phaleas does not specify

19. IV vii–ix, xi–xiii.
20. *Laws* 753a–d, 756b–e.

the amount of property to be possessed, nor in what form; nor does he realize that equality of property, though of some benefit in itself, is best combined with an education which will make it acceptable to the citizens. This reflection prompts Aristotle to write a short excursus on the relative importance of economics and character as causes of crime. He also criticizes Phaleas, as he has criticized Plato, for ignoring foreign affairs; but whereas our possession of Plato's text enables us to check the justice of this and other criticisms, we cannot in Phaleas' case say whether Aristotle reports him fairly or not. At all events, Phaleas seems to have been of some importance as a thinker who put his faith in one or two radical economic measures as cures for social and political unrest, rather than in law or education or elaborate constitutional arrangements.

1266a31 There are some other constitutions beside Plato's; their authors are sometimes statesmen[1] or philosophers, sometimes laymen. They all sketch constitutions that come nearer than either of Plato's to existing constitutions, under which people actually run their lives; for no other person has ever introduced such novelties as the sharing of children and wives, or common meals for women. They prefer to start from essentials: to some it seems vital to get the best possible regulation of possessions, for they say it is always about them that faction arises. This was the motive of Phaleas of Chalcedon, who was the first to propose that the property of the citizens should be equal. He thought that this was not difficult to do at the very foundation of a state, and that, although it was more difficult in states already set up and working, still all properties would quickly be brought to the same level, simply by arranging that the rich should bestow dowries but receive none, and the poor give no dowries but only receive them. Plato, when writing the *Laws*, thought that there ought up to a certain point to be free-

1. See I i.

dom from property-control, but that, as has been stated earlier, none of the citizens should have the right to own property more than five times as great as the smallest property owned.[2]

1266b8 But those who legislate along these lines must not forget, as indeed they do forget, that while fixing the amount of possessions they ought to fix the number of children too; for if the number of children becomes too great for the stock of possessions, it becomes impossible not to abrogate the law. And apart from the abrogation, many who were rich will become poor; and this is a most undesirable consequence, since you can hardly prevent such persons from becoming bent on revolution.

1266b14 That equality of possessions has considerable effect on the association which is the state[3] has, so we find, been realized by some even in times long past: witness the legislation of Solon;[4] and there are places where there is a law against unlimited acquisition of land. Laws likewise exist which prevent the sale of possessions, as for example in Locri, where the law is that they may be sold only when it can be shown that some conspicuous misfortune has occurred. Other laws require the ancient estates to be maintained intact. It was the abrogation of such a law that rendered the constitution of Leucas over-democratic; for it ceased to be possible to appoint to office only persons from the specified property-classes.

1266b24 Equality of possessions may exist and yet the level be fixed either too high, with resultant luxury, or too low, which leads to a life of penury. It is clear, therefore, that it is not enough for a legislator to equalize possessions: he must aim at fixing an amount midway

2. *Laws* 744 e; cf. II vi, n. 12.
3. *Koinōnia politikē*: cf. I i.
4. Solon (Archōn of Athens, appointed probably in 594) introduced a variety of economic measures designed to reduce the very great and oppressive differences of wealth existing at that time, though he certainly did not wish to *equalize* the property of all.

between extremes. But even if one were to fix a moderate amount for all, that would still be no use: for it is more necessary to equalize appetites than possessions, and that can only be done by adequate education under the laws. Perhaps, however, Phaleas would say that this is exactly what he himself meant; for he holds that in states there ought to be equality of education as well as equality of property. But one must say what exactly the education is to be; it is no use simply making it one and the same. 'One and the same' education might very well be of such a kind that it would produce men set on securing for themselves undue money or distinctions or both. And civil strife is caused by inequality in distinctions no less than by inequality in property, though for opposite reasons on either side; that is to say, the many are incensed by the inequality in property, whereas more accomplished people are incensed if honours are shared equally, for then, as the tag has it, 'good and bad are held in equal esteem'.[5]

1267a2 Phaleas holds that equality of possessions, by ensuring that no one will resort to stealing because he is cold or hungry, is a sufficient cure for crimes. But to secure the necessities of life is not the only purpose for which men turn criminal. They also wish to enjoy things and not go on desiring them; and if their desire goes beyond mere necessities, they will seek a remedy in crime. Nor is that the only motive; even men who feel no such desires wish to enjoy pleasures that bring no pain. Thus there are three[6] different sets of persons to be considered, and three different cures: for the first set, employment

5. Homer, *Iliad* IX, 319.
6. (i) Those who commit crimes to obtain the necessities of life; (ii) those who do so to obtain *more* than necessities to satisfy desires and obtain pleasure, (iii) those who want more than necessities in order to be able to live a life of 'pleasures that bring no pain'. In the last case, Aristotle seems to mean that 'philosophy' is a 'cure' in that leading a philosophic life makes many or all of one's desires for other things subside: the pleasures of philosophy make one independent of pleasure from other sources.

and moderate possessions; for the second, self-control. As for the third, if they wish to find independent enjoyment by themselves, philosophy alone, I think, will provide the cure; for unlike the other two kinds of desire, this one alone stands in no need of other people. As for major crimes, men commit them when their aims are extravagant, not just to provide themselves with necessities. Who ever heard of a man making himself a dictator in order to keep warm? For this reason there is more honour in slaying a tyrant than a thief.[7] So we may conclude that Phaleas' style of constitution would be a protection only against minor crimes.

1267a17 Moreover Phaleas is chiefly concerned to make the internal arrangements of his state work well, disregarding, as he ought not to do, relations with neighbouring and other foreign states. In framing a constitution it is essential to have regard to the acquiring of strength for war; yet Phaleas has said nothing about this. The same point applies to property, for it is essential that there should be resources sufficient not merely for the internal needs of the state but also to meet external dangers. For this purpose the total amount of property ought not to be so large that more powerful neighbours will covet it, and the owners be unable to repel the invasion; on the other hand it must not be so small that they cannot sustain a war even against an equal and similar foe. Phaleas fixed no limit; but how many possessions it is expedient to have is a question that must be answered. Perhaps the best formula would be that the total should not be so great as to make it profitable for a stronger power to go to war attracted by its great size; the inducements must be no more than they would be anyway, even in the absence of such possessions. For example, when Autophradates was about to lay siege to Atarneus, its ruler Eubulus[8] told

_____

7. I.e. once a man has the necessities of life, to become a tyrant is a greater crime than mere thieving.

8. Eubulus was a banker who in the confused political situation in Asia Minor, *c.* 359 B.C., had gained control of Atarneus and Assos.

him to consider how long it would take him to complete the capture of the place, and then to count the cost of a war of that duration. 'For', he added, 'I am willing now to abandon Atarneus in return for a smaller sum of money than that.' These words of Eubulus caused Autophradates to think again and to abandon the siege. *1267a37* So, while there is certainly some advantage in equality of possessions for the citizens as a safeguard against faction, its efficacy is not really very great. In the first place discontent will arise among the more accomplished people, who will think they deserve something better than equality. (This is the reason for the many obvious instances of revolt and faction inspired by them.) Secondly, the depravity of mankind is an insatiable thing. At first they are content with a dole of a mere two obols,[9] then, when that is traditional, they go on asking for more and their demands become unlimited. For there is no natural limit to wants and most people spend their lives trying to satisfy them. In such circumstances, therefore, a better point of departure than equalizing possessions would be to ensure that naturally reasonable people should not *wish* to get more than their share, and that the inferior should not be *able* to; and that can be achieved if they are weaker but not treated unjustly.

1267b9 There are errors also in what Phaleas has said about equality of possessions in itself. For it is only possession of land that he makes equal, forgetting that great wealth may also be had in the form of slaves, cattle and coined money; and one may have an immense stock of what is generally called movable property. Equality, or at least a moderate degree of control, should be aimed at in *all* these forms of property. Otherwise things must just be allowed to take their course.

1267b13 To judge from his legislation Phaleas is evidently framing a state with only a small number of

---

9. The reference is to the *diōbelia*, a grant (dating from the times of Pericles) given to the poorer Athenian citizens to enable them to attend the theatre.

citizens, at least if all the skilled workers are to be public slaves and not members of the citizen-body. But if those employed on public works are to be slaves owned by the state, one should employ the system in force at Epidamnus, which at one time Diophantus tried to introduce at Athens.[10]

These remarks on the constitution of Phaleas will put one in a position to judge what is good and what is bad in it.

II viii

(1267b22–1269a28)

THE CONSTITUTION OF HIPPODAMUS

Hippodamus evidently had flamboyance and a flair for publicity; and Aristotle, who was himself said to have taken pains over dress (Diogenes Laertius V 1), is obviously fascinated by his sartorial eccentricities. Like Phaleas and a good many other 'utopian' thinkers, Hippodamus likes to simplify and schematize: he proposes three classes, three divisions of the land to correspond, and three categories of laws. On the other hand he has a not unreasonable dissatisfaction with the simple 'yes or no' verdicts demanded in Athenian courts. Once again Aristotle's criticisms centre on a lack of clarity and detailed precision; and once again it is impossible for us to know now whether they are fair or captious. His central political concern in this chapter is with the question of who should 'share in the constitution', i.e. be a citizen and enjoy the appropriate privileges, such as eligibility for office. Underlying his comments is the assumption that possession of arms is a prerequisite for full citizenship and eligibility for office; and he criticizes Hippodamus for extending the citizenship too widely. In Greek

10. Cf. VII x, *fin.* Nothing further is known of Diophantus' proposal.

political theory the quotation 'What makes a citizen?' is crucial, and it is taken up at length in Book III.

In a long and splendid essay at the end of the chapter (1268b31 ff.) Aristotle devotes close attention to the implications of Hippodamus' proposal to give honours to those who discover some benefit to the state. This does indeed seem to be the most radical and far-reaching of Hippodamus' proposals, for it assumes, to some extent at least, that society is or should be in constant change. Aristotle is, of course, not thinking of technological discoveries, but if he had known of any, he would probably have been suspicious of them; certainly the nineteenth and twentieth centuries have shown how inventions very soon alter the whole politeia. He is thinking rather of new social and political ideas; and these in a settled regime of any type are always suspect. To mention such a topic is to raise one of the most important and difficult questions of politics. So long as constitutionalism and adherence to tradition act as safeguards against arbitrary and tyrannical government, so long must they be respected; and the political memory of the Greeks helped to make this conservative attitude very general. Aristotle admits that there have been improvements in the past and that there may be need for improvement at any time; but he does after all believe that all or most good innovations have already been made (cf. II v and VII x), and counsels extreme caution and reluctance. Plato would have agreed with him (Laws 797a–e). At bottom, both Plato and Aristotle believed – though for somewhat different metaphysical reasons – that it was in principle meaningful to talk of such a thing as a 'best' state, and that it should be possible with effort to achieve in practice a more or less close approximation to it. This done, change could only be for the worse. A proposal like Hippodamus', which actually encouraged change, would therefore be highly unwelcome to them.

1267b22   Hippodamus, son of Euryphon, came from

Miletus. It was he who invented the division of cities into precincts, and he also laid out the street-plan of the Piraeus. His ambition always to be different from other people made his life also peculiar in a variety of ways; and some thought that he was carrying his oddities too far with his long hair and expensive ornaments, wearing at the same time clothing that was cheap but warm, in summer and winter alike. He wished to be considered expert in the whole range of natural science too; and he was the first person not actually taking part in the workings of a constitution to attempt some description of the ideal one.

1267b30 Hippodamus planned a state with a population of 10,000, divided into three parts, one of skilled workers, one of farmers, and a third to bear arms and secure defence. The territory also was to be divided into three parts, a sacred, a public, and a private; the worship of the gods would be maintained out of the produce of the *sacred* land, the defenders out of the *common* land, and the *private* land would belong to the farmers.

1267b37 He also held the view that there were only three kinds of law, corresponding to the three grounds for lawsuits – outrage,[1] damage and homicide. He also wanted to legislate for a single supreme court, to which were to be referred all cases that appeared prima facie to have been badly judged; this court was to consist of selected elder persons. Verdicts in law-courts he thought ought to be given not by simply voting for or against, but each member of the court was to present a tablet, on which he was to state in writing the penalty, if it was a simple verdict of condemnation; but he was to leave the tablet blank if he was for a plain acquittal; and if it was partly the one and partly the other, he was to specify that. He thought present legislation bad in this respect, that by compelling jurymen to give a verdict either one way or the other, it made them false to their oath.

1268a6 He next set about enacting a law to the effect

1. *Hubris*

that all who made discoveries advantageous to their country should receive honours, and second, that the children of those who fell in war should be maintained at the expense of the state. (He was under the impression that this latter legislation was something entirely new; but it certainly obtains today at Athens and elsewhere.) The officials were all to be elected by the people, which was to consist of the three sections of the state just mentioned. Those elected would look after common interests and those of foreigners and of orphans.

1268a14 Such are the main features of Hippodamus' scheme, and those most deserving of comment. One's first point of criticism would be the division of the whole body of the citizens. For they all, skilled craftsmen, farmers, and those who carry arms, share in the constitution;[2] but the farmers have no arms, the craftsmen have neither land nor arms, and this makes them virtually the slaves of those who do possess arms. In these circumstances the sharing of all honours becomes an impossibility. For it is an absolute essential that Generals, and Guardians of Citizens, and in general those who hold the supreme offices, should be appointed from the ranks of those who possess arms. On the other hand, if they do not share in the constitution,[2] how can they be expected to be well disposed towards it? 'But', it may be said, 'those who possess arms must be superior in power to both the other sections.' But that is not easy unless they are numerous; and if they are numerous, what need is there for the rest to share in the constitution[2] and be in sovereign control of the appointment of officials?

1268a29 Again, what use are the farmers to the state? Skilled workers of course are essential; every state needs them, and they can support themselves from their skills, as in other states. But as for the farmers, if they were expected to provide maintenance for those possessing arms, then it would have been reasonable for them to

2. That is to say, enjoy citizenship, the right to hold office under the constitution.

be a part of the state. But actually that is not so: the land they work is their own and they work it for their own benefit.

1268a36 And as for the common land which will support the defenders, if they are to till it themselves, there will be no difference, as the legislator[3] intended there should be, between fighting men and farmers. And if there are to be certain others,[4] different from the fighters and from those farmers working their own property, that means that there will be a fourth section of the state, one with no share in anything but quite extraneous to the constitution. Or again, if one makes the same people cultivate the private and the common land, there will not be enough produce to enable each man to maintain two[5] households by farming. Why should they not *both* get their own maintenance *and* provide for the warriors directly from the same land and the same estates? There is much confusion here.

1268b4 His law relating to verdicts is no good either. He requires that even where the suit is written in simple terms,[6] the jurymen should make qualifications. But this is to turn juryman into arbitrator. Certainly that is what is practicable in arbitrations, even if there are several arbitrators, because they discuss their verdict among themselves. But it is not possible in a court of law, and most legislators go to the other extreme and make a point of *preventing* jurymen from having any opportunity to confer with each other.

1268b11 Again, confusion in the verdict will surely arise, because it may be the opinion of a juryman that a sum ought to be paid, but a lesser amount than the plaintiff demands. Suppose he demands twenty minae (or more): one juryman will say ten (or less), another five, another four (obviously this is the kind of division they

3. Hippodamus.
4. I.e. to work the common land in support of the fighters.
5. His own and that of a warrior.
6. I.e. requiring only 'guilty' or 'not guilty' as a verdict.

will resort to), and some will award the full amount claimed, others nothing. How then are the votes to be counted?

1268b17 Again, nothing forces a juryman to be false to his oath by giving a simple verdict for or against, provided that the indictment is written in simple terms,[6] and he gives his decision justly. For he who acquits does not say that nothing at all is due, but just that it is not twenty minae. The only person who would be false to his oath would be one who condemned the defendant while believing the twenty minae not to be due from him.

1268b22 And now for his suggestion that there should be some honours for those who discover something advantageous to the state. This sort of law looks well and sounds well, but it is very risky. It would encourage informers and in some cases lead to alterations to the constitution. This being so, we cannot separate it from another and wider question. Some people debate whether it is harmful or advantageous if states alter their ancestral law whenever a better one is found. If the answer to this question is that alteration is bad, then one can hardly give ready assent to Hippodamus' proposals. It is possible for people to bring in proposals for abrogating the laws or the constitution on the ground that such proposals are for the public good.

1268b31 Now that we have touched upon this matter it may be as well to say a little more about it, especially as there is, as I have said, debate on the point and a case could be made out also in favour of change. At any rate, if we look at the other sciences, it has definitely been beneficial – witness the changes in traditional methods of medicine and physical training, and generally in every skill and faculty. Now since we must regard statesmanship as one of these, clearly something similar ought to apply there too. And so indeed we could claim to find some indication of that, if we look at the facts and observe how uncivilized, how rough-and-ready, the old laws were.

Greeks used to go about carrying arms; they used to buy their brides from each other; and traces survive of other practices once doubtless customary, which merely make us smile today, such as the law relating to homicide at Cyme, by which, if the prosecutor can produce a certain number of witnesses, members of his own kin, then the defendant is guilty of murder.

1269a3 Generally, of course, it is the good, and not simply the traditional, that is aimed at. It would be foolish to adhere to the notions of primitive men, whether they were born from the earth or were survivors of some great catastrophe: we may reasonably suppose that they were on a level with ordinary, not very intelligent, people today, and lack of intelligence was said to be one of the marks of the earth-born.[7] We might go further and say that even those laws which have been written down are best regarded as not unchangeable. On the analogy of other skills, to set down in writing the whole organization of the state, down to the last detail, would be quite impossible; the general principle must be stated in writing, the action taken depends upon the particular case.[8]

1269a12 From these considerations it is clear that there are some occasions that call for change and that there are some laws which need to be changed. But looking at it in another way we must say that there will be need of the very greatest caution. In a particular case we may have to weigh a very small improvement against the danger of getting accustomed to casual abrogation of the laws; in such a case, obviously, we must tolerate a few errors on the part of lawmakers and rulers. A man will receive less benefit from changing the law than damage from becoming accustomed to disobey authority. For the example of the crafts is false; there is a difference between altering a craft and altering a law. The law has no power to secure obedience save the power of habit,

7. Cf. Plato, *Laws* 677b.
8. Cf. III xi *fin.*, *Nicomachean Ethics*, V x; Plato, *Politicus* 294a–c and *Laws* 925d ff.

and that takes a long time to become effective. Hence easy change from established laws to new laws means weakening the power of the law. Again, if changes in laws *are* to be permitted, it will have to be decided whether they may all be changed, and in every type of constitution, or not. And who is to make the changes? Anybody or only certain persons? That will make a considerable difference. We will now give up this discussion; it will be better resumed on other occasions.

II ix

(1269a29–1271b19)

CRITICISM OF THE SPARTAN CONSTITUTION

Having finished examining the proposals of the theorists (Plato, Phaleas, Hippodamus), Aristotle now turns to constitutions that are or have been actually in operation, Lacedaemonian, Cretan, Carthaginian – choosing these, he tells us at the end, because they are rightly admired.

A glance at the following notes on certain names and technical terms will help the reader to understand the points Aristotle makes in this long and important chapter.

Lycurgus, to whom Aristotle seems usually to be referring when he speaks of 'the lawgiver', was the traditional founder of the Spartan constitution. His date (and indeed his very existence) is uncertain, and the precise nature and extent of his work are matters of controversy.

Helots (literal meaning probably 'captives') were a class of state serfs (a convenient but anachronistic term), the descendants of originally independent peoples in Laconia and Messenia conquered by the Spartans at various times between perhaps the tenth and seventh centuries. They differed from ordinary slaves in various respects, and formed a class intermediate between them and the free

Spartans proper. Their broad counterpart in Thessaly were the penestai *(translated 'serfs').*

Peripheral populations (perioikoi, *'dwellers round')* *were small communities under Spartan control roughly encircling the Spartan territory. They paid Spartan taxes and were required to supply contingents of soldiers to fight in Sparta's wars; but they enjoyed only local administrative autonomy.*

The two Kings *were hereditary and belonged to two entirely separate royal houses; their functions and influence were not only political but military (as commanders-in-chief).*

The Ephors *were five officials who in addition to wide executive and judicial powers exercised close control over the conduct of the kings. They were elected annually by the citizens.*

The Board of Elders *(*gerousia*) had twenty-eight members over sixty years old, plus the kings. It was elected probably from a limited number of aristocratic families, and possessed extensive judicial and administrative functions, notably the preparation of business for the assembly of citizens. Its political influence and powers were great.*

The Spartiatae *were the full Spartan citizens.*

The Spartan constitution was widely praised in antiquity for its combination of these mutually checking and restraining components (see e.g. Plato, Laws 691–2), which was thought to ensure the stability of the state. Aristotle himself, though he has much fault to find with Sparta, notes in IV ix (cf. Thucydides I xviii) that in its balance between different principles her constitution resembles his own brand of 'polity'. Much, however, is obscure about Spartan constitutional history: for a good discussion, see W. G. Forrest, A History of Sparta, 950–192 BC *(London, 1968, 2nd ed. 1980).*

About the standards of value which Aristotle now applies to constitutions two points should be noted, because they are characteristic of his whole approach: first, the very best or ideal constitution may well differ from the type best suited to a particular place or time; and second, it is taken for granted that a citizen, if he is to develop the qualities worthy of a citizen, must not do work that is felt to be degrading. But it is recognized that if the citizens are not going to do their own dirty work, there must be a subordinate class to do it for them; and this class is bound to be a source of trouble. It is surprising that Aristotle has not more to say about this problem: he can think of no answer except repressive legislation; see however I vi for the 'friendship' he believes can exist between master and slave.

The Helots

1269a29 About the constitution of the Lacedaemonians, and about that of the Cretans and generally about others, there are two questions to be asked. First, are its enactments good or bad, judged by the standard of the absolutely best system? Second, does it contain anything that is not in keeping with the principles and style of the constitution which they have set out to achieve?

1269a34 Now it is agreed that a necessity for any state which is to operate a good constitution is freedom from essential[1] tasks; but how that condition is to be secured is not easy to see. For example, in Thessaly the serfs often attacked the Thessalians, just as the helots attacked the Spartans, always on the look-out for any mischance that may befall their masters. But nothing of the kind has so far occurred among the Cretans. The reason for this is perhaps that the neighbouring states, though they might well be at war with each other, never join up with the rebels; it is not in their interest to do so, since they too possess peripheral populations. Sparta's neighbours on the other hand, Argives, Messenians, Arcadians, were all hostile to her. Similarly there were from the start rebellions against the Thessalians, because they were still con-

1. I.e. menial, mechanical, routine; 'freedom' = *scholē*, 'leisure'.

stantly at war with their neighbours, Achaeans, Perrhae-bians, and Magnesians. And even if there is no other source of trouble, there is still the effort of management, of finding the right way to live with a subject population. If they are allowed too much licence, they become arrogant and begin to claim equal rights with their masters; if they are badly treated, they become resentful and rebellious. It is clear therefore that those who find themselves in such relations with their helotry have not yet found the best way.[2]

Spartan Women

1269b12 Again, the lack of control over Spartan women is detrimental both to the attainment of the aims of the constitution and to the happiness of the state. For just as man and wife are each part of a household, so we should regard a state also as divided into two parts approximately equal numerically, one of men, one of women. So, in all constitutions in which the position of women is ill-regulated, one half of the state must be regarded as not properly legislated for. And that is what has happened at Sparta. For there the lawgiver,[3] whose intention it was that the whole state should be tough, has obviously shown toughness himself as far as the men are concerned, but has been negligent over the women. For at Sparta women live intemperately, enjoying every licence and indulging in every luxury.

1269b23 An inevitable result under such a constitution is that esteem is given to wealth, particularly in cases when the men are dominated by the women; and this is a common state of affairs in military and warlike races, though not among the Celts and any others among whom male homosexuality is openly esteemed. Indeed it seems as if the first person to relate the myth of a union between

2. Cf. Plato, *Laws* 776 ff.

3. Presumably Lycurgus, and so throughout this chapter unless otherwise stated (see introductory note): cf. Plato, *Laws init*.

Ares and Aphrodite did not lack some rational basis for it: certainly all such people seem compulsively attracted by sexual relations, either with males or with females. This is why that state of affairs prevailed among the Spartans, where in the days of their supremacy a great deal was managed by women. And what is the difference between women ruling and rulers ruled by women? The result is the same. Boldness is not a quality useful in any of the affairs of daily life, but only, if at all, in war. Yet even here the influence of the Spartans' women has been very harmful. This was demonstrated when Laconia was invaded by the Thebans:[4] instead of playing a useful part, like women in other states, they caused more confusion than the enemy.

1269b39 Now it is not surprising that from the earliest times lack of control over women was a feature of Laconian society: there were long periods when the Spartan men were absent from their own land on military service, fighting against Argives, or again against Arcadians or Messenians. When they resumed their leisure, then predisposed to obedience by military life, which offers scope for many kinds[5] of virtue, they readily submitted themselves to their lawgiver. But not so the women. It is said that Lycurgus endeavoured to bring them under the control of his laws, but that when they resisted he gave up the attempt.[6] These then are the causes of what took place, and clearly therefore also the causes of the defect which we have been discussing. But our present inquiry is about what is right or wrong, not an attempt to decide what ought to be excused and what ought not.

Property

1270a11 If, as has been said earlier,[7] the position of

---

4. In 369.
5. Literally 'parts' (*merē*); cf. Plato, *Laws* 630 d ff.
6. Cf. Plato, *Laws* 779e ff., 804e ff.
7. In the 4th and 5th paragraphs of this chapter. See P. Cartledge, 'Spartan Wives: Liberation or Licence?', *Classical Quarterly*, 31 (1981), pp. 84–105.

women is wrong, not only does it look like a blot on the constitution in itself, but it seems to contribute something to the greed for money; for one might next go on to attack the Spartan inequality of property-ownership. For we find that some Spartans have come to have far too many possessions, others very few indeed; hence the land has fallen into the hands of a small number. Here there have been errors in the legal provisions too. For their lawgiver, while he quite rightly did not approve of buying and selling land in someone's possession, left it open to anyone to transfer it to other ownership by gift or bequest – and yet this inevitably leads to the same result. Moreover, something like two-fifths of all the land is possessed by women. There are two reasons for this: heiresses are numerous and dowries are large. It would have been better to have regulated dowries, prohibiting them altogether or making them small or at any rate moderate in size. But[8] as it is an heiress may be given in marriage to any person whatever. And if a man dies intestate, the person he leaves as heir[9] gives her to whom he likes. So although the land was sufficient to support 1,500 cavalry and 30,000 heavy infantry, the number fell to below 1,000. The sheer facts have shown that these arrangements were bad: one single blow[10] was too much for Sparta, and she succumbed owing to the shortage of men.

1270a34 It is said that in the time of their early kings the Spartans gave others a share in their constitution, so that in spite of long continuing wars there was not then any shortage of men. It is also said that at one time the Spartiatae had as many as 10,000. However, whether

8. The train of thought is probably, 'so far from there being such restrictions, heiresses, who may possess substantial property, may actually be given . . .'.

9. 'Heir' in a presumably very limited sense: he merely hands over the estate, with its owner the heiress whom he has 'inherited', to someone prepared to marry her.

10. The battle of Leuctra, against Thebes, in 371.

these statements are true or false, it is far better to keep up the numbers of males in a state by a levelling out of property. But the law on the begetting of children tends to militate against this reform. For the lawgiver, intending that the Spartiatae should be as numerous as possible, encourages the citizens to beget many children. For they have a law by which the father of three sons is exempt from military service, and the father of four from all taxes. But it is obvious that if many are born and the land distributed accordingly, many must inevitably become poor.

The Ephors

1270b6 Another defect in the Lacedaemonian constitution is seen in connection with the office of Ephor. The Ephorate independently controls the most important business. Its members come from among all the people, with the result that often men who are very poor find themselves on this board, and their lack of means used to make them open to bribery. (There have been many demonstrations of this in the past; and in our own day we have the affair of Andros, in which certain Ephors have been so corrupted by gifts of money that it is no thanks to them if their state was not utterly ruined.) And just because the power of the Ephors is excessive and virtually that of a tyrant, even the Spartan Kings were forced to curry favour with them.[11] And this has caused further damage to the constitution, for an aristocracy turned into a democracy.

1270b17 The Board of Ephors certainly keeps the constitution together: the people are kept quiet because it gives them a share in the highest office. So whether this is due to the lawgiver[12] or to good fortune, it suits the circumstances very well. The point is that if a constitution

11. *Dēmagōgein*, 'act like a demagogue, turn demagogue', in order to deal with them.

12. Either Theopompus, a king of Sparta in the eighth/seventh century (cf. V xi), or Lycurgus (see introductory note).

is to have a good prospect of stability, it must be such that all sections of the state accept it and want it to go on in the same way as before. The Kings have this feeling about the constitution because it confers dignity on themselves; the men of quality have it because of their membership of the Board of Elders (for this office is their reward for virtue), the people because of the universal basis of the Ephorate. But while it was necessary to elect Ephors from among all the citizens the present method of election is quite childish.[13]

1270b28　The Ephors also have supreme powers of jurisdiction in cases of importance; but considering that anybody at all may hold the office, it would be better that they should not have power to give verdicts on their own judgement, but only in accordance with written rules, i.e. as the laws direct. Nor does the way in which the Ephors live conform to the aims of the state. They live a life of undue ease, while the rest have a very high degree of austerity in living, so high indeed that they really cannot endure it but secretly get round the law and enjoy the pleasures of the body.

The Board of Elders

1270b35　There are drawbacks also to the authority exercised by the Elders. One might suppose that, so long as it consists of respectable men adequately trained with a view to every excellence, this institution is a good thing for the state. But the mind grows old no less than the body, so it is questionable whether they ought to have their lifelong supreme power to decide important cases. And when we find that their education has been of such a kind that even the lawgiver himself has no confidence in them as good men, the situation becomes dangerous. It is known that those who have taken on a share in this office conduct much public business by taking bribes and

13. It is usually assumed that the method employed was the same as for the election of the Elders; see note 15.

showing favouritism. For this reason it would be better that their proceedings should not be, as they are at present, exempt from any scrutiny.[14] It may be thought that the office of Ephor provides a scrutiny of all other authorities; but that is to give far too much to the Ephorate, and is not what we mean by requiring an authority to submit to scrutiny of its proceedings.

1271a9 And as for election of the Elders, the way in which the choice is made is silly,[15] and it is all wrong that a person who is going to be deemed worthy of the office should himself solicit it. Whether he wants to or not, the man to hold office is the man who is fit for it. But the lawgiver, in a way that is clearly typical of his whole approach to the constitution, begins by making the citizens ambitious and then uses their ambition as a means of getting the Elders elected; for no one who is not ambitious would ask to hold office. Yet the truth is that men's ambition and their desire to make money are among the most frequent causes of deliberate acts of injustice.

The Kings

1271a18 As to kingship, we may postpone[16] considering whether states are better with or without it; at any rate they would do better not to have Kings after the present Spartan fashion.[17] We say that in every case a King should be chosen in the light of his personal life. It is clear that even the Spartan lawgiver himself does not believe it possible to produce Kings of first quality; at all events, he has no confidence that they are good enough. This explains

14. The scrutiny or audit, *euthuna*, undergone by Athenian officials and those of many other Greek states on the expiry of their term of duty.

15. See Plutarch, *Lycurgus* 26: the choice was made by elaborately managed acclamation. For the following sentiments, cf. Plato, *Republic* 347b–d; 519b ff.

16. See III xiv–xviii.

17. I.e. on an hereditary basis.

why they used to send their personal enemies[18] to accompany them as ambassadors, and why they regarded disagreement between the two Kings as making for stability in the state.

The Common Meals

1271a26 Unsatisfactory also are the rules made by the person who first established the system of common meals,[19] called by the Lacedaemonians 'phiditia'. The gathering ought to be run at public expense, as in Crete. But at Sparta every individual has to contribute, though some of them are quite poor and unable to meet this expenditure, so that the result is the opposite of what the legislator intended. For common meals are intended to be a democratic practice, but under the regulations such as those laid down at Sparta it becomes anything but democratic. For it is not easy for those who cannot afford it to join in, yet this is their traditional way of delimiting the constitution – to exclude from it anyone who is unable to pay this particular due.

Some Further Criticisms

1271a37 (i) Some others too have objected to the law about Naval Commanders. The objections are well founded, for the arrangement is a cause of faction. This is because over and above the Kings, who are perpetual commanders of the forces, the naval command is set up, which is almost another Kingship. (ii) The principles of the lawgiver are open to a further criticism, which Plato has in fact made in his *Laws*:[20] their whole system of laws is directed to securing only a part of virtue, military

18. I.e. two Ephors.
19. 'Messes', *sussitia*, designed to foster social and military solidarity, and compulsory for all adult male Spartans if they were to remain full citizens. Cf. II x.
20. I *init.*, and 666e, 688a, 705d.

prowess, as being valuable for conquering. Hence the Spartans were stable enough while at war but began to decline once they reached a position of supremacy; they did not understand how to be at leisure, and never engaged in any kind of training higher than training for war. (iii) Another, and equally serious, error is that while they rightly hold that the good things which men fight to get are to be won more by virtue than by vice, they wrongly suppose that these good things are superior to the virtue. (iv) Public finance is another thing that is badly managed by the Spartiatae. They are obliged to undertake large wars, but there is never any money in the public treasury. Also they are very bad at paying taxes, for as most of the land is the property of the Spartiatae themselves, they do not inquire too closely into each other's contributions. And so a state of affairs has come about which is just the opposite of the happy conditions envisaged by the lawgiver: he has produced a state which has no money, but is full of individuals eager to make money for themselves.[21]

These are the main defects of the constitution of the Lacedaemonians; so let that suffice for the topic.

II x

(1271b20–1272b23)

CRITICISM OF THE CRETAN CONSTITUTION

The expression 'Cretan constitution' is not to be taken as referring to that of any one state: Crete had many city-states, many of which appear to have had a common pattern of constitution. Aristotle begins by discussing and accepting the tradition that the Spartan constitution was derived from the Cretan, and much of the chapter is devoted to a detailed comparison of the two. (For a dis-

21. See under 'property' earlier in this chapter.

cussion, see K. M. T. Chrimes, Ancient Sparta (Manchester, 1949), p. 209 ff., and R. F. Willetts, Ancient Crete, a Social History (London, 1965), p. 60 ff.) However, there are conspicuous omissions: property-ownership, inheritance, heiresses and the influence of women. Aristotle had found fault with Sparta on all these counts, but he ignores them in dealing with Crete, though from his point of view conditions were in general worse there. His criticisms of the Cretan constitution centre on its aristocratic bias, and its lack of any machinery to ensure that the constitution continues to function when the leading families fall out among themselves. On the other hand he thinks the Cretan common meals better organized than the Spartan; and he notes, as many writers in antiquity did, the special advantages of Crete's geographical position. But perhaps the most important theme in this chapter and the preceding one is that the various political forces in the state should all desire to keep the constitution as it is, for this makes for stability. There is here the germ of a theory of political consent, of which Rousseau's 'social contract' is the most celebrated example; cf. IV xi–xiii.

For 'peripheral populations', 'Ephors' and other technical terms in this chapter, see introduction to II ix.

1271b20 The Cretan constitution is similar to the Lacedaemonian; in some few particulars it is certainly no worse, but in general it is less finished. It is said, and it appears to be true, that to a very great extent the Cretan constitution was taken as a model by the Lacedaemonian. (Generally, later forms of constitution are more fully developed than earlier.) They say that Lycurgus, after laying down his guardianship of King Charillus,[1] went abroad and on that occasion spent most of his time in Crete. He chose Crete because the two peoples were akin, the Lyc-

---

1. Plutarch *Lycurgus* 3–4; cf. Herodotus I 65, Pausanias III 3.

tians being colonists[2] from Sparta; and when the colonists came, they found the inhabitants at that time living
under a legal system which they then adopted. Hence to
this day the peripheral populations use those laws unchanged, believing Minos[3] to have established the legal
system in the first place.

1271b32 The island of Crete appears to be both very
well placed and naturally suited to dominate the Hellenic
world. It lies right across our sea, on whose coasts all
around most of the Greeks are settled. At one end the
Peloponnese is not far away, and at the Asiatic end the
districts round Triopium and Rhodes are close at hand.
This enabled Minos to build up his maritime empire too:
he made some of the islands subject to himself, to others
he sent settlers; in the end he attacked Sicily, where he
met his death near Camicus.

1271b40 The Cretan system resembles the Laconian.
The helots farm for the Spartans, the peripheral populations for the Cretans. Both countries have common meals,
for which in ancient times the Spartans used not their
present name 'phiditia', but the same name as the Cretans:
'andria'.[4] This is a plain indication of its Cretan origin.
Similarly as regards the arrangement of the constitution:
the Cretans have 'Cosmoi', whose power the Spartan
Ephors have also; but there are ten of them, while the
Ephors number five. The Elders, who in Crete are known
as the Council, correspond. The Cretans used to have a
kingship, but they did away with it and the Cosmoi
exercise leadership in war. And all Cretans are members

2. A Greek 'colony' was not a 'subject territory' in the modern
sense, but simply a new state formed by citizens who left their
homeland (though the mother state would naturally exercise some
influence and control over the new foundation).

3. King of Crete in the remote past, famed as a legislator (cf.
Plato, *Laws init.*), and after his death one of the judges of the souls
in the underworld.

4. I.e. *men*'s meals or gatherings.

of the Assembly, but this body has no power to do anything except vote assent to measures decided upon by the Elders and the Cosmoi.

1272a12 The arrangements for the common meals are better among the Cretans than among the Spartans. At Sparta each man contributes a specified per capita amount; failure to pay excludes one from the constitution, as has been said earlier.[5] In Crete the basis is more communal: out of the entire agricultural produce, whether stock or crop, yielded by public land, and the tributes paid by the peripheral populations, one part is set aside for the gods and for the communal public services,[6] and another sum for the common meals. In this way all – men, women, and children alike – are maintained at the public expense.[7] The Cretan lawgiver regarded abstemiousness as beneficial and devoted much ingenuity to securing it, as also to keeping down the birth-rate by keeping men and women apart and by instituting sexual relations between males; whether he acted wisely or not will be discussed on another occasion.[8] It is clear then that better arrangements for communal meals have been made among the Cretans than among the Laconians.

1272a27 On the other hand their Cosmoi are an even worse arrangement than the Ephors: the chief defect of the Board of Ephors, its indiscriminate composition, is there too, but the constitutional advantage is absent. For at Sparta the people, because the Ephors are elected from among all, have a share in the most powerful office and are therefore disposed to keep the constitution as it is. But in Crete they choose the Cosmoi not from among

5. Cf. II ix, 2nd paragraph from end.
6. Literally 'liturgies' (*leitourgiai*), 'public services', payments to defray the cost of certain public functions (e.g. festivals). 'Communal' seems to indicate that in Crete such services were paid for not by wealthy individuals (as at Athens), but by the state.
7. Evidently enough was left over from the common meals for each man to take home something for his wife and children.
8. No such discussion is to be found in Aristotle.

everyone, but from certain families only; and they elect
the Elders from among those who have held the office of
Cosmos. And about them one might make the same comments as about the Spartan Elders: [9] their exemption from
scrutiny and their life-tenure are privileges in excess of
their merits; and their power to take decisions on their
own judgement, and not govern in accordance with written rules, is dangerous. The fact that the people are content not to have any share in the office of Cosmos is no
evidence of a sound arrangement. For there is no profit
to be made out of the office of Cosmos, as there is out of
the Ephorate; and Crete being an island, they live farther
away from those who would corrupt them.

1272b1 The methods employed to cure the defects of
this institution are outlandish, and more to be expected
in a power-group than in a constitution.[10] It often happens that Cosmoi are turned out of office by a conspiracy,
which may be engineered partly by some of their fellow-
rulers or by private persons. It is actually possible for
Cosmoi to resign office during their tenure; but all such
matters are better regulated by law and not left to the
personal decision of individuals, which is an unreliable
criterion. But worst of all is the condition where there are
no Cosmoi at all; and this often occurs, being brought
about by the action of powerful people who want to escape justice. All this makes it pretty clear that the Cretan
system, while it possesses a certain constitutional element,
is not really a constitution, but more of a power-group.[10]
The powerful men are wont to make up bands of their
friends and from among the people, and to cause suspen-
sion of all government and form factions and fight each
other. And that, surely, means nothing less than that for
the time being such a state is a state no longer, but its

9. See II ix.
10. A 'power-group' is a *dunasteia*, a cabal of 'powerful people'
(*dunatoi*) acting in an arbitrary and sharply oligarchial manner:
see IV v, vi.

political association[11] is breaking up. A state in this condition is indeed in danger, since those who wish to attack it are also those who have the power.

1272b16 However, as we have already remarked, Crete is kept stable by its geographical situation; its distance has kept foreigners out.[12] One result is that the Cretan peripheral populations remain settled, while the Lacedaemonian helots are often in rebellion. And the Cretans do not participate in any dominion overseas. But recently[13] a foreign war has reached the island, and the weakness of its laws has become apparent. So much for the Cretan constitution.

II xi

(*1272b24–1273b26*)

CRITICISM OF THE CARTHAGINIAN CONSTITUTION

Little detail is given, and that very obscurely, about the constitution of Carthage, the only non-Greek state here examined. Aristotle compares it with the Spartan, and therefore thinks he can describe it using Greek terms – Kings, Elders, Generals (for technical terms, see introduction to II ix). (The Romans, on the other hand, used the native word for the supreme Carthaginian officials, the 'Kings', latinizing it as Suffetes.) Aristotle treats the Carthaginian constitution as an example of the kind of aristocracy he calls a 'polity' (see introduction to II vi), but with 'deviations' (parekbaseis) towards oligarchy on the one hand and democracy on the other. He is well aware that 'the characteristic and vital force in Carthaginian politics was before all things money' (W. E. Heitland),

11. *Koinōnia politikē*, 'the association that takes the form of a *polis* (state)'; cf. I i.

12. Literally, 'its distance has created *xenēlasiai*,' i.e. 'extrusions of aliens', for which Sparta was notorious.

13. The event referred to is uncertain.

and this constitutes for him a serious 'deviation' in the direction of oligarchy from the standards of excellence and ability demanded by the aristocratic principle. As democratic, he mentions the powers of decision enjoyed by the popular assembly in opposition to the wishes of the Kings and Elders. What counted in favour of the Carthaginian constitution was that it was generally acceptable and continued to work.

Two further points of interest are: (a) In this and in other chapters (cf. II ix, first paragraph) Aristotle speaks of the 'principle' or 'aim' of a constitution, which its founders had in mind. This is very much in accord with the Greek habit of regarding a constitution or code of laws as set up once and for all by a legislator, and its various features as either conforming with or departing from that model. We should today be more inclined to stress the role of historical accident and conflicting religious, economic or political pressures, not only in the growth and development of the constitution, but also, and especially, as they affected the original legislators (if any) themselves, e.g. the Founding Fathers of America. Aristotle obviously appreciates such historical influences, but his language is some indication of a way of thought rather different from ours. (b) Aristotle sharply attacks the view of public office as something to be bought and sold as a source of profit (cf. IV vi and V viii). One is tempted to moralize: in some parts of the world today Aristotle's words still need to be taken to heart.

1272b24 The Carthaginians also are regarded as managing their constitution successfully, and in many respects in a distinctive manner, though in some particulars closely resembling the Lacedaemonians. Indeed these three constitutions, Cretan, Laconian, and Carthaginian, present a number of resemblances to each other and many differences from the rest. Many of the Carthaginian arrangements are good; and it is an indication that a constitution is well arranged when the people are content to abide by the constitutional system, and no faction worth mentioning has appeared, and no tyrant.

1272b33 Here are the resemblances to the Spartan constitution. The common meals of the clubs are like the phiditia, and the board of 104 members corresponds to the Ephors, but is better: its members are chosen on merit and not from all indiscriminately. Their Kings and Board of Elders are the counterpart of the Spartan Kings and Elders; and it is an advantage that the Kings are not drawn from one family alone, nor from any and every family. Election depends more on the eminence of one's family than on one's age, for worthless persons appointed to have supreme control of weighty affairs do a lot of damage, as they have already done to the Lacedaemonian state.[1]

1273a2 Most of the objections brought on the grounds that there are deviations[2] are applicable in common to all the three constitutions here mentioned. In relation to the principle of aristocracy, or 'polity', some features are objectionable because they deviate into oligarchy, others because they deviate into democracy. An example of the latter is the fact that at Carthage the Kings, acting in conjunction with the Elders, have sovereign power to refer or not to refer a matter to the people, provided they are unanimous; failing that, here too the people have power of decision.[3] Moreover, when a matter agreed upon by Kings and Elders is so referred, the people are not merely allowed by them to listen to the proposals of the officials, but they have sovereign power to make decisions

1. Cf. I ix, 'The Ephors', and I x.

2. From the perfection of the 'ideal' state, presumably, as distinct from that of the 'best possible' (i.e. the variety of aristocracy Aristotle calls a 'polity'): cf. II, ix *init*.

3. The Greek does not make it clear whether the unanimity and the 'power of decision' are about the referral itself, or about the actual matter under consideration; nor whether 'unanimity' (literally 'if all agree') means 'both of the two kings and all the elders' or (more probably) 'kings and elders' (thought of as two bodies, presumably with majority voting in the second).

on them; and it is open to all and sundry to oppose and speak against the proposals that have been referred to them. This feature does not exist in the other constitutions.

1273a13 Then there are oligarchical features. The Boards of Five,[4] which have supreme control over many important matters, not only fill up vacancies on their own by co-option but appoint members of the Hundred, the highest authority; moreover they enjoy a longer tenure of office than the rest: they begin to rule before they become members, and continue to do so after they have ceased to belong. On the other hand we must allow as aristocratic the fact that they receive no pay and are not chosen by lot, and one or two other features of that kind; for example all law-suits are decided by the committees, not, as at Sparta, some by one set of persons, others by another.

1273a21 The most conspicuous deviation of the Carthaginian system from the aristocratic towards the oligarchical is one which is quite in accord with the popular notion that rulers should be chosen not merely on merit but also on grounds of wealth. It is impossible, they argue, for a man without ample means to be a good ruler — that is, to have the leisure to be one. Now if election according to wealth is oligarchic, and on grounds of virtue aristocratic, a third system will be this one which underlies the constitutional arrangements of the Carthaginians, who have both these points in mind when they elect, and particularly when they elect the highest officials, i.e. the Kings and Generals.

1273a31 But this deviation from aristocracy must be regarded as an error on the part of the Carthaginian lawgiver. For it is most essential that from the very start provision be made for the best people to have leisure and not to depart in any way from standards of propriety, not only while in office but even as private citizens. But while we must look to wealth too,[5] for the sake of the leisure

4. 'Pentarchies'.
5. I.e. as well as to virtue (*aretē*).

it gives, it is a bad thing that the highest offices, of King and General, should be for sale. Where this practice is legal, wealth becomes of more esteem than virtue and causes the whole state to become bent on making money. Whatever is most valued by the highest authority inevitably makes the opinion of the rest of the citizens follow suit. And wherever virtue is not the most highly esteemed thing, there a securely aristocratic constitution is an impossibility. People who lay out sums of money in order to secure office get into the habit of looking, not unreasonably, for some return. Even the poor but reasonable man will want his profit, so it could hardly be expected that the not-so-honest, who has already put his hand in his pocket, should not want his profit too. Therefore it should be those who are best able to find spare time that should hold office. And even if the lawgiver has abandoned the idea of making those reasonable men wealthy, he ought to secure leisure for them, at least during their term of office. *1273b8* Another feature, which would seem objectionable, though the Carthaginians think highly of it, is plurality of office, the same man holding more than one. Surely work is best done when one task is performed by one man. The legislator ought to ensure this, and not require one and the same man to be player on the pipes and a shoemaker. So, too, where the state is not too small to allow of it, it is more statesmanlike,[6] as well as more democratic, that a number of people should share in the offices. For, as we have said,[7] in this way the work is more widely distributed and each individual task is performed more efficiently and more expeditiously. This can be illustrated from the sphere of the army and the navy; for in both these one might say that commanding and being commanded run right through all personnel.

6. *Politikōteron*, 'more fitted to (be the practice or policy of) a statesman, *politikos*', i.e. *a* citizen (*politēs*) in his capacity as an office-bearer in a state (*polis*); or perhaps 'more characteristic of a *polity*'.

7. Probably II ii, 3rd paragraph.

1273b18   But although their constitution is an oligarchy,[8] they are very successful in escaping faction, because from time to time a section of the people grows rich on being removed to the states. That is the way in which they cure the trouble and keep their constitution stable. But all that is Fortune's business, whereas it ought to be thanks to the legislator that they avoid faction. As it is, if any mischance were to occur and the mass of the ruled population were to rebel, the laws provide no remedy for restoring peace.

So much for my account of the Lacedaemonian, Cretan, and Carthaginian constitutions, all of which justly earn our respect.

II xii

(*1273b27–1274b28*)

SOLON AND SOME OTHER LAWGIVERS

This miscellaneous but very interesting chapter has the air of having been dashed off to complete as rapidly as possible the discussion of excellent constitutions actual and proposed, and of their framers and lawgivers. If the chapter is in fact by Aristotle, he may not have intended it to stand at this point; but its authenticity, in whole or part, has often been doubted (see commentaries). Its most important sections concern the conflict felt by Pittacus between equity on the one hand and law and order on the other, and the attempt to meet criticisms of Solon's legislation, which Aristotle admired (cf. e.g. IV

8. And therefore liable to dissolution by revolt of the less wealthy. Apparently the remedy was to enrich part of the common people on occasion by dispatching them to lucrative positions in 'the states' mentioned at the end of the sentence. Presumably these states were either Carthaginian 'colonies' (see II x, n. 2 and Plato, *Laws* 740e), or other places somehow subject to Carthaginian control.

*xi). The chapter ends with a rapid list of points 'peculiar'
to various legislators, which in part repeats briefly material
discussed earlier in the book.*

1273b27 Those who have voiced opinions on constitutions fall into two classes. We have already given some
account, so far as it is worth mentioning, of all of the
first class, that is, of those who took no part whatever in
political activity,[1] but remained private citizens all their
lives. The others, after personal experience of politics,
have become lawgivers either in their own or in certain
foreign cities. Some of these merely drafted laws, but
others, like Lycurgus and Solon, framed constitutions too;
for they established both constitutions and laws. Of the
Spartan constitution I have spoken already.[2]

1273b35 Some, who believe that Solon was a sound lawgiver, put forward the following reasons: (a) he abolished
the undiluted oligarchy; (b) he put an end to the enslavement of the people; and (c) he established the traditional
Athenian democracy by mixing the constitution well.
They explain that the mixture contains an oligarchical
element (the Council of the Areopagus),[3] an aristocratic

1. In this paragraph, 'political' has the sense 'to do with the
state (*polis*)' and 'experience of politics' = *politeuthentes*, 'having
taken part in state affairs'. 'Drafted laws' = *nomōn dēmiourgos*,
'workman, or maker, or framer, of laws'; cf. Pittacus in the final
paragraph of the chapter.

2. For Lycurgus and the Spartan constitution, see II ix. Solon
legislated for Athens in 594 B.C., or possibly somewhat later. His
chief reform was to abolish existing debts contracted on security of
land or person, and to forbid debts on security of person in the
future. He thus sharply curtailed the economic and political power
of the Eupatridae (rich nobles), who had by lending reduced many
poorer Athenians to slavery. See Aristotle, *Constitution of the
Athenians* 1–14.

3. Areopagus means 'Hill of Ares'. Before Solon the Council
consisted exclusively or mainly of Eupatridae; in the course of
time, under democratic pressure, it came to include members of
other classes also.

element (the fact that the officials are elected), and a democratic one (the courts). As a matter of fact it would seem
that Solon found the first two of these already in existence,
the council and the practice of electing officials, and merely
refrained from abolishing them. On the other hand, by
setting up courts drawn from the entire body of citizens,
he did establish democracy at Athens. It is in fact here
that some people find Solon at fault: they say that by
giving supreme power over all matters to the courts, appointed by lot, he ruined the other half of his work. As
soon as these courts became powerful, they began to do
everything with a view to pleasing the people, just as if
they were humouring a tyrant, and in this way converted
the constitution into the democracy as we now have it.
Ephialtes and Pericles reduced the power of the Council
of the Areopagus,[4] and Pericles introduced payment for
service in the courts; in this way each successive leader of
the people enlarged the democracy and advanced it to its
present scale.

1274a11 But it seems that all this took place not according to Solon's intention but as a result of circumstances.
For the Athenian sea-power in the Persian wars was due
to the Athenian people; this gave them a great opinion
of themselves, and they chose inferior men as popular
leaders when respectable men pursued policies not to their
liking. Certainly Solon himself seems to have given only
a necessary minimum of power to the people – the power
to elect officials and to require a scrutiny (for if they did
not have supreme power over even this, the people would
be no better than slaves or foes). He provided that all
officials were to be drawn from among the notables and
men of substance, that is to say the Pentacosiomedimnoi,

---

4. Ephialtes was a democratic politician. His measures of 462–1
deprived the Areopagus of political powers, and it then retained
only certain judicial functions, notably as the court for cases of
deliberate homicide. Pericles (495–429) was in 462–1 an associate of
Ephialtes.

the Zeugitae, and the third class, the 'Knights';[5] he excluded from office only the fourth property-class, the Thetes.

1274a22 Other lawgivers were Zaleucus, who made laws for the Epizephyrian Locrians, and Charondas of Catana, who made laws both for his own citizens and for the other states of Italy and Sicily that were of Chalcidian origin. (Some wish to include Onomacritus as the first expert in lawmaking, saying that he was a Locrian, that he trained in Crete during a visit there to practise his art of soothsaying, that Thales the Cretan was his friend, and that Lycurgus and Zaleucus heard Thales lecture and Charondas heard Zaleucus. But all that is somewhat to disregard chronology.)[6]

1274a31 Then there was Philolaus the Corinthian, who made laws for the Thebans. He was of the Bacchiad family, and became the lover of Diocles, a victor in the Olympic Games.[7] This Diocles, in disgust at the amorous passion for him of his mother Alcyone, left Corinth for Thebes, where he and Philolaus ended their days. Visitors are still shown their two tombs, which are easily visible one from the other; but one can be seen from Corinthian territory, the other not. The story is that they planned the sites of the two tombs themselves, Diocles so that the land of Corinth with its bitter memories of his suffering should be invisible from his grave, Philolaus that it might be visible from his. That is how they came to be living at

5. Solon's constitution distinguished four property-classes, based on annual income of measures (*medimnoi*) of corn or equivalent in money or other produce: Pentacosiomedimnoi ('500 measures men'), Knights (*Hippeis*, 'cavalry', 500–300 measures), Zeugitae (possibly 'yoke of oxen men', 300–200), and Thetes (labourers, less than 200).

6. Dates: Zaleucus and Thales, probably mid seventh century; Charondas, probably sixth century. This Cretan Thales (otherwise Thaletas) should not be confused with Thales the Milesian philosopher. The tangled details of this parenthesis apparently refer to attempts to trace the origin of the art of legislation to Crete; cf. II x *init*.

7. 728.

Thebes. Philolaus became their lawgiver, and among his measures there are some relating to the begetting of children. These the Thebans called 'laws of adoption'. They consist of an enactment, peculiar to Philolaus, which was designed to keep fixed the number of estates.

1274b5 As for Charondas, there is nothing peculiar to him except the suits for false witness (he was the first to permit notice to be given.)[8] In the careful detail of his laws he is more finished even than modern legislators. The feature peculiar to Phaleas[9] is his equalization of possessions; to Plato, communal ownership of possessions, wives, and children, and common meals for women;[10] also his law about intoxication, that the sober should preside at drinking parties;[11] and again that soldiers in their training should practise to become ambidextrous, instead of having one hand useful, the other useless.[12] There are laws of Draco,[13] but these were additions to an existing constitution. There is nothing peculiar to them worth mentioning except the severity of their heavy punishments.

1274b18 Pittacus[14] too was a maker of laws, not of a constitution; and a law peculiar to him states that if drunken men commit an offence they should pay a larger fine than sober men. Since more drunken men than sober commit crimes of violence, and ought to be pardoned more readily, he decided to disregard the question of pardoning them and concentrate on getting useful results.[15] The inhabitants of the city of Chalcis, in Thrace, had a lawgiver,

8. See n. 6. *Episkēpsis* is a technical term of Greek law: 'giving notice of intention to prosecute' (here an allegedly false witness).

9. II vii.

10. II i–vi.

11. *Laws* 640c–e, 671a–672a.

12. *Laws* 794d ff.

13. Draco produced Athens' first written legal code, probably in 621–20.

14. Ruler of Mytilene, 589–79.

15. The point of this somewhat paradoxical sentence seems to be that Pittacus, although accepting the *principle* that drunkenness is an excuse of a kind, decided, in view of the close correlation

Androdamas[16] of Rhegium, whose laws relate to homicide and heiresses, but I cannot mention any point that is peculiar to them.

Let this suffice for our survey of constitutions, actual and proposed.

---

between crime and drunkenness, that the principle had to be overridden on social grounds in favour of a policy of deterring intoxication by extra penalties.

16. Mentioned here only.

BOOK III

III i

HOW SHOULD WE DEFINE 'CITIZEN'?

The third book contains much of Aristotle's best work on politics and much that is of permanent interest. His material is very diverse, and it looks as if he may have assembled and utilized part of some earlier studies.

The major part of the book is devoted to constitutions – democratic, oligarchic, monarchic – a topic which had long been the kernel of Greek political thought. The first chapter opens with a difficult passage, some of which looks more like notes for a lecture than continuous discourse. He has hardly mentioned that he is about to discuss the constitution of a state, when he makes a series of observations not only about that but about the polis *or* state, *and the* politēs *or* citizen. *The connection between these observations is not clear, but the argument may have been something like this: One ought, before discussing* politeia, *to define* polis; *there is no unanimity about this definition, but, since a state is made up of its citizens, we should rather begin by defining citizen; there is just as much dispute about this definition, but it must be attempted, as a preliminary to discussing 'constitution', which is an organized system of relationships governing the state and the citizen.*

Aristotle accordingly discusses the definition of a citizen. It may seem odd to us thus to make the citizen prior to the state, but we should remember, first, that to say merely 'a citizen is a member of a state' involves asking 'what constitutes membership of a state?' – which is just the question now to be discussed; and second, that Aristotle's outlook is here, as so often, coloured by his biological studies: he is inclined to think of citizen as a kind of species and to look for the marks by which it may be recognized. He acknowledges in this first chapter, however, that the description of a citizen will vary according to the constitution he lives under, so that to look for the notion of the 'citizen' pure and simple, in some basic sense applicable to all citizens, may be mistaken in principle.

Nevertheless Aristotle attempts a general definition, namely that a citizen is one who 'participates in giving judgement and holding office'. This definition ought to jolt us into realizing that Aristotle would regard most of us – who rely on representatives to run our public affairs – as barely citizens at all; he would condemn modern democracy as insufficiently 'participatory'. On the other hand, even in a Greek democracy, a very large proportion of the population was excluded from office, notably women and slaves. For a stimulating discussion of these and other important questions, see M. I. Finley, Democracy Ancient and Modern *(London, 1973), esp. Ch. I.*

1274b32 In considering now the varieties and characteristics of constitutions, we must begin by looking at the state and asking what it is. There is no unanimity about this; for example, some say that an action was taken by the state, others that it was taken not by the state, but by the oligarchy or by the dictator. Now obviously the activities of statesman and legislator are wholly concerned with the state, and the constitution is a kind of organization of the state's inhabitants; but like any other whole that is made up of many parts, the state is to be classed as a composite thing; so clearly we must first try to isolate the citizen, for the state is an aggregate of citizens. So we must ask, Who is a citizen? and, Whom should we call one? *1275a2* Here too there is no unanimity, no agreement as to what constitutes a citizen; it often happens that one who is a citizen in a democracy is not a citizen in an oligarchy. (I think we may leave out of account those who merely acquire the title indirectly, e.g. the 'made' citizens.)[1]

1. Such citizens would acquire the status other than by birth

Nor does mere residence in a place confer citizenship: resident foreigners and slaves are not citizens, but do share domicile in the country. Another definition is 'those who have access to legal processes, who may prosecute or be prosecuted'. But this access is open to any person who is covered by a commercial treaty[2] – at any rate partially open, for a resident foreigner is in many places obliged to appoint a patron, so that not even this degree of participation is open to him unqualifiedly. (Likewise boys not yet old enough to be enrolled,[3] and old people who have retired from duty, must be termed citizens in a sense, but only with the addition of 'not fully' or 'superannuated' or some such term – not that it matters which word we use, since what we mean is clear enough). What we are looking for is the citizen proper, without any defect needing to be amended. Similar difficulties may be raised, and solved, about persons exiled or with civic disqualifications.

1275a22 What effectively distinguishes the citizen proper from all others is his participation in giving judgement and in holding office. Some offices are distinguished in respect of length of tenure, some not being tenable by the same person twice under any circumstances, or only after an interval of time. Others, such as membership of a jury or of an assembly,[4] have no such limitation. It might be objected that such persons are not really officials, and that these functions do not amount to participation in office. But they have the fullest sovereign power, and it would be ridiculous to deny their participation in office. In any case nomenclature ought not to make any difference; it is just that there is no name covering that which is common to a juryman and to a member of an assembly,

---

(presumably for services rendered, or *honoris causa*), but exercise none or only some of its privileges.
2. I.e. between states. 'Legal processes' = *dikaia*.
3. I.e. as citizens.
4. *Ekklēsia*, an assembly of all the citizens of a state.

which ought to be used of both. For the sake of a definition I suggest that we say 'unlimited[5] office'. We therefore define citizens as those who participate in this. Such a definition seems to cover, as nearly as may be, those to whom the term citizen is in fact applied.

1275a34 On the other hand we must remember that in the case of things in which the substrata differ in kind, one being primary, another secondary, and so on, there is nothing, or scarcely anything, which is common to all those things, in so far as they are the kind of thing they are.[6] Thus we see the various constitutions differing from each other in kind, some being prior to others – since those that have gone wrong or deviated must be posterior to those which are free from error. I will explain later what I mean by 'deviated'.[7] A citizen, therefore, will necessarily vary according to the constitution in each case.

1275b5 For this reason our definition of citizen is best applied in a democracy; in the other constitutions it *may* be applicable, but it need not necessarily be so. For in some constitutions there is no body comprising the people, nor a recognized assembly, but only an occasional rally; and justice may be administered piecemeal.[8] For example, at Sparta contract cases are tried by the Ephors, one or other of them, cases of homicide by the Elders, and other cases doubtless by other officials. Similarly at Carthage all cases are tried by officials.

1275b13 But our own definition of a citizen can be

5. I.e. in point of length of tenure.
6. A technically worded generalization prompted by the particular point which follows immediately. Constitutions ('substrata', 'underlying conditions') to which citizens ('things') belong, differ in kind and rank in an order of merit, so that (e.g.) a citizen in an oligarchy differs so radically from a citizen in a democracy as to preclude there being anything much in common between the two, in so far as they are *citizens* (and not simply men, for example).
7. III vi *fin.*, cf. II xi.
8. I.e. not in regular courts with juries of citizens, as in general at Athens, but by various separate and more select bodies or officials, as exemplified in the next sentence.

amended so as to apply to the other constitutions also. We simply replace our 'unlimited' office of juror or member of assembly by 'limited'.[5] For it is to all or some of these that the task of judging or deliberating is assigned, either on all matters or on some. From these considerations it has become clear who a citizen is: as soon as a man becomes entitled to participate in office, deliberative or judicial,[9] we deem him to be a citizen of that state; and a number of such persons large enough to secure a self-sufficient life we may, by and large, call a state.

III ii

(1275b22–1276a6)

A PRAGMATIC DEFINITION OF 'CITIZEN'

In this brief chapter, which coheres closely with III i, Aristotle points out that various common practical definitions of a citizen (e.g. as someone both of whose parents were citizens, or as a person who has been 'made' into a citizen by some state official empowered to do so) encounter certain difficulties. His own preference is to abandon such formal and legalistic criteria of citizenship in favour of a functional one: do candidates for the title 'citizen' share in deliberative and judicial office, as explained in III i? If so, they are citizens, and may be properly described thus irrespective of their parentage or the manner in which they came to exercise the required functions; and that a man may come to exercise them unjustly does not in itself disqualify him from actually being a citizen in practice. Aristotle's approach is thus both neat and pragmatic.

1275b22 For practical purposes a citizen is defined as one of citizen birth on *both* his father's *and* his mother's

9. *Kritikē,* 'to do with giving judgements'.

side; some would go further and demand citizen descent for two, three, or even more generations. But since these are only crude definitions, employed by states for practical purposes, some people pose the puzzle of how a great or great-great-grandfather's citizenship can itself be determined. Gorgias of Leontini, partly perhaps in puzzlement and partly in jest, said that, as mortars are what mortar-makers make, so Larissaeans are those made by the workmen, some of whom were Larissaean-makers.[1] The answer to such objectors is simple: if they participated in the constitution in the manner prescribed in our definition,[2] they were citizens. Of course, the criterion of having citizen-parents cannot be applied in the case of the original colonists or founders.

1275b34 I think however that there is perhaps a more important puzzle here, namely about those who got a share in the constitution because it had changed – as for example after the expulsion of the tyrants from Athens, when Cleisthenes enrolled many foreigners and slaves in the tribes.[3] The question here is not 'Are these persons citizens?', but whether they are citizens justly or unjustly. Some would go further and question whether anyone can be a citizen unless he is justly so, on the ground that unjust and false mean the same thing. But when persons exercise their office unjustly, we continue to say that they rule, though unjustly; and as the citizen has been defined by some kind of office (i.e. if he shares in such and such an office, he is, as we said, a citizen), we cannot deny the propriety of using the term even in these cases.

---

1. Gorgias was a famous Sicilian 'sophist', who paid a visit to Athens in 427. *Dēmiourgos* was the Greek word for 'workman', and, in some states including apparently Larissa, for a certain type of public official; and the word 'Larissaean' was used to describe both a citizen of Larissa and a kind of pot made there. Gorgias' point is that to be 'made' a Larissaean (citizen) by a 'workman' (official) is a perfectly good criterion of citizenship.

2. At the end of III i.

3. Thus making them citizens, in 510. (I omit *metoikous* from the text, as a gloss on *xenous*.)

CONTINUITY OF IDENTITY OF THE STATE

*The pragmatic note struck at the end of the preceding
chapter prompts Aristotle to resume a crucial practical
difficulty he had raised at the beginning of III i: when
a state's constitution changes (e.g. from oligarchy to democracy), certain persons are admitted to or deprived of
citizenship. If the new government repudiates debts contracted by the old, are we entitled to protest, on the
grounds that only the constitution has changed, whereas
the state remains in some sense the same? Or does a change
of constitution entail a 'different' state, characterized by a
complete lack of legal and civic continuity with its predecessor? In brief, what are the criteria of continuity of a
state, and should the state for this purpose be identified
with its constitution at a given moment?*

*Aristotle first reviews and dismisses some relatively sim-
plistic criteria based on considerations of territory and
population, and then seeks guidance from the plausible
analogies of 'choruses' (the groups of actors who danced
and sang in Greek drama), and musical 'modes' or 'styles'.
The same notes, differently arranged, produce different
styles; similarly, while the people that make up a state
may not change during a revolution, they may nevertheless, as a result of that revolution, be 'associated' differently to make a different constitution; and different constitutions, because some or all of those who are citizens
under one constitution will not be citizens under another,
thus entail* different *states. This is not such a weird conclusion as it may seem. Aristotle would not wish to deny
that a state continues to exist after a change of constitution: clearly it is not the case that one state literally ceases
to exist and another comes into being. His point is that
since a change of constitution entails a change in the
citizen-body – i.e. in those who hold deliberative and*

judicial office (see III i) – the state has become different in kind: it is not the state it was before, in spite of obvious material continuities of site, buildings, population, etc.

But this conclusion hardly settles the question of the justice of a regime's repudiation of the commitments of its predecessor in power. Aristotle's decision to make the form of constitution the criterion of continuity lends colour to the claim that a new form of government is not bound by all the contractual obligations of an old. Yet he does not want us to jump to this conclusion, for he indicates there is more to be said on the question; but in fact he never takes it up again. The first paragraph, however, suggests in passing a possible criterion: did the previous constitution promote the general, as distinct from a sectional, interest?

1276a6 This question of justice or the lack of it cannot be separated from the dispute we have already mentioned,[1] which arises from the difficulty some people raise as to whether it was or was not the state that acted – for example when a change takes place from oligarchy to tyranny or democracy. There are those[2] who after such a change claim that they are no longer obliged to fulfil the terms of a contract; for it had been entered into, so they say, not by the state but by the tyrant. Similarly they would disown other obligations, if these have been incurred under one of those types of constitution which rest on force and disregard the common interest. It follows that if there is a democracy of this type, we must say that the acts of this constitution are acts of the state to the same degree[3] as those flowing from the oligarchy or tyranny are.

1. III i *ad init.*
2. Presumably members of the new regime. 'Entered into': literally 'took', presumably the money or goods, without giving the agreed return.
3. I.e. not at all. One cannot have it both ways: if the acts of a tyrant may be disowned on the grounds that he is not acting in the common interest, so too may those of a democracy, if its aims are similarly unacceptable.

1276a17 And this topic seems to be part of yet another question – how are we to tell whether a state is still the same state or a different one? We might try to investigate this question using territory and inhabitants as criteria; but this would not carry us very far, since it is quite possible to divide both territory and population into two, putting some people in one part and some into the other. That is not a very serious difficulty: it arises from our use of the word *polis* in more than one sense.[4] Such a puzzle is therefore resolved easily enough.

1276a24 Another question is this: when a population lives in the same place, what is the criterion for regarding the state as a unity? It cannot be the walls, for it would be possible to put one wall round the whole Peloponnese. Babylon is perhaps a similar case, and any other state with a circumference that embraces a nation rather than a state. (It is said of Babylon that its capture was, two days later, still unknown to a part of the city.) These questions of the state's size – both how big it should be and whether it helps to have the population drawn from one nation or more than one – are problems to which it will be useful to return later,[5] since the statesman has to keep them in mind.

1276a34 But when the same population continues to dwell in the same territory, must we say that the state remains the same so long as there is continuity of race among that population, even though one generation of people dies and another is born – just as a river or spring is commonly said to be the same, although different water passes into and out of it all the time?[6] Alternatively, ought we to speak of the *population* as being the same for the reasons stated, but say that the *state* is different?

4. I.e. the social and political sense, and the territorial.
5. V iii and VII iv.
6. Aristotle is probably thinking of Heraclitus' celebrated remarks on unity and change, notably 'Upon those who step into the same rivers ever-changing waters flow' (fr. 12 in H. Diels and W. Kranz, *Die Fragmente der Vorsokratiker* I, 6th ed., Berlin, 1951–2).

For the state is a kind of association – an association of citizens in a constitution; so when the constitution changes and becomes different in kind, the state also would seem necessarily not to be the same. We may use the analogy of a chorus, which may at one time perform in a tragedy and at another in a comedy, so that we say it is different – yet often enough it is composed of the same persons. And the same principle is applicable to other associations and combinations, which are different if the combination in question differs in kind. For example, we say the same musical notes are fitted together differently, to produce either the Dorian or the Phrygian mode. If this is right, it is clear that the main criterion of the continued identity of a state ought to be its constitution. This leaves it quite open either to change or not to change the *name* of a state, both when the population is the same and when it is different.

But whether, when a state's constitution is changed, it is just to disown obligations or to discharge them – that is another question.

III iv

(1276b16–1277b32)

HOW FAR SHOULD THE GOOD MAN
AND THE GOOD CITIZEN BE DISTINGUISHED?

Aristotle has discussed, but has not really finished discussing, citizen and state in relation to constitution. He has had difficulty in defining citizen in such a way as to be applicable to all forms of constitution. This same difficulty now reappears in another form: in attempting to find out what a good *citizen is, he discovers that here too the answer depends largely on the* politeia, *constitution, in which the citizenship is held. Perhaps this is our cue to remind ourselves of the inadequacy of 'constitution' as a translation of* politeia, *which embraces the whole social, political and economic organization of the state; and also that 'virtue'* (aretē, *'excellence', 'efficiency') is often conceived in terms of civic function rather than of character or mental or spiritual state: 'what I can do' as well as 'what I inwardly am'. What follows now, about the good man, 'sound' citizen, and good ruler or official, will be clearer if these points are borne in mind. (In this chapter,* spoudaios, *'sound', usually of the* citizen, *is distinguished in translation from* agathos, *'good', usually of the individual* man – *though what if anything hinges on this point of vocabulary is by no means clear; indeed, in this chapter the two terms are commonly interpreted as virtual synonyms – but see R. Develin, 'The good man and the good citizen in Aristotle's* Politics', Phronesis, *18 (1973), pp. 71–9.)*

Aristotle argues that the good citizen can be a good man only in the 'best' state, and only then when he is performing the function of ruling, not when he is being ruled. Such a doctrine sounds to us arid and unhelpful. Why does Aristotle hold it?

The first four paragraphs argue that what makes a good citizen is the contribution his 'virtue' makes to the stability and well-being of the constitution; but of constitutions there are many different kinds, so the 'virtue' of a good citizen *will vary according to the constitution under which he lives. It cannot, therefore, be the same as the invariable 'perfect' virtue of the good* man. *Even in the 'best' state, the inevitable differentiation of function among the citizens prevents the virtue of the good citizen from being identical with that of the good man, which is single, and the same in all good men.*

The next two paragraphs concede that the two virtues may coincide in particular cases, i.e. when the good man is, in his capacity as good citizen, ruling well – for that entails the exercise of wisdom (phronēsis) *which is an essential part of the 'perfect' virtue of a good man. But part of the virtue of a good citizen is to be ruled well also, which does not require wisdom, and is less praiseworthy. Only when the good citizen is ruling is his virtue identical with that of the good man. Two more paragraphs then distinguish the citizen's alternation of ruling and being ruled from the permanent relationship of ruler and ruled seen in slavery. A final paragraph points out that the particular virtues, e.g. wisdom, differ according as to whether they are exercised by ruler or ruled. This consideration too militates against the view that the virtue of the good citizen and the good man are identical, for the virtue of the latter is exercised only when ruling.*

The last paragraph of the chapter perhaps suggests that Aristotle found these conclusions somewhat unpalatable. His dilemma arises, as so often, from his belief in natural teleology. Man has certain faculties to use, including the noblest, the intellectual. A man cannot be 'good' if he is not using his faculties: there is a kind of moral imperative to use them (cf. introduction to III vi). Now a man who is ruled has to hold his reasoning faculty in abeyance, to the extent that he must do as he is told and not exercise judgement or take a decision of his own or direct other people. He cannot, therefore, be a 'good' man. He may be a good citizen, *of a particular constitution; but unless he is ruling well over fellow-citizens, having first learned to do so by being ruled, he is not exercising his human faculties to the full, and is not 'good'. The 'good man' looks as though he will be a rather rare phenomenon (cf. the exacting criteria and apparent rarity of* phronēsis, *practical wisdom, in* Nicomachean Ethics, *VI xiii); and at the end of the present chapter we learn that men who are being ruled will need mere 'right opinion', not* phronēsis *(cf. Plato,* Republic *IV). Aristotle is thinking in terms of an intellectual and political élite.*

*Aristotle could have escaped his dilemma simply by challenging his own assumption that 'goodness' or 'virtue' (*aretē*) cannot be complete without the exercise of certain functions. In so far as 'good' is a term of moral approbation, why should it depend on the exercise of the 'noble'* *faculty of reason for the purpose of ruling? Could not an unintelligent person, who never rules, be 'good'? Back would come Aristotle's answer: 'As a citizen, yes; as a man, no'. We may think this queer; but at least his very acute discussion does have the considerable merit of focusing our attention on the question, 'What do we mean when we say a man is "good"?'.*

These seem to be the central issues of the chapter, but there is much else of interest: for a full discussion, see the commentaries, especially Newman I 234 ff. Some sentences are very difficult, partly because of textual cruces.

1276b16 Connected with the matters just discussed is the question whether we ought to regard the virtue of a good man and that of a sound citizen as the same virtue, or not. If this is a point to be investigated, we really must try to form some rough conception of the virtue of a citizen.

1276b20 So then: we say a citizen is a member of an association, just as a sailor is; and each member of the crew has his different function and a name to fit it – rower, helmsman, look-out, and the rest. Clearly the most exact description of each individual will be a special description of his virtue; but equally there will also be a general description that will fit them all, because there is a task in which they all play a part – the safe conduct[1] of the voyage; for each member of the crew aims at securing that. Similarly the task of all the citizens, however different they may be, is the stability[1] of the association, that is, the constitution. Therefore the virtue of the citizen must be in relation to the constitution; and as there are more kinds of constitution than one, there cannot be just one single *and perfect* virtue of the sound citizen. On the other hand we do say that the good *man* is good because of one single virtue which *is* perfect virtue. Clearly then

1. *Sōtēria*, 'safety', 'stability', a major preoccupation of Greek states, and an important topic in the analysis of the causes of constitutional change in V–VI.

it is possible to be a sound citizen without having that virtue which makes a sound man.

1276b35 Look now at the problem from another angle and consider the same point in relation to the best constitution. That is to say, if it is impossible for a state to consist entirely of sound *men*, still each of them must do, and do well, his proper work; and doing it well depends on his virtue. But since it is impossible for all the *citizens* to be alike, there cannot be one virtue of citizen and good man alike. For the virtue of the sound citizen must be possessed by all (and if it is, then that state is necessarily best). *But* if it is inevitable that not all the citizens in a sound state are good,[2] it is impossible for all to have the virtue of the good man.

1277a5 Again, a state is made up of unlike parts. As an animate creature consists of body and soul, and soul consists of reasoning and desiring, and a household consists of husband and wife, and property consists of master and slave, so also a state is made up of these and many other sorts of people besides, all different. The virtue of all the citizens cannot, therefore, be *one*, any more than in a troupe of dancers the goodness of the leader and that of the followers are one.

1277a12 Now while all this shows clearly that they are not the same in general, the question may be asked whether it is not possible in a particular case for the same virtue to belong both to the sound citizen and the sound man. We would answer that there is such a case, since we maintain that a sound ruler is both good and wise,[3] whereas wisdom is not essential for a citizen. Some say that from the very start there is a different kind of education for rulers. They instance (a) the obvious training of the sons of royalty in horsemanship and war, and (b) a saying of Euripides, which is supposed to refer to the education of a ruler: 'No frills in education, please ... only what the

2. It *is* inevitable, because of their inevitable diversity of function, and therefore of virtue.

3. *Phronimos*, 'possessing practical wisdom', *phronēsis*.

state doth need.'[4] But though we may say that the virtue of good ruler and good man is the same, yet, since he too that is ruled is a citizen, we cannot say in general that the virtue of citizen and man are one, but only that they may be in the case of a particular citizen.[5] For certainly the virtue of ruler and citizen are not the same. And that doubtless is the reason why Jason of Pherae said that he went hungry whenever he ceased to be tyrant, not knowing how to live as a private person.

1277a25 But surely men praise the ability to rule and to be ruled, and the virtue of a citizen of repute seems to be just this – to be able to rule and be ruled well. If then we say that the virtue of the good man is to do with ruling, and that of the citizen to do with both ruling and being ruled, the two things cannot be praiseworthy to the same degree.

1277a29 So since on occasions they seem different, and ruler and ruled ought not to learn the same things, whereas the citizen ought to know both and share in both, one could see from the following.[6]

1277a33 For there is such a thing as rule by a master, which we say is concerned with necessary tasks; but the master has no necessity to know more than how to *use* such labour. Anything else, I mean to be able actually to be a servant and do the chores, is simply slave-like. (We speak of several kinds of slave, corresponding to the several varieties of operation. One variety is performed by manual workers, who, as the term itself indicates, live by their hands; among these are the skilled mechanics.) Hence, in some places, only with the arrival of extreme democracies have workmen attained to participation in office. The work then of those who are subject to rule is not work which either the good statesman or the good

---

4. From Euripides' *Aeolus*: part of lines 2 and 3 of fr. 16 in A. Nauck, *Tragicorum Graecorum Fragmenta* (2nd ed., Leipzig, 1889).
5. I.e. one who is ruling wisely and well in a 'best' state.
6. This unintelligible sentence reflects the apparently garbled and lacunose condition of the Greek.

citizen ought to learn, except occasionally for the personal use he may require to make of it. For then the distinction between master and slave just ceases to apply.

1277b7 But there is another kind of rule – that exercised over men who are free, and similar in birth. This we call rule by a statesman.[7] It is this that a ruler must first learn through being ruled, just as one learns to command cavalry by serving under a cavalry-commander and to be a general by serving under a general, and by commanding a battalion and a company. This too is a healthy saying, namely that it is not possible to be a good ruler without first having been ruled. Not that good ruling and good obedience are the same virtue – only that the good citizen must have the knowledge and ability both to rule and be ruled. That is what we mean by the virtue of a citizen – understanding the governing of free men from both points of view.

1277b16 Returning now to the good *man*, we find the same two qualities. And this is true even though the self-control and justice exercised in ruling are not the same in kind.[8] For clearly the virtue of the good man, who is free but governed, for example his justice, will not be always one and the same: it will take different forms according to whether he is to rule or be ruled, just as self-control and courage vary as between men and women. A man would seem a coward if he had only the courage of a woman, a woman a chatterbox if she were only as discreet as a good man. Men and women have different parts to play in managing the household: his to win, hers to preserve. But the only virtue special to a ruler is practical wisdom; all the others must be possessed, so it seems, both by rulers and by ruled. The virtue of a person being ruled is not practical wisdom but correct opinion; he is rather like a person who makes the pipes, while the ruler is the one who can play them.

7. I.e. of citizens over fellow-citizens, by turns; cf. I i.
8. I.e. not the same as the self-control and justice exercised in being ruled.

III iv

These considerations have made clear whether the virtue of the good man and that of the sound citizen are the same or different, and the sense in which they are the same and the sense in which they are different.

III v

(*1277b33–1278b5*)

OUGHT WORKERS TO BE CITIZENS?

Aristotle now returns to citizenship. He is aware that in some states the banausoi, *mechanics, have full citizenship; but in his view they cannot, by the nature of their occupation, possess the qualities and abilities necessary for a citizen. Does this call for a new definition? Aristotle does not think so. He holds that citizens are a particular class of men, to which no one who is constantly engaged in commercial or manual labour can belong, at any rate in the 'best' state. Such people simply do not have the time and opportunity to fulfil the essential function of a citizen, to rule (while holding office) and to be ruled by turn. Mechanics, labourers, etc. are no doubt essential to a state; but that is not in itself a qualification for citizenship, which is a matter not merely of life but of the 'good' life, in which a man exercises those high faculties possessed by him as a human being, notably that of reason.*

1277b33 There remains still a question about the citizen. Is a citizen really 'one who has the chance to participate in offices', or are we to count mechanics too as citizens? If we do the latter, i.e. give them the title citizen though they do not share in government, then the virtue of the citizen ceases to be that of every citizen, since the mechanic too is a citizen. On the other hand, if he is not a citizen, where *does* he belong, since he is not a foreign resident or a visitor either? But perhaps this kind of reasoning does not really result in any absurdity. After all, slaves do not belong to any of the above-mentioned categories, nor do freed slaves: true it is that we must not give the name citizen to all persons whose presence is necessary for the existence of the state. (Nor yet are children citizens in an unqualified sense, like grown men; children can be called citizens only in a hypothetical sense:[1] they *are* citizens, but incomplete ones.) Indeed, in ancient times in certain countries the mechanics *were* slaves or foreigners, and therefore mostly still are. But[2] the best state will not make the mechanic a citizen. But if even he is to be a citizen, then at any rate what we have called the virtue of a citizen cannot be ascribed to everyone, nor yet to free men alone, but simply to those who are in fact relieved of necessary tasks. Some tasks of this kind are discharged by services to an individual, by slaves, others by mechanics and hired labourers, who serve the public at large.

1278a13 A little further examination will show how it stands with these people, and our earlier statement of the position will itself suffice to make matters clear:[3] as there are several constitutions, so there must be several kinds of citizen, particularly of citizen under a ruler. Thus in one constitution it will be necessary, in another impossible, for the mechanic and the hired labourer to be a citizen. It would, for example, be impossible in any constitution called aristocratic or any other in which honours[4] depend on merit and virtue; for it is quite impossible, while living the life of mechanic or hireling, to occupy oneself as virtue demands. In oligarchies it is not possible for a hireling to be a citizen, because of the high property-qualifications required for participating in office; but it may be possible for a mechanic, since in fact most skilled workers become rich. In Thebes, however, there was a law requiring an

1. I.e. the hypothesis (*hupothesis*) that they will grow up to *become* citizens.

2. Supply something like, 'without actually going to *that* extreme . . .'.

3. Probably a reference to III i.

4. *Timai*, 'status', 'respect', 'privileges', such as are peculiarly gained from holding office.

interval of ten years to elapse between giving up trade and participating in office.

1278a26   In many constitutions the law admits to citizenship a certain number even of foreigners; in some democracies the son of a citizen mother is a citizen, and in many places the same applies to illegitimate children. Lack of population is the usual reason for resorting to laws such as these. But when, after making such persons citizens because of a dearth of legitimate citizens, the state has filled up its numbers, it gradually reduces them, dropping first the sons of slave father or slave mother, then sons of citizen mother but not father, and finally they confine citizenship to those of citizen birth on both sides.

1278a34   From all this two points emerge clearly: first, that there are several kinds of citizen, but second, that a citizen in the fullest sense is one who has a share in honours.[4] We are reminded of Homer's 'Like some immigrant settler, without honour'.[5] For he who has no share in honours[4] is no better than a resident alien. (Sometimes it is not publicly stated what practice is being followed, so that the fellow-inhabitants[6] may be deceived.)

1278a40   We have now answered the question whether it is the same or a different virtue that makes a good man and a sound citizen, and have shown that in one state they will be the same person, and in another different; and that where they are the same, not every sound citizen will be a good man, but only the statesman, that is one who is in sovereign control, or capable of being in control, either alone or in conjunction with others, of the administration of public affairs.

5. *Iliad*, IX 648, XVI 59.
6. *Sunoikountōn*, i.e. that part of the total population which is excluded from citizenship etc., and merely *lives in* the same state together with its citizens.

III vi

CORRECT AND DEVIATED CONSTITUTIONS
DISTINGUISHED

In this chapter Aristotle first briefly classifies constitutions according to the 'sovereign' or ruling element in each; then, in the light of his teleological view of the state as existing to serve the common good, pronounces judgement on them according to whether the 'sovereign' element serves its own interests only or those of all the citizens.

His contrast between political rule and the rule of master over slave is revealing: whereas political authority should be exercised in the interests of the ruled, a master's authority is primarily for his own benefit, and only incidentally for that of the slave. The crucial difference, evidently, is that citizens are equal, and those in power are not essentially superior to the ruled; but a slave is inferior to his master (in point of rationality and hence capacity for natural 'political' life as a citizen), so that his master's interests are paramount. Not that Aristotle means to license ill-treatment or unscrupulous exploitation of slaves: as he remarks, authority over slaves in bad condition is a poor thing, and slaves in fact benefit, *in virtue of their natural capacities and functions, from their relationship with their masters; in this sense master and slave have the 'same' interest in maintaining the relationship. Obviously Aristotle's argument from inferiority of interests is bound to be repugnant to anyone with egalitarian views about the rights of man. It does however make sense within the framework of a belief that the 'political' life lived by a citizen of a* polis *is supremely 'natural' and 'best', for 'natural' interests are the highest interests of all. 'Nature' seems to carry strong social and political imperatives.*

1278b6 Having settled these questions, we must proceed to our next and ask whether we are to posit only one constitution or more than one; and if more than one, what they are and how many, and what the differences are between them. The 'constitution' of a state is the organization of the offices,[1] and in particular of the one that is sovereign over all the others. Now in every case the citizen-body of a state is sovereign; the citizen-body *is* the constitution. Thus in democracies the people are sovereign, in oligarchies the few. That, we say, is what makes the one constitution differ from the other; and the same criterion can be applied to the others also.

1278b15 We ought at the outset to state the purpose for which the state has come to be, as well as the number of kinds of authority controlling men and their life as members of an association. At the beginning of this work, when we drew a distinction between household-management and mastership, we also stated that by nature man is a political animal.[2] Hence men have a desire for life together, even when they have no need to seek each other's help. Nevertheless, common interest too is a factor in bringing them together, in so far as it contributes to the good life of each. The *good* life is indeed their chief end, both communally and individually; but they form and continue to maintain a political association[3] for the sake of life itself. Perhaps we may say that there is an element of good even in mere living, provided that life is not excessively beset with troubles. Certainly most men, in their desire to keep alive, are prepared to face a great deal of suffering, as if finding in life itself a certain well-being and a natural sweetness.

1278b30 But to return to authority: it is not difficult to

---

1. In this chapter both 'office' and 'authority' translate *archē*, literally 'rule'. 'Rule of a master' translates *despoteia*.

2. *Politikon zōon*, 'an animal whose nature is to live in a *polis* (state)'; cf. I ii, n. 14.

3. *Politikē koinōnia*, 'the association that takes the form of a *polis* (state)'; cf. I i.

distinguish its recognized styles (I often speak about their definition in my public lectures).[4] First, although the natural slave and the natural master really have the same interest, rule of master over slave is exercised primarily for the benefit of the master and only incidentally for the benefit of the slave, because if the slave deteriorates the master's rule over him is inevitably impaired.

1278b37 Then there is the authority of a man over his wife, his children, and his whole household, to which we give the name 'household-management'. This is exercised either for the benefit of those subject to the authority, or for some benefit common to both parties. In itself it is for the benefit of the subjects, as we see by the analogy of the other skills, such as that of a doctor or of an athlete's trainer, who would only incidentally be concerned with their own interests. (For of course there is nothing to prevent a trainer on occasion being himself a member of the team in training, as the man who steers the ship is always one of the members of the ship's company. The trainer or pilot looks to the good of those under his authority, but when he himself is one of them he gets the same benefit out of it incidentally as they do, in that the pilot is a member of the ship's company, and the trainer becomes one of those in training, while yet remaining their trainer.)

1279a8 That is why,[5] whenever authority in the *state* is constituted on a basis of equality and similarly between citizens, they expect to take turns in exercising it. This principle is very old but in earlier times it was applied in a natural and proper manner: men expected each to take a turn at public service,[6] and during tenure of office to look after the interests of someone else, who then did the same for him. But nowadays there is more to be gained out of public affairs and offices, so men want to be

4. Or, 'external ("extra-mural"?) or published treatises'.
5. I.e. since a ruler looks after the interests of the ruled, the former claims in due course reciprocal service from the latter.
6. *Leitourgein*; cf. IV iv, n. 11.

in office continuously. They could hardly be more zealous in their place-hunting if they were ill and their recovery depended on securing office.

1279a16   It is clear then that those constitutions which aim at the common good are right, as being in accord with absolute justice; while those which aim only at the good of the rulers are wrong. They are all deviations from the right constitutions. They are like the rule of master over slave, whereas the state is an association of free men.

III vii

(*1279a22–1279b10*)

CLASSIFICATION OF CORRECT AND DEVIATED CONSTITUTIONS

This chapter carries forward the theme of its predecessor, by distinguishing three 'correct' constitutions and three 'deviations'. The three correct kinds aim at the common interest: kingship, aristocracy, 'polity'; the three others aim at the sectional interest of the rulers: tyranny, oligarchy, democracy. In each set the first type is the rule of one, the second the rule of a few, and the third the rule of the many. These distinctions are somewhat rough-and-ready, as Aristotle himself recognizes in the next chapter.

1279a22   Having drawn these distinctions we must next consider what constitutions there are and how many. We begin with those that are correct, since when these have been defined it will be easy to see the deviations. As we have seen, 'constitution' and 'citizen-body' mean the same thing, and the citizen-body is the sovereign power in states. Sovereignty necessarily resides either in one man, or in a few, or in the many. Whenever the one, the few, or the many rule with a view to the common good, these constitutions must be correct; but if they look to the private advantage, be it of the one or the few or the mass, they

are deviations. For either we must say that those who do
not participate are not citizens, or they must share in the
benefit.[1]

1279a32 The usual names for right constitutions are as
follows: (a) Monarchy[2] aiming at the common interest:
kingship. (b) Rule of more than one man but only a few:
aristocracy (so called either because the *best* men rule or
because it aims at what is *best* for the state and all its
members).[3] (c) Political control exercised by the mass of
the populace in the common interest: polity. This is the
name common to all constitutions.[4] It is reasonable to use
this term, because, while it is possible for one man or a few
to be outstanding in point of virtue, it is difficult for a
larger number to reach a high standard in all forms of
virtue – with the conspicuous exception of military virtue,
which is found in a great many people. And that is why in
this constitution the defensive element is the most sovereign body, and those who share in the constitution are
those who bear arms.

1279b4 The corresponding deviations are: from kingship, tyranny; from aristocracy, oligarchy; from polity,
democracy. For tyranny is monarchy[2] for the benefit of the
monarch, oligarchy for the benefit of the men of means,
democracy for the benefit of the men without means.
None of the three aims to be of profit to the common
interest.

III viii

(*1279b11–1280a6*)

AN ECONOMIC CLASSIFICATION OF CONSTITUTIONS

*The classification of constitutions in the preceding chap-
ter was on the basis of the number and aims of the rulers.*

1. If, that is, they are to be called citizens.
2. 'Monarch' means literally 'the rule of one'.
3. *Aristos* means 'best'.
4. *Politeia* means 'constitution'.

Now, in a somewhat Marxist vein, Aristotle argues that the really crucial criterion of classification is an economic one (cf. IV iv init.): an oligarchy is the rule of the wealthy, whether they are few or many (though in practice they are invariably few), and democracy the rule of the poor, whether they are many or few (though in practice they are invariably many). 'Democracy' is in fact to Aristotle and the Greeks in general a brutally realistic word: its literal meaning is 'power of the people' (dēmos), and it means what it says — rule by a particular class, the numerous poor, and in their own interests. Today we think of 'democracy' as being, ideally at any rate, 'rule by and for everybody at large', whether rich or poor.

1279b11 We must however go into a little more detail about what each of these constitutions is. Certain difficulties are involved, which one whose aim is strictly practical might be allowed to pass over; but a man who examines each subject from a philosophical standpoint cannot neglect them: he has to omit nothing, and state the truth about each topic.

1279b16 Tyranny, as has been said, is a monarchy which is exercised like a mastership[1] over the association which is the state; oligarchy occurs when the sovereign power of the constitution is in the hands of those with possessions, democracy when it is in the hands of those who have no stock of possessions and are without means. The first difficulty concerns definitions. Suppose the majority to be well-off, and to be sovereign in the state; then we have a democracy, since the mass of the people is sovereign. So too, if it is somewhere the case that those who do not own property, while fewer in number than those who do, are more powerful and in sovereign control of the constitution, then that is called an oligarchy, since the few are sovereign. It looks therefore as if there were something wrong with our way of defining constitutions.[2]

1. I.e. over slaves; the reference is to the end of III vi.
2. Because we expect to find the ruling class in democracy to be *poor*, and in an oligarchy to be *rich*.

1279b26 Even if we try to include both criteria of nomenclature, combining wealth with fewness of numbers in the one case (calling it oligarchy when those who are both wealthy and few hold office), lack of wealth with large numbers in the other (calling it democracy when those who are both poor and numerous hold office) – even then we are only raising a fresh difficulty. For if there is not in fact any other constitution than those with which we have been dealing,[3] what names can we give to the two just mentioned, one in which the wealthy are more numerous, and one in which the poor are less numerous, each category being in its own case in sovereign control of the constitution? The argument seems to show that it is a matter of accident whether those who are sovereign be few or many (few in oligarchies, many in democracies): it just happens that way because everywhere the rich are few and the poor are many. So in fact the grounds of difference have been given wrongly: what really differentiates oligarchy and democracy is wealth or the lack of it. It inevitably follows that where men rule because of the possession of wealth, whether their number be large or small, that is oligarchy, and when the poor rule, that is democracy. But, as we have said, in actual fact the former are few, the latter many. Few are wealthy, but all share freedom alike: and these are the grounds of their respective claims to the constitution.[4]

3. In III vii.
4. I.e. to control it, by being citizens and therefore entitled to hold office.

(1280a7–1281a10)

THE JUST DISTRIBUTION OF POLITICAL POWER

Another possible criterion for the distribution of political power is justice. Now differences in ethical standards – between what counts as 'just' in one state and what counts as such in another – could indeed provide an excellent way of classifying and of comparing the various forms of society. But Aristotle's use of the new criterion, which he discusses in Chapters ix–xiii, is hardly what we expect. By 'justice' in this chapter he means distributive justice, in a political *context: what share of political power is it 'just' that each man should have? An oligarch will answer, 'the rich should have more, the poor less'; the democrat will say, 'all men who are equal, i.e. in being of free birth, should have share in political power on an equal basis'. Aristotle objects to both these answers as resting on at best a partial notion of justice. He accepts the notion that the state should confer political power, privilege and status in proportion to 'value received', i.e. in proportion to the contribution men make to the total purpose for which the state exists, the good life, which entails the exercise of all the distinctly human virtues. Such a distribution would be 'just' in a 'complete' sense, because it depends on a man's contribution not to partial ends such as wealth, but to the overall end of the association we call a state.*

So the question that faces Aristotle is, What kind of superiority is to be regarded as constituting a claim to office and privilege? As we would expect, he puts good birth and ownership of property on the list, and the moral qualities of justice and courage; a high level of culture and education too will be a token of merit in one who is to take part in the working of a state which aims at securing the good life. Men are not equal in these respects, and any state which ignores this fact and thinks in terms of absolute equality must be one of the wrong types, a 'deviation' (cf. III xiii). The upper groups will always be superior in education and ability; but the numerical superiority of other sections of the population must also be taken into account.

The description of 'deviation' given in ix–xiii differs from that given in vi–vii, but does not contradict it: Aristotle is drawing out the implications *of his earlier account. 'Deviated' constitutions, according to vi–vii, are those in which the interests of one section of the community take precedence over those of the others. Consequently, absolute equality has to be condemned, since it fails to satisfy the criterion of a 'correct' constitution, that it should seek the good of all.*

These considerations prompt Aristotle to discuss why, on this view, mere geographical proximity of residence, or trading agreements or a military alliance between various groups of people, do not make a state in the true sense of the word. Such arrangements may indeed serve the material interests of all, but they suffer from the crucial limitation that they do not, at least directly, help to make the citizens more 'politically' virtuous, i.e. more able to play their part in a 'good' state (polis). A state will no doubt make trading and defensive treaties etc.; but they are not its raison d'être. *Or are they? An objector may well retort that historically at any rate these were precisely the purposes for which states were founded – for mutual protection and to ensure a food supply. Why should we attach to the state any other purpose than these limited utilitarian ones? In any case, he might complain, the notions of 'political' virtue and the 'good life' are very hard to describe exactly. It must be admitted that on this point Aristotle is in this chapter both brief and vague; however, he does give fuller accounts elsewhere, notably in the first three chapters of VII. But just how far does he mean to go when he insists (in the third paragraph) that a 'true' state must concern itself with the moral virtue of its citi-*

zens? For the controversy on this point, see e.g. l–lii in Barker's translation of the Politics, *and D. J. Allan, 'Individual and state in the* Ethics *and* Politics', *in* La Politique d'Aristote, Fondation Hardt, Entretiens XI (Geneva, 1965) (see Select Bibliographies).

1280a7 First we must grasp what definitions of oligarchy and democracy men put forward, and in particular what is the oligarchic and what is the democratic view of justice. For all adhere to a justice of some kind, but they do not proceed beyond a certain point, and are not referring to the whole of justice in the sovereign sense when they speak of it. Thus it is thought that justice is equality; and so it is, but not for all persons, only for those that are equal. Inequality also is thought to be just; and so it is, but not for all, only for the unequal. We make bad mistakes if we neglect this 'for whom' when we are deciding what is just. The reason is that we are making judgements about ourselves, and people are generally bad judges where their own interests are involved. So, as justice is relative to people, and applies in the same ratio to the things and to the persons (as pointed out in my *Ethics*),[1] these disputants, while agreeing as to equality of the thing, disagree about the persons for whom,[2] and this chiefly for the reason already stated, that they are judging their own case, and therefore badly.

1280a21 There is also this further reason, namely that both parties are talking about justice in a *limited* sense, and so imagine themselves to be talking about justice unqualifiedly. Thus it is an error when men unequal in one respect, e.g. money, suppose themselves unequal in all, just as it is an error when men equal in one respect,

---

1. I.e. it is just to give more (property, privileges, etc) to the more deserving (persons), less to the less deserving. The reference is to *Nicomachean Ethics*, V iii.

2. I.e. to agree that two things are equal (in size, value, etc.) is easy; to agree that two *persons* are equal (in worth or merit) is difficult, because the criteria are highly disputable.

e.g. in being free, suppose themselves equal in every respect. To argue thus is to neglect the decisive point. If persons originally come together and form an association for the sake of property, then they share in the state[3] in proportion to their ownership of property. This is the apparent strength of the oligarchs' view that it is *not* just that out of a sum of a hundred minae he that contributed only one should receive equal shares with him who found the remaining ninety-nine; and that this applies equally to the original sum and to any profits subsequently made. But a state's purpose is not merely to provide a living but to make a life that is good. Otherwise it might be made up of slaves or animals other than man, and that is impossible, because slaves and animals do not participate in happiness,[4] nor in a life that involves choice.

1280a34 A state's purpose is also to provide something more than a military pact of protection against injustice, or to facilitate mutual acquaintance and the exchange of goods, for in that case Tyrrhenians and Carthaginians, and all others with commercial treaties with each other, would be taken as citizens of a single state. Certainly they have import agreements, treaties to prevent injustice, and written documents governing their military alliance. But in the first place each has its separate officials: there are none in common to which they are both equally subject for these purposes. Secondly, neither side is concerned with the *quality* of the other, or with preventing the behaviour of any person covered by the agreements from being unjust or wicked, but only with the prevention of injustice as between each other. But all who are anxious to ensure government under good laws make it their business to have an eye to the virtue and vice of the citizens. It thus becomes evident that that which is genuinely and not just

3. I.e. the association in question: see I i.
4. 'Happiness' is the customary but inadequate translation of *eudaimonia*, the state of well-being which consists in living in the exercise of all, especially the highest (i.e. rational and ethical), faculties of man.

nominally called a state must concern itself with virtue. Otherwise the association is a mere military alliance, differing only in location and restricted territorial extent from an alliance whose parties are at a distance from each other; and under such conditions law becomes a mere agreement, or, as Lycophron[5] the sophist put it, 'a mutual guarantor of justice',[6] but quite unable to make citizens good and just.

1280b12 That this is true will be clear from some further illustrations. Suppose you merge the territories into one, making the walls of Corinth and Megara contiguous: that still does not make a single state of them, nor would it even if they established rights of marriage between the two, though this is one of the ties peculiarly characteristic of states. Or again, suppose you had 10,000 people living apart from each other, but near enough not to become dissociated: carpenter, farmer, shoemakers and suchlike are there, and furthermore they have laws prohibiting injustice in their transactions with each other; yet, so long as their association does not go beyond such things as commercial exchange and military alliance, that is still not a state. And why not? you may ask. The reason is certainly not that the association is loosely knit. For even if they actually moved close together, and maintained an association such as I have described, with each man still treating his own household like a state, and if they mutually supported each other, as in a defensive alliance, against injustice only, even then that would not be considered a state, not at any rate in the strict sense, since the nature of their intercourse is the same whether they move close together or stay apart.

1280b29 It is clear therefore that the state is not an

5. Lycophron's date is uncertain. He was probably a pupil of Gorgias (*c.* 483–376), and had sceptical views about the merits of noble birth. Little else is known of him. On his passage, see R. G. Mulgan, *Journal of the History of Ideas*, 40 (1979), pp. 121–8, and W. K. C. Guthrie's reply (p. 128).

6. *Dikaia* (neuter plural), literally 'just things'; perhaps 'just claims'.

association of people dwelling in the same place, established to prevent its members from committing injustice against each other, and to promote transactions. Certainly all these features must be present if there is to be a state; but even the presence of every one of them does not make a state *ipso facto*. The state is an association intended to enable its members, in their households and the kinships,[7] to live *well*; its purpose is a perfect and self-sufficient life. However, this will not be attained unless they occupy one and the same territory and intermarry. It is indeed on that account that we find in states connections between relatives by marriage, brotherhoods, sacrifices to the gods, and the various civilized pursuits of a life lived together. All these activities are the product of affection, for it is our affection for others that causes us to choose to live together; thus they all contribute towards that good life which is the purpose of the state; and a state is an association of kinships[7] and villages which aims at a perfect and self-sufficient life – and that, we hold, means living happily and nobly.[8]

1281a2 So we must lay it down that the association which is a state exists not for the purpose of living together but for the sake of noble[8] actions. Those who contribute most to this kind of association are for that very reason entitled to a larger share in the state than those who, though they may be equal or even superior in free birth and in family, are inferior in the virtue that belongs to a citizen. Similarly they are entitled to a larger share than those who are superior in riches but inferior in virtue.

All this makes it clear that all those who dispute about constitutions are using the term 'justice' in a limited sense.

7. *Genē*, 'kinship-groups', 'clans'.
8. *Kalos*, 'fine', 'good'.

III x

JUSTICE AND SOVEREIGNTY

This short chapter is a good example of Aristotle's 'apore-tic' style, in which he makes a number of suggestions in swift succession, only to dismiss them. The opening ques-tion, 'What should be the sovereign authority of the state?' links the chapter to the beginning of III vi; and the question of the justice of the actions of various possible 'sovereign authorities' links the discussion as a whole to the preceding chapter, on the just distribution of power. The candidates for sovereignty Aristotle lists for considera-tion in this chapter are (i) the mass of the people, who are poor; (ii) a tyrant; (iii) the few, who are rich; (iv) 'respect-able' people (epieikeis); (v) the one most worthy man (spoudaiotatos); (vi) law.

In the case of (i)–(iii), Aristotle is at pains to point out that an authority may commit unjust acts; he instances the taking of the property of other sections of the popula-tion, and makes the useful point that sovereignty does not actually confer justice on anything the sovereign power may do, even if it is 'just' that the rulers in question should hold the sovereignty in the first place. (He perhaps im-plies, but does not make, a reverse point: that few and slight unjust acts of rulers holding sovereign authority do not in themselves make it unjust that they should hold it.) The justice of holding authority and the justice displayed in exercising it in action are indeed different, and the dis-tinction is important; but the chapter is too staccato to reveal Aristotle's views on their exact relationship. The chapter closes with the sober reflection that making law sovereign instead of men solves no difficulties: law can and does reflect the bias of its framers.

1281a11 Another question is 'Where ought the sovereign

power of the state to reside?' With the mass of the people? With the rich? With the respectable? With one man, the best of all? Or a tyrant? There are objections to all these. Thus suppose the poor use their numerical superiority to make a distribution of the property of the rich: is not that unjust? 'No, by Zeus,' it may be said, 'it has been done justly, by a decision of the sovereign power.' But what else can we call the very height of injustice? And if the majority, having laid their hands on everything, again distribute the possessions of the few, they are obviously destroying the state. But virtue does not destroy its possessor, nor is justice destructive of the state. So it is clear that this law too cannot be just. Or, secondly, if it *is* just, any actions taken by a tyrant also must be just: his superior strength enables him to use force, just as the mass of the people use force on the rich. Thirdly, is it just for the few and the wealthy to rule? If so, and they too do this and plunder and help themselves to the goods of the mass, then that is just. And if *that* is so, then it is just in the former case also. The answer clearly is that all these three states of affairs are bad and not just.

1281a28 The fourth alternative, that the respectable should rule and have sovereign power over everything, means that all the rest must be without esteem, being debarred from the honour of holding office under the constitution. For offices, we say, are honours; and if the same persons hold office all the time, the rest must be without honour. Is then the fifth alternative better, that one man, the most worthy, should rule? But this is yet more oligarchical, because it leaves still larger numbers without honour. It might be objected that it is a bad thing for any human being, subject to the affections that enter the soul, to have sovereign power, which ought to be reserved for the law. But that will not make any difference to the problem-cases we have been discussing: there may be a law, but it may have a bias towards oligarchy or democracy, so that exactly the same results will ensue.

III xi

(1281a39–1282b13)

THE WISDOM OF COLLECTIVE JUDGEMENTS

Aristotle now takes one of the candidates for sovereignty which he had listed and discussed summarily in the last chapter, the mass of the people, and seems, at first blush, to be espousing a major democratic principle: 'Many heads are better than one.' There is, he argues, some advantage in giving the people political power, at least to the extent of allowing them to elect officials and scrutinize their conduct: for the fact is that collective decisions, even by persons not individually distinguished for practical wisdom (phronēsis), are commonly at least as good as those reached by a select group of 'sound' men. It is interesting to note that Aristotle here concedes, in the first paragraph, a degree of phronēsis and aretē (moral virtue) to the ordinary man; contrast Nicomachean Ethics, VI xiii, where both seem to require rare intellectual qualities (and cf. introduction to III iv).

Socrates and Plato had been inclined to argue that politics is or should be a skill, with recognized modes of procedure, a precise set of ends, and agreed criteria for assessing whether these ends have been achieved. Such a skill they believed to be a rare accomplishment, not to be found among the populace at large. In general terms, Aristotle shares these beliefs; hence his judicious recognition of the wisdom of collective decisions by the people may well seem more surprising than it really is. His point is not that collective decisions are or must be good because they are made by the people, who, being a majority, have some sort of entitlement to have their own way; it is that decisions about the 'good' life in a polis are analogous to those made by a skilled practitioner in an art or profession, but that to judge from experience they are as likely to be made correctly by the many as by the few. In this chapter, then,

Aristotle merely recognizes a limited efficiency in popular judgement. For a discussion, see the reference to Braun's first 1959 article in the second collection of essays in the Select Bibliographies.

Why *is popular judgement efficient? Aristotle's answer is brief and somewhat mechanical: one man judges one 'part' (of a work of art or political problem) better than others, and another man another part, so that the many collectively may judge better than an individual expert. Is it not also a matter of uncanny group-intuition? (Compare Plato's recognition of the curious moral intuitions of even rogues, at* Laws *950bc.) It is hard to resist quoting one of the stately nineteenth-century quotations Newman prints in his commentary (III 215): 'Canning used to say that the House of Commons as a body had better taste than the man of best taste in it, and I am very much inclined to think that Canning was right' (Lord Macaulay, Letter of February 1831).*

Like its predecessor, this chapter concludes with a ringing declaration of faith in the rule of law; but the discussion of it is again brief and inconclusive.

1281a39 The other possibilities are to be discussed elsewhere;[1] at the moment it would seem that one view put forward – namely that the mass of the people ought to be sovereign, rather than the best but few – is not without difficulty, but has perhaps some truth in it. For it is possible that the many, no one of whom taken singly is a sound man, may yet, taken all together, be better than the few, not individually but collectively, in the same way that a feast to which all contribute is better than one supplied at one man's expense. For even where there are many people, each has some share of virtue and practical wisdom; and when they are brought together, just as in the mass they become as it were one man with many pairs of feet and hands and many senses, so also do they become

1. III xii–xvii, IV, VI.

one in regard to character and intelligence. That is why the many are better judges of works of music and poetry: some judge some parts, some others, but their collective pronouncement is a verdict upon all the parts. And it is this that gives sound men their superiority over any individual man from the masses. Handsome men differ from ugly, it is said, and paintings from actual objects, just because they draw together into one what was previously scattered here and there, though any one of the features taken separately, the eye of one man, some other part of another, might well be more handsome than in the picture.

1281b15 But it is not at all certain that this superiority of the many over the sound few is possible in the case of every people and every large number. There are some, by heaven, among whom it would be impossible: otherwise the theory would apply to wild animals – and yet some men are hardly any better than wild animals. But there is no reason why in a given case of a large number we should not accept the truth of the point we have made.

1281b21 These considerations enable us to solve the former problem,[2] and also another and related question – in what spheres is this sovereignty of the free men, the mass of the citizens, to be exercised? We must remember that they are not men of wealth, and have no claim to virtue in anything. To let them share in the highest offices is to take a risk: inevitably, their unjust standards will cause them to commit injustice, and their lack of judgement will lead them into error. On the other hand there is a risk in not giving them a share, and in their non-participation, for when there are many who have no property and no honours they inevitably constitute a huge hostile element in the state. But it can still remain open to them to participate in deliberating and judging.

1281b32 It was for this reason that both Solon[3] and some of the other lawgivers give to the people power to elect officials and to demand an account from them at the end

2. Apparently that of III x, 'who should be sovereign?'
3. Cf. II xii, and Aristotle, *Constitution of the Athenians* 7–8.

of their tenure, but no right individually to hold such offices. This was on the principle that the whole body acting together has the necessary perception,[4] even though each is individually only partly qualified to judge. By thus mixing with the better sort, they render good service in their states, in something like the way that a combination of coarse foods with refined renders the whole diet more nutritious than a small amount of the latter.

1281b38 But such an arrangement of the constitution raises a number of difficulties. First, the proper person to judge whether a piece of medical work has been properly done is the same sort of person as is actually engaged on such work, on curing the patient of his present sickness – in other words the medical practitioner himself. And this is equally true of the other skills and empirical crafts. As then it is among doctors that a doctor should give an account of himself, so also should other professional men among their peers. By doctor I mean not only the ordinary practitioner and the master-craftsman, but also those who have been trained in the art, such as are to be found in pretty well all skills. And we let these trained persons judge no less than we let the experts.

1282a7 Second, in the matter of elections the same would seem to apply. Choosing aright is a task for the experts – those in surveying choose surveyors, those in navigation choose navigators, and so on. Admittedly in some jobs and some skills you will find laymen who share in the choice, but not more than the experts. So it would seem that on this argument the mass of the people should not be given the sovereign power either of choosing officials or of calling them to account.

1282a14 Perhaps, however, not all these arguments are right. First, there is the argument which we used a while back[5] – that provided the mass of the people is not too slave-like, each individual will indeed be a worse judge

4. Or perhaps 'sense': the word is *aisthēsis*, which picks up 'senses' (*aisthēseis*, plural) in the first paragraph.
5. In the first paragraph of this chapter.

than the experts, but collectively they will be better, or at any rate no worse. Secondly, there are tasks of which the actual doer will be neither the best nor the only judge, cases in which even those who do not possess the skill form an opinion on the finished product. An obvious example is house-building: the builder can certainly form an opinion on a house, but the user, the household-manager, will be an even better judge. So too the user of a rudder, the helmsman, is a better judge of it than the carpenters who made it; and it is the diner not the cook that pronounces upon the merits of a dinner. I think perhaps these two arguments are sufficient to resolve the question.

1282a24 But there is another and connected difficulty. It seems odd that inferior persons should have sovereign control over more important matters than the respectable sort; yet the choice of officials and the scrutiny of their work are a very important matter indeed. But as we have said, in some constitutions they *are* assigned to the people, the assembly having sovereign control of *all* such matters; yet although members of the assembly, and also of the council, and of the panels of jurymen, are recruited on low property-qualifications and are of any age, nevertheless for treasury officials, generals, and the supreme offices a high property-qualification is demanded.

1282a32 This difficulty too can be met, and this practice[6] too perhaps justified, by arguments similar to those which we have just used: it is not the individual juryman, councillor, or member of assembly who rules, but the court, the council and the people; and of these each individual mentioned – I mean the councillor, assembly-member and juryman – is a part. So it is quite just that the mass of the people should be in sovereign control of more important things, since people, council, and law-court all comprise many persons. And as for property-qualifications, the sum total of property owned by them is larger than that of

6. Of allowing to the people the power of choosing officials and scrutinizing their conduct.

those who, singly or with a few colleagues, hold the highest offices.

1282a41 These matters may be regarded as settled in that way; but we must look back at our original problem,[7] from which nothing emerges so clearly as the fact that the laws, if rightly established, ought to be sovereign, and also that officials, whether individually or as a body, ought to have sovereign power to act in all those various matters about which the laws cannot possibly give detailed guidance; for it is never easy to frame general regulations covering every particular. We said 'laws rightly established', but we have not yet discovered what sort of laws these ought to be, so the old problem[8] remains. For as constitutions vary, simultaneously and in like manner the laws too inevitably vary, and are sound or bad, just or unjust; but this much is clear, that the constitution must set the pattern for the laws. If however that is so, laws framed in accordance with one of the right types of constitution will inevitably be just, but if according to one of the deviations, unjust.[9]

III xii

(*1282b14–1283a22*)

JUSTICE AND EQUALITY

This chapter, being reminiscent of I i ad init. and of the opening chapters of the Nicomachean Ethics, *looks like something of a fresh start; but it turns out to raise much the same problem as was discussed in III ix, and to treat it in much the same way (see introduction to that chapter, and cf. V i). On the notion of 'proportionate' equality (i.e. greater shares for greater merit, as distinct from iden-*

---

7. That broached in III x.
8. III x *ad fin.*
9. For 'correct' and 'deviated' constitutions, see III vi–vii.

tical shares irrespective of merit), useful background reading would be Plato, Laws 756e–758a.

1282b14 In every kind of knowledge and skill the end which is aimed at is a good. This good is greatest, and is a 'good' in the highest sense, when that knowledge or skill is the most sovereign one, i.e. the faculty of statecraft.[1] In the state, the good aimed at is justice; and that means what is for the benefit of the whole community. Now all men believe that justice means equality in some sense, and they are in limited agreement with the philosophy of justice which I explained in my *Ethics*:[2] they hold that justice is some entity which is relative to persons, and that equality must be equal for equals. The question we must keep in mind is, equality or inequality in what sort of thing? For this is a problem, and one for which we need political philosophy.[3]

1282b23 It is possible to argue that superiority in *any* good whatever justifies unequal distribution of offices, given that in all other respects than this the persons are not different but similar – for differences in them would mean different justice and different deserts. But surely, if that be granted, we shall have to allow that superiority in height or complexion or any other good thing will confer an advantage in political rights.[4] Is not the fallacy here pretty obvious? A comparison with other kinds of knowledge and faculties shows that it is. For if, say, pipe-players are equal in skill, we must not give an advantage in instruments to those of better birth, for that would not enable them to play any better. The use of the better instrument ought to belong to the better performer.

1282b34 If this is not sufficiently clear, it will become so if we sharpen the example. If one man is outstandingly superior in pipe-playing, but far inferior in birth or good looks (even supposing that birth and good looks are each a

1. *Politikē dunamis.*
2. *Nicomachean Ethics*, V vi.
3. *Politikē philosophia*, 'philosophy about the *polis* (state)'.
4. *Politika dikaia*, 'just things in the context of the *polis*'.

greater good than the skill of pipe-playing, and its superiority to them is greater in proportion than the superiority of this player's ability to that of the rest), even then, I say, he should still get the best pipes. For superiority both in wealth and in birth ought to contribute to the quality of the performance – to which these qualities in fact contribute nothing at all.

1283a3 Moreover, according to that way of reasoning, every good thing would be commensurable with every other good thing. For if marks are given for a particular degree of tallness, then tallness in general would be in competition with both wealth and freedom. So if we say that X has greater superiority in height than Y has in virtue, then even if in general virtue is of greater importance than height, we are making everything commensurable with everything; since if one amount is greater than some other, clearly there is another which is equal.[5] But such mensuration is quite impossible here, so it is clear that in matters relating to the state men are quite right not to take any and every kind of inequality into account in competing for offices, and only those differences which contribute to making up the state as a whole should be urged in the competition. Such qualities as superior swiftness of foot, however important that may be in winning honour in athletic contests, should not entitle one to take more than the next man.

1283a16 Hence those of noble birth or who are free or have wealth are quite right to lay claim to honours, since the members of the state must be free and must have taxable property (you could no more make a state out of paupers than out of slaves). But obviously something more is needed besides: I mean justice, and the virtue that is proper to citizens.[6] For without these additions it is not

5. E.g. if a given amount, *a*, of (say) wealth is 'greater' (or 'better', *kreitton*) than a given degree, *d*, of virtue, there must be *some* amount of wealth, less than *a*, which is *equal* to *d*.

6. *Politikē aretē*, especially in their capacity as *politikoi*: see introduction to I i.

possible for the state to be managed. More exactly, whereas without free population and wealth there cannot be a state at all, without justice and virtue it cannot be managed well.

III xiii

(1283a23–1284b34)

THE SOLE PROPER CLAIM TO POLITICAL POWER

In the early paragraphs of this chapter Aristotle examines how the various claims to political power (notably wealth, birth and superior strength of numbers) may compete. He admits that each claim has a certain partial or relative 'justice', but he denies that any of them is 'just' in an absolute sense. Each demands exclusive consideration at the expense of all the others: whichever is adopted, any man, or set of men, who excelled in that respect, would have to be given power, even if he excelled in no other. For instance, on the criterion of wealth, one supremely rich man would have to be allowed to rule, even if he were also a supreme rogue. Aristotle discusses various cases where difficulties could occur: a single man could deploy greater strength than the masses, whose claim to rule normally depends on precisely this – superior strength; or a few persons claiming to rule on the grounds of over-whelming wealth may nevertheless be poorer than the masses collectively (though not individually). All such problems arise if we adopt one claim in preference to the rest: each taken by itself is, as we might say, 'socially divisive'.

This latter point is the key to Aristotle's solution. The only claim that is absolutely just is that of 'virtue' (aretē), that is, the moral and intellectual ability always needed in a 'statesman', a citizen who is ruled and rules by turn in the interests of the whole state, not in those of just one part which might advance one of the 'partial' claims (e.g.

the masses, who might advance the claim of superior numbers). When a man excels to a superlative degree in 'virtue', he must be reckoned as a 'god among men' and given supreme power above the law. It is not clear, however, here at least, why superlative ability in ruling and being ruled ought to exempt one *from the latter. But Aristotle follows whither he thinks the argument leads him, and comes right out and says that such a person ought to be a permanent king in the state, claiming the glad obedience of all others.*

One could argue that Aristotle is here showing himself to be Platonist in spite of himself: Plato too had envisaged (notably in the Republic *and* Politicus*) a supreme individual or individuals above the law and ruling in the interests of the state. But the positions of the two philosophers are instructively different. Plato's supreme rulers would have owed their power to their metaphysical insight into the supreme moral values, Aristotle's to (as it were) a claim for a* quid pro quo *from the state. If each person with a 'partial' claim to power (wealth, etc.) deserves some political power in return for the partial contribution he makes to the common good (see III ix), the person with the 'absolute' claim (virtue) apparently deserves absolute political power in return for his total contribution to that good. Aristotle's approach is thus less metaphysical than 'transactional'.*

The chapter closes with the tantalizing statement that those who excel in 'the virtue of a statesman' (in the special sense of this latter word) should be permanent kings, but Aristotle does not enlarge on how they may be identified, appointed, or dismissed. He may perhaps even see outstanding individuals as more of a problem than an asset: certainly he seems to have a certain sympathy with the practice of ostracism, of which he has a brief but interesting historical discussion towards the end of the chapter.

1283a23 Some or all of these things would seem to have

a proper claim to be contributions to a state's existence; but I repeat that, in order to secure the good life, education and virtue would have the most just claim of all. But since those who are equal in one particular ought not to enjoy equality in all things, nor those who are unequal in one respect have inequality in all, it follows that all constitutions in which such a state of affairs prevails must be deviations.[1]

1283a29 It has already been stated that while all men have some kind of justice in their claims, not all of them have a claim that is just in an absolute sense.[2] (a) The *rich* argue that they have a greater share in the land, and the land is of social[3] interest; and further, that they are more to be relied upon to fulfil their contracts. (b) The claims of the *free* and *well-born* are closely related: the more nobly born are more fully citizens than the non-noble, good birth being held in esteem in every country; and the offspring of the better sort are likely to be better men, for good birth is excellence[4] of stock. (c) Next we shall mention the equally just claims of *virtue*, for we always speak of justice as a social[3] virtue, and one which is sure to bring all the other virtues along with it. (d) And surely the *majority* have a better claim than the minority, as being stronger, richer and better, if we balance the larger numbers against the smaller.

1283a42 Now suppose all these to be present in a single city – that is to say, the good, the rich and the well-born, and beside them a mass of citizens – will there or will there not be dispute as to which should rule? Now in the three types of constitution of which we spoke earlier the decision provokes no dispute, because they differ from each other in just this respect, sovereignty being exercised in oligarchy by the rich, in aristocracy by the sound, and so on. But we have to ask ourselves how to reach a conclusion

1. III vi–vii, and cf. introduction to III ix.
2. Cf. III ix.
3. *Koinos, koinōnikos*, 'in common', 'communal'.
4. *Aretē*, 'virtue'.

when these elements are present at one and the same time. Suppose for example that those who have virtue are exceedingly few in number – how is the matter to be settled? Are we to regard their fewness in the light of the work to be done, asking whether they are strong enough to run the state? Or are we to ask whether their numbers are sufficient to *make* a state?

1283b13 The problem arises in regard to all claimants to honours in the state. Those who base their claim to rule on wealth would seem to have no just claim at all, nor those who base themselves on birth; for if one man is very much richer than the rest, then clearly by the same principle of justice,[5] he will have to be sole ruler over them all, and similarly one who is superior in good birth will have to rule over all whose claim is based on free status. This same thing could well happen where the constitution is an aristocracy, based on virtue; for if one man is better than all the sound men in the citizen-body, then on the same principle of justice[5] he ought to be sovereign over them. Again, suppose that the multitude ought to be sovereign because they are stronger than the few, and suppose one man, or more than one but still fewer than the many, to be stronger than the rest – then these would have to be sovereign rather than the multitude.

1283b27 All these considerations seem to show that none of these criteria is right by which one set of men claim that they themselves should rule and all the rest be subject to them. For surely, whether their claim to sovereignty over the citizen-body rests on wealth or on virtue, it remains true that against their arguments the multitude will have some justice on their side; for it is quite possible on occasion for the multitude to be better than the few, and richer too, when considered not singly but together.

1283b35 So it is possible in this fashion to meet also a difficulty which some people pose and debate, namely

5. *Dikaion*, i.e. the 'partly just' principle based on wealth or merit, invoked by *more* than one 'rich' or 'better' person to establish *their* right to rule.

whether a lawgiver, who seeks to lay down the laws that are most right, ought, given the circumstance mentioned,[6] to legislate for the benefit of the majority or for the benefit of the better sort. By 'right' we ought to mean 'equally' right, i.e. right with respect to the benefit of the whole state and the common[3] interest of the citizens. (A citizen is in general one who has a share in ruling and in being ruled; but he will not be identical in every kind of constitution. So far as the best constitution is concerned, he is a man who is able and who chooses to rule and to be ruled with a view to a life that is in accordance with virtue.)

1284a3 But if there is one man (or several, but not enough to make up the whole complement of a state) of such superlative virtue that the capacity for statecraft[7] and the virtue of all the rest are simply not to be compared with his (or theirs), such men we must take not to be part of the state. To judge them worthy of mere equality with the rest would be to do them an injustice, so far unequal to them are they in virtue and in the capacity for statecraft.[7] We may reasonably regard such a one as a god among men[8] – which shows, clearly, that legislation too must apply only to equals in birth and capacity. But there is no law that embraces men of that calibre: they are themselves law, and anyone who tried to legislate for them would be snubbed for his pains. They might well say what the lions in Antisthenes' fable said to the hares who asserted their claim to equality with them.[9]

1284a17 It is for this kind of reason that democratically organized states establish also the practice of ostracism. They appear to attach such immense importance to the

6. In the second part of the preceding sentence. 'Right' = *orthos*, 'straight', 'correct'.

7. *Politikē dunamis*, the ability to contribute to the life of the state (*polis*) by proper discharge of the functions of a citizen (*politēs*) in his capacity as a 'statesman' (*politikos*), i.e. one who rules and is ruled by turn.

8. Cf. Plato, *Politicus* 303b.

9. 'Show us your claws and your teeth.' Antisthenes was a devoted follower of Socrates, and wrote extensively on ethical topics.

principle of equality above all else that they ostracized and removed out of the state for fixed periods anyone whose power was deemed to be excessive, whether this power was due to wealth or popularity or any other influence in the state. (Here is an example from mythology: the Argonauts left Heracles behind for some such reason – because the Argo would not have on board one so vastly bigger than the rest of the crew.) This is why critics of tyranny who disapprove of the advice given by Periander are not to be considered fully justified. It is said that to Thrasybulus' messenger, who had come for advice, Periander returned no answer; but while walking in a field, reduced all the stalks to one level by lopping off the tallest. The messenger did not understand the motive for this action, but reported the action to Thrasybulus, who perceived that he ought to remove the outstanding men.[10] The method is useful not only to tyrants, and tyrants are not alone in practising it: oligarchies and democracies are in just the same position, for ostracism has very much the same effect as lopping off and exiling the leading men. And it is the regular practice of the holders of sovereign power, in their dealings with other states and with foreign nations. For example, the Athenians, as soon as their empire[11] was strong enough, reduced Lesbos, Chios, and Samos to submission,[12] contrary to the terms of the agreement; and the Persian king often trimmed the Medes, Babylonians, and others who prided themselves on their earlier supremacy.[11] Indeed this whole question concerns all constitutions, not merely the divergent ones, which resort to such methods for their own advantage, but also right forms of constitution, which aim at the common[3] good.

10. Periander was tyrant of Corinth from c. 625 to 585, Thrasybulus being tyrant of the Miletus at about the same time; see Herodotus, V 92, and V x, n. 11, and V xi, n. 2.

11. *Archē*, 'rule'.

12. In 427 (Thucydides III 2 ff., 36 ff.), 424 (Thucydides IV 51), and 440–39 (Thucydides I 115–18) respectively.

1284b7 This same point may be observed also in the other skills and fields of knowledge. A painter would not allow his representation to have one foot disproportionately large, however magnificent the foot might be. A shipbuilder would not let the stern, or any other part of the ship, be out of proportion. A chorus-master will not allow among the members a performer whose voice is finer and more powerful than all the others. On this showing there is no reason at all why monarchs should not remain on good terms with their states, provided that in taking this action[13] their own rule is beneficial to those states. Therefore the theory behind ostracism has some measure of political justice,[14] in cases of admitted disproportion. Of course if the lawgiver can so construct the constitution from the start that there will never be any need of this kind of medicine, so much the better. Otherwise the best we can do, if occasion arises, is to put matters right by some such method. (In fact this is not the way it worked out in the states, because instead of seeking the advantage of their own constitution, men used ostracism as a weapon in factional strife.)

1284b22 So in the deviation forms of constitution ostracism is obviously exercised for some personal benefit,[15] and is just; though it is perhaps equally obvious that it is just in a limited sense only. But when it comes to the best type of constitution, there is a real difficulty, not in the cases of superiority in the other goods, such as strength[16] or riches or popularity, but where a man is pre-eminent in virtue. What are we to do then? Men will not say that such a person ought to be banished or deported; nor yet that they ought to rule over him, for that would be like claiming to rule over Zeus, by dividing up the offices.[17] It only

13 Of removing rivals.
14. *Politikon dikaion*, cf. III xii, n. 4.
15. Of the ruling element, whatever this happens to be.
16. Or 'influence': cf. earlier in this chapter, 1284a21.
17. That is, presumably, by holding offices turn and turn about with Zeus; cf. III xvii *ad fin*.

remains therefore to let nature take its course; he will govern and we will all gladly obey him. Thus such men will be permanent kings in their states.

III xiv

(1284b35–1285b33)

FIVE TYPES OF KINGSHIP

In III vii six forms of constitution were set out, three 'right' (kingship, aristocracy, polity), and three 'deviations' (tyranny, oligarchy, democracy). Kingship and tyranny were both 'rule by one man', the literal meaning of the Greek word monarchia, *monarchy. The intervening discussions about justice and sovereignty in the state have been carried on with the rule of the few or of the many as a constitutional background, and there has been no mention of monarchy – naturally enough, since it would be only slightly relevant to questions about sovereignty and the just distribution of political power, and not relevant at all if the monarchy's powers are unlimited. But obviously not all monarchies have such powers, and most of this chapter is devoted to discussing four types of limited monarchy (the Spartan, the non-Greek, 'aisumnēteia', and the 'heroic'), in the light of four main criteria: (a) whether they are subject to law, (b) whether their tenure is for life or for a set term, (c) whether they are elective, (d) whether they are over willing subjects. Confusingly, Aristotle calls all these four monarchies 'kingships', but admits that two are effectively tyrannies. Lastly he describes a fifth kind of monarchy, which presumably looks* back *to the unfettered kingship of the 'god among men' envisaged at the end of the last chapter, and* forward *to the 'absolute' kingship mentioned at the beginning of the next. The discussion is pleasingly enriched by Aristotle's intimate knowledge of Greek history, and by his felicitous quotations from Homer and Alcaeus.*

1284b35 After what has just been said it will be a good
thing to change the subject and consider kingship, since
we hold that it is one of the right forms of constitution.
We have to inquire whether or not a king's rule, rather
than some other constitution, is advantageous for the good
management of any country or state, or if it is advantageous for some and not for others. But first we must
decide whether there is only one kind of kingship or
several different varieties of it. It is easy to see that there
are several kinds, and that the mode of rule is not the
same in every case.

1285a3 The clearest example of kingship according to
law is the one to be found in the Spartan constitution. It
is, however, not sovereign over everything; though when
a king goes out of the country he is leader in all matters
relating to the war, and to the kings[1] is committed also
the care of religious matters. So such a kingship is like a
perpetual generalship held on terms of personal authority,
in that the king has no sovereign power to put anyone to
death except for cowardice, as on military expeditions of
old, by law of force. There is a clear example in Homer:
Agamemnon put up with being abused in meetings of
assemblies, but once an expedition had begun, he had
sovereign power of life and death. So much is implied in
his words: 'Anyone whom I shall catch absent from the
fighting ... his body shall become the prey of dogs and
birds, and no escape, for the power of death is in my
hand.'[2] This then is one type of kingship – a generalship
tenable for life, which may be acquired either by birth or
by election.

1285a16 Alongside this there is another type of
monarchy, such as kingships found among certain non-
Greeks. All these have power approximating to that of
tyrannies, but they are legally established and ancestral.
For it is because non-Greeks are by natural character

1. There were two of them: cf. II ix.
2. *Iliad*, II 391-3, with some omissions and the addition of 'for
... hand'.

more slavish than Greeks (and the Asiatics than the Europeans) that they tolerate master-like rule without resentment. Therefore, while such kingships are for these reasons like tyrannies, their legality and ancestral status make them safe. And for the same reason the ruler has a royal, not a tyrant's bodyguard; for a king's bodyguard is composed of citizens carrying arms, a tyrant's of foreigners. And the king rules over willing subjects according to law, the tyrant over unwilling subjects; so that whereas the one draws his bodyguard from among his citizens, the other uses it against them.

1285a29 These then are two types of monarchy; and there is a third, which used to exist among Greeks of old. This third type is called *aisumnētēs*, and was in rough terms an elective tyranny. It differs from the non-Greek monarchy only in not being ancestral; it is equally subject to law. The rulers held office sometimes for life, sometimes for a stated period or until certain things should be accomplished; for example the people of Mytilene elected Pittacus for the purpose of repelling the exiles who tried to come back led by Antimenides and the poet Alcaeus.[3] That Pittacus was chosen is clear from one of Alcaeus' banqueting songs in which he grumbles that 'With mass-adulation they appointed low-born Pittacus to be tyrant of their easy-going and unlucky state'. Of these kinds of rule, we may say that by being like that of a master, they are and were like tyrannies; but royal, in being elective, and in being exercised over willing subjects.

1285b3 There is a fourth kind of royal monarchy, which existed in heroic times. It was both ancestral and subject to law, and willingly accepted by its subjects. The first of these kings had been benefactors of the mass of the people in the arts of peace or in warfare, or in welding the people together, or in providing them with land. So they became kings, willingly accepted by their subjects, and ancestrally established in the eyes of their successors in the next gen-

3. About 590; fr. 160 of Alcaeus in J. M. Edmonds, *Lyra Graeca* I (Loeb Classical Library, 2nd ed., 1928). See also F. E. Romer, p. 487 below.

eration. They held sovereign control of leadership in war, and of sacrifices not reserved for priests. They also gave judgements at law; some did this on oath, some without oath, the oath being the raising aloft of the royal sceptre. In early times these kings ruled continuously over the affairs of the city, of the country, and across the borders; but later in some cases they themselves relinquished some of their duties, in others they were deprived of them by the populace. The duty of offering sacrifices was in some states the only one which was left in the hands of the kings; and even where one could justifiably say a kingship did still exist, they retained only the leadership of armies on expeditions beyond the borders.

1285b20 These then are the four forms of kingship: (a) that of heroic times, willingly accepted by the people and exercised on certain specified conditions, the king being general, judge, and religious head; (b) the non-Greek rule, acquired by birth, exercised as by a master, and subject to law; (c) what men call *aisumnēteia*, i.e. an elective dictatorship; and (d) the Lacedaemonian, in rough terms an hereditary permanent generalship. These then are the distinguishing marks of these four kinds. But there is also a fifth, in which one man single-handed is in sovereign control of everything, in the same way as each state or foreign nation controls its own public affairs. This fifth kind comes under the same heading as household-management, for just as household-management is, as it were, the kingship of the household, so this kingship is the household-management of a state, or of a foreign nation or nations.

III xv

(*1285b33–1286b40*)

THE RELATION OF KINGSHIP AND LAW (1)

In this chapter a number of related problems are raised, discussed and dropped in somewhat bewildering succes-

sion. The central themes are (a) the contrast, indeed the tension, between the personal rule of a king and the rule of law, and (b) the assessment of their relative merits.

The first four types of kingship described in the preceding chapter were all in some way restricted; the fifth was unrestricted. Hence there are really only two main classes. Of the four limited monarchies the Lacedaemonian is now taken for comparison because it is the most restricted of all. But for that very reason it is not typical of monarchy; and since limitation of royal authority involves some distribution of power, which takes place also under any other system of government, it seems that only absolute kingship needs to be discussed. Now this at once raises a problem. When Aristotle was discussing distribution of power under oligarchy or democracy, he came to the conclusion (at the end of III xi) that where possible the law should be sovereign. But at the end of the last chapter and the beginning of this, he postulates a king who makes his own laws and whose superlative excellence appears to entitle him to do so. The answer to the question what is to be done in such an event is not given till the last two chapters of the book (xvii–xviii), and the discussion in the present chapter and the next has relevance to any form of state in which personal authority and legal authority could exist side by side. On the Platonic background, see e.g. Politicus 294a ff.

Towards the end of the chapter Aristotle digresses to speculate on the origin of kingship and on the course of early constitutional development. The reconstruction he gives in IV xiii is different; but in an age when adequate source-material for writing exact and detailed history of early times barely existed, it is hardly surprising that both Plato's and Aristotle's historical accounts are somewhat generalized and free, and commonly adjusted to the theme in hand.

The chapter closes with a discussion of some practical difficulties of kingship; the observation that even the rule *of law needs to be backed by a degree of force is chilly and realistic.*

1285b33 We may say then that there are really only two types of kingship to be considered – the foregoing and the Lacedaemonian. Most of the others fall between these two extremes, as having sovereign power over fewer matters than absolute kingship has, but over more than the Lacedaemonian. So there are two questions to be asked, first whether or not it is expedient for states to have a perpetual general, appointed either on grounds of birth or by turns, and second whether or not it is expedient that one man should have sovereign powers in all matters. The former question, relating to generalship of the kind mentioned, is of a type concerned with laws rather than constitutions, since it is possible for such a thing to exist under any constitution. I am therefore leaving it aside and concentrating on the other style of kingship, since it is a type of constitution. We must therefore examine it and run over the problems that we find there.

1286a7 We begin by asking whether it is more expedient to be ruled by the best man or by the best laws. Those who believe that to be ruled by a king is expedient think that the laws enunciate only general principles and do not give day-to-day instructions on matters as they arise; and so, they argue, in any skill it is foolish to be guided always by written rules. In Egypt a doctor is allowed, rightly, to depart from his treatment if the patient is not well after four days; if he does so earlier, he does it at his own risk. For the same reason, it is obvious that the constitution which goes by laws and written rules is not the best. On the other hand, rulers cannot do without that general principle in addition: it provides something which, being without personal feelings, is better than that which by its nature does feel. Every human soul must have feelings, whereas a law has none; but in compensation, one might say, a man will give sounder counsel than law in individual cases.

1286a21 It seems clear then that this man must be a lawgiver, and that laws must be laid down, which shall be sovereign in all cases, except those in which they go awry.[1] But when the law either cannot decide at all or will only decide badly, ought the power to rule to rest with the one best man or with all? In our own day verdicts are given, deliberations are carried on, and decisions are arrived at by men acting together; and all these decisions refer to separate problems and individual cases. Now any one of these individuals, measured by his own contribution alone, may be inferior. But the state consists of many men, and this gives it the same kind of superiority as a communally provided banquet has over a single simple meal. So a crowd is, on numerous occasions, actually a better judge than one man, whoever he may be.[2] Again, the many are less easily corrupted. As a larger amount of water is less easily polluted, so the multitude is less easily corrupted than the few. The judgement of one man is bound to be corrupted if he is in a bad temper or has very strong feelings about something. But in the other case it would take a lot of doing to arrange for all simultaneously to lose their temper and go wrong.

1286a36 But we must make sure, first, that the multitude are also the free-born, and second that they depart from the provisions of the law only in cases which the law itself inevitably fails to cover. This second proviso may not be at all easy where numbers are large; but if the good, that is good men and good citizens, are in the majority, then when we put the question, 'which is the less liable to be corrupted, the sole ruler or the numerical majority who are all good?', the answer is obviously, 'the majority'. And if it is urged that the many will split into factions, which the one cannot do, perhaps the answer must be that they too are sound souls,[3] no less than your 'one man'. If then we

---

1. *Parekbainein*, the verb used to describe a constitution as 'deviant' (e.g. III vi). 'This man' is presumably the ruler.
2. Cf. III xi.
3. *Spoudaioi tēn psuchēn*, literally 'sound in respect of soul'.

are to describe this rule of the majority who are all good men as aristocracy,[4] and the rule of one as a kingship, then aristocracy in a state will be preferable to kingship, whether or not rule is exercised by armed force, provided it is possible to get a homogeneous majority.

1286b8 Perhaps we have here a clue to the reason why royal rule used to exist formerly, namely the difficulty of finding enough men of outstanding virtue, all the greater since in those days the states they inhabited were small. An especial function of good men is to confer benefits, and it was in recognition of the benefits that they had conferred that men were appointed to be kings. Then, when a large number of men of similar virtue became available, people no longer tolerated one-man rule but looked for something communal, and set up a constitution. But the good men did not remain good: they began to make money out of that which was the common property of all. And to some such development we may plausibly ascribe the origin of oligarchies, since men made wealth a thing of honour. The next change was to tyrannies, and from tyrannies to democracy. For the struggle to get rich at all costs tended to reduce numbers,[5] and so increased the power of the multitude, who rose up and formed democracies. And now that there has been a further increase in the size of states, one might say that it is hard to avoid having a democratic constitution.

1286b22 If anyone should hold that it is best for states to be ruled by kings, he will have to consider a question relating to the king's children. Are his offspring also to be kings? Considering what kind of persons some of these have turned out to be, we would have to say that hereditary succession is harmful. You may say the king, having sovereign power, will not in that case[6] hand over to his

4. 'Aristocracy' means literally, 'power (held by) the best'.

5. The numbers of the rich rulers, presumably: wealth, the qualification for ruling, became concentrated in fewer and fewer hands.

6. These last three words are not in the Greek. I take the point to be that the king will not hand over to one of his sons if none of them is suitable.

children. But it is hard to believe that: it is a difficult achievement, which expects too much virtue of human nature.

1286b27 Then there is this question of armed force: is the intending king to have about him a force with which he will be able to impose his will on those who seek to resist his rule? How else is he to exercise his authority? For even if his sovereignty is such that he can act only in accordance with law, and do nothing of his own volition that is illegal, it will still be necessary for him to have sufficient armed force to give the laws protection. This question, in so far as it relates to this kind of king,[7] is perhaps not difficult to answer. He must indeed have a force, and it should be made strong enough to overpower one man or a band of men, but not the multitude. This is the principle which was followed in earlier times, when guards were assigned to a man who was being appointed as 'tyrant' or *'aisumnētēs'*, as they called him, of the state; so too, when Dionysius asked for these guards, somebody advised the Syracusans to limit them to just the number required for that purpose.

III xvi

(*1287a1–1287b36*)

THE RELATION OF KINGSHIP AND LAW (2)

Aristotle has wandered away from the question posed at the beginning of III xv. All these discussions about the relations between monarchy and law seem to have been concerned not with absolute but with 'legal' monarchy – a subject which he professed to have put aside in order to consider 'absolute' monarchy. To this he now returns, repeats something of what he said at the beginning of Chapter xv, and then once again discusses the authority of

7. I.e. one who rules according to law.

the law and the authority of the individual. It looks as if there may have been at one time a double set of Aristotle's notes; yet although xv and xvi overlap a good deal, xvi does contain a number of new points, notably: (a) That law is in some sense a 'mean'. Aristotle was in general inclined to think of virtues as means between extremes *(see* Nicomachean Ethics, *II vi–ix), and we have here evidently an attempt to extend the analysis to law. From the drift of his discussion, it looks as if he thought of law as a mean in the sense that it constitutes a compromise between unfettered personal discretion on the one hand and slavish adherence to written rules on the other (cf.* Plato, Laws *875d ff, 925d–926a). Or is his point simply that law is a mean in the sense that it is impartial? (b) That law is in some sense 'natural'. Again, Aristotle does not discuss the point at length. The argument seems to rest on the natural equality of men, which entitles them all to a share of ruling according to some agreed and hence 'legal' system of alternation.*

However, it should be noted that the entire chapter is written rather confusingly: ostensibly, at any rate, it is an account of the arguments of certain anti-monarchical polemicists, and it is not clear precisely where Aristotle's own comments, if any, begin and end.

1287a1 We must now turn to consider our next subject, the king whose every act is in accordance with his own personal volition. For the king who is 'subject to law' does not, as has already been said,[1] amount to a form of constitution, because perpetual generalships may exist in democracy or in aristocracy or in any other constitution, and it is not unusual to put one man in sovereign control of the whole administration – witness the government of Epidamnus and, to a lesser extent, of Opus. But we are now speaking of 'absolute' kingship, meaning by that one whereby the king rules over everything according to his own volition. *1287a10* There are some who hold that it is not even in

1. III xv *init.*

accordance with nature[2] that one man should be sovereign over all the citizens, when the state is made up of persons who are alike. For, they say, those who are by nature alike must get the same natural justice and deserts; and so, if it is bad for the health of unequal persons to have equal food or clothing, this is also applicable to honours; and the converse also is true. Justice therefore demands that no one should do more ruling than being ruled, but that all should have their turn. So we are back again with law, for organization *is* law. It follows therefore that it is preferable that law should rule rather than any single one of the citizens. And following this same line of reasoning further, we must add that even if it is better that certain persons rule, these persons should be appointed as guardians of the laws and as their servants. Offices there must be, they say, but it is not just that there should be only one man in office, at any rate where all men are alike.

1287a23 Again, though there are matters about which the law appears incapable of giving a decision, in such cases a human being too would be unable to find an answer. It is in order to meet such situations that the law expressly educates the officials, and empowers them to decide and to deal with these undetermined matters to the very best of their just judgement.[3] Moreover, it allows for amendments to be made, wherever after experiment a new proposal is thought to be better than the established practice. Therefore he who asks law to rule is asking God and intelligence and no others to rule; while he who asks for the rule of a human being is importing a wild beast too; for desire is like a wild beast, and anger perverts rulers and the very best of men. Hence law is intelligence without appetition.

1287a32 Another argument is that which employs an analogy with medicine or other professional skills, and alleges that it is a bad thing to practise medicine according to written rules, it being preferable to call in those who

2. 'Much less expedient', Newman.
3. The formulation echoes that of the Athenian juryman's oath.

possess the skills. But this analogy is false. The doctor does not do anything for friendship's sake that is against his rational judgement: he cures his patient and takes his fee; but people in offices of state usually do all manner of things to show favour or disfavour. If you suspected that the doctors had been bribed by your enemies to make an end of you, then you would naturally prefer to get treatment according to written rules. Again, doctors when ill call in other doctors to treat them, and trainers other trainers when they themselves go into training – on the principle that it is impossible to give true judgement when their own interests and their own feelings are involved. So it is clear that the search for what is just is a search for the mean; for the law is the mean. Further, customary laws influence us more crucially,[4] and in more crucial[4] matters, than written laws; so that though a man, as ruler, is less fallible than written laws, he is no less fallible than customary laws.

1287b8 Of course, if a man is the only ruler, there will be much that he cannot easily supervise; he will therefore need to have several other officials appointed by him, so what difference does it make whether they were there at the beginning of his rule or were appointed subsequently by him in virtue of his position as sole ruler? Besides, if, as has been said before, a sound man has a right to rule because he is better, then two good men are better than one. Hence the expression 'Let two go together', and Agamemnon's prayer, 'Would that I had ten such counsellors.'[5]

1287b15 In our own day too the officials (for instance judges) have the sovereign power to give decisions about some matters on which the law is not able to decide. But it is universally agreed that where the law is capable, it is the law's rule and decisions that will be best. But there are

---

4. *Kurios*, usually 'sovereign'. 'Customary' = literally 'laws by habit' (*ethos, ethē*), which we obey more or less without thinking. The paragraph seems to argue against Plato, *Politicus* 296b ff.

5. Homer, *Iliad* X 224 and II 372.

things which can and others which cannot be included in laws; and it is the latter that give rise to difficulties and raise the old question: Which is preferable, the rule of the best man or the rule of the best law? Among the matters which cannot be included in laws are those which are the subjects of deliberation. Yet they[6] do not deny the inevitability of such decisions being taken by a man; they merely say that there should be not one man only but many.

1287b25 An individual ruler, if he has been well educated by law, gives good decisions; but he has only one pair of eyes and ears, one pair of feet and hands, and it would be a paradox if he had better vision in judgement and action than many men with many pairs. Monarchical rulers, as we see even in our own times, appoint large numbers of men to be their eyes and ears, hands and feet; for such people as are friendly to themselves and to their rule, they make sharers in it. If they are not friends, they will not act according to the monarch's intentions. On the other hand if they *are* friends, both of the monarch and his rule, then, since a friend is equal and similar, if the monarch thinks that these men ought to rule, he thinks thereby that equal and similar persons ought similarly to rule.

These, roughly stated, are the contentions of the opponents of kingship.

III xvii

(*1287b36–1288a32*)

THE HIGHEST FORM OF KINGSHIP

In this chapter Aristotle completes his discussion of kingship and law, and decides, as he has already suggested at the end of III xiii, that when a single individual is utterly

6. Presumably the advocates of the rule of law, or simply men in general.

outstanding in virtue, he ought to be given a permanent all-powerful and 'absolute' kingship, above the law. Two related points (among many it would be possible to make about this fascinating thesis) may be indicated here: (1) Aristotle seems not to envisage such a ruler ceasing to be wholly virtuous: indeed he apparently thinks that such virtue may be transmitted genetically, or at least by education within the same family. 'Once wholly virtuous, always so' would seem to us political naïveté; or does Aristotle conceive such a king merely as a theoretical possibility? (2) In the very suggestive second paragraph, Aristotle describes three kinds of society, and the kind of ruler which each naturally produces and which is suitable for it; one of these three is the 'royal' society, which produces the wholly virtuous and absolute king. Here again, the possibility of change seems not to be allowed for: could not societies, by internal change, progress to or regress from this ideal? Aristotle was certainly aware of the fact that a state may change its constitution over a period, and his analysis here seems curiously static – though it is admittedly brief and exploratory.

1287b36 But these observations, though valid in some cases, are perhaps not valid in others. For while in the natural order of things 'just' and 'expedient' vary in sense according to whether the ruler is a master, king or statesman,[1] there is no natural sense in which they can apply to the rule of a tyrant, nor to any of the other constitutions which are deviations, for they develop in a manner contrary to nature. But from what has already been said, it is clear that, among those who are equal and alike, it is neither just nor expedient that one single man should be sovereign over all the rest, whether he rule with laws or without (he himself then being law instead), or whether he is a good man ruling over good men, or not-good over not-good; nor even if he is superior in virtue – except in

1. 'Statesmen' are fellow-citizens, who rule turn and turn about: see I i.

certain circumstances. What these circumstances are I must now state, though to some extent they have been stated already.[2] But first I must define what is meant by the terms 'royal', 'aristocratic', and 'of statesmen'.[1]

1288a8 A populace is 'royal' if it is of such a kind as naturally to produce a breed[3] of outstanding virtue fitting it for leadership in the state. A populace is 'aristocratic' if it is such as naturally to produce a breed able to be governed as befits free persons by those whose virtue equips them to be leaders in the holding of office in the state. A populace is 'of statesmen'[1] if it is one in which there naturally grows up a breed of citizens able to rule and be ruled according to a law which distributes offices on a basis of merit to those who are well-off financially.

1288a15 When therefore either a whole family or a single individual among people at large can be found, whose virtue is so outstanding as to outstrip that of all the rest, then it becomes just that this family should be royal and sovereign over all things, and that this one man should be king. For, as has been said earlier, this meets the requirements of that justice which men are wont to demand in setting up constitutions, whether they are making them aristocratic or oligarchic, or, again, democratic. For they all base claims on superiority, though the superiority is not the same in each case. It also accords with the position adopted previously,[2] for of course it would be improper that such a man[4] should be put to death or exiled or ostracized or required to be ruled over in his turn.[5] For while the part[5] is not naturally superior to the whole, yet superiority is exactly the position of one so outstandingly excellent as I have described. There is therefore nothing

2. III xiii, *ad fin*.
3. *Genos*, so too 'family' subsequently.
4. Of utterly outstanding virtue.
5. *Meros*, 'part'; *kata meros*, 'in turn', 'alternately'. The point is that rule by turns is suitable for parts; but parts are not superior to the whole; 'such a man' *is* superior to the whole; therefore rule by turns is not suitable for him.

for it but to obey such a man and accept him as sovereign, not in alternation[5] but absolutely.

1288a30 On kingship then and on its various forms and whether or not it is advantageous for states, and for which states, and in what circumstances, to all those questions let these be our answers.

III xviii

(*1288a32–1288b4*)

THE EDUCATION OF THE IDEAL KING

In the preceding chapters Aristotle has given really very little detail about absolute kingship, either the kind of man he needs to be, or the circumstances in which absolutism is a good thing. This makes it impossible to say with certainty whether he had Alexander the Great in mind or not. On the whole it seems unlikely: see V. Ehrenberg, Alexander and the Greeks *(Oxford, 1938), ch. 3, but cf. H. Kelsen, 'Aristotle and Hellenic-Macedonian policy', in* Articles on Aristotle II *(see Select Bibliographies). At least we can say that there is no mention of great conquests as a necessary qualification for monarchy.*

The chapter is by way of a tail-piece to the book and looks forward to the discussions of Book VII. It makes a single and valuable point about the education which produces the ideal monarch: that it will be virtually identical to that of the 'sound' man who is a citizen of the best state. It is this person, somehow writ large, who seems to be the absolutely virtuous absolute king Aristotle envisages.

1288a32 But since we say that there are three right constitutions,[1] and that of these the best must be of necessity that which is managed by the best men (and that may mean one man alone, or one entire family,[2] or a populace

1. See III vii.
2. *Genos*, cf. III xvii.

outstanding in virtue, some able to rule, others to be ruled, with a view to the most desirable life), and since further it was shown in the initial discussions[3] that in the best state it is bound to be the case that the virtue of a man and of a citizen are identical, then it follows clearly that the method and means one would employ to establish a state under an aristocracy or king, and those by which a sound man is produced, are the same, so that the education and morals[4] that make a man sound, and those that will make him fit to play the part of a statesman or of a king, are also more or less identical.

1288b2 Now that these matters have been settled we must next endeavour to describe how the *best* constitution naturally comes about and how it is naturally established.

The promise to examine the best constitution is redeemed in Books VII and VIII (hence it was for a time customary for editors to renumber these two books and print them after Book III). In the Books IV–VI the emphasis is however not on the absolutely best constitution but on the most serviceable kind for actual use. To this the name 'polity' is given, as in III vii. There is a general cohesiveness about Books IV, V and VI (see, in the Reviser's Introduction, 'The Contents and Structure of the Politics'*), and in the second chapter of Book IV Aristotle gives a partial table of contents. But when it comes down to detail there is much disarray.*

3. III iv–v.
4. *Ethē*: cf. III xvi, n. 4.

BOOK IV

IV i

(1288b10–1289a25)

THE TASKS OF POLITICAL THEORY

At the beginning of Book IV Aristotle's discussion takes a more practical turn. The political theorist, he maintains, must investigate four kinds of constitutions:
1. *The ideal or absolutely best conceivable, without regard to actual circumstances.*
2. *The best attainable in the circumstances that prevail.*
3. *Constitutions inferior to 1 and 2, which evidently may be worth putting into practice and preserving.*
4. *An all-purpose constitution which would suit all states. He must also appreciate that there are several different kinds of each of the main constitutions (that there are, e.g., several different varieties of democracy), and that each variety requires different laws. This programme of study is embarked upon in chapter iii.*

To attain (1) and (2) would be the concern of a 'utopian' political theorist such as Plato: the Republic *presumably describes, in his view, the first kind of constitution, the* Laws *the second (but note the wider horizons of* Laws *739ab ff.). Aristotle, however, evinces a certain impatience with utopianism: he is prepared to offer help to constitutions far removed from the ideal – and, interestingly enough, not by sudden or radical constitutional change, nor by demanding a fresh start, but by 'Fabian' gradualism and piecemeal 'social engineering', and with the consent of the inhabitants of the state concerned. The whole chapter is a salutary reminder that in spite of all Aristotle's theoretical discussion, and his keen interest in the utopias he describes in Book II, his* Politics *has an essentially practical purpose.*

1288b10   In all the skills and sciences which do not

235

operate piecemeal but give complete coverage to some class of objects, it is the task of a single skill or science to investigate what suits each individual class. For instance, what kind of training is advantageous for what kind of body, and what training is best? For the best must necessarily suit the body which is best endowed and best equipped. It is a further task of gymnastic to investigate what single form of training for everyone will serve the greatest number. And even if a man has no ambition to acquire the condition or the knowledge[1] appropriate for athletic contests, it is none the less the business of the teacher or gymnastic trainer to impart that[2] degree of ability too. We see the same principle at work in medicine, shipbuilding, clothing and every other skill.

1288b21 So it is clearly true also that it is the task of one and the same science to consider the best constitution, what it is and what it would be like if it were constructed exactly as one would wish, without any hindrance from outside. Another of its tasks is to consider what constitution is suited to what persons, because for many the best is perhaps impossible to attain; so the good lawgiver and the genuine statesman will have to bear in mind both the 'absolutely best' constitution and the 'best in the circumstances'. There is also a third, which starts from an assumption – I mean he must be able to consider also a constitution which is given, both how it could come into being, and how once in being it may last longest. I am speaking particularly of a state which happens to operate neither the best constitution (being without provision even for its basic needs), nor the one possible in the actual circumstances, but a worse. Besides these there is a fourth he must recognize – the constitution which will suit pretty well all states. This is why the majority of those who give their views on constitutions, however well they may do it in other respects, fall down on questions of utility. For we must consider not only the best constitution but also

1. *Epistēmē*, translated as 'science' elsewhere in this chapter.
2. I.e. the lesser.

the possible, and likewise also that which is easier and more within the reach of[3] all states.

1288b39 But there are of course some today who concentrate on the search for the highest constitution, which needs ample resources; others talk rather about some common[3] constitution, yet dismiss entirely the constitutions that actually exist and simply give their approval to the Lacedaemonian or some other. But what is needed is the introduction of a system which the people involved will be easily persuaded to accept, and will easily be able to bring in, starting from the system they actually have. Hence it is a no less difficult task to put a constitution back on its feet than to create one from the start, just as relearning a lesson is no less hard than learning it in the first place. Thus it is another of the duties of a statesman, in addition to those stated, to be able to render assistance to actually existing constitutions, as noted before.[4] But he cannot do this without knowing how many forms of constitution there are. Some people think that there is only one democracy and only one oligarchy. This is not true, and therefore one should not forget how many differences there are between constitutions and how many different ways there are of combining them.

1289a11 This same practical wisdom enables one to discern both which laws are best, and which of them suit each constitution. For one ought to lay down laws to fit constitutions (as indeed is always done), not constitutions to fit laws. A constitution is the arrangement which a state adopts for the distribution of offices, and for the determination of sovereignty in the constitution and of the end which the particular association aims at realizing. Laws distinguishable from descriptions of constitutions are those according to which the rulers shall rule and shall watch out for those that transgress them. This makes it quite clear that even for the purpose of laying down laws it is necessary to start with a grasp of the varieties of con-

3. *Koinos.*
4. In the preceding paragraph? Or perhaps III viii is meant.

stitutions and the definition of each, because it is impossible for the same laws to be good for all oligarchies and all democracies, since there is more than one form of each, both of oligarchy and of democracy.

IV ii

(1289a26–1289b26)

CONSTITUTIONS PLACED IN ORDER OF MERIT

It is difficult to know what to make of this chapter. It may be merely an alternative draft of the programme of inquiry outlined in IV i, to which its final paragraph is fairly similar. If however it was meant to be taken as a confirmation and development of it, then the train of thought would seem to be: 'We envisage an inquiry into constitutions, and we have previously distinguished six. But by virtue of having already discussed the "best" constitution, we have in effect dealt with two of the three "correct" ones. (Implication: there is an order of merit among these.) Now the three "perverted" constitutions also may be graded; but in order not of merit, but demerit. But leaving questions of grading aside, we must, before discussing the various constitutions, distinguish the sub-varieties of each' (cf. IV i ad fin.). The programme of inquiry is therefore now restated with variations of emphasis, to prepare afresh for IV iii ff.; in this revision, greater emphasis is given to the relevance of the sub-varieties, and one further and final item (e) is added to the list of topics to be investigated. But even if this reconstruction is correct, the programme of inquiry of IV i and ii is followed only approximately in the subsequent chapters and books: it refers primarily to IV iii–xiii, but topics (d) and (e) at the end of the chapter appear to look ahead to V and VI (see notes to text). On the significance of this for the composition and structure of the Politics, see the Select Bibliographies (esp. commentaries).

1289a26 In our first inquiry[1] into constitutions we analysed them as follows: the *right* constitutions, three in
number – kingship, aristocracy, and polity – and the
deviations from these, likewise three in number – tyranny from kingship, oligarchy from aristocracy, democracy from polity. Aristocracy and kingship have been
discussed already[2] (because the inquiry into the best
constitution is identical with discussion of these two
words, as both have the same aim, that is virtue endowed
with material goods), and the distinctions between them
have been drawn;[3] we have also determined when it is
that kingship is to be adopted.[4] It therefore remains to
discuss polity,[5] which is called by the name which is
common to them all, and then the other three: oligarchy, democracy and tyranny.

1289a38 As to these three deviations, which is worst
and which second worst – this is obvious, for the deviation from the first and most divine must be the worst.
Now kingship, unless it is receiving a name to which
it is not entitled, must exist in virtue of the great superiority of the person who reigns. Accordingly, tyranny
is the worst, and is farthest away from polity; oligarchy
comes second, for aristocracy is very different from this
kind of constitution; while democracy is the most moderate of the deviations. One of my predecessors[6] has
expressed such views on these matters, but he takes a
different standpoint from mine. He thinks that where
all are reasonable enough (when oligarchy, for instance,
and the rest are of a serviceable standard), then democracy is the worst of them; but when all are bad, democracy is the best. My view is simply that these
constitutions are erroneous; and it is therefore improper

---

1. Evidently III vii in particular.
2. III xiv–xviii.
3. III vii, xv, xvii.
4. III xvii.
5. See especially IV viii and ix.
6. Probably a reference to Plato, *Politicus* 303ab.

to speak of one oligarchy as better than another, but only as less bad.

1289b11   But let us leave such estimates aside and go on to analyse: (a) How many varieties of constitutions there are, on the assumption that there is more than one form of oligarchy and democracy. (b) Which is the most universal[7] constitution, and which is the most preferable constitution after the best; and which other, if any, though aristocratic and well-constructed, is even so suitable for most states – what constitution will answer to that description? (c) Among other constitutions too, which is preferable for whom, since probably for some democracy is essential, rather than oligarchy, for others oligarchy rather than democracy. (d) In what manner one who wishes to set up these constitutions should go to work in each several case, I mean each particular form both of democracy and of oligarchy.[8] And lastly (e), when we have given as good and succinct an account of all these as we can, we must tackle the question which are those processes that destroy constitutions, and which are those that keep them stable, both in general and in each particular case; and also what causes most naturally give rise to these processes.[9]

IV iii

(*1289b27–1290a29*)

WHY THERE ARE SEVERAL CONSTITUTIONS

Somewhat unexpectedly, in view of the 'programme' of IV i–ii, Aristotle now tells us briefly why there are several different constitutions. States have various 'parts' (households, professional groups, etc.) in various combinations, and the resulting variety of economic and social pressures inevitably produces a variety of constitutions.

7. *Koinos.*   8. VI i–vii.   9. V *in toto.*

Aristotle considers unsatisfactory the popular view that there are fundamentally only two constitutions, democracy and oligarchy, the others being grouped roughly under one or other of these headings; it would be truer, he suggests, to think of one or two 'well-formed' constitutions, the others being 'deviations' from them. He thus prefers a classification based on 'value judgements' to a purely descriptive one. In effect the chapter prepares us for the several different kinds of constitution we shall meet in subsequent chapters, by contrasting a popular classification with a philosophical, which looks for the reasons for the complexity of constitutional forms and seeks to grade them on moral criteria.

1289b27 The reason for the plurality of constitutions lies in the plurality of parts in every state. We observe in the first place that all states are composed of households, and then that of this total number of persons some must be wealthy, others poor, others in the middle between them; furthermore the rich and the poor are respectively armed and unarmed. We also observe that the people are divided into three classes, agricultural, commercial, and mechanical workers. There are also differences among the upper classes, according to their wealth and the extent of their possessions. We ask, for example, how many horses a man keeps. (Horse-rearing is always difficult without wealth. Hence in ancient times the states whose power lay in their horses had oligarchies, and they made use of their horses in war against states whose borders were contiguous. We see this in Chalcis and Eretria and, on the Asiatic side, Magnesia on the Maeander, and other areas.) In addition to wealth there are other *differentiae*, of family, virtue, and any other similar feature we described as 'part' of a state, when in our discussion of aristocracy we were analysing the essential parts of any state.[1]

1290a3 Sometimes all these parts have a share in the

1. Possibly III xii *ad fin.*

241

constitution, sometimes a large number of them, sometimes fewer. It thus becomes clear that there must be several constitutions differing in kind from each other, since the parts differ in kind among themselves. For a constitution is the arrangement of the offices, which are everywhere distributed either according to the power of the participants, or on an equal basis, that is, equality as between the propertyless, for example, or as between the propertied, or some other equality as between them both. There must therefore be as many constitutions as there are arrangements of the superiorities and differences between the parts.

1290a13 But they are commonly reckoned to be two: in the same way as the winds are sometimes classified into northerly and southerly, the rest being deviations from these, so there are supposed to be two constitutions – democracy and oligarchy. For people treat aristocracy as a type of oligarchy, it being oligarchy in a way, and polity, as we call it, as a type of democracy, as the west wind is taken to be a sort of north wind and the east a sort of south wind. The same kind of duality some people find also in music; they lay down two types of mode, Dorian and Phrygian,[2] and give one or other of these names to all the other arrangements of notes. People have therefore formed a firm habit of looking at constitutions in this way. But our own classification is better, as well as more accurate, because the well-formed constitutions are two (or perhaps only one), and all others are deviations, either from the absolutely best or from the harmonious and well-balanced mixture.[3] These deviations we label oligarchical, if they are too strict and master-like,[4] but democratic if they are loose and relaxed.

2. The Dorian and Phrygian 'modes' (*harmoniai*) were two of several Greek 'styles' of music, each of which tended to be associated with particular kinds of theme and treatment. See further VIII v–vii.

3. Literally, *tēs eu kekramenēs harmonias*, 'from the well-mixed mode'.

4. *Despotikos*, 'like a mastership (of slaves)'.

(*1290a30–1292a39*)

THE PARTS OF THE STATE
AND THE CLASSIFICATION OF DEMOCRACIES

This long and difficult chapter contains several repetitions and inconsistencies which suggest that the material which Aristotle left has fallen into disarray. Comment is devoted to elucidation of the structure of the chapter as it stands. I have divided it into five sections:

Definitions of democracy and oligarchy.
  Democracy and oligarchy are commonly defined in excessively simple terms. Numbers are not in themselves decisive (cf. III viii): e.g. democracy is the rule of the poor, the dēmos, be they few or many; and they are usually the latter. Wealth and status, as well as numbers, are crucial for classification.

The parts of the state, and resulting variety among constitutions (1).
  Constitutions are of several kinds, because every state has several parts which can be combined in various ways, just as different kinds of animals could be produced by different combinations of different varieties of 'parts' (i.e. different sorts of mouth, stomach, limb etc.). A list of the parts of a state is now embarked upon.

Plato on the parts of the state.
  A digression in refutation of Plato's views in the Republic on the minimum number of parts essential to a state if it is to be self-sufficient.

The parts of the state, and resulting variety among constitutions (2).
  A resumption of the list of the parts. Often enough, one man can perform more than one function in the

*state; but no man can be both poor and rich, so it is
easy to regard the large numbers of the poor and the
small numbers of the rich as 'opposites' among the
parts of the state. Hence constitutions are thought to
be two: democracy and oligarchy.*

Varieties of democracy.
*Democracy (and oligarchy) will obviously take various
forms according to the type of person dominant in it
– traders, fishermen, artisans etc. A list of five kinds
of democracy follows. The chapter closes with a discussion of the last and most extreme and tyrannical
form, where the people decide everything by decree
at the bidding of demagogues, and dispense with the
rule of law.*

*Summarized thus, and surveyed as a whole, the chapter
presents an understandable if ungainly sequence of argument. Space forbids discussion of the many points of
political and philosophical interest, and I fasten on one
only, which we have had occasion to notice before (see
introduction to III viii): the constant assumption that*
dēmokratia *means exactly, and starkly, what it says –
power exercised by the* dēmos, *that is, by a particular
social class,* in its own interest.

Definitions of Democracy and Oligarchy

1290a30 It is a mistake, which some people habitually
make today, to describe democracy and oligarchy in
terms too simple and absolute, saying that there is a
democracy where the mass of the people is sovereign
(as if the majority[1] were not also sovereign in oligarchies and everywhere), and an oligarchy where few
are sovereign in the constitution. Suppose a total of
1,300; 1,000 of these are rich, and they give no share in
office to the 300 poor, who also are free men and in other

1. I.e. of participants in the constitution.

respects like them; no one would say that these 1,300 lived under a democracy. Or again, suppose the poor to be few, but to be stronger than the well-to-do, who are more numerous than they: no one would call such a constitution oligarchical, where a share in honours is not given to the others, the rich. Therefore we should say rather that it is a democracy whenever the free are sovereign, oligarchy when the rich are sovereign; but what actually *occurs* is that the former are many, the latter few: many are free, few are rich. Otherwise,[2] if the offices were distributed on a basis of height, as is said by some to be done in Ethiopia, or of handsome appearance, then there would be an oligarchy, because the numbers of tall or handsome are small.

1290b7 Nevertheless even these considerations,[3] on their own, are not adequate to define these constitutions. Both democracy and oligarchy consist of a number of parts; and whenever the free are not numerous, but rule over a majority who are not free, we still cannot say that it is a democracy, nor that it is an oligarchy where the rich rule in virtue of superior numbers. The former situation existed in Apollonia on the Ionian Gulf, and on Thera; for in each of these states honours were restricted to a minority – those persons of distinguished ancestry who had taken part in the original settlements. The other state of affairs existed at one time in Colophon, where before the war with Lydia[4] the majority had amassed substantial possessions. A democracy exists whenever those who are free and are not well-off, being in the majority, are in sovereign control of government, an oligarchy when control lies with the rich and better-born, these being few.

2. I.e. if we consider the *number* of rulers as the sole criterion of nomenclature.

3. Wealth and freedom, as opposed to numbers.

4. Early seventh century, when Gyges was king of Lydia.

The Parts of the State, and Resulting Variety among Constitutions (1)

1290b21 That constitutions are several, and the reason why they are several, has now been shown. Let us now start from the point mentioned before,[5] and show that they are even more numerous than was stated, and say what they are and from what cause. We agree that every state is composed of many parts, not just one. Now if our chosen subject were forms of animal life, we should first have to answer the question 'What is it essential for every animal to have?' And among those essentials we should have to include some of the organs of sense-perception, and something for the processing and reception of nourishment, such as mouth and stomach, and in addition parts of the body which enable the animal in question to move about. If these were all that we had to consider and there were differences between them (several different kinds of mouth, for instance, of stomach, of sense-organs, and of parts to do with loco-motion), then the number of ways of combining these will necessarily make a number of different kinds of animals. For it is impossible for one and the same animal to have several different kinds of mouth or ear. So when you have taken all the possible couplings of these one with another, they will produce forms of animal; and the number of forms of animal will be equal to the number of combinations of essential parts.

1290b38 We may apply this to the constitutions mentioned; for states too are made up not of one but of many parts, as has often been said. These are (a) the bulk of the people concerned with food-production, called tillers of the soil; (b) the part called mechanical, by which we mean people who follow those skills which are indispensable to the running of a state (these skills are further divided into the absolutely essential and those

5. IV iii *ad init.*

who minister to luxury or the good life); (c) the commercial, by which we mean that section which spends its time on buying and selling, merchant commerce and retail trade; (d) the section comprising hired labourers; (e) the element which will defend in time of war. This last is just as indispensable as the others, if the population is not to be a slave to aggressors. For of course no state can possibly have a claim to the name, if it is naturally a slave to others: a state is self-sufficient, which is just what a slave is not.

Plato on the Parts of the State

1291a10 For this reason I find the treatment given to this topic in the *Republic*[6] to be more clever than adequate. For Socrates says that a city is compounded of four absolutely essential elements, and that these are the weaver, the farmer, the shoemaker and the builder; then, deeming these to be not self-sufficient, he adds metalworkers and those in charge of indispensable livestock, then the merchant and the retailer. This becomes the full complement of the 'first' state, apparently on the supposition that every state is formed to satisfy minimum needs and not rather for a finer purpose; and also that its need for shoemakers is equal to its need for farmers. To defenders in war he assigns no part until territorial expansion involves them in contact with neighbours and war breaks out.

1291a22 But surely there also ought to be among the four, or any other number of associates, one whose duty it will be to decide upon and render justice. If the soul is to be regarded as part of a living creature even more than its body, then in states too we must regard the corresponding elements as being parts in a fuller sense than those which merely conduce to utility and necessity: I mean such things as the fighting force and all

6. 369b–371e.

those connected with the judicial administration of justice;[7] and over and above these, that deliberative element which represents political wisdom in action.[8] It is irrelevant to my argument whether these qualities are to be found separately in several people or in the same; it is quite normal for the same persons to be found bearing arms and tilling the soil. If then those on both lists[9] are to be counted as parts of the state, it is clear that at least[10] the heavy-armed military element is an essential one.

The Parts of the State, and Resulting Variety among Constitutions (2)

1291a33 Those who render service[11] by their possessions are a seventh part; we call them the well-to-do. An eighth part is composed of those who are on official business, i.e. who render service[11] in connection with the offices – since a state cannot do without officials. So there must be persons capable of holding office and rendering service[11] of this kind to the state, either continuously or by turns. There remain those who have in fact just been distinguished,[12] the deliberators and those who give decisions where matters of justice are in dispute.

1291a40 Now if these elements must exist in states, and

7. *Dikaiosunē dikastikē*, 'justice in trials', as determined by jurymen (*dikastai*); cf. I ii, n. 24.

8. *Syneseōs politikēs ergon*, a fine expression, literally 'activity of insight connected with the *polis*'.

9. I.e. the occupations present in Plato's 'first' state, and Aristotle's additions.

10. I.e. to say nothing of other kinds of fighter.

11. Literally, 'render *leitourgiai*, public services' (cf. II x, n. 6). 'Liturgies' were compulsory payments by the richer citizens towards the expenses of certain public functions, e.g. of dramatic and musical festivals. In the case of the eighth part the point is presumably that to hold office is a 'contribution' or 'expenditure' of a kind, analogous to the expenditure of money by the seventh part: cf. III vi.

12. In the preceding paragraph.

exist in a fine and just manner, it becomes essential that some of the citizens should be possessed of virtue. Many suppose that the other capacities may very well coexist in the same persons: the same people may be defenders, farmers, skilled workmen, and judges and deliberators too. All these have some claim to virtue also, and believe themselves to be capable of most of the offices. But the same people cannot be both rich and poor, and that is why the prime division of a state into parts seems to be into poor and the well-to-do. Further, owing to the fact that the one group is for the most part numerically small, the other large, these two parts appear as opposites among the parts of the state. So the constitutions are accordingly constructed to reflect the predominance of one or other of these, and there seem to be two constitutions – democracy and oligarchy.

Varieties of Democracy

1291b14 That constitutions are several and for what reasons they are several, has been mentioned before; let us now show that there are several forms both of oligarchy and of democracy. But this is clear even from what has been said already. There is on the one hand the people, on the other the notables, as we call them. Of each of these there are several kinds. For example, of the people one kind is engaged in agriculture, another in skills, and yet another in commerce, in buying and selling. Another kind takes to the sea, and there they fight or trade or carry passengers or catch fish. (In many places the sections of the population engaged in one or other of these occupations are large: fishermen are numerous at Tarentum and Byzantium, traders at Aegina and Chios; at Athens many are engaged on triremes, at Tenedos in passenger traffic.) To these we may add the labouring class and those whose possessions are so small that they cannot have any time off, also those who are not of free birth on both sides, and any other similar kind of multitude. The distinguishing marks of the notables are wealth, good birth, virtue, education and the other things listed under the same heading.[13]

1291b30 The first variety of democracy is that which is so called because it is based chiefly on the principle of equality. In such a democracy the law interprets equality as meaning that the poor shall not enjoy any more advantage than the rich, that neither shall be sovereign, but both shall be exactly similar. For if, as is held by some, freedom is especially to be found in democracy, and also equality, this condition is most fully realized when all alike share most fully in the constitution. But since the people are a majority, and the decision of the majority is sovereign, this must be a democracy. Here, then, is one type of democracy.

1291b39 Another type has a property-qualification for office, but only a modest one, so that he who gets the requisite amount is allowed to share in office, but ceases to do so if he loses it. Another type is when all citizens share unless they fail to pass a scrutiny,[14] but the law rules. Another type is when everyone shares, provided only that he is a citizen, but again the law rules. Another type of democracy is the same in other respects, but the multitude is sovereign and not the law. This occurs when the decrees are sovereign over the provisions of the law.

1292a7 It is the demagogues who bring about this state of affairs. When states are democratically governed according to law, there are no demagogues, and the best citizens are securely in the saddle; but where the laws are not sovereign, there you find demagogues. The people becomes a monarch, one person composed of many, for the many are sovereign, not as individuals but as an aggregate. What kind of multiple rulership,

13. Literally, 'according to the same difference, i.e. distinguishing principle'. That is to say, under one heading come advantages (wealth, etc.); under another, disadvantages.

14. As to birth, it seems; cf. IV vi, n. 3.

collective or of several individuals, Homer meant,[15] when he spoke of it as being a bad thing, I do not know. But at all events, such a people, in its role as a monarch, not being controlled by law, aims at sole power[16] and becomes like a master, giving honour to those who curry its favour. Such a democracy is the counterpart of tyranny among monarchies. Hence its general character too is exactly the same: both play the master over the better sort of person, and the decrees of democracy are the directives of tyranny; the tyrant's flatterer is the same as, or analogous to, the demagogue, each exercising influence in his sphere, flatterers on tyrants, demagogues on peoples such as I have described. They are able to do this primarily because they bring every question before the people, and make its decrees sovereign instead of the laws. This greatly enhances their personal power because, while the people is sovereign over all, *they* rule over the people's opinion, since the multitude follows their lead. Moreover, the accusers of the officials claim that the decision ought to belong to the people; the people need no second invitation, and so all the offices are brought low.

1292a31 So if you were to say that such a democracy is not a constitution at all, your strictures would seem to be perfectly right. Where laws do not rule, there is no constitution. The law ought to rule over all, in general terms, and the officials ought to make rulings in individual cases; then we can decide we have a constitution. So if democracy is one of the constitutions, it is clear that this kind of set-up, where everything is governed by decree, is not a democracy at all, in the real sense; for no decree can have general validity. So much for the classification of democracy.

15. *Iliad*, II 204–5.
16. Literally, *monarchia*, 'rule by one'.

THE CLASSIFICATION OF OLIGARCHIES

Aristotle now fulfils the promise of the preceding chapter, to give a list of the various kinds of oligarchy, and appends a brief but valuable reminder that constitutions are not static, and do not always lend themselves to tidy classification: a democracy, for instance, may be a democracy in law, but an oligarchy in temper and operation; and these 'mixed' situations are produced particularly by changes of constitution. There is an important political truth here: a given formal or legal constitution may, in sufficiently determined hands, be 'manipulated' for ends radically different from its ostensible aims; this is indeed a danger inherent in the discretion allowed to officials under almost any constitution. Aristotle however barely begins to discuss this possibility, though the last sentence of the chapter suggests that he was aware of it.

1292a39 Of oligarchy there are four types. In (a), access to office is restricted by a property-qualification such that the not so well-off, though more numerous, have no share in the constitution, but a share is open to him who acquires property. In (b), there is a very high property-qualification, and they themselves[1] choose those who are without.[2] (If this choice is made from among all these,[2] the practice is considered to be aristocratic, if from a limited group only, oligarchical.) (c) This is hereditary, son succeeding father in office. (d) This also is hereditary, but the officials rule, not the law. This type of oligarchy holds among oligarchies a position analogous to

1. Probably existing 'sharers in the constitution': see the penultimate paragraph of IV vi.
2. I.e. 'those without a share in the constitution', though qualified in point of property.

that of tyranny among monarchies, and among democracies to that extreme democracy of which we have just been speaking. An oligarchy of this type is in fact called a 'power-group'.

1292b11 This completes our list of types of oligarchy and democracy; but it should not be forgotten that things often turn out differently in practice. There are plenty of instances of a constitution which according to its law is not democratic, but which owing to custom and training is democratic in its workings; conversely, there are in other places constitutions which according to law incline towards democracy, but by reason of their customs and training operate more like oligarchies. This is especially apt to happen after a change of constitution. The citizens do not at once discard their old ways, but are at first content to gain only moderate advantages from their victory over the opposing side, whichever that may be. The result is that the existing laws continue to be valid, but power is in the hands of those who have brought about the change in the constitution.

IV vi

(*1292b22–1293a34*)

FOUR TYPES OF DEMOCRACY AND FOUR OF OLIGARCHY

After the digression in the second part of IV v, Aristotle now gives a list of four kinds of democracy and then four of oligarchy; this latter list reads like an expansion of the first part of IV v, and the chapter as a whole has many points of affinity with IV iv and IV xiii.

The classification of democracies and oligarchies in this chapter is made in terms of what Aristotle sees as an inverse ratio *between the amount of property possessed by the politically dominant part of the state, and the rule of law: the greater the property, the greater the oppor-*

tunity for that part to seize the reins of power for itself, and the less willingness to let law rule. Aristotle thinks this analysis holds good both for oligarchy and for democracy; in the latter case, it was notoriously a mark of extreme democracy actually to pay holders of office a kind of salary out of state revenues, a practice which facilitated control of government by the poorer sections of the population. Connections between wealth and political power fascinated Plato too (see e.g. Republic VIII–IX and Laws 756b–e, 758b).

On payments to office-holders, cf. II xi, V viii, and M. H. Hansen, 'Misthos [pay] for magistrates in classical Athens', Symbolae Osloenses, 54 (1979), pp. 5–22.

1292b21 The statements already made have listed clearly enough the forms of democracy and oligarchy. For either all the aforementioned parts of the people must have a share in the constitution, or only some and not others. When the farming element, and the element in possession of a moderate amount of property, is the sovereign in the constitution, the constitution is operated in accordance with the laws, because so long as they work they have enough to live on; but they cannot afford to take time off,[1] so they put the law in charge and attend only the necessary meetings of the Assembly. But the rest of the population, as soon as they acquire enough property to qualify them according to the law, also have the right to participate. Thus *all* who have acquired it have that right. For where some do not enjoy the right to participate on any terms, that is a mark of oligarchy. But to have the right to take time off is not possible without revenue.[2] This then is one form of democracy, and these are its causes.

1. In order to hold office.
2. The text and meaning of this sentence are uncertain. As it stands, the train of thought seems to be '. . . but democracies, in imposing no property-qualification, do not solve the problem: participation still requires office-holders to be compensated from revenue for "loss of income" '.

1292b34 Another form of democracy is based on the next distinction: birth. Here office is open to all about whose birth there is no question,[3] but only those participate who can take time off. In such a democracy the laws rule because there is no revenue. A third form of democracy allows participation to all who are *free*, although they do not in fact participate for the reason already stated; so here too the law inevitably rules. The fourth type of democracy is in point of time the last to develop in states. The reason for this lies in their growth. Not only are they much larger than they originally were, but they have much larger revenues. Thus all participate, because the mass of the people preponderates; and even the poor, being able to have time off, take part in the administration of the constitution, receiving pay for doing so. In fact, the mass of the poor take the most time off: they have no encumbrances, while the wealthy, who have private affairs to look after, often do not take part in the Assembly and courts of law. Thus in this fourth kind of democracy it is not the laws that are sovereign in the constitution, but the mass of the poor.

1293a10 So much for the list of kinds of democracy and their characteristics, and the constraints that produce them. Here is the succession of types that can be observed in oligarchies. First, where those who own possessions are many but the amount that they own is on the small side and not too much, they allow participation in government to everyone who acquires possessions; and because of the large numbers who thus become members of the citizen-body, the laws and not the men are necessarily sovereign. This is because the further they are removed from the exercise of rule by a single person,[4] and possess neither so much that they can afford to neglect it and take time off, nor so little that they are maintained by the state, the more they are bound to

3. *Anupeuthunoi*: cf. IV iv, n. 14.
4. *Monarchia*.

think it best that the laws should rule for them, and not they themselves.

1293a21 Next, when the owners are fewer than in the previous case and their possessions larger, we have the second type of oligarchy. Having more power, they expect to make their position more profitable. So they restrict entry into the citizen-body from outside their number to those of their own choosing; but because they are not yet sufficiently powerful to rule without law, they lay down a law to fit the case;[5] if they intensify the process, and become fewer in number and greater in possessions, the third stage of oligarchy is reached. In this they keep offices in their own hands, but do so in accordance with a law which provides for sons succeeding their fathers at their death.

1293a30 The final stage is reached when they overtop all the rest in possessions and in numbers of friends; this kind of power-group is near to single rule,[4] the men being sovereign and not the law. This is the fourth form of oligarchy, corresponding to the last form of democracy.

IV vii

(*1293a35–1293b21*)

VARIETIES OF ARISTOCRACY

Aristocracy in the strict sense has already been dealt with in Book III, to which reference is made in this chapter. But since the essential thing about an aristocratic constitution is that it is composed of the best men, the word is often loosely applied to any constitution, such as that of Carthage and Sparta, which officially or unofficially attaches importance to choosing the best men, even when it is oligarchical in its pursuit of wealth, or democratic in its concern for the common people. Such constitutions

5. I.e. a law providing for the restricted entry, presumably.

show a mixture of aims, but they are not formally mixed constitutions like polity, which also, when it inclines towards oligarchy, is apt to get the epithet 'aristocratic'.

1293a35 There are besides democracy and oligarchy two constitutions, one[1] of which is generally recognized and has been included as one type in the list of four – monarchy, oligarchy, democracy, and what goes by the name of aristocracy. The other makes a fifth on that list, and is called by the name which is common to them all, for men call it 'polity'; but since it is rarely found in practice it is overlooked by the typologists of constitutions, who therefore, like Plato, give a list of only four in their *Constitutions*. Now the aristocracy which we dealt with earlier[2] in this work is aptly named, for this name is justly given only to that constitution which is composed of those who are without qualification best in virtue, not simply to one composed of those who are good in relation to some assumed situation. For only in the former type of aristocracy are good man and good citizen one and the same without qualification;[3] the good men in other cases are good only in relation to their own constitution.

1293b7 However, the name aristocracy is used of some constitutions to mark a distinction both from oligarchically run constitutions and from what we call polity – that is to say, it describes a constitution in which election to office depends on merit, not only on wealth. This constitution differs from the other two,[4] and is called aristocratic. For even in constitutions which do not publicly promote virtue there are nevertheless persons of good reputation who are regarded as respectable men.

1. Aristocracy.
2. III iv, v, vii, xv, xviii contain relevant material.
3. Cf. III iv. On the 'assumed situation' (*hupothesis*), cf. IV xi, n. 9.
4. Oligarchy and polity.

So where, as at Carthage, the constitution has a threefold aim, wealth, virtue and the good of the people, it is aristocratic; so too is that of Sparta, where there is a dual purpose only, virtue and the good of the people, and thus a mixing of the two (democracy and virtue). So we may say that apart from aristocracy properly so called, which is the best, there are these two[5] and also a third which occurs when what we call polity inclines rather towards oligarchy.[6]

IV viii

(1293b22–1294a29)

POLITY DISTINGUISHED FROM ARISTOCRACY

The main burden of this subtle and difficult chapter is to present polity as a mixture of oligarchy and democracy, and to combat the common tendency to call 'aristocracies' such of those mixtures as lean towards oligarchy. Since in the latter case the influence of wealth makes it confusingly easy to regard the mixture as an aristocracy (see note 3), Aristotle evidently wishes to restrict the use of 'polity' to those mixtures which do not produce the features characteristic of aristocracy (e.g. education, good government, virtue), or at any rate do not count them as qualifications for 'honours'. This thesis requires Aristotle to distinguish rather carefully not only between aristocracy and polity, but also between aristocracy and oligarchy.

The description of 'mixture of oligarchy and democracy' is not as it stands particularly illuminating, and in the next chapter Aristotle seeks to explain it in more detail.

1293b22 We have still to discuss what we call polity (and also tyranny). We have placed it here because it is

5. Carthage and Sparta.
6. Aristocracy is characteristically oligarchic: see III vii, IV ii.

not a deviation, and neither are the above-mentioned aristocracies. In strict truth they have *all* deviated from the most correct constitution, and so are counted among the deviations which we spoke of originally, and which are themselves deviations from *them*.[1] It is reasonable to defer mention of tyranny till the end because in comparison with the rest it is least of all a constitution, which is what our inquiry is about. Having explained why this arrangement has been adopted, I must proceed to discuss polity; for now that oligarchy and democracy have been explained, the function of polity becomes clearer, since, to put it in a word, polity is a mixture of oligarchy and democracy.

1293b34 But it is those mixtures which lean more towards democracy which are generally called polities, and those which lean towards oligarchy are called aristocracies, because education and good birth belong more to the better off. Moreover the well-to-do appear to *have* those things for the sake of which malefactors commit crimes; hence the rich are called 'people of quality' and 'notables'. Since therefore aristocracy aims at distributing the highest positions to the best of the citizens, it is said that oligarchies also are composed on the whole of 'people of quality'. But one thing I think is quite impossible: that a state which is controlled not by the best but by the worst[2] should be governed by good laws, and likewise that a state without such government should be ruled by the best. It is not government by good laws where the laws enacted are good but not obeyed. 'Government by good laws' should therefore be understood in two senses: obedience to the laws laid down, and well-enacted laws laid down by which people abide (it is quite possible to be obedient to badly enacted laws). And a further

1. I.e. from polity and the aristocracies mentioned. The reference is perhaps to III vii, where polity is briefly described; cf. II vi, 1265b26.

2. *Mē aristokratoumenē*, 'run not as an *aristo*cracy (*aristos* = 'best man'), but *ponērokratoumenē*, 'run by the bad' (*ponēroi*, i.e. oligarchs).

distinction is possible: obedience may be given either to the best laws available to them in the circumstances, or to the absolutely best.

1294a9 It is the especial mark of aristocracy that the distribution of honours should have been made in accordance with the virtue of the recipients. Virtue is the definitive principle of aristocracy, as wealth is of oligarchy, and freedom of democracy. The principle of majority-decision belongs to all three: in oligarchies and in aristocracies and in democracies, whatever has been decided by the larger part of those who participate in the constitution is sovereign. For most states, the form 'polity' is a misnomer, because the aim of the mixture is merely to have regard to the interests of both well-to-do and poor, both wealth and freedom, whereas almost everywhere the well-to-do and the people of quality are coextensive.[3] But since there are the *three* grounds for claiming equality in a constitution, freedom, wealth and virtue (a fourth claim, called 'good birth', arises out of the two last of these three, for good birth is wealth plus virtue going back to one's forbears), it is clear that the term polity should be applied to the dual mixture of well-to-do and poor, and the term aristocracy kept for the triple mixture. This is the most genuine of aristocracies after the true and primary.[4]

1294a29 I have now shown that there are other types of constitution besides monarchy, democracy, and oligarchy, and what their characters are. It is clear too how one aristocracy differs from another, and how polities differ from aristocracy; and that the two are closely related.

3. Wealth commonly leads to the virtues characteristic of an aristocracy of the 'people of quality' (*kaloi kagathoi*); only when it does *not* do we have a polity, as distinct from an aristocracy.

4. The triple mixture consists of freedom, wealth and virtue; the dual omits virtue. The 'true and primary' aristocracy pays regard to virtue *alone*.

IV ix

(1294a30–1294b41)

POLITY AS A MIXTURE OF OLIGARCHY AND DEMOCRACY

Aristotle now gives some practical advice on how a polity may be established by 'mixing' oligarchy and democracy. We may either (a) adopt the law of both, or (b) take neither's law as it stands, but effect a compromise, or (c) take parts of the law of each. Elucidation of (a) comes in the second paragraph of IV xiii.

Once again we see the perennial fascination of the Spartan constitution: cf. II ix and Plato, Laws 682e ff. and 712d ff.

1294a30 Our next task is to continue on from what has been said and describe how what we call polity develops in relation to democracy and oligarchy, and what has to be done in order to establish it. The definitive features of democracy and oligarchy will emerge at the same time; for we have to grasp the differences between these two, and then take as it were a 'tally' from each of them to put together.

1294a35 Now one may mix or combine in one or other of three definitive ways. The first is to take the legislation of both. For example, in the matter of judging, in oligarchies they impose a fine on the wealthy for non-attendance as jurymen in the law-courts, and they do not pay the poor for their attendance; in democracies no fines for non-attendance are imposed on the wealthy, and the poor receive pay for their services. Both these together constitute something in common and midway between them, and would therefore, as a mixture of the two, be characteristic of a polity. That is one way of joining the two. A second way is to take something intermediate between the two sets of provisions. Thus for membership of

261

the assembly in democracies there is no property-qualification (or only a very small one), whereas in oligarchies the property-assessment is high. Here something common is provided by neither, but by an assessment fixed midway between. The third method is from two sets of regulations to take one part from the oligarchical law, the other part from the democratic. For example, the filling of offices: to do this by lot is regarded as democratic, by selection oligarchic; a property-qualification is oligarchic, its absence democratic. Take therefore one from each, the oligarchical election of officials and the democratic freedom from property-qualification, and the result is both polity-like and aristocratic. So much for the *method* of mixing.

1294b14 A definitive feature of the *well*-mixed democracy and oligarchy is that it is possible to describe the same constitution either as democracy or as oligarchy. It is clearly the very excellence of the blending that creates this impression in those who thus describe it. A middle position has the same characteristic: each of the two extremes appears in it. This is exactly what happens in the case of the constitution of the Lacedaemonians. Many people try to describe it as a democracy, because the system has a number of democratic features: first the rearing of the children, under which the sons of the rich are reared in the same way as the sons of the poor and receive an education which the sons of the poor could also receive; then similarly in the next age group, and when they are grown up, the arrangements for feeding in the communal messes are the same for all, for thus there is no outward mark of distinction between rich and poor; and the rich wear clothing which any poor man could get for himself. There is also the fact that the people choose the members of the Council of Elders and share in the Ephorate, the two most important offices in the state. Others call it an oligarchy because of its many oligarchical features: the absence of the use of the lot, all officials being elected; the power of few to pronounce binding sentence of death or exile, and many other similar points. A constitution which is a really well-made combination of oligarchy and democracy ought to look like both and like neither.

1294b36 It should be kept stable by means of itself and not through outside agencies. It is not doing that when the number of those who wish it to continue make a majority (a condition which can equally arise in a bad constitution), but only when no section whatever of the state would even wish to have a different constitution. We have now mentioned the way in which polity ought to be established, and likewise the so-called aristocracies.

IV x

(1295a1–1295a24)

THREE FORMS OF TYRANNY

In the following short chapter on tyranny in relation to other types of monarchy Aristotle harks back to certain previous discussions (III xiv–xvii). That which is technically the rule of a tyrant need not necessarily be without law, and such rule has obvious resemblances to kingship. Discussion of tyranny, he claims, is therefore justified.

1295a1 It remained for us to say something about tyranny, not because there is much to say, but so that it might take its place in our inquiry; for even to it we assign a place of a sort in a list of constitutions. We defined kingship in an earlier part of this work and discussed whether, in the most usual sense of the word 'kingship', it was or was not a good thing for states, and also who is to be appointed king, and how and from what source. When dealing with kingship we also defined two forms of tyranny, because the power exercised by a tyrant in both cases in some sense overlaps with kingship too, both forms of rule being according to law. (For example, among certain non-Greeks, sole rulers with absolute personal power are *elected* to that office; and among ancient Greeks of long ago there arose sole rulers of this type, called *aisumnētai*.) In certain respects these two forms of tyranny differ from each other; but they were king-like because they were according to law, and because the sole rule was over willing subjects; yet they were tyrannical, because rule was exercised as by a master, according to the personal decisions of the tyrants.

1295a17 There is a third type of tyranny, thought to be the most extreme because it is the exact converse of absolute kingship. Any sole ruler, who is not required to give an account of himself, and who rules over subjects all equal or superior to himself to suit his own interest and not theirs, can only be exercising a tyranny of this third kind. Hence it is endured unwillingly, for no one willingly submits to such rule if he is a free man. These then are the kinds of tyranny, and the number of them; and they arise for the reasons given.

IV xi

(1295a25–1296b12)

THE MERITS OF THE MIDDLE CONSTITUTION

The 'middle' constitution which Aristotle recommends so enthusiastically in this important chapter seems to be the 'mixed' constitution of IV viii and ix (cf. III vii), considered from sociological, psychological and economic points of view rather than from a strictly constitutional one. He advocates that a large number of the citizens should each have moderate and adequate property, less than that of the rich and more than that of the poor. The effect of such a 'middle' population will be to diminish conflict between rich and poor, and to prevent the constitution from being an extreme one. In short, this chapter gives the conditions in which the technical, political and constitutional arrangements of the 'mixed' constitution or 'polity' are likely to prove acceptable and workable.

Aristotle attempts to justify the argument of this chapter by reference to one of his best-known philosophical principles, namely that virtue is a mean between two extremes. This ethical rule of thumb suggests the doctrine of a constitutional middle way easily enough, yet somewhat unconvincingly: what real parallel or affinity is there between a mean in conduct and a mean in the level of wealth of a section of the population or in the character of a constitution? Evidently Aristotle would make the connection by arguing that a middle class with a moderate income is disposed to 'mean' conduct, which suits a 'mixed' constitution. But this, if true, can be so only 'for the most part', to use one of Aristotle's favourite expressions: rich men have been known to act moderately, and people of moderate wealth can be savage in its defence.

In order to avoid possibly misleading associations with the technical Marxist concept of 'class', or with modern middle classes, I have, at the cost of some slight awkwardness, excluded the term 'middle class' from the translation. Aristotle usually says in this chapter merely hoi mesoi, *'the middle people', or* to meson *(neuter singular), 'the middle'; the nearest he comes to the notion of class is in his use of the word* meros, *'part' or 'section', e.g. at the beginning of the third paragraph, and in IV xii. As he makes clear at the beginning of the third paragraph, his analysis in this chapter of the structure of the state is based firmly on the amount of wealth possessed by each 'part'.*

1295a25 What is the best constitution and what is the best life for the majority of states and the majority of men? We have in mind men whose virtue does not rise above that of ordinary people, and whose education does not depend on the luck either of their natural ability or of their resources; and who have not an ideally perfect constitution, but, first, a way of living in which as many as possible can join and, second, a constitution within the compass of the greatest number of states. The 'aristocracies', as they are called, that we have just been discussing[1] do not fall within the competence of most states, but some of them do approximate closely to what we call polity (hence we ought to speak of both constitutions as though they were one and the same).

1295a34 The decision on all these points rests on the same set of elementary principles. If we were right when in our *Ethics*[2] we stated that virtue is a mean, and that the happy life is a life without hindrance in its accordance with virtue, then the best life must be the middle life, consisting in a mean which is open to men of every kind to attain. And the same principles must be applicable to the virtue or badness of constitutions and states. For the constitution of a state is in a sense the way it lives.

1295b1 In all states there are three state-sections: the very well-off, the very badly off, and thirdly those in between. Since therefore it is agreed that moderation and a middle position are best, it is clear that, in the matter of the goods of fortune also, to own a middling amount is best of all. This condition is most easily obedient to reason, and following reason is just what is difficult both for the exceedingly rich, handsome, strong and well-born, and for their opposites, the extremely poor, the weak, and those grossly deprived of honour. The former incline more to arrogance and crime on a large scale, the latter are more than averagely prone to wicked ways and petty crime. The unjust deeds of the one class are due to an arrogant spirit, the unjust deeds of the other to wickedness. Add the fact that it is among the members of the middle section that you find least reluctance to hold office as well as least eagerness to do so; and both these attitudes, eagerness and reluctance, are detrimental to states.

1295b13 There are other drawbacks about the two extremes. Those who have a superabundance of good for-

1. IV vii–viii.
2. E.g. *Nicomachean Ethics* I x, II ii, vi, VII xiii, X vii.

266

tune, strength, riches, friends, and so forth, neither wish to submit to rule nor understand how to do so; and this is engrained in them from childhood at home: even at school they are so full of *la dolce vita* that they have never grown used to being ruled. Those on the other hand who are greatly deficient in these qualities are too subservient. So they do not know how to rule, but only how to be ruled as a slave is; while the others do not know how to be ruled in any way at all, and can command only like a master ruling over slaves. The result is a state not of free men but of slaves and masters, the former full of envy, the latter of contempt. Nothing could be farther removed from friendship or from partnership in a state.[3] Sharing is a token of friendship; one does not want to share even a journey with one's enemies. The state aims to consist as far as possible of those who are like and equal, a condition found chiefly among the middle people. And so the best-run constitution is certain to be found in this state, whose composition is, we maintain, the natural one for a state to have.

1295b28 It is the middle citizens in a state who are the most secure: they neither covet, like the poor, the possessions of others, nor do others covet theirs as the poor covet those of the rich. So they live without risk, not scheming and not being schemed against. Phocylides' prayer was therefore justified when he wrote, 'Those in the middle have many advantages; that is where I wish to be in the state.'[4]

1295b34 It is clear then both that the best partnership in a state[3] is the one which operates through the middle people, and also that those states in which the middle element is large, and stronger if possible than the other two together, or at any rate stronger than either of them alone, have every chance of having a well-run constitution.

3. *Politikē koinōnia*, 'partnership/association that takes the form of a state'; cf. I i.
4. Fr. 12 in E. Diehl, *Anthologia Lyrica Graeca* (Leipzig, 1949–52), fasc. I. Phocylides was a gnomic poet of sixth-century Miletus.

For the addition of its weight to either side will turn the balance and prevent excess at the opposing extremes. For this reason it is a most happy state of affairs when those who take part in the constitution have a middling, adequate amount of property; since where one set of people possess a great deal and the other nothing, the result is either extreme democracy or unmixed oligarchy, or a tyranny due to the excesses of either. For tyranny often emerges from an over-enthusiastic democracy or from an oligarchy, but much more rarely from intermediate constitutions or from those close to them. The reason for this we will speak of later when we deal with changes in constitutions.[5]

1296a7 The superiority of the middle constitution is clear also from the fact that it alone is free from factions. Where the middle element is large, there least of all arise factions and divisions among the citizens. And big states are freer from faction, for this same reason, namely that their middle element is large. In small states it is easy for the whole body of citizens to become divided into two, which leaves no middle at all, and nearly everybody either rich or poor. Democracies too are safer than oligarchies in this respect and longer-lasting thanks to their middle people, who are more numerous and take a larger share of honours in democracies than in oligarchies. For when in their absence the unpropertied preponderate in numbers, trouble arises and they soon come to grief. An indication of the truth of what we have been saying is to be found in the fact that the best lawgivers have come from the middle citizens – Solon, for example, whose middle position is revealed in his poems, and Lycurgus, who was not a king, and Charondas and most of the rest.[6]

1296a22 These facts also show why most states are either democratic or oligarchic; for the middle being frequently small, whichever of the two extremes is on top, those with

5. V viii.
6. For Solon see II vii, n. 4 and II xii, n. 2; for Lycurgus see II ix, introduction; for Charondas see I ii, n. 7 and II xii.

possessions or the common people, abandons the middle and conducts the constitution according to its own notions, and so the result is either democracy or oligarchy. Then again, owing to constant strife and faction between the people and the wealthy, neither side, whichever of the two succeeds in gaining the mastery, ever sets up a constitution which is equally based and acceptable all round. Taking supremacy in the constitution as a prize of victory they proceed to set up a democracy or an oligarchy as the case may be. Also, those[7] who came to exercise leadership among the Greek states installed democracies or oligarchies in them according to the constitution which each had at home, looking entirely to their own advantage, not to that of the states themselves. So for these reasons the middle constitution has never occurred anywhere, or only seldom and sporadically. Only one[8] of a long succession of leaders was prevailed upon to allow a system of this kind. And to this day into whatever state you go, you will find that they have got into the habit of not even wanting equality: their aim is to rule, failing which they accept a condition of defeat.

1296b2 Which constitution is best, and why, will be clear from the above. As for the rest, the different kinds of oligarchy and democracy which we say there are, it is not difficult to arrange them in order of merit, this one better, that one worse, and so on; for now that the best is decided upon, proximity to it must denote better, and the farther away one moves from the middle, the worse; unless of course one judges by a reference to a given situation;[9] for often enough, although one constitution is more desirable, there is nothing to stop another from being, for some people, more advantageous.

7. The Athenians and the Spartans.
8. Solon? See n. 6. A. I. Dovatur, *Philologus*, 116 (1972), pp 309–11, suggests Alexander the Great; G. Huxley, *On Aristotle and Greek Society* (Belfast, 1979), pp. 55–6, argues for Hermias of Atarneus.
9. *Hupothesis*, i.e. a particular set of circumstances demanding *ad hoc* modification of the preferences of theory; cf. IV vii *ad init*.

WHY DEMOCRATS AND OLIGARCHS
SHOULD CULTIVATE THE MIDDLE GROUND

*This somewhat obscurely articulated chapter is a good
example of the informal and semi-systematic way in which
Aristotle's thought is apt to move. I interpret as follows.
Chapter xi (of Book IV) had concluded that in certain
circumstances the best or preferable constitution, the
'mixed' one based on the 'middle people', may be abandoned in favour of one more 'advantageous'. Aristotle
now naturally, and in apparent abandonment of the subject of the 'middle' people, is prompted to ask the
question: what constitution is 'advantageous' to what
sort of person? Obviously democracy to the many poor,
oligarchy to the wealthy few; but there will be no stability
in such constitutions unless the element that wishes it to
continue is 'stronger' than that which does not. Aristotle
suggests, if I understand him aright, that the numbers of
the poor may be 'stronger' than the 'quality' of the rich
(their wealth, education, etc.); or this 'quality' may be
'stronger' (meaning 'more influential', presumably) than
the numbers of the poor; in the former case, a democracy
is natural, in the latter an oligarchy. There is some point,
presumably varying from case to case, at which the ratio
between number and quality shifts decisively one way or
the other; and the greater the imbalance, the more
extreme will be the democracy or oligarchy that
results.*

*Now comes, at the beginning of the third paragraph,
the crucial junction of thought: both democracy and
oligarchy should always (sc. in spite of being, as such,
'advantageous' to their respective adherents) somehow
accommodate the 'middle people' – because thus the
'stronger' element will be even stronger, and the constitu-*

tion will be more stable; and of course without stability the constitution will not be as advantageous to the 'stronger' element as it might be. Stability is therefore in a sense the key to the chapter, which turns out to have been concerned all along, like its predecessor, with the constitutional merits of an influential 'middle people'. In effect it argues that even partisans of 'extreme' constitutions have or should have, on their own showing, an interest in cultivating the middle ground.

In the final paragraph, Aristotle notes that makers of aristocratic constitutions commit the mistake of trying to ensure stability not by 'mixing' their constitutions but by tricking the people. In the next chapter he proceeds to list some of the subterfuges employed.

1296b13 It is proper to follow what has been said by a discussion of the question of what constitution is advantageous for what persons, and what kind of constitution for what kind of men. First, we must grasp a principle which is universally applicable to them all: it is essential that that part of the state which desires the permanence of the constitution should be stronger than that which does not.

1296b17 Now every state can be measured either qualitatively – I mean by such qualities as freedom, wealth, education, and good birth – or quantitatively, that is by numerical superiority. Look at the parts which make up a state: it is possible that quality may be present in one, quantity in another (e.g. the non-noble may be numerically greater than the noble, the poor than the rich), but without quantitative superiority being enough to compensate for the qualitative inferiority. These must therefore be weighed one against the other. Where the number of the poor is sufficiently large to exceed the given ratio, there democracy naturally arises; and the type of democracy will depend on the type of people which has the numerical superiority in each case. Thus, if those who cultivate the soil make up the superior numbers, the democracy will come first[1] on the scale; if those engaged in mechanical work and receiving pay for it predominate, then it will come last,[1] and similarly with the rest in between. Where, on the other hand, the rich and notable people have a greater qualitative superiority than quantitative inferiority, there an oligarchy naturally arises, and once again its type will depend on the degree of superiority in those who form the oligarchical body.

1296b34 But at all times a legislator ought to endeavour to include the middle people in the constitution. If he is framing laws that are oligarchical in character, he should have the middle people always in view; if democratic, he should again make them attractive to those in the middle. Wherever the middle people outweigh a combination of the two extremes, or even one only, then there is a good chance of permanence for the constitution. There is no danger of rich and poor making common cause against *them*; for neither will want to be slaves to the other, and if they are looking for a constitution more acceptable[2] to both, they will not find any better than this. Their mistrust of each other would make it impossible for them to accept alternation in office. But in all places the mediator is best trusted by the parties, and the one in the middle is a mediator.

1297a6 The better mixed a constitution is, the longer it will last. It is a mistake made by many, even by those seeking to make an aristocratic constitution, not only to give too great a preponderance to the rich, but to cheat the people. In the long run mistaken good inevitably gives rise to unmistakable evil; for the greedy grabbing of the rich does more harm to the constitution than that of the people.

1. I.e. respectively the weak and the extreme form of democracy; cf. IV vi.
2. *Koinoteros*; cf. II vi, n. 3 and IV i, n. 3.

RIGHT AND WRONG STRATAGEMS TO ENSURE
A MAJORITY FOR THE CONSTITUTION

In the preceding chapters Aristotle has dwelt on the importance to a constitution of gaining the adherence of the majority (cf. introduction to II x), and in closing IV xii he had mentioned how this may be achieved by trickery. A list of such tricks is now given. Oligarchy can be made to appear less objectionable to the people in five ways, which may even strengthen its position. It is evidently less easy for democracies to delude oligarchs, and the question becomes merged in the general question of mixing the two into a moderate constitution. But it is by no means clear in this chapter when Aristotle is using politeia in the general sense of constitution and when he means 'polity'.

In the third paragraph Aristotle recommends a legitimate device, of allowing only arms-bearers to 'share in the constitution'; since Greek soldiers commonly had to supply their own equipment, this is in effect to fix a property-qualification that will exclude the poor but still ensure that supporters of the constitution are in a majority. (The recommendation does not spring from any particular admiration for soldiers as such.) After a brief historical review of the role of the armed forces as it affected constitutions, Aristotle rounds off his present set of topics by a summary that only partly corresponds to the first three items in the 'table of contents' given in IV i–ii.

1297a14 There are five devices which are employed against the people in order to give a constitution a more attractive appearance. They concern the Assembly, the offices of power, the law-courts, the carrying of arms, and physical training. Thus first, membership of the Assembly may be open to all, fines for non-attendance being imposed only on the rich (or much larger fines on them than on others). Next the offices: those with a certain property-qualification are not allowed to decline office by oath,[1] but the poor are. Thirdly the law-courts: fines are imposed on the rich if they do not serve as jurymen, but the poor are exempt (or else, as in Charondas'[2] laws, there are small fines in the latter case, large in the other). Sometimes membership both of Assembly and juries is thrown open to any persons who have their names put on the roll; but if, being thus enrolled, they fail to serve in the Assembly or the court, they incur large fines. It is the deliberate intention that the threat of a fine should cause people to avoid enrolment, and that non-enrolment should lead to their serving neither in law-court nor in Assembly. Similar regulations are made about carrying arms and gymnastic training: it is lawful for the poor not to possess arms, whereas the rich are fined if they do not have them. And if they fail to attend gymnasia, there is a penalty for the rich but none for the poor, so that the possibility of a penalty may cause the rich to attend; while the poor, having no penalty to fear, may absent themselves.

1297a34 These are oligarchical devices in the framing of laws; in democracies they are made in the opposite sense. They provide pay for the poor who serve in assembly or law-court, and impose no fine on the rich for non-attendance. That is why, if it is desired to make a just mixture of oligarchy and democracy, obviously the thing to do is to draw upon both sides and include both the payment for the one and the fine for the other. In this way all would have a share; otherwise the resultant constitution will be in the hands of one set or the other.

1297b1 Citizenship ought to be reserved for those who carry arms.[3] This means imposing a property-qualification,

---

1. I.e. an oath that one cannot afford to hold the position.
2. See I ii, n. 7 and II xii.
3. Literally, 'the *politeia*, constitution, should be made up exclusively of those who carry arms', i.e. they alone should be *politai*, citizens. By *politeia* Aristotle may however mean polity: see introduction to chapter.

whose amount cannot be settled absolutely and once and for all. The level must be fixed no lower than is absolutely necessary to ensure that the number of those who share in the constitution is larger than those who do not. For the poor are generally content enough, even if they do not share in honours, provided only that they are not liable to be ill-treated or deprived of any of their possessions. (That, however, is far from easy to achieve: members of a citizen-body do not always behave considerately.) And in time of war those who have no resources of their own are reluctant to serve as soldiers unless they are fed, but are quite ready to fight if rations are provided.

1297b12 In some places the constitution includes those who have served as hoplites[4] as well as those serving currently; this was the case in Malis, but only those on active service were elected to hold office. The earliest constitution (after the kingships) among the Greeks was in fact composed of warriors, of the cavalry in the first place, because it was in them that strength and superiority in war were to be found (for without organized formations a hoplite force is useless, and the ancients had no fund of experience of such things and no tactical procedures[5] for them, so that their strength rested with their cavalry). Then when states became larger and those with arms became stronger, the number of sharers in the constitution became larger. For this reason what we nowadays call 'polities' were formerly called democracies. But the constitutions of those early times were, understandably enough, oligarchical or royal; for owing to the smallness of the population their middle element was not large, and so, being neither numerous nor well organized, they were content to allow others to rule.

1297b28 We have now stated why constitutions are several in number, why there are others besides those commonly mentioned (there is not one kind only of democracy, and the same applies to the rest), and further

4. Heavy-armed infantry.
5. *Taxeis*, 'systems'.

what the differences are and the causes of them; and in addition which, speaking generally, is the best of the constitutions, and which kind among the others suits which kind of person.

IV xiv

(1297b35–1299a2)

THE DELIBERATIVE ELEMENT IN THE CONSTITUTION

Discussion of 'stratagems' in the preceding chapter now evidently prompts Aristotle to deal in the remainder of this book with various patterns of constitutional machinery that may be found 'expedient' in different constitutions – a topic which follows on here naturally enough, since there is practical value in it, and the book began with a reminder of the need to be practical as well as theoretical. Whatever be the form of government, it must provide for three things: (a) discussion and decision about what is to be done, (b) officers of state of all grades to carry out the policy, and (c) a judicial system. The combinations and permutations of the appointment of, and relationships between, the personnel of the deliberative, administrative and judicial functions of government are extremely complex and defy summary. On the assumption that Aristotle is not inventing them, or not all of them, out of his head as an academic exercise, they may serve to point up the immense variety of constitutional procedure evolved by the ancient Greek city-states, which we tend to forget through our customary concentration on some of the better-known examples (Athens in particular) of the major forms of constitution (democracy, oligarchy, etc.). As Aristotle often remarks, and as is abundantly clear from the Politics *as a whole, none of these forms was monolithic.*

We should beware of supposing that Aristotle's three-fold division of powers corresponds more than very

*roughly to the fairly sharp modern 'separation of powers'
as between legislature, executive and judiciary: he
evidently envisages considerable overlapping of functions.
Here again he reflects ancient Greek practice.*

1297b35 In dealing with our next topic we must speak
again about the constitutions, both in general terms applicable to all and also severally, using the appropriate
starting point. There are three elements in each constitution in respect of which every serious lawgiver must look
for what is advantageous to it; if these are well arranged,
the constitution is bound to be well arranged, and the
differences in constitutions are bound to correspond to the
differences between each of these elements. The three are,
first, the deliberative, which discusses everything of common importance; second, the officials (here we ask what
they ought to be, the limits of their sovereign powers, and
the methods by which they are selected); and third, the
judicial element.

1298a3 The sovereign powers of the deliberative element
cover decisions as to war and peace, the making and dis-
solving of alliances, legislation, the penalties of death,
exile and confiscation of goods, the choosing of officials,
and the scrutiny of their conduct on expiry of tenure. The
right to decide on all these matters must *either* be given
to all the citizens, *or* all to some (e.g. to one or more
officials, or some to some officials, others to others), *or*
some of them to all, others to some. To allow everyone
to decide, and on all matters, is democratic;[1] for such
equality is what the common people seek.[1]

1298a11 The principle that everyone should deliberate
may be applied in various ways: first, they may all perform the work but by turns rather than collectively (as in
the constitution of Telecles[2] the Milesian); and in others
there is an arrangement whereby the boards of officials
deliberate jointly, but everyone enters upon office in turn,

1. *Dēmotikon* = 'democratic', *dēmos* = 'common people'.
2. Not otherwise known.

from the tribes and the smallest parts until the whole process is complete, coming together only for legislation and for constitutional matters, and to hear pronouncements from the officials. A second method involves the collective action of everyone; but they come together only for the purposes of electing officials, making laws, deciding on war and peace, and holding scrutinies, the remaining matters being deliberated on by officials appointed for the purpose in each case, these officials being appointed either by lot or by election from among all. A third method is for the citizens to meet about offices and scrutinies, and to deliberate on wars and alliances, but for the other matters to be managed by the officials, as many of them as possible elected; and for such officials expert knowledge is an essential prerequisite. Under the fourth method all come together to deliberate about everything, and the officials take no decisions but only carry out preliminary investigations. This is the way a modern extreme democracy works, which we maintain corresponds to an oligarchy that is run by a power-group, and to a monarchy that is a tyranny.[3]

1298a33 All these four methods are democratic; but where only some deliberate about all matters, the principle is oligarchic. This principle likewise can be applied in several different ways: first, when those eligible to participate in deliberation are elected on the basis of a property-qualification that is not too high, and are on that account fairly numerous, when they obey the law and do not change what it forbids them to change, and when the attainment of the required property level permits one to participate – then, though an oligarchy, such a constitution by reason of its moderation is like a polity. Next, when not all participate in deliberation but only those elected, and they rule according to law no less than in the previous case, then that is oligarchic. When again those who control the deliberating themselves choose their

3. Cf. IV iv *ad fin.*, VI vi *fin.*

own members, and son succeeds father, and they control
the laws, that arrangement is necessarily and in the most
extreme degree oligarchical. Finally, when certain persons
have control of certain matters, such as when all control
war and peace and scrutinies, and the remaining business
is controlled by the officials who are appointed by election
and not by lot, the constitution is an aristocracy. When
some matters are under the control of elected persons,
others of those chosen by lot, and these latter are taken
either from all or from a pre-elected few, or the elected
and the lot-chosen function together, then some of these
features are characteristic of an aristocratic constitution,[4]
others of polity itself.

1298b11   We have now distinguished in this manner the
deliberative element in relation to the constitutions, and
the administration of each constitution is as indicated by
our analysis. But for what is nowadays reckoned to be a
democracy in the fullest sense (I mean one in which the
people is sovereign even over the laws) it is advantageous
to adopt, in order to encourage better deliberation, a
procedure used by oligarchies for their courts. I am referring to their practice of prescribing fines for failure to
serve as jurymen as a means of making sure that those
whom they want to serve really do appear in court (while
democrats provide pay for the poor). To do this in relation to the assembly would, as I say, be beneficial, as it
will ensure the presence of the notables as well as of the
people, and they will deliberate the better when each
side does so with the other. It is a good thing also that the
membership of the deliberative element should be determined either by election or lot, and, if by lot, then an
equal number from the sections of the population; and
also, whenever the democrats among the citizens are
numerically much superior, it is a good thing *either* not
to provide pay for them all for their attendance, but to

4. Or, 'of a polity with an aristocratic leaning' (*politeia aristo-
kratikē*).

pay only a number equal to the number of notables, *or* to eliminate the excess[5] by lot.

1298b26 In *oligarchies*, on the other hand, it will be found expedient to pick certain extra members from the mass of the people, or else, as is done in some constitutions, to set up a committee (pre-councillors, law-guardians, are the names given), and then to deal only with such business as has already been pre-deliberated by them. In this way the people will participate in deliberation without being able to set aside any of the provisions of the constitution. Alternatively, they should pass resolutions that are identical to, or at any rate not inconsistent with, the recommendations.[6] A further alternative is to bestow only advisory powers on everyone, reserving full deliberative powers for the officials. One should in fact do just the opposite of what is done in constitutions:[7] one should make the people sovereign when it rejects, not sovereign when it comes to approval, in which case there must be a reference back to the officials. In constitutions[7] they act in the reverse manner: the small body is sovereign in rejection, but not in approval, in which case the matter is always referred back to the larger body. This then is the way in which an analysis should be given of the deliberative and sovereign element in the constitution.

IV xv

(1299a3–1300b12)

THE EXECUTIVE ELEMENT IN THE CONSTITUTION

Aristotle now turns to the second of the three 'elements' he had enumerated at the beginning of IV xiv, the execu-

5. I.e. the number of persons by which the democrats exceed the notables (*gnōrimoi*).

6. Of the committee.

7. Or, 'polities'.

tive (or, as he puts it, the archai, *the 'offices' or 'officials').
He raises a large number of issues: (a) What kinds of
official are there? (b) Who appoints them? (c) From whom
are they appointed? (d) How are they appointed? (e) What
is their tenure of office? (f) What are their function and
powers? (g) How do the various officials operate in relation to each other? (h) Which officials, modes of appointment, powers and tenure etc. are appropriate for which
constitutions?*

*Aristotle's long and discursive treatment of these topics
is rich in observation and analysis, and two features of the
chapter are of special interest: (1) His attempt, in the
second paragraph, to isolate just what we mean by
'official', as distinct from persons merely 'in charge' of
something. As can be seen from Newman's comments and
references* ad loc. *(cf. also* III i *and Plato,* Laws *767a,
768c) the controversy was a live one. Aristotle briefly tries
various lines of approach and plumps provisionally for
the rather widely drawn criterion that officials deliberate,
decide and give orders – the last function being crucial.
But after these inconclusive remarks he drops the search
for definition as being of academic interest only. (2) His
elaborate analysis, towards the end of the chapter, of the
ways in which the various features of appointment may
be combined. Admittedly, this matter is of practical interest, as particular constitutions find it expedient to combine them in particular ways; yet, as he virtually admits,
he carries the mechanical analysis beyond the point where
it could serve any useful purpose. One wishes he had
devoted less energy to this enterprise and more to the
philosophically interesting question, 'What is an official
as distinct from a mere functionary?'*

1299a3 Next, we turn to classify the officials. Great
variety is also to be found in this element in the
constitution: questions arise about their number and the
scope of their sovereign powers, about the length of
tenure of office of each (it is made six months in some

cases, in others less, in others a year, but in yet others longer periods). Should tenure be perpetual, or for a very long term? And if neither of these, then the question arises whether the same persons should hold office repeatedly, or for one period only, being ineligible for a second. Then there is the officials' appointment – from whom are they to be drawn, by whom appointed, and in what manner? We ought to be able in all these matters to determine how many different ways are possible and then match them up, looking to see what sorts of officials are best for what sorts of constitution.

1299a14   Another question – and even this is not easy to answer – is, which kinds ought to be called 'officials'? The association which we call the state[1] needs a great many people to take charge of various things, so many that we should not designate them *all* as officials, neither those appointed by lot nor those elected. I am thinking in the first instance of the priests, whose position is quite different from the offices of state. Then there are the heralds and the trainers of choruses,[2] and envoys to be sent abroad, all these being appointed by election. Some responsibilities affect the state, and of these some affect all the citizens, for the purposes of a particular activity (e.g. a general, while they are under arms), others a section only (e.g. a controller of women or children). Other responsibilities affect the household;[3] for example, they frequently elect persons to measure out corn. There are also ancillary responsibilities which, when resources permit, will be performed by slaves. Roughly speaking, we may say that officials are those empowered to deliberate and make decisions on certain matters and to issue orders; and particularly the last, since this is the essence of rule. All this makes hardly any difference in practice; disputes about the terms have not resulted in any decision. But it

1. See I i.
2. *Chorēgoi*, persons appointed to meet the expenses of dramatic performances.
3. *Oikonomikai epimēleiai*, 'economic' responsibilities.

is a question which is open to further intellectual investigation.

1299a31 Turning to more difficult questions, we ask what kind of officials, and how many, are essential – essential, that is, if there is to be a state at all; we ask also what kind, while not essential, are yet useful for a sound constitution. Such questions need to be discussed in relation to every constitution, and in particular in relation to small states. For in the large states it is both possible and necessary to assign separate tasks to separate officials, one to each man because the large number of citizens makes it possible for many of them to sit on the committees, so that one man never holds the same office twice, or only after a long interval, and because every job gets done better when it is the responsibility of one official, not of many. In the smaller states, on the other hand, a number of offices have to be concentrated in a few hands (on account of the small population it is not easy for many to hold office, for who will there be to succeed?). However, sometimes the small states require the same officials and laws as the large; but whereas the small need the same persons to serve frequently, in the others this need arises only at long intervals. Thus there is really no reason why a number of different responsibilities should not be assigned together, because they will not hinder each other, and as a way of counteracting lack of manpower it is essential to make committees serve more than one purpose. (A hook will hang a roast as well as a lamp.) If therefore we can say how many officials are essential for any state at all, and how many are not essential but still ought to be there, then knowing all this we shall find it easier to deduce what sorts of offices are fit to be amalgamated into one.

1299b14 Another point not to be overlooked is fittingly mentioned here. What sort of matters ought to be supervised by many boards for different places, and which other sorts by a single official, whose authority is sovereign everywhere? I am thinking of such matters as keeping order in the market. Should there be a separate market-controller in every place, or one for everywhere? Should divisions be made according to the work or according to the persons? Is all regulation of good order a task for one man, or should there be a separate one for women and children? Similar questions arise when we consider offices in relation to constitutions. Does each constitution make some difference, or none, to the *type* of offices? Thus, are the same offices sovereign in democracy, in oligarchy, in aristocracy, and in monarchy, even though they are filled not from equal nor even similar people, but from different people in different constitutions – in aristocracies from the educated, in oligarchies from the rich, in democracies from the free? Or are there some offices that correspond precisely to the differences in the officials,[4] and in some places do the same offices serve best, in others different ones? For it may happen that here an extensive role, there a minor, for the same office fits the situation best.

1299b30 There are however offices peculiar to certain situations and not found everywhere, for example that of 'pre-councillors'. This is not a democratic institution, but the council itself is; for a body of this kind whose responsibility is to deliberate on business beforehand is necessary so that the people shall get through their work. If this council consists of only a few men, it is oligarchical. But *pre*-councillors must necessarily be few in number; therefore they are always an oligarchical feature. Where both offices exist, there the pre-councillors stand over the members of the council; for the councillor is a democratic

---

4. Who of course vary in character, tastes, views, etc., as indicated, according to the constitution under which they live. Aristotle debates the compatibility of various offices in various constitutions. The last few lines of this paragraph are however not entirely clear, and I have interpreted some details of the Greek in a way which may not command assent: see my note in *Liverpool Classical Monthly*, 4 (1979), pp. 93–5.

institution, whereas the 'pre-councillor' is an oligarchic one.

1299b38 The function of even the council may be weakened at the other end also, as in those democracies in which the people itself meets and takes a hand in everything. This is apt to happen wherever members of the assembly are well paid for their attendance, because this gives them time off to come to frequent meetings and decide everything themselves. A controller of children, a controller of women, and officers with sovereign powers to discharge responsibilities similar to these, are an aristocratic feature, not a democratic one (for who could prevent the wives of the poor from going out when they want to?). It is not oligarchic either, for the wives of oligarchs are rich and pampered.

1300a8 So much for the present on these matters; I must next try to describe from the beginning the ways of appointing officials. The alternative ways in which this can be done fall into three definitive groups, the combination and permutation of which will necessarily be found to include all the methods. First we ask who are those who make the appointments, second from among whom do they make them, third in what manner it is done. To each of these three questions there are three different answers: either all citizens appoint or only some do; appointments are made either from all citizens or from some specified persons,[5] the qualification for appointment being property-group or birth or virtue or some similar thing (as at Megara, where only those qualified who had been among the returning exiles who had fought together against the people);[6] and all this may be either by lot or by election. These coupled alternatives yield further couplings as follows: some appoint to some offices, all appoint

5. Abbreviated to 'some' in what follows, when the reference is to persons: 'some' as opposed to 'all'. 'Some' is also used in reference to offices/officials: 'some' as opposed to 'others'.
6. The reference is uncertain.

to others; some offices are filled from all, others from some; some are filled by lot, others by election.[7]

1300a22 [8]For each of these alternatives there is a choice of four methods: *all* appoint from all by election or all from all by lot; or all appoint from some by election or all from some by lot (and if from all, either by sections, for instance tribe, deme, or brotherhood, and so on through all the citizens, or else from all on every occasion); or partly one way and partly the other.[9] Again, if the appointers are only *some*, not all, the appointments may be made either by election from among all or by lot from among all, or by election from some, or by lot from some, or partly one way and partly the other – I mean partly by election from all, partly by lot, and partly by election from some, partly by lot. This gives twelve methods, apart from the two couplings.

1300a31 Of these modes of appointment, three are democratic – all appoint from all either by lot or by election or by both, that is, to some offices by lot, to others by election. But that not all should appoint at one time,[10] and either from among all or from some, by lot or election or both, or some officials from all and others from some, either by lot or election or both (that is, some by lot, some by election) – *that* is a characteristic of a polity. When some appoint from all, by lot or election or both (some officers by lot and others by election), that is oligarchical, and the more so when they appoint from both.[11] To

7. The essence of this paragraph is as follows. (A) *Appointers*: (i) All, (ii) some, (iii) all to some offices, some to others. (B) *Appointed*: (i) All, (ii) some, (iii) all to some offices, some to others. (C) *Mode*: (i) Election, (ii) lot, (iii) election for some offices, lot for others. Confusingly, all cases of (iii) are reserved for the last sentence of the paragraph.

8. On the two ferociously complex and textually corrupt paragraphs that follow, see Newman's commentary, Ross's and Barker's translations, and the appendix to this chapter.

9. I.e. the use of election for some offices, the lot for others.

10. I.e. all appointers fill some offices, some fill others.

11. I.e. some offices filled from among all, others from among some.

appoint[12] some officials from all, and others from only some, or some by election and others by lot, is characteristic of a polity, but with a bias towards aristocracy. But it is oligarchic when some appoint from some by election, and when some appoint from some by lot (it makes no difference that this is not in fact done), and when some appoint from some by both methods. When only some appoint from among all, and when all elect from some, that is aristocratic.

1300b5 Such then is the number, and classification in relation to the different constitutions, of the methods of appointing officials. Which method is best for what people, and how the appointments should be made, are questions which can only become clear in conjunction with decisions about what offices there are and what powers they have. By 'power' of an office I mean such things as sovereign control of revenue and of security; for the power of a general is different in kind from the function of controlling commercial contracts.

Appendix to IV xv

As Rackham remarks in the Loeb translation, 1300a22–b5 is a 'dizzy passage' (locus vertiginosus). If I understand it aright, the text down to a31 may be schematized as shown in the diagram. (In 1300a23 I read 'four', not 'six'.)

These are the 'twelve methods': 1–4 and 7–10 each describe a method of appointment to all offices; 5–6 and 11–12 each describe a method of appointment coupling election and lot, in the sense that some offices are filled by election, others by lot. (Line 5 is in effect a conflation of 1 and 2, 6 of 3 and 4, and so on.) The 'two couplings', which are not represented in the diagram below, are Ai + Aii (all appoint to some offices, some to others), and Bi + Bii (all are appointed to some offices, some to others). Each of the six 'alternatives', all couplings apart, has 'four methods', represented by the four ticks in each column which have two companions in the same horizontal

---

12. The appointers here are presumably 'all'.

'These (six) alternatives'
(1300a22)

THE APPOINTERS		THE APPOINTED		THE OFFICES	
All Ai	*Some* Aii	*All* Bi	*Some* Bii	*Election* Ci	*Lot* Cii
✓		✓		✓	
✓		✓			✓
✓			✓	✓	
✓			✓		✓
✓		✓		✓ +	✓
✓			✓	✓ +	✓
	✓	✓		✓	
	✓	✓			✓
	✓		✓	✓	
	✓		✓		✓
	✓	✓		✓ +	✓
	✓		✓	✓ +	✓

line; e.g. there are four ways of conducting an election by choosing officials from 'some' (Bii) of the persons qualified. Hence, the two missing couplings apart, A, B, and C have a total of 'twelve methods' (p. 286, middle).

In the second paragraph of the passage, Aristotle isolates which methods are characteristic of which constitutions, and complicates the picture still further by making use of all couplings, Ai + Aii and Bi + Bii as well as Ci + Cii (which is the most frequent): see footnotes for the less obvious instances.

IV xvi

(1300b13–1301a15)

THE JUDICIAL ELEMENT IN THE CONSTITUTION

Finally, Aristotle treats the third of the 'elements' enumerated in IV xiv, the judicial system. This chapter

exhibits broadly the same features as the preceding two:
it contains an analysis of types of court, a description of
how appointments of jurymen are made, and notes on
which modes of appointment suit which constitutions.

Aristotle assumes that there will be a separate court
for each of the eight main types of suit. The first of these
to be mentioned is the euthuna, *a scrutiny or investiga-*
tion made of an outgoing official's conduct. It is strange
that there is no mention of suits about legacies and about
property generally, which we know to have been of
frequent occurrence. But the whole chapter is only a
series of scraps and unfulfilled intentions.

1300b13 Of the three elements, only the judiciary now
remains to be discussed. Here too the various procedures
may be reviewed on the same principle. Courts of law
differ in three definitive respects: (a) *from whom* the
members are drawn, (b) the matters *about which* they
have jurisdiction, (c) the *manner* of appointment. In
regard to the first we ask whether members are drawn
from all or from some; in regard to the second we ask how
many types of court there are; in regard to the third we
ask whether appointment is by lot or by election.

1300b18 I begin with the second of these, the number of
types of court. There are eight of these, concerning
(1) scrutinies, (2) offences against the public interest, (3)
matters relating to the constitution, (4) disputes between
officials and private persons about the imposition of fines,
(5) private transactions of some magnitude, (6) homicide,
(7) foreigners, (8) minor transactions involving sums between one drachma and five, or a little more (for even
these require a legal decision, though not a body of jurymen). Under (6), there are four kinds of homicide court
(whether with the same or a different set of judges), concerning (i) deliberate slaying, (ii) unintentional slaying,
(iii) cases where the offence is admitted but justification
is claimed, and (iv) cases where the charge is brought
against persons exiled for murder, with a view to their

return. A reputed example of this is the court in Phreatto[1] at Athens; but such cases are rare at all times, even in large states. Under (7), there are two kinds, one for foreigners disputing with foreigners, the other for foreigners disputing with citizens. I will say no more about these,[2] or about the homicide courts, or about those concerning foreigners, but will speak of those relating to the state; for if these are mismanaged, divisions follow, and changes in constitutions.

1300b38 If all judge all the matters listed, they must be appointed either (i) by lot or (ii) by election, or (iii) partly one way and partly the other, or else, although dealing with the same matters, (iv) some by lot and others by election.[3] Thus there are four procedures, and four others where the appointments to the jury are made on a sectional basis. For once again, those who judge on all matters may be taken from some only, and may be appointed either by election or by lot (or partly by election and partly by lot); or some courts dealing with the same matters may consist both of elected members and of members appointed by lot. These then, as stated, are the procedures corresponding to those already listed.[4] But we may in addition have the same pairings, part of a court being appointed from among all, part from some, or from both together, as happens for instance if members of the same court are appointed some from all, others from some, and either by election or by lot or by both. The possible procedures relating to courts of law have now been stated; of these the first (from all and about all matters) is democratic, the second (from some and about

1. For a discussion of this court, see D. M. MacDowell, *Athenian Homicide Law in the Age of the Orators* (Manchester, 1963), pp. 82–4.

2. The minor transactions of court (8), which in the Greek text immediately precede 'I will say . . .'.

3. I.e. *either* all panels are (i) chosen by lot *or* (ii) elected, *or* (iii) some cases go to elected panels, some to panels chosen by lot, *or* (iv) some cases go to *mixed* panels.

4. In IV xv, presumably.

all matters) is oligarchic, the third (partly from all and partly from some) is characteristic of aristocracy and polity.

BOOK V

V i

EQUALITY, JUSTICE AND CONSTITUTIONAL CHANGE

The fifth book fulfils one of the promises made in IV ii – to discuss both the preservation and the dissolution of constitutions, and the respective causes. Minor changes not amounting to dissolution are mentioned briefly; but Aristotle is thinking chiefly of revolutions, carried through by violence or trickery (see V iv ad fin.), and resulting in a new constitution. This was the type of change most familiar and most feared; hence Aristotle shows some anxiety to avoid all change and to cultivate stability. Discontent is a constant threat to stability; and inequality, being a kind of injustice, is a potent cause of discontent; and as there is more equality in democracy than in oligarchy, the former is generally the more stable. The Greek word stasis, *which bulks large in this book, is not exactly 'revolution', but the state of affairs that leads to it, when tension has become so great that an outbreak of violence between opposing sides is on the cards. My usual translation of* stasis *is 'faction'.*

It is worth noting here a crucial point about stasis *and constitutional change in ancient Greece. The aim of those who wished for change was usually not simply to replace one policy by another within the same constitutional arrangements; it was to replace one complete constitution by another – to recast the whole set of rules by which political decisions were made.*

The first four chapters of the book discuss constitutional changes and their causes in fairly general terms, and the opening chapter is a fine example of Aristotle's shrewd analysis. He is here concerned not merely to list what circumstances lead to what changes, but to penetrate to the psychological or intellectual or 'ideological' sources of social conflict. These sources he locates in differing notions of distributive justice, which in turn depend on different criteria for measuring the equality and inequality of men. True to his intention to give practical advice, he counsels (as did Plato in the Laws *756e) the use of a judicious combination of 'arithmetical' equality and equality by ratio* (logos), *i.e. according to* axia, *value (i.e. merit or desert). For a discussion of these ideas in Greek thought, see F. D. Harvey, 'Two concepts of equality',* Classica et Mediaevalia, *26 (1965), pp. 101–46, and 27 (1966), 99–100.*

1301a19 We have now dealt with nearly all the matters that we promised, but we have still to discuss (a) what the sources are of change in constitutions, and the nature and number of these sources; (b) what the destructive agencies are that affect each constitution, and (c) from what kinds into what kinds they generally change. We must likewise consider (d) what factors make for the preservation of constitutions, both in general and of each kind separately, and also (e) by what means each of the constitutions could best be preserved.

1301a25 We should begin by assuming the fundamental starting point. Many constitutions have come about because although everyone agrees on justice, i.e. proportionate equality, they go wrong in achieving it, as mentioned before.[1] Democracy arose from the idea that those who are equal in any respect are equal absolutely. All are alike free, therefore they claim that they are all equal absolutely. Oligarchy arose from the assumption that those who are *un*equal[2] in some one respect are *completely* unequal: being unequal in wealth they assume themselves to be unequal[2] absolutely. The next step is when the democrats, on the ground that they are equal, claim equal participation in everything; while the oligarchs, on the ground that they are unequal, seek to get a larger share,

1. See III ix, xii–xiii.　　2. I.e. superior.

because 'larger' is unequal. Now all these constitutions have a sort of justice in them, but from an absolute standpoint they have gone wrong. And this is why, whenever either side does not share in the constitution according to their fundamental assumption in each case, they form factions. Those who are of outstanding virtue would have by far the greatest justification for forming factions (they are the only people to whom the term 'absolutely unequal' can be properly applied), but they least often do so. Then there are those who being superior in birth claim that they are too good for mere equality, just because of this inequality of birth; for those who have inherited virtue and wealth from their forbears are commonly reckoned nobly-born. These are, generally speaking, the origins of factions, the founts from which they spring.

1301b6 Hence the changes which take place may be of two kinds, according to whether they involve a complete abandonment of an existing constitution for another, or not. Examples of the former are from democracy to oligarchy, from oligarchy to democracy, from these to polity and aristocracy, or the reverse. In the other case they prefer the established arrangement (oligarchy or monarchy, for instance), but want to run it themselves. Or again it may be a matter of degree: they may wish an existing oligarchy to become more broadly or less broadly based, an existing democracy to become more democratic or less, and similarly with the other constitutions, either a relaxation or a tightening up. There are also attempts to change only a part of the constitution – the establishment or abolition of a particular office, for example the alleged attempt by Lysander to abolish the monarchy,[3] or of King Pausanias to abolish the Ephorate. In Epidamnus too there was a partial change in the constitution: they instituted a council in place of the tribe leaders, and it is still the rule that whenever any officer is appointed by vote, the existing officers, out of all the

3. Of Sparta, *c.* 399 (cf. V vii, n. 3); for Pausanias, see V vii, 1st paragraph.

members of the citizen-body, *must* be present at the public gathering. The sole archon too was an oligarchical feature of this constitution.

1301b26 Inequality is everywhere at the bottom of faction, for in general faction arises from men's striving for what is equal. I am speaking of states where there is no proportion in the unequals' inequality (a perpetual monarchy ruling over equals, for instance, is unequal). Now there are two kinds of equality, the one being numerical, the other of value. I use 'numerically equal' to cover that which is equal and the same in respect of either size or quantity, and 'equal in value' for that which is equal by ratio. Thus numerically the difference between three and two is the same as the difference between two and one, so that the amounts of difference are numerically equal. But the relationship of four to two is, by ratio, equal to the relationship of two to one: two is exactly the same fraction of four as one is of two, namely a half. But while men agree that absolute justice is justice based on value, they differ, as has been said before, in that one group believes that if they are equal in any respect, they are equal all round; while the others claim that if they are not equal in any respect, they ought to have unequal treatment in all matters. It is for this reason that there are, broadly speaking, two kinds of constitution, democracy and oligarchy. The number of people in whom noble birth and virtue are found is very small, but those other features are present in a larger number, so that while you could not find anywhere a hundred good men of noble birth, you could in many places find many rich and poor.[4]

1302a2 To lay it down that the equality shall be exclusively of one kind or the other is a bad thing, as is shown by what happens in practice: no constitution that is constructed on such a basis lasts long. The reason for this is that to start from an initial and fundamental error makes

4. Whose joint presence leads to the formation of oligarchies and democracies. Many *good* men would lead presumably to some form of aristocracy.

it impossible not to run into disaster at the end. Therefore we must make use both of numerical equality and of equality of value. Nevertheless democracy is safer and less liable to faction than oligarchy. In oligarchies, two factions arise, one between the oligarchs and the people, and one of the oligarchs among themselves. In democracies, on the other hand, the only faction that arises is against oligarchy;[5] *internal* faction within a democracy virtually never occurs. Also, a constitution of the middle people is nearer to democracy than is a constitution of the few, and is of all such constitutions the safest.

V ii

(*1302a16–1302b5*)

SOURCES OF CONSTITUTIONAL CHANGE (1)

Aristotle now analyses the causes of faction and constitutional change under three heads: (a) the condition of men, by which he seems to mean chiefly a psychological *state apt to prompt them to form factions; (b) the things about or for which the factions are formed; (c)* social *factors that produce the 'condition' of (a). His description of (a) draws on V i: the 'condition' is at bottom discontent at the absence of equality and justice, in whatever sense these terms are understood by the person feeling the discontent. Under (b) come honour and profit, in the sense that men form factions in order to attain them. Honour and profit are also listed under (c), as* causes *of the 'condition' of (a), along with ill-treatment, contempt, etc.: men become disposed to form factions because they* see *unjust gains of profit and honour by others. Group (c) concludes with a bare list of influences that produce men inclined to faction, presumably over a fairly lengthy period of time.*

5. I.e. in effect against those persons who *favour* oligarchy.

1302a16 Since we are considering the sources of factions and changes affecting the constitution, we must begin by getting a general grasp of their origins and causes. These fall into three main groups, and we must classify them in outline accordingly: first we have to understand the conditions that lead to faction, secondly, the objects aimed at, and thirdly all the various origins of political unrest and of factions among the citizens.

1302a22 That which causes conditions leading to change is chiefly and generally what we have just been speaking of:[1] inequality. For those who are bent on equality resort to faction if they believe that though having less, they are yet the equals of those who have more. And so too do those who aim at inequality and excess, if they think that though unequal, they do not have more, but equal or less. (These desires are sometimes just, sometimes not.) The lesser form factions in order to be equal, the equal in order to be greater. These then are conditions predisposing to faction. Second, as to what is at issue between the factions: we find this to be profit and honour, also their opposites; for it is in striving to avoid dishonour and loss, whether for their friends' sake or for their own, that men resort to factions in their states. Thirdly, the origins and causes of the changes[2] – in the sense of things which make men feel in the way described and strive for the objects mentioned – there are perhaps seven of these, but the list could well be extended. Two of them are the same as already stated: (i) profit and (ii) honour, but operating in a different way. They play a part now, not by stimulating men to fight against each other in order to acquire them, as in the former description, but because men see others getting a larger share of them, some unjustly, some justly. The five other causes in this group are (iii) ill-treatment, (iv) fear, (v) preponderance, (vi) contemptuous attitudes, and (vii) disproportionate increase. To these we may add, as stimuli of a different sort, (viii) the soliciting

1. V i.
2. I.e. presumably changes from one constitution to another.

of votes, (ix) lack of vigilance, (x) imperceptible changes, and (xi) dissimilarity.

V iii

(*1302b5–1303b17*)

SOURCES OF CONSTITUTIONAL CHANGE (2)

This chapter describes the operation of the influences listed at the end of V ii (the enumeration – i, ii etc. – is the same in both chapters). Aristotle gives fairly extended treatment to the last of them, 'dissimilarity', by which he apparently means dissimilarity of family or lineage or state. The conflicts he describes under this head do not seem to have been inspired by ideological or religious beliefs in the essential superiority or inferiority of certain races – at least so far as one can tell from his account; and in this respect modern racial conflicts are often more complicated than those he mentions here (but cf. VII vii, init.). In the paragraph devoted to 'disproportionate increase' we again notice one of Aristotle's favourite analogies, that between body and state (cf. introduction to I i, and references there). Of the final four influences (viii–xi), Aristotle notes that three lead to revolution without faction. Finally, he discusses (xii) the influence of geography.

1302b5 What effect (iii) ill-treatment and (i) profit have, and how they operate as causes, hardly needs to be pointed out. When those in office ill-treat others and get larger shares for themselves, men form factions both against each other and against the constitution to which they[1] owe their power to act; and these greater shares are won sometimes at the expense of individuals, sometimes at the expense of the common interest. Obvious also is

---

1. The officials, presumably.

the effect of (ii) honour, and how it can operate as a cause of faction: those who see others honoured, and are themselves not honoured, turn to faction; and the situation is certainly unjust whenever either the honour or the lack of it is contrary to deserts, but it is just whenever it is in accordance with them. Next, (v) preponderance: this is to be seen in any case where one or more men exercise power out of all proportion to the state or to the power of the citizen-body. Monarchy and a power-group commonly emerge, one or other of them, from these conditions. That is why the practice of ostracism is followed in some places, Argos and Athens for example. But it is much better to look ahead and prevent the rise of such excessive predominance than to let it appear and look for a remedy afterwards.

1302b21 As for (iv) fear, it operates in two ways: those who have committed a crime turn to faction because they fear punishment; and those who expect to be wronged by others want to forestall it, like the notables at Rhodes, who conspired against the people on account of lawsuits that were being brought against them.[2] (vi) Contemptuous attitudes too lead to faction and revolt. In oligarchies, for instance, when those who have no share in the constitution are more numerous, they deem themselves more powerful. This attitude is also found in democracies, when the wealthy show their contempt of disorder and lack of government. At Thebes the state was so badly managed after the battle of Oenophyta[3] that the democracy was wrecked; so too was that of Megara, because of a defeat produced by disorder and lack of government, and similarly in Syracuse before the tyranny of Gelon,[4] and in the case of the democracy at Rhodes before the uprising.

1302b33 How (vii) disproportionate increase may be-

---

2. See V v, n. 2. Many of the other historical details of this paragraph are too vague for certain identification and dating.

3. Where Thebes fought Athens in 456.

4. 485–478; cf. V x, 1312b10 ff.

come a cause of constitutional change may be illustrated
by a comparison with our bodies. The body consists of
parts, and all increase must be in proportion, so that the
proper balance of the whole may remain intact, since
otherwise the body becomes useless,[5] as would happen if
feet four cubits long grew on a body two spans high, or if
the body were to change into the shape of some other
animal, because of disproportion in the *kind* of growth,
not only in the amount. So too a state consists of parts,
one of which may increase without being noticed. For
example, in democracies and polities there is apt to be an
increase in the number of those who are not well-off.
Sometimes this is due simply to chance events. Thus at
Tarentum many of the notables were defeated and slain
by the Iapygians; then, soon after the Persian wars, a
democracy took the place of a polity. So too at Argos,
when as a result of the slaying by Cleomenes the Spartan
of the 'seventh-day people'[6] they were obliged to bring in
some of the peripheral populations. At Athens, losses in
land-battles reduced the numbers of notables because
during the war against Sparta it was from a list of *their*
names that the soldiery was drawn. This kind of thing[7]
may occur, though more rarely, in democracies too, for
when the number of the notables grows, or their possessions increase, changes to oligarchies or power-groups
result.

1303a13 Changes of constitution can take place even
without faction, because of (viii) soliciting of votes, (ix)
lack of vigilance, and (x) change so gradual as to be imperceptible. (viii) At Heraea they changed from holding
elections to drawing lots, simply because they found that
the successful candidates were those who solicited votes.

---

5. *Phtheiretai*, 'is spoiled, wrecked', the same verb as was used to
describe the destruction of democracy in the preceding paragraph.
Cf. I ii, n. 20.

6. I.e. 'those who died on the seventh day (of the month)'; or
perhaps 'those in the seventh tribe'. The date is probably 494.

7. I.e. disproportion.

(ix) It is owing to lack of vigilance that those who are not friendly to the constitution are sometimes allowed to get into the supreme offices. This is what happened at Oreus, where Heracleodorus became one of the officials and set up a polity,[8] or rather a democracy, in place of the oligarchy, which was overthrown. (x) Then there is extreme gradualness: it very often happens that a considerable change in a country's customs takes place imperceptibly, each little change slipping by unnoticed. Thus in Ambracia the property-qualification for office was small, but it was gradually reduced and became so low that it might as well have been abolished altogether.

1303a25 Then there is (xi) difference of stock, which remains a stimulus to faction until such time as the two groups learn to live together; for just as a state cannot be made out of any and every collection of people, so neither can it be made in any space of time at will. Hence faction has been exceedingly common when the population has included an extraneous element, whether these have joined in the founding or have been taken on later. Thus Achaeans were associated with Troezenians in the founding of Sybaris,[9] then, becoming more numerous, they cast out the Troezenians. (This was the origin of the curse of the Sybarites.) In Thurii too Sybarites quarrelled with the rest of the founders, claiming greater shares on the grounds that the land belonged to them, and they were expelled. At Byzantium the fresh colonists hatched a plot, but were found out and expelled after a fight. The people of Antissa after receiving Chian exiles fought with them and threw them out. The people of Zancle accepted a number of Samians, but they themselves were forced to leave. The people of Apollonia on the Euxine Sea brought in additional settlers, and then turned to faction. At Syracuse after the period of tyranny they made citizens of the foreigners, the mercenary soldiers, and then formed factions and turned to fighting. Most of the Amphipolitans

8. Perhaps in 377.   9. About 720.

were expelled by the Chalcidic settlers whom they had
brought in.

1303b4   [10]In oligarchies the many rebel on the ground of
not being justly dealt with, on the ground that although
they are equal they are not getting equal treament, as I
said earlier. In democracies it is the notables who rebel,
because, though not equal,[11] they get merely equal treatment.

1303b7   Sometimes there are (xii) geographical reasons
for faction: the lie of the land may not be conducive to
the unity of the state. Thus at Clazomenae those on the
Mole were at variance with those on the Island, likewise
the Colophonians and Notians. At Athens there is a difference between the dwellers in the city itself and those in
Piraeus; the latter are more emphatically democratic in
outlook. We know how in warfare the crossing of water-
courses, even of quite small ones, tends to cause troops to
split up. So it seems that every distinction leads to division.
Perhaps the greatest division is between virtue and vice,
after that the distinction between wealth and poverty, and
the rest after that in varying degrees. In this final group
comes the one we have mentioned.[12]

V iv

(*1303b17–1304b18*)

THE IMMEDIATE OCCASIONS OF
CONSTITUTIONAL CHANGE

*The first four paragraphs of this chapter recognize that
the* immediate *causes of factions, which in themselves may
concern important issues, may be quite trivial – typically
a quarrel between powerful persons, which serves to bring
the discontents of opposing sides to 'flashpoint' and ulti-*

10. This paragraph seems misplaced at this point.
11. I.e. they are superior.
12. I.e. the geographical.

mately involves the whole state. (Aristotle does not say so, but presumably antecedent conditions would have to be suitable: no quarrel could have such an effect if feelings on either side were not already exacerbated.) The next paragraph in effect links the theme of trivial or accidental or unlooked-for causes to a theme of V iii: excessive preponderance of one part of the state; for a preponderance may come about for reasons that have nothing to do with the faction which it ultimately provokes. These themes lend themselves to anecdotes, and Aristotle draws tellingly on his store of historical instances. He then briefly notes that faction may also arise, under certain conditions, when opposing parts of the state are equally balanced. A few remarks on the use of force and fraud conclude his discussion of constitutional change in general, and in V v he turns to particular constitutions.

1303b17 Now factions, though arising from small matters, are not concerned with them but with large issues; and even small factions are important when they occur among those in sovereign power. An example of this happened at Syracuse in early times,[1] when the constitution changed as a consequence of faction between two young men, both from among the office-holders, caused by a love-affair. When one of the two was away from home, the other seduced the boy-beloved of his friend. He in turn showed his indignation by inducing the other's wife to come to him. As a result, all members of the citizen-body were enlisted on one side or the other, and were divided into two factions. It is therefore essential to guard against this kind of thing at the very start and resolve all factions among leaders and those in powerful positions. The false step is at the beginning, but 'well begun is half done', as the proverb says, so that a small error at the start is

1. Perhaps in 485, before Gelon's tyranny, or a little earlier: cf. V iii, n. 4.

equivalent in the same proportion[2] to those of the later stages.

1303b31 Disputes among the notables generally have an effect on the whole state, as happened in Hestiaea after the Persian wars, when two brothers quarrelled over the distribution of their father's estate. One of them, the poorer, when his brother did not openly declare the amount of the property or reveal the cache which the father had discovered, won the support of the democrats. The other, who possessed a great deal, was supported by the wealthier class.

1303b37 At Delphi a quarrel arising from a marriage-alliance was at the bottom of all the later factions. The intended bridegroom, forecasting bad luck by an omen which he saw when he came to fetch his bride, went away without her. Her family considered that they had been ill-treated, and when the young man was sacrificing, they planted some temple-property, and subsequently put him to death for sacrilege.

1304a4 At Mytilene,[3] too, faction arising out of heiresses was at the root of many troubles, including that war with the Athenians in which Paches captured their state. Timophanes, one of the wealthy, died and left two daughters. A certain Dexander wanted them for his two sons, but was rejected and came away empty-handed. Then, being local commissioner[4] for Athenian affairs, he started the faction which spurred Athens into action. At Phocis faction arose out of an heiress, between Mnaseas father of

2. I.e. a bad start which vitiates the first half is as serious as all the mistakes of the second half, and so stands in the 'same proportion' to the whole as they all do, i.e. the proportion of a half. Aristotle may be punning on the word *archē*, which means not only 'start' but 'rule'/'ruler'/'official'; if so, perhaps 'stages' (*merē*) ought to be rendered 'parts' (of the state).

3. 428; cf. Thucydides III i ff.

4. *Proxenos*, 'representative' of a foreign state, but not a citizen of it. Dexander would therefore have been a Mytilenean, not an Athenian.

Mnason and Euthycrates father of Onomarchus; and this faction became the origin for the Phocians of the Sacred War.[5] At Epidamnus also a change of constitution arose out of matrimonial affairs. Someone had promised his daughter in marriage; the father of the intended bridegroom became one of the officials and imposed a fine on this man who, feeling insulted, attracted to his side those who were not sharers in the constitution.

1304a17 Another set of causes which may lead to change into democracy, into oligarchy, or into polity, is to be seen when a committee or a part of the state becomes great in size or esteem. Thus at Athens the Council of the Areopagus, after having been greatly in esteem during the Persian wars, was considered to have tightened up the constitution. Then conversely the Athenian democracy was strengthened by the crowd who served in the navy and who had been responsible for the victory at Salamis, because the leadership of Athens thus gained rested on sea-power. At Argos the notables gained much credit for the battle against the Spartans at Mantinea and tried to use the occasion to put down the democracy; while at Syracuse responsibility for the victory in the war against the Athenians belonged to the people, who changed the constitution from a polity into a democracy. At Chalcis the people joined with the notables in removing the tyrant Phoxus and then seized hold of the constitution; and in Ambracia the people joined with his attackers to cast out the tyrant Periander and got the constitution into their own hands.[6]

1304a33 The important thing to remember is that those who are responsible for the acquisition of power, whether they be private individuals or officials or tribes, or whatever aggregate or part you will, it is they who provoke faction. They may do so indirectly, as when the rest, jealous of the honour bestowed on them, start up the faction, but also directly, when they themselves are so

5. 355–347, against Thebes.
6. About 581; cf. V x, n. 14. Ambracia was a city in N.W. Greece.

preponderant that they are no longer content to remain on terms of equality with the rest.

1304a38   Constitutional changes are provoked also when what are regarded as opposing sections of the population are evenly balanced, such as the rich element and the people, but there is no middle element or only a very small one. For when one section of the population, whichever it may be, is preponderant, the other is not likely to risk opposing those who are obviously stronger. It is for this reason that those who are superior in virtue hardly ever start a faction: they amount to a few against many.

1304b5   Generally, then, in all types of constitution the causes and beginnings of factions and of changes are as I have described. As to method, violence and trickery are both used, violence sometimes immediately, at the beginning, but sometimes by way of subsequent compulsion. The use of trickery also is dual. In the one case they are successful in their deceit, and their change of the constitution is at first readily accepted, but subsequently they use force to keep control of it in spite of opposition. An example of this is seen in the rule of the Four Hundred:[7] they deluded the Athenians by saying that the king of Persia was going to supply money for the war against Sparta. This was not true, but they went on trying to keep control of the constitution. In the other case they use persuasion from the start and then go on using it in such a way that their rule is willingly accepted.

What has been said above describes in general terms change in all constitutions.

7. In Athens, 411.

V v

(1304b19–1305a36)

WHY DEMOCRACIES ARE OVERTHROWN

Having dealt with the general causes of constitutional change, Aristotle now turns to the particular causes of change in particular constitutions. The central theme of this chapter is that democracy is apt to be overthrown because of its own internal excesses: democratic leaders (demagogues), in their zeal to gain and retain the support of the common people, take such stringent measures against the wealthier classes as to provoke them forcibly to resist; and the result is often oligarchy. (In earlier times, for accidental reasons which Aristotle analyses, popular leaders were able to establish tyrannies.) Aristotle was, of course, not particularly well-disposed to democracy (though his treatment of oligarchs in V vi is just as un-sympathetic), and his suggestion that the upper classes were 'obliged' to resist 'unprincipled' popular leaders has the ring of polemic. Plato's picturesque and more ex-plicitly hostile account of democracy and its decline should be compared (Republic, 555 ff.).

This chapter is full of examples taken from Greek his-tory: but Aristotle's references, while self-explanatory as far as they go, are fairly swift: for full discussions the reader should consult the commentaries and R. Weil, Aristote et l'histoire: essai sur la 'Politique' *(Paris, 1960).*

1304b19 But we must take each type of constitution separately and observe how these general tendencies work out in practice. In democracies the most potent cause of revolution is the unprincipled character of popular leaders. Sometimes they bring malicious prosecutions against the owners of possessions one by one, and so cause them to join forces; for common fear makes the bitterest of foes cooperate. At other times they openly egg on the multitude against them. There are many instances of the kind of thing I mean.

1304b25 At Cos the democracy was replaced when wicked popular leaders arose, the more notable citizens combining against them.[1] Similarly at Rhodes, when the popular leaders *both* provided pay for the public office *and* tried to stop the refunding to naval commanders of the expenses which they had incurred. These, therefore, weary of the lawsuits brought against them, were obliged to form an association and put down the democracy.[2] At Heraclea too the democracy was brought low just after the foundation of the colony – and all because of their own leaders, whose unjust treatment of the notables caused them to leave; finally the exiles gathered forces, returned, and put down the democracy. The democracy at Megara too was dissolved in a similar way: here the popular leaders, in order to confiscate their money, banished many of the notables; this went on until the number of those thus exiled became so large that they returned, won a battle against the people, and set up the oligarchy.[3] The same thing happened also at Cyme in the time of the democracy whose fall was brought about by Thrasymachus.

1305a2 From inspection of the other cases also you can see that changes take place pretty well after the same manner: in order to win the favour of the multitude they treat the notables unjustly and cause them to unite. Sometimes they make them split up their possessions or income in order to finance their public duties;[4] sometimes they bring slanderous accusations against the rich with a view to confiscating their money.

1305a7 In earlier times a change from democracy to

1. Perhaps in 357.

2. Probably in 390, perhaps in 357; cf. V iii. The suits would have been brought by contractors for equipment etc. who had not been paid by the naval commanders (*triērarchoi*).

3. Heraclea Pontica was founded as a colony of Megara about 560. 'Confiscate' = dēm*euein*.

4. *Leitourgiai*: see IV iv, n. 11.

tyranny took place whenever popular leader and military leader were one person; indeed most of the early tyrants started by being popular leaders. The reason why this does not occur nowadays is that in the old times popular leaders were drawn from those who led the troops, for as yet there were no skilled speakers. Today with the spread of skill in oratory the able speakers become popular leaders, but owing to their ignorance of warfare they do not attempt to seize power, except in a few insignificant instances. Another reason why tyrannies arose more frequently in the past than they do today is that certain individuals had offices of great power entrusted to them: at Miletus, for instance, tyranny arose out of the office of presidency, for the president had many and great sovereign powers.[5]

1305a18 A further reason is that cities were smaller in those days and the people lived all over the countryside, busy with their labours there; so their champions, if they were military men, used to aim at tyranny. They would all do this because they had the confidence of the people, a confidence based on hostility to the rich. At Athens, for example, Peisistratus led a revolt against the dwellers on the plain;[6] at Megara Theagenes found the rich men's cattle put out to graze on the others' land by the river and slaughtered them;[7] and Dionysius, accuser of Daphnaeus and the rich, was judged to be deserving of his office of tyrant because this hostility won him trust as a man of the people.[8]

1305a28 Change also takes place in another direction – from ancestral democracy to the modern. For when

5. The reference is possibly to Thrasybulus' seizure of a tyranny, *c*. 610. The precise functions and powers of the Milesian 'president' (*prutanis*) at this time are obscure.

6. Peisistratus was tyrant of Athens from 561 to 527, apart from certain intervals spent in exile. The 'dwellers on the plain' were wealthy land-owners.

7. The date of Theagenes' tyranny is during the second half of the seventh century.

8. Dionysius I was tyrant of Syracuse from 405 to 367.

officials are chosen by election, and not on the basis of property-classes, and the people are the electors, those who are eager to secure election lead the people on and on, until they make them sovereign even over the laws. A remedy to prevent or diminish this tendency is to make the tribes nominate the officials and not the whole people.[9]

Such are, in general, the causes of all changes as they affect democracies.

V vi

(1305a37–1306b21)

WHY OLIGARCHIES ARE OVERTHROWN

Aristotle seems to think of the causes of the overthrow of oligarchies as falling broadly into two classes, internal and external. Yet his exposition makes it clear that the distinction is not particularly neat: in the third paragraph, for instance, demagogues within an oligarchy rely on the support of the people, whom they encourage to exert external pressure. Nevertheless, Aristotle evidently thinks of this as an 'internal' cause, in the sense that it is rivalry among the oligarchs that causes them to seek among the people a wider base of support. In practice, as he recognizes, internal and external causes react on each other in a variety of complex ways. His presentation is slightly confused by his tendency to 'exalt the occasions of constitutional change into causes' (Newman IV, 345), as for example in the case of the purely personal animosities in paragraph six, which must have been merely the accidental trigger for the expression of more widespread discontents (cf. V iv). But rough-and-ready as some of his analysis may be, its fullness of detail is impressive, and

---

9. Election by tribes could take various forms. The advantage that Aristotle sees here is that it hinders the *direct* relationship between people and popular leader.

serves to remind us once more that Greek constitutional forms were not monolithic but exhibited tremendous variety of origin, rise and fall. Indeed, Aristotle concludes the chapter by remarking that oligarchies and democracies change not only into each other but into different species of the same form.

1305a37 Turning now to changes in oligarchies, we find that the two chief ways in which they occur are the most conspicuous. One is when the oligarchs wrong the multitude, in which case any champion is good enough, particularly when the multitude happens to be led by someone from the oligarchy itself, like Lygdamis at Naxos who afterwards actually ruled as tyrant there.

1305b1 There are also various ways in which faction originating from other people may cause an oligarchy to fall. Sometimes the initiative comes from the rich themselves, from those of them who are not included among the officials, when the number of those enjoying such honours is very small. This has been known to occur in Massalia, in Istros, in Heraclea, and in other states. Those who had no share in the offices kept on agitating until first elder brothers and then the younger were admitted to a share. For in some places it is not permitted that father and son should hold office simultaneously, in others not elder and younger brothers. At Massalia, the oligarchy changed into something rather like a polity, but at Istros it ended by becoming a democracy, and at Heraclea the few were increased to 600. At Cnidos too change was due to strife among the notables themselves, owing to the fact that the numbers participating were small, and, as has been mentioned, if a father did so, a son might not, and of a number of brothers only the eldest. The people intervened in the faction, chose a champion from among the notables, and carried out a successful *coup* (faction makes an easy prey). At Erythrae too in early times, under the oligarchy of the Basilidae, in spite of the excellent way

314

in which those included in the constitution were discharging their responsibilities, the people, chafing at rule by a few, changed the constitution.

1305b22 The other type of internal change in oligarchies arises directly out of the oligarchs' own rivalry, which turns them into demagogues. Now there are two kinds of demagogy, one which functions within the ranks of the few themselves (for a demagogue can arise even when there are very few indeed), the other when members of an oligarchy act as demagogues to the common crowd. Examples of the first are the demagogy which made Charicles' men powerful during the time of the Thirty[1] at Athens, likewise that of Phrynichus' associates during the time of the Four Hundred.[2] Of the second, a good example was Larissa, where the Citizen-Guardians played the demagogue to the common crowd because they were elected by them. And this second kind is apt to occur in any oligarchy where the officials are not elected by the persons from whom they are drawn, but offices are dependent on a high property-qualification or on membership of a political club, and the electors are the hoplites or the people, as happened at Abydos; also where the courts are not manned by the citizen-body,[3] for demagogy to influence verdicts[4] may lead to change in constitution, as happened at Heraclea on the Euxine; and further whenever one set tries to reduce the size of the oligarchy still more, for then the seekers of equality[5] are forced to summon the people to their aid.

1305b39 Then too there are oligarchies where change is due to the spending of private resources on extravagant living. For persons of this type too seek to make innovations, either aiming at tyranny themselves or putting up

1. The 'Thirty Tyrants' who held power in Athens 404–403.
2. The Athenian oligarchy of 411.
3. Aristotle seems to mean, 'not manned *exclusively* by . . .'.
4. I.e. in trials in which the demagogues are litigants.
5. I.e. those who are now excluded.

some other person. Thus at Syracuse it was Hipparinus who did this to Dionysius,[6] and at Amphipolis the additional Chalcidic settlers were brought by a man called Cleotimus, who on their arrival formed them into a faction against the well-to-do; and at Aegina the person who had carried through the negotiations with Chares tried to change the constitution for some similar reason.[7] Sometimes they do not wait, but try to make changes immediately; sometimes they secretly help themselves to public funds, and then either they themselves form factions against each other, or else others form factions against them, in order to combat the theft, as happened at Apollonia on the Euxine Sea.

1306a9 An oligarchy which is of one mind with itself is not easily destroyed from within; a good example is the constitution at Pharsalus, where a few men continue to have sovereign authority over many simply because they treat each other properly. Oligarchies are also destroyed when an attempt is made to set up one oligarchy within another. This occurs whenever, with a total citizen-body that is not large, not all the few share in the highest offices. It once happened in Elis, where the constitution was in few hands, and very few persons were ever added to the Elders, because the existing members held office for life and the total was fixed at ninety; moreover the method of election favoured the group in power,[8] and was like that of the Elders at Sparta.

1306a19 Change away from oligarchies takes place both in war and in peace – in war, because they are obliged, owing to their mistrust of the people, to employ mercenary soldiers; for the man to whom they have committed the command of these troops often becomes tyrant, as Timophanes[9] did at Corinth; and if there are several of

6. Dionysius I, tyrant of Syracuse from 405 to 367.
7. I.e. because he had run out of money.
8. 'Favoured the group in power': *dunasteutikē*, literally, 'appropriate to a power-group' (*dunasteia*, cf. II x, n. 10).
9. Assassinated by his brother Timoleon, *c.* 365.

them, they set up a power-group of their own. Sometimes, just for fear of these results, being obliged to employ the people in defence, they give the multitude a share in the constitution. In peace, on the other hand, owing to their mutual mistrust, they commit the country's defence to mercenary soldiers with a neutral commander, who sometimes gets sovereign power over both parties, as happened at Larissa during the rule of the Aleuadae who were associates of Simus; so too in the case of Iphiades at Abydos, when he led one of the clubs of that time.

1306a31   Factions also occur because one set among the oligarchs themselves is thrown out by another, and because factions arise out of lawsuits or dealings connected with a marriage. Some factions of matrimonial origin have been mentioned already;[10] to these may be added the knights' oligarchy at Eretria, which was brought low by Diagoras, who had suffered an injustice connected with a marriage. The factions at Heraclea and at Thebes were due to a law-court verdict: the court at Heraclea inflicted punishment on Eurytion on a charge of adultery – justly, but in a spirit of faction; while at Thebes the court found against Archias, and their enemies were so hot against them that the men were tied in the pillory in the market-place. Many oligarchies have fallen owing to their excessively despotic[11] rule, brought low by some of their own members who disapproved: the oligarchy at Cnidos, for example, and that at Chios.

1306b6   A combination of circumstances sometimes leads to change both in what we call polities and in those oligarchies in which entry to the council, the law-courts and other offices is open only to those of a certain property-qualification. For often the qualification, when it is first fixed, is well suited to its purpose at the time: in an oligarchy it ensures that few participate in the constitution, in the polity all the middle people. But prosperity ensues, thanks to a period of peace or some other good fortune,

10. V iv.
11. *Despotikos*, i.e. 'like that of a master (*despotēs*) over slaves'.

and it comes about that the same amounts of property are worth many times as much as before in the scale of assessment, and so everyone comes to share in everything, the change occurring either quickly or gradually and little by little, without being realized.

1306b16   Such then are the causes of change and faction in oligarchies. We may add this general remark: both oligarchies and democracies sometimes develop not into their opposites but into constitutions still of the same class. For example a democracy or an oligarchy that is bound by laws may change into a democracy or an oligarchy with sovereign power, or vice versa.[12]

V vii

(*1306b22–1307b26*)

THE CAUSES OF FACTIONS IN ARISTOCRACIES

*Factions and constitutional changes in aristocracies are discussed next. Aristocracy is based not on numbers but on virtue (*aretē*); yet it is clearly a form of oligarchy, since the virtuous are always few. But Aristotle's favoured 'polity' too is based on virtue and is therefore a kind of aristocracy, which is at the same time more democratic than oligarchic. So aristocracy and polity, and the 'extreme' constitutions, oligarchy and democracy, all feature in the rather complex discussion of this chapter, to which IV vii–ix are essential background reading.*

As Newman notes (IV 366), most of Aristotle's historical examples in this chapter are taken from Sparta. This concentration may be fortuitous; but if not, the reason is surely that he regarded Sparta as a 'mixed' constitution or 'polity' (IV ix), which is closely related to aristocracy.

The remarks in the penultimate paragraph about the

12. Cf. IV iv–v.

dangers of change are almost Platonic, at any rate in theme if not in tone: cf. for example Laws *796e ff.*

1306b22 One reason for factions in aristocracies is the fact that only a few people share in honours. This, as we have noted,[1] disturbs oligarchies too; for aristocracy too is a kind of oligarchy, the rulers in both being limited to a few; and although the reason for the limitation is not the same, aristocracy too is for this reason thought of as oligarchy. Such faction is bound to occur: (a) whenever there is some group of people who have convinced themselves that they are equals in virtue: for example at Sparta those known as Partheniae[2] (who were descended from the Equals) started a plot, but were found out and shipped off as colonists to Tarentum; (b) when some great men, in no whit inferior in virtue, are dishonoured by some who are more highly honoured, as was Lysander by the Kings;[3] (c) when a man of courage gets no share in honour, like Cinadon who got up the attack on the Spartiatae in the time of Agesilaus;[4] (d) when there is a wide disparity of wealth between rich and poor; this condition is particularly likely to come about in time of war, and it too occurred at Sparta, at the time of the Messenian war, as can be seen from the poem of Tyrtaeus called 'Eunomia':[5] some people were so hard pressed by the war that they demanded a redistribution of land; (e) when one

1. V vi *ad init.*
2. 'Sons of maidens', born as a result of a drive to replenish the population, depleted during the first Messenian war (eighth century). The 'Equals' (cf. 'Peers') were the Spartiatae, the full Spartan citizens, who had equal political rights: see II ix. 'Equal' in this and the preceding sentence = *homoioi*, not *isoi*.
3. Lysander was a Spartan general whose policies were frustrated by the Spartan Kings, 405–395.
4. 398.
5. 'Good Order', *Eunomia*. Tyrtaeus composed in Sparta about the middle of the seventh century; the Messenian war mentioned here was the second.

man is powerful and is capable of becoming more so: he aims at becoming sole ruler, as apparently Pausanias at Sparta, who led their forces in the Persian war, and Hanno at Carthage.

1307a5 But the chief cause of overthrow, both of polity and of aristocracy, is a deviation from justice in the constitution itself. Thus in polity the origin is in the failure to secure a proper mixture of oligarchy and democracy, in aristocracy in the failure to mix these and virtue, but especially the pair – democracy and oligarchy. For not only polities but also most of those constitutions called aristocracies aim at mixing these two; and the difference between aristocracies and constitutions called polities lies in this point,[6] and it is this that makes some more and others less stable. Those that lean rather towards oligarchy are called aristocracies, those that lean towards the mass of the people are called polities; and the effect is to make polities safer than aristocracies. This is due to the fact that greater size means greater strength; for where people have equal shares, they are more content, but those who have the advantages of riches, if they enjoy a preponderance in the constitution, seek to ill-treat others and enhance their own fortunes.

1307a20 As a general rule, if a constitution has a tendency in one direction, those on one side or the other who augment their strength under it will produce changes in the same direction, polity tending towards democracy, aristocracy towards oligarchy. But the opposite is also possible: aristocracy may shift towards democracy, when the poorer people suppose themselves wronged and exercise a pull in that direction; and polity may change to oligarchy, once it loses the only qualities that make it last, namely private property and equality according to deserts. This occurred at Thurii.[7] On the one hand, because the property-qualification for holding office was rather high, it was reduced and the number of boards

6. I.e. in how the mixing is done.
7. Perhaps in 413.

increased. On the other, the notables illegally got possession of all the land, being enabled to win the advantage as the constitution was biased towards oligarchy. Then the people, trained in arms during the war, became stronger than the garrison troops. So in the end the possessors of more than their share of land gave it up.

1307a34 A further consequence of the fact that all aristocratic constitutions are oligarchic in character is that the notables win even greater advantage; for example at Sparta, where properties keep coming into the hands of the few. In both also the notables have greater freedom to do as they please and marry as they please. It was just this that ruined the city of Locri: a connection by marriage was formed with the tyrant Dionysius,[8] a thing which would never have happened in a democracy, or even in an aristocracy in which the elements had been properly mixed.

1307a40 Changes in aristocracies generally take place unobserved, because the dissolution is a gradual process. We have already stated[9] this as a general principle applicable to all constitutions, namely that even a small thing may cause changes. If for example people abandon some small feature of their constitution, next time they will with an easier mind tamper with some other and slightly more important feature, until in the end they tamper with the whole structure. The constitution of Thurii affords one example.[10] There the generalship could legally be held only every fifth year by the same man. Some of the younger men grew combative, and the rank and file of the garrison troops esteemed them highly. This group had no use for the men of affairs and believed that they would easily prevail. They first set about annulling that

8. Dionysius I, tyrant of Syracuse from 405 to 367. An offspring of the marriage, Dionysius II, exercised a harsh tyranny over Locri, 356–346.

9. V iii–iv.

10. Newman believes it 'likely' that the following events may be dated to the fourth century.

law, so as to make it possible for the same men to be general continuously; for they saw that the people would eagerly vote them into office. Those of the officials who were charged with responsibility in the matter, Councillors as they were called, while at first inclined to oppose, were eventually won over with the rest; they supposed that after tampering with that law the young men would be leaving the rest of the constitution intact. But later, when other things were tampered with which they wanted to stop, they proved powerless to do anything. So the whole set-up of the constitution was altered and it passed into the hands of the power-group that had started the process of innovation.

1307b19 All constitutions are changed from the outside as well as from within: for example, if a neighbouring constitution is of the opposite kind and is not far away, or, if far away, especially powerful. The Athenians and the Lacedaemonians illustrated this in their day: the Athenians everywhere brought low the oligarchies, the Lacedaemonians the democracies.

So much then for the origins of constitutional change and of factions.

V viii

(*1307b26–1309a32*)

HOW CONSTITUTIONS MAY BE PRESERVED (1)

Chapters viii and ix describe methods of ensuring the stability of the three constitutions (democracy, oligarchy and aristocracy) whose dissolutions have been examined in v–vii. Both chapters are remarkable for their total lack of reference to historical examples: it is as though Aristotle, while able earlier to display plenty of historical instances of the collapse of constitutions, could now find none of their successful maintenance. That is difficult to believe, for some Greek states kept the same constitution

for long periods. What he seems to have done, as he prac-
tically admits in the first paragraph, is to write these two
chapters largely by advising measures which are implicit
in, and may be deduced from, the disastrous policies de-
scribed in v–vii, in the sense that the former reverse the
latter and so correct their mistakes. We may feel he would
have been wise to strengthen his counsel by pointing to
actual examples of its successful application. It is a curi-
ously disembodied way of giving practical advice, how-
ever good the advice itself is – as indeed it is good, em-
bracing many prudent and sensible adjustments designed
to prevent any one 'part' of the constitution from becom-
ing predominant and so distorting its balance. These
adjustments are evidently to be continuous: Aristotle is
very far from suggesting that it is possible to set up a
constitution and then expect it to function without atten-
tion.

Aristotle must have been well aware (cf. IV vi) of the
difference between receiving payment from public funds
and stealing from them; yet in this chapter he seems to
describe the former in terms of the latter; cf. II xi.

1307b26 Our next topic is the preservation of constitutions both in general and in particular cases. The first and
obvious point to make is that if indeed we do understand
the causes of their destruction, then we understand also
the causes of their preservation. For opposites are productive of opposites, and destruction is the opposite of
preservation.

1307b30 Now in constitutions that are well-blended it is
essential to take many precautions, and certainly against
anything being done contrary to the laws; and it is essential in particular to guard against the insignificant breach.
Illegality creeps in unobserved; it is like small items of
expenditure which when oft-repeated make away with a
man's possessions. The spending goes unnoticed because
the money is not spent all at once, and this is just what
leads the mind astray. It is like the sophistic argument

which says 'If each is small, all is small', which is true and not true: the whole or the all may be made up of small amounts without being small itself. One precaution to be taken, then, is in regard to the beginning;[1] and equally we must not trust those arguments of sophistry that are designed to delude the multitude, for the facts prove them false. The sort of constitutional sophistries I mean have already been explained.[2]

1308a3 We must next observe that some aristocracies (and oligarchies too) remain stable, not because their constitutions are secure, but because those who hold office give proper treatment both to the members of the citizen-body and to those outside the constitution; that is to say, they do not treat the latter unjustly, but allow their leaders to participate in the constitution; they do not treat the ambitious unjustly by dishonouring them, nor the mass of the people in the matter of profit; and among themselves and the rest of those who share in the constitution they treat each other in a democratic spirit, that is to say, on an equal footing, since the equality over the whole populace which is a democrat's aim is not only just but advantageous as between persons who are alike. Hence if the size of the citizen-body is large, there is advantage in having many of the democratic rules such as tenure of office for only six months, so as to give all, being similar, a share in it; their similarity makes them, as it were, into a *dēmos*, which is why, as we have observed, very often demagogues arise even among them.[3] Also, since it is not as easy to do wrong in a short as in a long tenure of office, these oligarchies and aristocracies are less likely to fall into the hands of power-groups; for tyrannies arise in oligarchies and democracies for precisely that reason: either the greatest men in each case – demagogues

---

1. Of illegality, or change, presumably; cf. 1308a34 and V iv, n. 2.
2. IV xiii *ad init.*
3. *Dēmos* = 'people', *dēm*agogues are 'people-leaders'. The reference is to V vi.

in the one, power-group leaders in the other – aim at tyranny for themselves, or else those who hold the highest offices do so, if they hold them for a long period.

1308a24 Constitutions enjoy stability not only when any possible destroyers are at a distance, but sometimes just because they are close by; for through fear of them men keep a firm hold on their own constitution. So it becomes the duty of those who have the interests of the constitution at heart to create terrors so that all may be on the look-out and, like sentries at night, not allow their watch on the constitution to relax; the distant fear must be brought home. They must also take further precautions, by means of legislation, against the rivalries and factions of the notables, and restrain those not involved before they too make the rivalry their own; it is not every man but only a statesman who can discern in its early stages the harm that is being done.

1308a35 Changes in oligarchies and polities may be due to the property-qualifications remaining fixed while the money in circulation is greatly increasing.[4] When this situation occurs the best thing to do is to assess the total communal valuation and compare the new total with the old. In some states people are assessed every year, in which case the calculation must be based on that period; but in the larger states it should be done every second or every fourth year. And if the value is then found to be much greater or much smaller than it was when the level qualifying[5] for the constitution was laid down, it should be lawful to increase the property-qualifications or lower them; if the value has gone up, they are increased in proportion to the rise, whereas if the value has fallen, they are decreased to a lower level. If the situation is not met in this way and no adjustments are made in oligarchies and

---

4. Cf. V vi, *fin.*
5. I.e. entitling one to be a citizen (*politēs*), a member of the citizen-body (*politeuma*), i.e. one who 'shares in' the constitution (*politeia*).

polities, then in the latter case[6] change is liable to take place from polity to oligarchy, or from oligarchy to power-group; in the former,[7] the changes will be from polity to democracy and from oligarchy to polity or democracy.

1308b10 It is a practice common to democracy, oligarchy, monarchy and every constitution not to augment the power of any one man out of proportion, but to try to bestow on him either minor honours tenable for long periods or major ones tenable only for a short time; for men become corrupt, and not everyone can master the intoxication of success. Or if that is not possible, at any rate they avoid heaping honours on a man all in a bunch and then removing them in a bunch; the process should be gradual. And they try especially to manage matters by laws in such a way that no person becomes pre-eminent through the power either of his wealth or of his friends; or if that cannot be done, to require such men to remove themselves, and out of the country at that. But since men introduce innovations for reasons connected with their private lives too, an authority ought to be set up to exercise supervision over those whose activities are not in keeping with the interests of the constitution – of oligarchy in an oligarchy and of democracy in a democracy, and likewise in each of the rest.

1308b24 For the same reasons exceptional prosperity in one section of the state is to be guarded against. The danger can be remedied by entrusting offices and the conduct of affairs to the opposing sections.[8] (By 'opposing' I mean the respectable sort as contrasted with the generality, and the wealthy as contrasted with the indigent.) An endeavour should be made either to merge the poor population with the rich or to augment the middle; this dissolves the factions that are due to the inequality.

1308b31 It is most important in every constitution that the legal and other administrative arrangements[9] should

6. I.e. when the total value has decreased.
7. I.e. when the total value has increased.
8. I.e. to *both* sections.

be such that holding office is not a source of profit. This point needs to be particularly watched in constitutions that are oligarchically framed. For the many do not so much resent being debarred from office, indeed they are glad to be allowed time to attend to their own affairs, but they do not like to think that officials are stealing public money. Their resentment then becomes twofold: they are deprived of both honours and profit. Also, it is only by observing this principle that it ever becomes possible for democracy and aristocracy to coexist, because it will then be possible for both the notables and the multitude to get what they want; for it is democratic that holding offices should be open to all, aristocratic that the notables should fill them, and this is exactly what will happen when there is no profit to be made out of the offices. For those who are not well-off will not want office unless there is profit in it, preferring to look after their own affairs, while the rich will be able to accept office, as they need no supplement from public funds. The effect of this will be that the poor will become better off through spending their time at their work, and the notables will not be ruled by anybody and everybody. In order to prevent theft from public funds, the handing over of them to a successor should take place in the presence of all the citizens, and duplicates of the lists should be made available to brotherhoods, companies, and tribes. And in order to encourage the holding of offices without profit, there should be honours laid down by law for those who win a distinguished reputation in them.

1309a14 In democracies the rich ought to be treated with restraint: there should be no redistribution of property, nor of income, such as goes on unnoticed in some constitutions. It is better, even if they want to, not to let the rich undertake costly but useless public services[10] – for instance financing a torch-race or the training of a chorus, or the like. In an oligarchy, on the other hand,

9. *Oikonomia.*
10. *Leitourgiai*, see IV iv, n. 11.

special attention must be paid to the welfare of those who are not well-off: to them should be assigned those offices which yield some gain; ill-treatment of them by one of the rich should carry a severer penalty than one committed among the poor themselves; there should be no right of free testamentary disposition, but only kin should inherit; and the same person should not be permitted to inherit more than one estate. In this way disparity of possessions will be less, and a greater number of the poor will join the ranks of the well-to-do.

1309a27 It always pays, whether in a democracy or an oligarchy, to give equality or even preference in other matters to those whose participation in the constitution is less, to the rich in a democracy, to the poor in an oligarchy. This does not mean that they should be given sovereign offices; these should be reserved exclusively, or at any rate mostly, for participants in the constitution.

V ix

(1309a33–1310a38)

HOW CONSTITUTIONS MAY BE PRESERVED (2)

This chapter continues and concludes the theme of its predecessor. It discusses, inter alia, the character of those in power, their relationship with the ruled, and the nature and purpose of education – which, if it is to promote stability, must be calculated to produce people who favour and fit in with the constitution in question. But perhaps the shrewdest sections are directed against extremists of whatever persuasion: only by incorporating elements of opposing constitutions can a given constitution survive. A democracy, for instance, which adopts rigorous and thoroughgoing democratic measures is more likely to be destroyed by violent reaction from the rich than one which pays some attention to their interests: overtaut bows snap. The advice Aristotle gives in this chapter, as

*in many another, is calm and sensible: stability depends
on the 'middle way'; cf. IV xi–xii.*

1309a33 There are three essentials for the holders of the
sovereign offices: goodwill towards the established constitution, tremendous capability for the work involved in
the office, and in each constitution the kind of virtue and
notions of justice that are calculated to suit the particular
constitution in question. (Justice is not the same in every
constitution, so that differences in notions of justice are
inevitable.)[1] But there is a question here: when all these
qualities are not to be found in the same person, how is
the choice to be made? If one man is fit to be a general,
but is a low fellow and without goodwill towards the constitution, while another is just and has that goodwill, how
is one to choose between them? It seems that we must
look to two points: what quality do all men have in
abundance, and what quality do they all have less of? In
the case of generalship, we must regard experience more
than virtue, as men possess the skill of a general less abundantly than integrity.[2] It is the other way round in the
case of an office which involves stewardship and safe
custody of goods: this requires virtue above the average
but no knowledge that is not to be found among all men.
And another question might be asked: if both goodwill
towards the constitution and capability are present, what
need is there of virtue? Will not these two of themselves
bring about good results? As against that it may be said
that men may possess these two qualities and still be
morally incapable;[3] and if in spite of knowing,[4] and hav-

1. Cf. I ii *fin.* 'Notion of justice' = *dikaiosunē*. 'Justice' =
dikaion: cf. III ix, xii–xiii, V i–ii.

2. *Epieikeia.*

3. *Akrateis* (noun *akrasia*) 'weak', 'to know what is right but to
be unable to resist temptation to do wrong' (see especially *Nicomachean Ethics* VII). *Akrasia* is a condition which, as Aristotle
implies, calls for the cultivation of virtue by education and the
formation of good habits.

4. *Sc.* 'what their own interests are', or possibly 'their moral
duty'.

ing goodwill towards *themselves*, they nevertheless fail to serve their own interests, is there anything to prevent some of them being incapable of serving the common interest too?

1309b14 In general, all those legal provisions which we say are advantageous to the constitution in each case, all these are constitutional safeguards, including that oft-mentioned and most important principle – to ensure that the number of those who wish the constitution to be maintained is greater than that of those who do not. Moreover, there is one thing that must not be overlooked, though it is at present overlooked in constitutions that deviate – the principle of the middle way. Many steps thought of as democratic lead to the fall of a democracy, and the corresponding thing happens in oligarchies. Some people, believing that this virtue is a single one,[5] push it to extremes. They fail to realize that a nose which deviates from the perfect straightness by being either hooked or snub is still a fine nose and looks good as well; but if the process is carried to excess,[6] first it will lose the proportion which belongs to this part of the body, and finally it will not look like a nose at all, because of the extreme to which either the hook or the snub has been pushed at the expense of its opposite; and this is true of other parts of the body also. So it is with constitutions: both oligarchy and democracy may be tolerably good, though they diverge from the best arrangement; but if one carries either of them to excess, the constitution will first become worse and finally not a constitution at all. Therefore both the lawgiver and the statesman must know what kinds of democratic measures preserve and what kinds undermine democracy, and what kinds of oligarchical measures do the same for oligarchy.

5. I.e. they do not realize that just as each constitution, e.g. democracy, can take more than one form, and be more or less extreme (cf. IV i–vii), so too 'this virtue' (i.e. the particular virtue, or indeed virtues, suitable to the constitution in question) can (and presumably must) take several forms.

6. I.e. in sculpture or painting.

For it is not possible for either oligarchy or democracy to exist and continue to exist without both the wealthy and the mass of the people. If the distinction between them is abolished by the levelling of possessions, the resulting constitution will of necessity be a different one; that is to say, constitutions are themselves destroyed by the destruction of that very distinction, through legislation carried to excess.

1310a2 These mistakes are made both in democracy and in oligarchy. In democracies they are made by the demagogues, whenever the mass of the people has sovereign power over the laws: they make one state into two by their attacks on the rich. Yet they ought, for the sake of stability, to behave in just the opposite way, and always appear to be speaking on behalf of the rich. So too in oligarchies its members should always appear to speak on behalf of the people; and the oath which they take should be the very reverse of that which is in fact taken by them today – for in some oligarchies today their oath is: 'I will be hostile to the people and do all I can against them.' Both their assumptions and their ostensible conduct ought to be the opposite of this, and the declaration they ought to take on oath is: 'I will do no wrong to the people.'

1310a12 But of all the safeguards that we hear spoken of as helping to maintain constitutional stability, the most important, but today universally neglected, is education for the way of living that belongs to the constitution in each case. It is useless to have the most beneficial laws, fully agreed upon by all who are members of the constitution, if they are not going to be trained and have their habits formed in the spirit of that constitution – in a democratic spirit, that is, if the laws are democratic, but oligarchically if they are oligarchic; for as one individual may be morally incapable,[3] so may a whole state. Now to have been educated for the constitution does not mean simply doing the things that members of an oligarchy or democratically minded people enjoy doing, but doing what will enable them to live as oligarchs or as democrats, as the case may be.

1310a22 However, what actually happens is that in oligarchies the sons of the rulers enjoy ease and comfort, and the sons of the poor, being trained and inured to toil, are both more willing and better able to introduce innovations. And what has come to prevail in democracies is the very reverse of beneficial, in those, that is, which are regarded as the most democratically run. The reason for this lies in the failure properly to define liberty. For there are two marks by which democracy is thought to be defined: 'sovereignty of the majority' and 'liberty'. 'Just' is equated with what is equal, and the decision of the majority as to what is equal is regarded as sovereign; and liberty is seen in terms of doing what one wants. So in such a democracy each lives as he likes and for his 'fancy of the moment', as Euripides says.[7] This is bad. It ought not to be regarded as slavery to live according to the constitution, but rather as self-preservation.

The sources of change and destruction of constitutions, as well as the means of preserving and maintaining them, are for the most part as I have described.

V x

(*1310a39–1313a17*)

THE ORIGINS AND DOWNFALL OF MONARCHY

In spite of the last sentence of V ix, Aristotle has discussed the preservation and destruction of oligarchy and democracy only. He now discusses, in V x and xi, the various origins and downfalls of monarchy, a word which means literally 'the rule of one' and therefore embraces both tyranny and kingship; the differences between these two

7. Fr. 891 in A. Nauck, *Tragicorum Graecorum Fragmenta* (2nd ed., Berlin, 1889). For the comment in the next two sentences, cf. Aristotle, *Metaphysics* Λ x, 1075a18 ff.

are described in paragraphs 3–5. Four causes of their over-throw are distinguished: (a) injustice (especially hubris, *treating others with overbearing arrogance); (b) anger, hatred and fear; (c) contempt; (d) ambition and desire for gain. Of these, (a) refers to the actions of the monarch, while (b–d) are the feelings and motives of his subjects. In short, personal animosities play a large role in the over-throw of monarchies. Towards the end of the chapter (1312a39 ff.) Aristotle divides the causes of destruction into the external and the internal; and the latter prompt him to give further examples of personal enmities. Before going on to speak briefly of the possibility of revolution in a good monarchy, he sums up on tyranny by recalling that oligarchies and democracies of the wrong type could also be destroyed either from without or from within, and that if from within, the causes there too are generally moral and psychological.*

The chapter is very long, and by contrast with its two predecessors is replete with historical references (which I have annotated fairly lightly, many being in any case obscure). Anyone with an interest in ancient scandal, particularly the sexual kind, will find much to engage him, but there is a certain tedium in these lists of examples: in places Aristotle seems to be (as it were) copy-ing out his card-index. Yet, as always in Aristotle, we see a powerful intellect arranging, classifying and analysing a bewildering variety of material ranging over several centuries of Greek history. And much of the value of this chapter lies in observations and discussions that are almost incidental to its main theme, e.g. the brief remarks on the different effects of anger and hatred (1312b27 ff.), the nice description of extreme democracies and extreme oli-garchies as tyrannies held by more than one person (1312b37, cf. 1312b5–6), and the psychological analysis of the various kinds of contempt (1311b40 ff.). What Ari-stotle is presumably doing here is to draw on and apply the results of his own detailed analysis of the emotions in the second book of his Art of Rhetoric. *This, the first comprehensive and systematic study of the emotions by a Western philosopher, makes invaluable background reading to this chapter of the* Politics.

1310a39 It remains to deal with monarchy, and to establish both the causes of its destruction and the means of its preservation. What we find happening in both kingship and tyranny follows closely what has been said about constitutions in general; for kingship has the same basis[1] as aristocracy, and tyranny is a compound of extreme oligarchy and democracy. This is precisely what makes tyranny most hurtful to the ruled: it is made up of two bad types and contains the deviations and errors that derive from both. As for origins, the two styles of monarchy arise directly out of that which contrasts with them. Kingship develops with the aim of helping the respectable men against the people: a king is created from among respectable men on account of his superiority in virtue or deeds of virtue, or the superiority of his virtuous family. The tyrant springs from the people, from the populace, and directs his efforts against the notables, to the end that the people may not be wronged by them. This is clear from the record; for it is fairly generally true to say that tyrants have mostly begun as demagogues, being trusted because they abused the notables.

1310b16 Certainly in cities that have grown to considerable size this is the way tyrannies originate. But there have been other ways: some early tyrannies arose out of kingships that had deviated from ancestral traditions and were aiming at making their rule more masterlike; others arose from those who had been elected into the sovereign offices (in very early times the peoples elected to office[2] and religious missions for long periods of tenure). Tyrannies have also come into being when oligarchies have chosen one man and invested him with sovereign powers in the

1. Virtue (*aretē*): cf. IV ii and 1310b31 ff.
2. *Dēmiourgiai*: cf. III ii, n. 1.

highest offices. In all these ways the opportunity to prevail lay ready to hand, provided only that the will was there, for the power existed either in the royal rule or in the honour.[3] Some examples of tyrannies of different origins are: (a) from an established kingship: Pheidon of Argos and others; (b) from honours:[3] Phalaris and the tyrants of Ionia; (c) from the position of demagogue: Panaetius of Leontini, Cypselus of Corinth, Peisistratus[4] of Athens, Dionysius[5] of Syracuse and others in the same way.

1310b31 Kingship, as we have remarked, is organized on the same basis as aristocracy: merit – either individual virtue, or birth, or distinguished service, or all these together with a capacity for doing things. For it is just those who have done good service or have the capacity to do it, either for states or for foreign nations, that have been honoured with the position of king. Some, like Codrus,[6] saved their people by war from slavery; others, like Cyrus,[7] set them free or acquired territory or settled it, like the kings of the Lacedaemonians, of the Molossians, and of the Macedonians.

1310b40 A king aims to be a protector – of the owners of possessions against unjust losses, of the people against any ill-treatment. But a tyrant, as has often been said,[8] does not look to the public interest at all, unless it happens to contribute to his personal benefit. The tyrant's aim is pleasure: the king aims at what is good.[9] Hence they differ even in the advantages they seek: the tyrant

---

3. Offices, in effect. Phalaris, tyrant of Agrigentum in S.W. Sicily, c. 570–c. 554, was noted for his brazen bull in which he roasted victims alive.

4. Tyrant of Athens 561–527, with intermissions. For Cypselus, see V xi, n. 5.

5. Dionysius I, tyrant of Syracuse from 405 to 367.

6. An early, perhaps legendary, king of Athens. Learning that the Dorians would defeat Athens if he survived, he gave his life to save his city.

7. Cyrus freed Persia from the Medes in the mid sixth century.

8. E.g. III vii *ad fin.*

9. *To kalon.*

grasps at money, the king at honour. A king's bodyguard is made up of citizens, a tyrant's of foreigners.[10]

1311a8 That tyranny has the disadvantages of both democracy and oligarchy is clear. From oligarchy it derives two things: (1) the notion of wealth as the end to be pursued (certainly wealth is essential to it, as it provides the only way of keeping up a bodyguard and a luxurious way of living), and (2) mistrust of the populace; hence it deprives them of weapons, harms the common crowd and relegates them from the city to live in scattered communities. These features are common to oligarchy and tyranny. From democracy is derived hostility to the notables, whom the tyrant brings low by open methods or secret, and sends into exile as being rivals and hindrances to his rule. These, of course, are the people who also originate plots for his overthrow, some themselves wishing to be rulers, others not to submit like slaves. We are reminded of the advice given by Periander to Thrasybulus,[11] to lop off the tallest stalks, implying that he should always remove the outstanding among the citizens.

1311a22 Now it has been said, or at any rate suggested, that the same origins of change must be supposed to operate in monarchies as in constitutions in general. For injustice (particularly in the form of ill-treatment),[12] and contempt and fear, often cause those who are ruled to rebel against monarchies; and loss of private possessions is also sometimes a cause. And the ends are the same too: great wealth and great honour are characteristic of the sole ruler, king or tyrant, and these are things which all men want for themselves. Attacks on rulers may be directed against their persons or against their office. If men have been ill-treated, their attack will be on the tyrant's person; for ill-treatment may take many forms

10. I.e. mercenaries.
11. See III xiii, n. 10, and V xi.
12. *Hubris*: here apparently, and probably throughout the chapter, with special reference to the overbearing arrogance with which injustice and injury may be inflicted.

and each will provoke anger. And most angry attackers are keener on vengeance than on supremacy.

1311a36 Here are some examples. (a) The fall of the Peisistratidae, whose insults to Harmodius and outrage to his sister caused Harmodius to attack on her account, and Aristogeiton on account of Harmodius.[13] (b) The occasion for the attack on Periander,[14] tyrant of Ambracia, was that when he was drinking in company with his boy-beloved he asked the lad whether he was yet with child by him. (c) Pausanias's attack on Philip[15] was due to the fact that he allowed him to be ill-treated by Attalus's men. (d) Amyntas the Little was attacked by Derdas for boasting about the flower of Derdas's youth.[16] (e) Evagoras[17] of Cyprus was attacked and murdered by the eunuch, who felt ill-treated because his wife had been seduced by Evagoras's son. Many attacks on rulers have arisen out of resentment caused by a monarch's offences against his subjects' persons,[18] such as (f) Crataeas's attack on Archelaus.[19] Crataeas was always resentful of the liaison, and the slightest excuse was enough; but there was also, perhaps, the reason that the king had promised one of his two daughters to him but gave him neither. (Involved in a war against Sirrhas and Arrhabaeus, he gave the older to the king of Elimea and the younger to Amyntas his son, thinking that this was the best way to avoid discord between him and his son by Cleopatra.) But at the bottom of the coolness between them was Crataeas's disgust with granting erotic favours. And for the same reason, Hellenocrates of Larissa joined in the attack. Archelaus had made

13. 514. Hippias, son and successor of Peisistratus (see n. 4), fell four years later.

14. Cf. V iv, n. 6.

15. Of Macedonia, 336 (which is evidence for the late date of at least this part of the *Politics*); cf. n. 32.

16. Literally, 'for vaunting over' it, i.e. for having made Derdas his boy-beloved.

17. Ruler of Salamis in Cyprus from 411 until his death in 374.

18. I.e. sexual offences.

19. King of Macedonia from *c*. 413 to 399.

sexual use of his young body but did not, as he had promised, let him return to his home town. Hellanocrates concluded that the liaison had been inspired by arrogance[12] and not by passionate love. (g) At Aenos, Python and Heracleides killed Cotys[20] to avenge their father, and Adamas deserted Cotys, feeling arrogantly ill-treated because he had as a boy suffered castration at his hands.

1311b23 There are many cases also of anger being aroused by blows and assaults on the person, the victims of which, feeling themselves arrogantly ill-treated,[12] have killed or tried to kill the perpetrators, who include even members of official circles and of royal power-groups. In Mytilene, for example, when the Penthilidae[21] went about in gangs, carrying clubs and beating up people, Megacles with the help of friends attacked them and put them down. Later Smerdes, because he had been dragged out from beside his wife and beaten, killed Penthilus. Then there was the attack on Archelaus instigated and led by Decamnichus. The reason for his anger was that Archelaus had given him to the poet Euripides to be scourged; and Euripides was angry because Decamnichus had made some remark about the poet's foul-smelling breath.[22] There were many other plots and assassinations arising out of causes of this kind.

1311b36 Similarly when fear is the reason; for this too was one of the list of causes,[23] both in constitutions in general and under the rule of one man. For example, Artapanes murdered Xerxes[24] because he feared the accusation that he had hanged Darius not on Xerxes' orders, but thinking that Xerxes would excuse him, being at dinner and unlikely to remember.

20. King of Thrace, 382–359.
21. The ruling family of early Mytilene.
22. See n. 19 Euripides (*c.* 485–*c.* 406) spent the last few years of his life at Archelaus' court.
23. Earlier in this chapter, 1311a22ff.
24. King of Persia 485–465. Darius was Xerxes' son, Artapanes his chief bodyguard.

1311b40 Thirdly, contempt. Sardanapalus[25] rendered himself contemptible by being seen carding wool with the women, and was murdered by someone who saw him. (At least, that is the story of the legend-tellers; and if it is not true of him, it is pretty sure to be true of someone else.) Dion's attack on the younger Dionysius[26] was due to contempt: he saw that the tyrant was never sober and the citizens shared his contempt for him. Sometimes even some of a monarch's friends despise him so much that they attack him. His reliance on them allows them to despise him and makes them confident that he will never notice anything. And those whose aim is to seize power for themselves are also, up to a point, actuated by contempt when they attack: they feel they are strong enough and contemn the risk, and their strength causes them to undertake the attack lightly, as do commanders of armies when they attack their monarchs. A case in point is Cyrus, who despised Astyages,[27] both his power and his manner of life: the power had become inert, the life one of self-indulgence. Similar was the attack of Seuthes the Thracian, while a general, on Amadocus. Some attack for a mixture of these reasons; Mithridates for instance, attacked Ariobarzanes both because he despised him and because he wanted to profit. Attacks that are inspired by contempt are generally carried out by men who are by nature bold, and also hold military office[28] in the service of a monarch. For courage combined with physical power makes men bold, and for this double reason they are confident of easy success before they make their attack.

1312a21 But when the reason for an attack is ambition, a different style of cause operates from those already mentioned. It is not true to say that, just as some men attack tyrants because they have an eye on the immense profits

25. King of the Assyrians, 668–626.
26. Tyrant of Syracuse, 367–356 and 346–343. Cf. nn. 29 and 33.
27. King of Media, overthrown by Cyrus in 559.
28. Literally 'honour' (*timē*).

and honours which accrue to them, *every* ambitious attacker chooses to take the risk in that spirit. The fact is that, while the former act for the reason given, the latter act as they would on any other exceptional venture that offers men a chance of making themselves famous and notable: they attack a monarch in order to win glory for themselves, not because they want his monarchy. Still, there are not very many who go ahead for this reason: there must be in addition disregard of personal safety, should the venture miscarry. They should not lose sight of Dion's attitude, difficult though it is for many men to adopt it. Dion [29] took only a few men with him against Dionysius, saying he felt that whenever he could advance with success, he was satisfied to have completed that much of the enterprise; thus, if it should happen that after taking but a few steps in that country he should be slain, he would have died a death that pleased him.

1312a39 One of the ways tyranny, like each of the other constitutions, may be destroyed is from without, if there is a more powerful constitution that is opposed to it; the desire to destroy it will certainly exist because of the opposition of aims, and when power is added to desire men always act. The constitutions are opposed thus: democracy is opposed to tyranny, on Hesiod's principle[30] that 'two potters never agree'; for democracy is the extreme form of tyranny. Kingship and aristocracy are also opposed to tyranny, being opposite to it as constitutions; and for this reason the Lacedaemonians brought low very many tyrannies, as did also the Syracusans during the time when they had a good constitution. Another way is from within, when there is faction among those who share the tyrant's power, for example the tyranny of Gelon's

29. Dion, a relative of Dionysius I (see n. 5), tried to educate Dionysius II (see n. 26) along Platonic lines, and later turned against his pupil. See Plato, *Letters* III, VII and VIII.
30. *Works and Days* 25.

circle,[31] and, more recently,[32] that of Dionysius. In the former, Thrasybulus, brother of Hiero, established an influence like a demagogue's over Gelon's son, and led him into a life of sensual pleasure. His purpose was to be ruler himself. The family got together a conspiracy with the aim of bringing about the fall of Thrasybulus, not of the tyranny as a whole. But their supporters in the conspiracy, seizing their chance, threw out the lot of them. In the other case Dion led a force against Dionysius,[33] to whom he was related by marriage, and enlisted popular support; he threw out Dionysius but was afterwards slain himself.

1312b17 The two chief reasons for attacks on a tyranny are hatred and contempt. Hatred of tyrants is always present, but in many cases their fall comes from their being despised. This can be seen from the fact that men who have themselves won the position have generally maintained their rule, but those who had acquired it from a predecessor nearly all lose it straight away. Living only to enjoy themselves, they soon become easy to despise and give their attackers plenty of chances. We ought to include anger as part of hatred, since in a way it leads to the same actions. But anger is often more active than hatred. Angry men go into the attack with greater intensity just because this feeling does not involve their reasoning powers, which hatred uses more. To be ill-treated makes men follow their passions rather than their reason, and this is just what brought about the fall of the tyranny of the Peisistratidae[13] and many of the others. Anger is accompanied by pain, which makes it difficult to exercise reason, whereas hostility is not painful. In short then the same causes which we said[34] destroyed unmixed and extreme oligar-

31. See V iii, n. 4.
32. Nῦν, 'in our day', referring to 356; but in view of n. 15, hardly a secure indication of the date of this chapter.
33. Dionysius II (see nn. 26 and 29).
34. V iii, v, vi.

chies and extreme democracies are just those which must be regarded as destroying tyrannies too; for these extreme forms are really distributed[35] tyrannies.

1312b38 Kingship least suffers destruction from without; it is therefore long-lasting. When kingships are destroyed it is most often from within, and in two ways: one, when those who participate in the royal rule form factions among themselves, the other when kings try to run affairs too tyrannically, claiming sovereign power over more than they are legally entitled to. But nowadays kingships no longer arise, and such as do are more like a tyranny or a monarchy.[36] For kingship is government by consent as well as sovereignty over more important affairs; the number of persons who are all on a similar level is large, and none of them stands out enough to measure up to the greatness and grandeur of the office. So for this reason men do not readily consent to be ruled by such people, and if by force or by fraud one of them attains that position, that is regarded as a tyranny without further ado.

1313a10 We must add a further cause of downfall to those stated, one that is characteristic of hereditary kingships. Those who inherit are often persons whom it is easy to despise; and though they possess the honour of a king, not the power of a tyrant, they ill-treat others. The overthrow of kingship is then easy, for when people cease to wish him to be king, a king will be at once a king no more; but a tyrant is still a tyrant even though people do not want him.

For these reasons and others like them monarchies suffer destruction.

35. Literally 'divided', i.e. among several people.
36. Aristotle seems here to treat *monarchia* as a *disreputable* form of sole rule, like tyranny, as opposed to kingship, an acceptable form.

V xi

(1313a18–1315b10)

METHODS OF PRESERVING MONARCHIES, WITH PARTICULAR REFERENCE TO TYRANNY

Dealing next with ways of preventing revolution in monarchies, Aristotle again has much more to say about tyranny than about kingship, which being based on consent is much more stable. Tyranny is based on force and, traditionally, maintained by force. The other way for a tyrant to maintain his position is to cultivate certain features of kingship, which Aristotle enumerates at length. These 'two quite different methods by which tyrannies may be preserved' are well described by Newman (IV 448): 'The two ways of preserving a tyranny differ in this: ... in the first it is taken for granted that the subjects of a tyrant are necessarily hostile to him and the aim is to make them unable *to conspire against him ... whereas in the second the aim is to make the subjects of the tyrant* indisposed *to conspire against him....'*

It may seem strange that Aristotle devotes so much attention to describing measures by which a tyrant could maintain his position, for obviously he disapproves of tyranny as such. Yet we may suspect that the lonely figure of the tyrant exercised a certain fascination over him; and since he has described the means of preserving other constitutions, it is possible that a donnish rigour and desire for completeness of treatment led him to give an equal attention to tyranny. His main reason, however, presumably appears in the closing words of the chapter: a tyrant who adopts certain features of kingship will be to that extent a less bad *ruler – a tyrant still, to be sure, but perhaps a tolerable, 'half-good' tyrant. Aristotle may have supposed that the chapter could serve the beneficent practical purpose of persuading at least some tyrants, in the interests of maintaining their position, to modify their rule in a desirable direction.*

1313a18 As to the preservation of monarchies, the general principle of opposite causes still holds good, but special principles are applicable to each. (A) Kingships are preserved by tending towards greater moderation. The fewer those spheres of activity where a king's power is sovereign, the longer the regime will inevitably survive undiminished. They themselves become less like masters, and more like their subjects in character, and therefore arouse less envy among them. That is the secret of the long life of the Molossian kingdom; and as for the Lacedaemonian, we can first point to the reason that from the very start the ruling was divided between two Kings; secondly, Theopompus,[1] in addition to other measures of moderation, instituted as a check the office of the Ephors. This diminution of the royal power had in the long run the effect of strengthening the kingship, so in a sense Theopompus did not reduce it but increased it, as he himself is reported to have said in reply to his wife, when she asked if he was not ashamed to be passing the kingdom on to his sons in a lesser state than he had inherited it from his father. 'Certainly not,' he replied, 'the kingdom that I pass on is longer-lasting.'

1313a34 There are two quite opposed methods by which (B) tyrannies are preserved. I deal first with the traditional method, the principle followed by most tyrants in exercising their dominion. Periander of Corinth[2] is credited with having introduced many of the ways of applying it, but the Persian government offers many parallels. Here belong all the old[3] hints for the preservation (so far as possible) of tyranny: (i) 'Lop off the eminent and get rid of men of independent spirit'; (ii) 'Don't allow getting together in messes or clubs, or education or anything of

1. A king of Sparta, eighth–seventh century.
2. See III xiii, n. 10, and V x, n. 11.
3. Possibly a reference to V x, fifth paragraph.

that kind; these are the breeding grounds of independence and confidence, two things which a tyrant must
guard against'; (iii) 'Do not allow schools or other gatherings where men pursue learning together, and do everything to ensure that people do not get to know each other
well, for such knowledge increases mutual confidence';
(iv) 'Keep the dwellers in the city always within view and
require them to spend much time at the palace gates;
their activities then will not be kept secret, and by constantly performing servile actions they will become used
to having little spirit of their own.' There are other pre-
cepts of tyranny of the same kind, all of them having the
same effect, among the Persians and other non-Greeks.
Similarly a tyrant should endeavour (v) to keep himself
aware of everything that is said or done among his subjects: he should have spies like the 'Tittle-Tattle Women'
of Syracuse, or the Eavesdroppers whom Hiero[4] used to
send to any place where there was a meeting or gathering
of people. Men speak less freely for fear of such men, and
if they do open their mouths, they are more likely to be
detected.

1313b16 Another way is to stir up strife and set friends
against friends, people against notables and the rich
against each other. It is also in the interests of a tyrant to
make his subjects poor, so that he may be able to afford
the cost of his bodyguard, while the people are so occupied with their daily tasks that they have no time for
plotting. As examples of such measures, all having the
same effect – of keeping subjects perpetually at work and
in poverty – we may mention the pyramids of Egypt, the
numerous offerings made by the Cypselids,[5] the building
of the temple of Zeus Olympius by the Peisistratidae,[6]
and some of the works at Samos, under Polycrates.[7] Sub-

4. Tyrant of Syracuse, 478–467.

5. Cypselus was tyrant of Corinth, *c.* 657–*c.* 625, and was succeeded
by his son Periander (see n. 2), who died in 585.

6. See V x, nn. 4 and 13.

7. Tyrant of Samos in the late sixth century.

jects are also kept poor by payment of taxes, as at Syracuse under Dionysius,[8] where in five years the value of everything possessed was paid in. The tyrant is also very ready to make war; for this keeps his subjects occupied and in continued need of a leader. Friends are a source of stability to a kingship, but not to a tyrant; it is part of his policy to mistrust them more than anyone, as having more than anyone the power to do what all the others merely wish.[9]

1313b32 The features of extreme democracy are also all characteristic of a tyrant's policy: the dominance of women in the home, and slack control of slaves. The reason for both features is the same. Tyrants expect in this way to get information against the men, for women and slaves do not plot against tyrants: keep them satisfied and they must always be supporters of tyrannies – and of democracies, for the people too likes to be sole ruler. So for this reason, the flatterer too is held in honour by both: in democracies, the popular leader, because he is the flatterer of the mob; at a tyrant's court, those who keep him company in an obsequious spirit, which is the function of flattery. This makes tyranny favour the baser sort, in the sense that a tyrant loves to be flattered, and no man of free spirit will oblige him. Respectable men give friendship, or at any rate refrain from flattery, and base men are useful for base deeds ('nail on nail', as the saying goes).[10]

1314a5 The typical tyrant dislikes proud and free-spirited people. He regards himself as the only person entitled to those qualities; and anyone who shows a rival pride and a spirit of freedom destroys the supremacy and master-like character of the tyranny. Thus the tyrant hates such people as destroyers of his rule. He is also inclined to

8. See V x, n. 5.

9. I.e. to attack him.

10. Aristotle uses the saying loosely: it commonly referred to the expulsion of like by like (cf. the drunkard's hopeful cure: 'a hair of the dog that bit me').

cultivate the company of foreigners and eat with them rather than with citizens of his own state; for the latter he sees as potential enemies, the former as not making rival claims.

1314a12 All these and their like are marks of tyranny and ways of maintaining it; and they are utterly depraved. They may all be grouped under three heads, corresponding to tyranny's three aims, namely that its subjects shall (a) have little spirit of their own, (b) have no trust in each other, and (c) have no means of carrying out anything. As to (a), the point is that resistance is not planned by puny spirits against anyone. As to (b), no tyranny is ever brought low until a certain degree of mutual confidence is established; hence tyrants are hostile to respectable men, as being dangerous to their rule, not only because of their repugnance to being ruled as though by a master, but because they command confidence, both among themselves and others, and abstain from making accusations against each other or anybody else. As to (c), no one attempts what is quite beyond his powers, so nobody attempts to destroy even a tyranny if the power to do so is not there. These then are the three definitive ends to which the tyrant's plans relate: all his acts might be referred to these three principles – he wants his subjects to have no mutual confidence, no power and little spirit.

1314a29 So much for one method of preserving tyrannies; the other requires care to be exercised in virtually the opposite direction. To understand it, we take our cue from the destruction of kingships. Just as one way of setting a kingdom on the road to destruction is to make its rule more tyrannical, so conversely it preserves a tyranny to make it more kingly, always guarding just one thing – the power of the ruler, power enabling him to govern not only those who wish him to but also those who do not. For if he abandons that, he abandons his whole position as tyrant. This serves as his permanent fundamental principle; for the rest, in his every real or pretended act he must be adept at playing in the role of a king.

1314a40   Thus in the first place he will appear to think of the general good; he will not spend large sums on giving bounties such as arouse the people's indignation, as when the gifts are extracted from *their* toil and labour, while *he* gives lavishly to his mistresses, to foreigners, and to his skilled craftsmen. And in this connection he will render an account of his revenue and expenditure – a practice adopted by some tyrants in the past. Such a mode of administration will help him to look like a household-manager[11] and not a tyrant. And he does not have to fear shortage of money, being sovereign over the state. Indeed, if a ruler goes abroad much, it is actually more expedient for him to follow this policy[12] than to collect and leave behind a vast sum. There will be less likelihood that those in charge of his finances will try to get the control of affairs into their own hands; and when tyrants are away they are more nervous about those in charge of their finances than about the citizens: the citizens go abroad with him, the financial officers remain behind. Again, when he collects taxes or demands public services,[13] it should appear that he is doing these things to further his management,[11] and for his military needs at a particular juncture; and generally he should make himself look like a guardian and steward not of his own resources but of the public's.

1314b18   In his dealings he should always give the impression of dignity,[14] not of harshness, of being the kind of person who inspires not fear but respect in those who meet him. This is not easy if he is really despised. Hence if he cannot manage to cultivate any of the other virtues, he should aim at least at valour in warfare, and establish for himself a military reputation. Neither he nor any of his entourage should be seen to violate[15] any of his youth-

11. *Oikonomos, oikonomia.*
12. I.e. of publishing accounts.
13. See IV iv, n. 11.
14. *Semnos,* translated by 'proud' earlier in this chapter.
15. *Hubrizō, hubris;* cf. V x, n. 12.

ful subjects, male or female; and this applies equally to
the women of his court in their behaviour towards other
women. (Female sexual assaults[15] too have often caused
tyrannies to fall.) His behaviour must also be unlike that
of some tyrants nowadays in regard to indulgence of the
body: they start at dawn and continue for days on end,
and even do so for the express purpose of letting others
see their indulgence and marvel at how happy and
supremely fortunate they are. In such matters moderation
is best, or at least to avoid indulgence in full view of
others. It is not the sober but the tipsy man who is easily
got at and easily despised, not the wide-awake but the
slumberer. And he must do the opposite of practically
all the things mentioned long before:[16] thus in the arrangement and adornment of the city he should be a
trustee rather than a tyrant.

1314b38 In religion he should always be more obviously
in earnest than anyone else, but not so as to give an impression of brainlessness. Men are less fearful of being
treated illegally by such a person, whom they regard as
a religious man and one who pays regard to the gods; and
they plot against him less if they believe that he has even
the gods on his side. Again, when any of his subjects show
a marked capacity for anything, he should honour them
so much that they come to believe that even by independent citizens they could not have been given greater
honour. Such honours he should bestow in person, leaving punishments to be imposed by others, whether officials
or courts. There is a protective principle here which
applies equally to all kinds of monarchy – not to make
any one man great; if need be, let there be several (they
will watch each other). If in practice it is found necessary
so to single out one man, let him not be one of bold
character. Such a character is always ready for the attack,
whatever the business in hand. And if it is decided to

16. Possibly a reference to the public works described in the
3rd paragraph of this chapter: the wise tyrant will undertake them,
but in a different spirit.

dismiss him from power, this should be done gradually: do not remove his whole competence at one blow.

1315a14 He should abstain from all ill-treatment[17] in all its forms, and two in particular – offences against the person and against youth. This precaution must be taken especially in regard to ambitious men; for while the money-loving chiefly resent slights which affect their money, the ambitious and respectable resent attacks on their honour. Hence either he must not employ such men or, if he inflicts punishment, it should obviously be inflicted in a fatherly spirit and not as a slight. His liaisons with young persons should spring from love, not simply from the opportunities open to him; and generally any apparent diminution of honours should be bought off by greater ones bestowed. Of all those who make attacks on a tyrant's life, the most to be watched and feared are those who reck nothing of their own life provided they can take his. Therefore he should be wary of such men when they think that they are ill-used[17] (themselves or the objects of their care). When anger is the spring of their action men are unsparing of themselves. As Heraclitus once said, 'Anger is a difficult enemy; he buys with his life.'[18]

1315a31 Since states are made up of two sections, those who have property and those who do not, both, if possible, ought to believe that they owe their safety to the regime, and neither ought to treat the other unjustly. But whichever of the two sections is the more powerful, its members ought to be thoroughly embraced by the regime, so that, with this backing for his interests, the tyrant may be able to avoid the necessity of such measures as the liberation of slaves and the confiscation of arms. For it is sufficient for the purpose of being stronger than his

17. *Hubrizesthai*, cf. n. 15.
18. A partly verbatim report of fr. 85 in H. Diels and W. Kranz, *Die Fragmente der Vorsokratiker*, I (6th ed., Berlin, 1951–2). 'Life' = *psuchē*, in this translation usually rendered 'soul'. Heraclitus of Ephesus wrote around the turn of the sixth and fifth centuries.

attackers if one or other of the two sections be added to his power.

1315a40   It would be superfluous to go into any further details about such matters. The general purpose is clear: a tyrant should not appear like a tyrant in the eyes of his subjects, but like a king and a manager of a household;[11] not a person who is out for his own gain but as a trustee of the affairs of others, aiming not at a life of excess, but at one of moderation; and as someone who moreover makes friends with the notables but is also the people's leader. If he acts thus, his rule is bound to be not only better and more enviable (he will not be hated and feared, and his rule will be exercised over better men, not men reduced to impotent submission), but also more lasting; and he himself will have either the right disposition or at least a half-good disposition with respect to virtue, a man not wicked but half-wicked.

V xii

(*1315b11–1316b27*)

THE IMPERMANENCE OF TYRANNIES;
PLATO ON CONSTITUTIONAL CHANGE

In spite of all his 'tips to tyrants' in the preceding chapter, Aristotle has to recognize that tyrannies and oligarchies rarely last long; and in the first two paragraphs of this final chapter of Book V he gives some examples of the most durable.

The remainder of the chapter is somewhat difficult, being another of Aristotle's puzzlingly unsympathetic criticisms of Plato, of which we have many examples in II. It is as though, at the end of his account of constitutional change, he felt that it could be rivalled or challenged by Plato's, which he therefore tried to dismiss with a few well-chosen broadsides. In the eighth and ninth books of the Republic *Plato gave an imaginary account* of changes from one form of constitution to another; though based on observed fact, it was essentially a psychological study, of the progressive deterioration from the finest aristocracy to the worst tyranny; it was not intended as a factual or systematic analysis of all forms of constitutional change, nor as direct political advice to rulers. Aristotle seems almost perversely determined not to enter into the spirit of the thing: the essence of his attack is that the causes of change in constitutions are in fact far more various and complex than they are described as being in the Republic. Plato would have responded, one supposes, with agreement and a pitying smile, and with a just reminder of the special focus of his own account. Discussion about the nature and causes of constitutional change was no doubt carried on both inside and outside the Academy (where Aristotle studied for twenty years), and to read this chapter together with Republic VIII and IX is to overhear controversy.

In the third paragraph Aristotle refers allusively to a complex and controversial passage of the Republic (546b ff.), in which Plato suggests, apparently somewhat playfully, that the initial deterioration in the ideal constitution might be described mathematically, in terms of the 'nuptial number'. If it is not too pretentious so to describe it, this could be regarded as an early attempt to apply mathematical techniques to genetic and social change. Aristotle's criticism is that it is far too generalized, and could equally well apply to any other constitution, not only the 'best'. Indeed, the whole of the second part of the chapter is a good example of Aristotle's healthy mistrust of generalization, which stems from his fundamental belief that each separate constitution has its own special causes of change which it is the business of the political theorists to collect, describe and analyse as a basis for giving political advice designed to further the 'good' life.

On the interpretation of the 'nuptial number', see J. Adam, Plato's Republic (Cambridge, 1902, repr. 1963), II pp. 201–9, 264–312.

1315b11   Still, oligarchy and tyranny are shorter-lived than any other constitution. The longest tyranny was the Sicyonian, that of Orthagoras and his sons: it lasted a hundred years. This was because they treated their subjects with moderation and in many matters subjected themselves to the rule of law:[1] and Cleisthenes was a warlike person and therefore not one to be easily despised. In general, they maintained themselves as the people's leaders by repeated acts of care for them. (At any rate, it is said that Cleisthenes set a wreath upon the head of an adjudicator who had declared someone else the winner; and some say that the seated statue to be seen in the market-place is of the man who gave that decision.) It is said of Peisistratus[2], too, that he was once summoned to appear before the court of the Areopagus, and submitted.

1315b22   Second place goes to the tyranny of the Cypselids[3] at Corinth, which lasted seventy-three and a half years. Cypselus was tyrant for thirty years, Periander for forty and a half, and Psammitichus, son of Gorgus, for three. The reasons for their success are the same. Cypselus was a leader of the people and all through his reign continued without an armed guard; Periander was more of the typical tyrant, but he was warlike. Third is the tyranny of the Peisistratidae[2] at Athens. This was not continuous, for twice during his tyranny Peisistratus was exiled. Thus he was a tyrant for seventeen years out of thirty-three; his sons reigned for eighteen years, making thirty-five years in all. Of the rest there is the Syracusan, of Hiero and Gelon,[4] but even this did not endure for longer than eighteen years. Gelon was tyrant for seven years and died in the eighth, Hiero for ten; and Thrasy-

1. Literally, 'were slaves to the laws'. The tyranny of Orthagoras' family lasted from *c.* 665 to *c.* 565; Cleisthenes was tyrant from *c.* 600 to 570.

2. See V v, n. 6 and V x, nn. 4 and 13.

3. See III xiii, n. 10, V x, V xi, n. 5. Gorgus was Periander's successor.

4. See V iii, n. 4 and V xi, n. 4. Thrasybulus succeeded Hiero in 467.

bulus was driven out in the eleventh month. But all round, tyrannies have not lasted long.

1315b40 I have now said virtually all I have to say on these topics, having described in relation both to monarchies and to constitutions in general the causes of their destruction and the ways in which they are preserved. But in the *Republic* Socrates discourses, though in an unsatisfactory manner, on their changes. He starts from the first and ideally best constitution, but the change which he discerns in it is not peculiar to it. For he says that change is due to the fact that nothing stays the same but changes within a certain cycle; and that this periodicity has its origin in those entities 'in which a basic proportion of four to three, coupled with five, produces two harmonies', meaning by that, when the number on this diagram is cubed.[5] This implies that nature at a certain moment produces bad men, beyond the reach of education. This is perhaps in itself unexceptionable; it may well be that there are people who are incapable of being educated and becoming sound men. But why should this be a change affecting peculiarly what he calls the best constitution, any more than any other constitution or anything else that comes into existence? And throughout that period of time which he speaks of as changing all things, do even things which started to come into existence at different times change at the same time? I mean, if something came into being the day before the turning point,[6] does it then change along with the rest?

1316a17 My second criticism is this: why should this constitution change into the Laconian?[7] All constitutions more often change into their opposites than into those like them. The same argument also applies to the subsequent changes which he gives – from the Laconian to

5. See *Republic* 546c.
6. Of the cycle; presumably the moment when the 'best' constitution begins to deteriorate.
7. *Republic* 544c ff. 'This' constitution is 'the best'.

oligarchy and from that to democracy and from democracy to tyranny. Surely there are also changes in the reverse direction, as from democracy to oligarchy, and to this even more than to monarchy.

1316a25 Moreover, he stops at tyranny and does not say whether or not it will suffer change, nor, if it does, what will cause the change, and into what sort of constitution. The reason is that he would have found it difficult to say, for tyranny is an indeterminate thing. According to Socrates' theory it ought to change into the constitution which is first and best; the process would then become continuous and circular. But tyranny can also change into tyranny, as at Sicyon from that of Myron to that of Cleisthenes, or to oligarchy, like the tyranny of Antileon at Chalcis, or to democracy, as did that of Gelon's family at Syracuse,[4] or into aristocracy, as that of Charillus[8] at Lacedaemon, or as at Carthage. Change may also take place from oligarchy to tyranny, which is what happened to most of the older Sicilian oligarchies, in Leontini to the tyranny of Panaetius, in Gela to that of Cleander, in Rhegium to that Anaxilaus, and in many other cities likewise.

1316a39 It is also an odd notion that change into oligarchy is due to the fact that those who hold office are fond of money and makers of money, and not rather to the fact that those with vast possessions think it unjust that those who do not have property should participate in the state on equal terms with those who do. And in many oligarchies it is not possible to make money:[9] there are laws to prevent it. On the other hand, in democratic Carthage they do make money and have not yet changed their constitution.

1316b6 Equally odd is his statement that the oligarchical state is two states, one of the rich and one of the poor.[10] But why is this oligarchy of which he speaks different in

---

8. See references at II x, n. 1.
9. I.e. from commerce: *Republic* 550e. Cf. I ix and III v.
10. *Republic* 551d.

this respect from the Laconian, or any other in which not all are equally possessed of property, or in which not all are equally good men? Without any person becoming poorer than he was, men none the less change from oligarchy to democracy, if the poor become more numerous, and from democracy to oligarchy when the wealthy are stronger than the multitude, so long as the one party is alert and the other negligent. Though there are many causes that give rise to the changes, he mentions but one, namely that by their extravagant living men get heavily burdened by payments of interest and become poor, implying that all or most of them were rich at the start.[11] But this is not true. Certainly, whenever some of the leading men lose their wealth, they do try to make innovations; but when some of the others lose theirs, nothing happens out of the ordinary. And if change does take place on such an occasion, even then it does not tend towards a democracy, any more than towards some other constitution. What counts in creating faction and constitutional change is whether honours and privileges are shared, and whether people are unjustly treated or ill-used, even when they have not squandered their possessions through enjoying the possibility of doing exactly what they like – an opportunity which he says is furnished by an excess of liberty. And there are many different oligarchies and democracies, but Socrates speaks of their changes as if there were only one of either.

11. *Republic* 555d. 'The changes' are from oligarchy to democracy.

BOOK VI

VI i

(*1316b31–1317a39*)

HOW DO CONSTITUTIONS FUNCTION BEST?

The sixth book, which refers frequently to points made in the fourth and fifth, deals with the question how constitutions can be made to work best. Chapters i–v discuss democracy, and vi–vii oligarchy; but in viii the book seems to break off unfinished. Chapter i is programmatic, and contains little that is fresh: in the first half Aristotle simply distinguishes his themes from others tackled or projected; in the second, he isolates two reasons why democratic constitutions exist in more forms than one (cf. IV vi).

1316b30 So far[1] we have listed and counted the varieties of a constitution's deliberative and sovereign element, and of its system of offices and courts, and what kinds of them are arranged so as to suit what kind of constitution; we have also discussed[2] the causes, and the kinds of circumstances, that lead to the destruction and preservation of constitutions. But since there are in fact several sorts of democracy and of the other constitutions, it might not come amiss to pick up the remaining threads of that inquiry and to state what particular procedure is appropriate and expedient in each case.[3]
1316b39 We have also to consider how all the various arrangements of the elements[4] we listed may be combined, for a combination of two arrangements makes the constitutions overlap: an aristocracy may become oligarchic, a polity more democratic. In speaking of com-

1. IV xiv–xvi.
2. In Book V as a whole.
3. VI iv, in the case of democracy.
4. Executive, judicial, deliberative: see IV xiv, *init.*

binations which ought to be investigated but never have been,[5] I mean, for example, cases such as these: when there is an oligarchical bias in the arrangement of the deliberative element and in the elections of officials, but an aristocratic bias in the courts; or if these and the deliberative functions are assigned on oligarchic principles, the electoral on aristocratic; or any other procedure by which not all the elements appropriate to a given constitution are combined in it.

1317a10 Again, while we have already spoken[6] of the kinds of democracy suitable for a specific kind of state, and what kind of oligarchy for what kind of populace, and, of the other constitutional types, which is advantageous to whom, there is still something to be said. We ought to show not only, of these constitutions, which kind is best for states, but also how both these and the others ought to be contructed. Let us now deal briefly with this question, beginning with democracy; this will at the same time throw light on its opposite, the constitution which is called by some oligarchy.

1317a18 To carry out this inquiry we must take all the features of popular rule, i.e. all that are considered to be entailed by democracy. For out of combinations of these emerge the forms of democracy, and the existence of more than one democracy, all of them different. There are two reasons why there are several democracies; first, the one already mentioned,[7] that peoples differ: one populace may be agricultural, another engaged in mechanical tasks and labour for hire; and when the first of these is added to the second, or the third to both, not only is the *quality* of the democracy altered (in that it becomes better or worse), but also its *identity*.[8] The other reason is the one under discussion: all these features which are entailed by democracy and are regarded as

5. Nor does Aristotle himself discuss them.
6. IV xii.
7. E.g. IV vi, cf. xv.
8. I.e. it becomes a different *kind* of democracy.

appropriate to this constitution make the democracies different, according to whether few or several or all of these features which are entailed by democracy are combined in them. It is useful to be able to distinguish each feature for the purpose both of setting up whichever of these democracies one prefers, and of making amendments. Those who set up constitutions try to bring to the foundation all the features appropriate to their fundamental principle, but they are wrong in so doing, as has been stated earlier when the dissolution and preservation of constitutions was under discussion.[9]

Let us now discuss the claims, the ethical standards,[10] and the aims of the various constitutions.

VI ii

(1317a40–1318a10)

PRINCIPLES AND PRACTICES OF DEMOCRACIES

In this splendidly meaty chapter Aristotle examines the 'claims, ethical standards and aims' (see VI i ad fin.) of democracy. The second paragraph contains one of the most succinct yet most comprehensive summaries to be found anywhere of democratic principles as they were applied in practice in ancient Greece.

It is, however, the analysis and reflection of the first and third paragraphs that will repay study. In the first, if I interpret aright, Aristotle analyses the relationship between liberty and equality. Liberty has two 'marks': (a) ruling and being ruled by turn; (b) living as one pleases. Equality justifies (a) on moral grounds: it is just that all should have an equal share of the privilege of ruling; and it also ensures this sharing in practice, by allowing the populace to enforce it by its majority of 'equal' votes. On the other hand, (b) conflicts with (a):

9. V ix.   10. *Ēthē*

one would rather never *be ruled. Nevertheless the democrat recognizes that the willingness to be ruled is a guarantee of the freedom to rule, and in thus yielding place
in his turn to the next ruler he facilitates equality of the
enjoyment of the privilege of ruling. Liberty and equality
thus intimately support each other.*

*The final paragraph is difficult to follow, but seems
to pick up a point in the first, that the majority is
sovereign. Now inevitably in most states that majority
will be the poor, who regard democracy as a device for
maintaining their own ascendancy and interests. Aristotle now briefly and tantalizingly envisages a 'thorough-
going' democracy in which the poor do not have sole
sovereignty – perhaps merely because they do not constitute a majority, or because democracy is not seen by
them as an instrument of social warfare. In that case, 'of
the people' in the text will mean 'of the whole people',
and Aristotle will be contemplating something like a
modern Western democracy, which, in theory at any
rate, is for the benefit of the whole population of the
state, not merely that of the poor.*

1317a40 A basic principle of the democratic constitution is liberty. People constantly make this statement,
implying that only in this constitution do men share
in liberty; for every democracy, they say, has liberty for
its aim. 'Ruling and being ruled in turn' is one element
in liberty, and the democratic idea of justice is in fact
numerical equality, not equality based on merit; and
when this idea of what is just prevails, the multitude
must be sovereign, and whatever the majority decides is
final and constitutes justice. For, they say, there must
be equality for each of the citizens. The result is that
in democracies the poor have more sovereign power than
the rich; for they are more numerous, and the decisions
of the majority are sovereign. So this is one mark of
liberty, one which all democrats make a definitive principle of their constitution. Another is to live as you like.

For this, they say, is a function of being free, since its opposite, living not as you like, is the function of one enslaved. This is the second defining principle of democracy, and from it has come the ideal of 'not being ruled', not by anyone at all if possible, or at least only in alternation. This[1] is a contribution towards that liberty which is based on equality.

1317b17 From these fundamentals, and from rule thus conceived, are derived the following features of democracy: (a) Elections to office by all from among all. (b) Rule of all over each and of each by turns over all. (c) Offices filled by lot, either all or at any rate those not calling for experience or skill. (d) No tenure of office dependent on the possession of a property qualification, or only on the lowest possible. (e) The same man not to hold the same office twice, or only rarely, or only a few apart from those connected with warfare. (f) Short terms for all offices or for as many as possible. (g) All to sit on juries, chosen from all and adjudicating on all or most matters, i.e. the most important and supreme, such as those affecting the constitution, scrutinies, and contracts between individuals. (h) The assembly as the sovereign authority in everything, or at least the most important matters, officials having no sovereign power over any, or over as few as possible. (The council is of all offices the most democratic as long as all members do not receive lavish pay; for lavish pay all round has the effect of robbing this office too of its power; for the people, when well-paid, takes all decisions into its own hands, as has been mentioned in the inquiry preceding this.)[2] Next, (i) payment for services, in the assembly, in the law-courts, and in the offices, is regular for all (or at any rate the offices, the law-courts, council, and the sovereign

---

1. I.e., I take it, 'to be ruled by alternation'. More fully and literally, '. . . and it [the second defining principle (?)] makes a contribution *in this way*', i.e. by operating not in the full form of 'live as you like'/'not being ruled at all', but in the modified form of 'to be ruled by alternation'.

2. IV xv.

meetings of the assembly, or in the offices where it is obligatory to have meals together). Again (j), as birth, wealth, and education are the defining marks of oligarchy, so their opposites, low birth, low incomes, and mechanical occupations, are regarded as typical of democracy. (k) No official has perpetual tenure, and if any such office remains in being after an early change, it is shorn of its power and its holders selected by lot from among picked candidates.[3]

1318a3 These are the common characteristics of democracies. And from the idea of justice that is by common consent democratic – justice based on numerical equality for all – springs what is reckoned to be the most thorough-going democracy and *dēmos*;[4] for equality exists if the poor exercise no more influence in ruling than the rich, and do not have sole sovereign power, but all exercise it together on the basis of numerical equality. In this sense, they could think of the constitution as possessing equality and freedom.

VI iii

(*1318a11–1318b5*)

WAYS OF ACHIEVING EQUALITY

This chapter is a fascinating discussion of the democratic concept of equality, and makes various practical suggestions for reconciling the democratic demand for arithmetical equality (i.e. equality of voting power for each individual), and for majority rule, with the oligarchic demand for that kind of 'proportionate' equality that gives greater power to greater wealth. (For Aristotle's discussion of these two 'equalities', see III ix, xii, and V i.) Each side wants power to lie in something 'greater':

3. Or perhaps '. . . by lot instead of by election'.

4. The last two words presumably amount to '. . . and the most inclusive idea of what makes a "people" ', i.e. rich and poor together.

numbers and property respectively. The system Aristotle describes in the second paragraph ensures that on at least some occasions both the greater numbers of persons and the greater amount of property will be on the winning side (as explained in note 5). But because of the 'weighting' given to the rich in terms of votes (as for example in note 1), there could also be occasions when the numerical majority consisting largely of poor persons could be outvoted by the numerical minority consisting largely of the rich. One wonders if the compromise Aristotle puts forward would have satisfied either party.

The technicalities of the first two sentences are a little tricky, and I have attempted to elucidate them in Liverpool Classical Monthly, *4 (1979), pp. 98–9; cf. also Rackham's notes in the Loeb edition.*

1318a11 The next question is, how will they obtain equality? Ought the property-qualifications to be divided,[1] those of 500 persons for the benefit of a 1,000, so that the 1,000 have the same power as the 500? Or should one refuse to establish equality on these lines, and make the division as before, but then from the 500 take the same number of persons as from the 1,000, and give to these supreme control of elections and law-courts?[2] Will

1. E.g. if the minimum qualification for political rights is 2x of property, then 500 rich men, each of whom owns 2x, will qualify; but 1,000 poor, each of whom owns 1x, will not. Equality of power is achieved by 'dividing' the minimum qualification 2x into a fraction of itself, 1x. Each poor man has now 1x of power, each rich man 2x. Since $500 \times 2 = 1,000 \times 1$, the two blocks have equal power. Cf. VI iv, end of 3rd paragraph, and VI vi.

2. In the first alternative, there are two blocks, 1,000 and 500; whether they meet separately or together is not clear (though the example explained in note 5 suggests the latter); in either case they would be equal in 'power'. In the second alternative, each block is given the same number of *representatives*, presumably to some larger body. In both alternatives, therefore, the wealthy *individual* is in a sense given a 'weighting', but the wealthy *block* is not: its power is no greater than that of the other and poorer block.

this constitution then be most just in accordance with the democratic conception of justice, or will one based on the majority? For the champions of democracy say that what the majority decide is just, while the partisans of oligarchy say that it is whatever is decided upon by those with greater possessions, asserting that size of fortune is the proper criterion to use. But both these views involve inequality and injustice. If we take the view that justice is what the few decide, we have a tyranny; for if one man has property greater than all the other wealthy persons, according to oligarchic justice he alone has a just title to rule. If we take justice to be what is decided by a numerical majority, they will act unjustly, confiscating the property of the rich and less numerous, as has been said before.[3]

1318a27 In order to ascertain what an equality might be upon which both parties will agree, we must start by examining the definitions of justice from which they severally begin. Thus it is said that whatever seems right to the majority of the citizens ought to be binding. So be it – but not universally or in every case. Since it happens that the state is made up of two parts, the rich and the poor, we grant that whatever seems good to both groups, or to a majority in each, shall be binding. But if their decisions disagree, the answer should be whatever is decided by the majority, i.e. by those of the higher total property-assessment.[4] Suppose for example that there are ten of one group and twenty of the other, and a resolution has been supported by (A) six of the rich and five of the poor and opposed by (B) the four remaining rich and the fifteen remaining poor, then whichever have the highest total property-assessment, the property of both rich and poor being reckoned in each

3. III x.
4. The crucial point here is that whereas in an oligarchy the rich would exercise final power alone, and in a democracy the poor, under Aristotle's proposal *both* sides would have *some* voice, proportionate to their property, in the making of decisions.

set, their decision is to be binding.[5] If they turn out to be equal, that should not be regarded as a difficulty any different from that posed by an equality of votes in an assembly or law-court: the matter must be decided by lot or in some other recognized manner.

1318b1 And however difficult it may be to find out the truth about equality and justice, yet it is easier than to get men's agreement when you are trying to persuade them to forgo some greater share that lies within their grasp. It is always the weaker who go in search of justice and equality; the strong reck nothing of them.

VI iv

(*1318b6–1319b32*)

THE BEST DEMOCRACY

This is the core chapter in the first part of the book (Chapters i–v, on democracy). Aristotle argues that democracy works best when the population consists largely of country-dwellers, not town-dwellers, because the former are disinclined to exercise too frequently the democratic right of attendance at the meetings of the assembly in the city; and he dwells at some length on the sterling merits of an agricultural population. Ancient literature is full of more or less romantic praises of country life, but Aristotle's assessment is relatively cool and dispassionate, being strictly for the purpose of assessing political and constitutional advantages. Towards the middle and end of the chapter he notes and recommends certain measures of crucial importance to an 'agrarian' democracy; they affect mainly the related problems of land-tenure and qualification for citizenship.

5. In this example, if each of ten rich men has 2x property and 2 votes, and each of twenty poor men 1x property and 1 vote, then side A has (6 × 2) + (5 × 1) votes = 17, and side B has (4 × 2) + (15 × 1) votes = 23. Side B therefore wins.

This 'best' democracy is not an extreme democracy; and in this connection we encounter, not for the first time in the Politics, *a doctrine of political checks and balances (cf. introduction to II ix). Aristotle believes that the extreme forms of any constitution are less durable than the moderate or 'mixed' (see e.g. IV xi–xii, VI v–vi). Hence in an agrarian democracy the 'notables' and 'middle people' have an important role: it is they who will do most of the ruling (they have the leisure), but subject to election and formal 'scrutiny' (euthuna, see II ix, n. 14), by the poorer people. Thus the richer citizens will not feel resentful at a democracy run by, and largely in the interests of, the poor; and they will lend the state culture, administrative wisdom, and stability. On the other hand they cannot, in language reminiscent of VI ii, 'do as they please': there is always the agrarian population to check them by its power of election and scrutiny.*

1318b6 Of the four democracies the best is that which is first in order, as was said in the preceding parts of our work.[1] It is also the oldest of all. I am referring to the 'first' as it would be in a classification by peoples. An agrarian people is the best; so that it is possible to construct a democracy, too,[2] anywhere where the population subsists on agriculture or pasturing stock. For having no great abundance of possessions, they are kept busy and rarely attend the assembly; and since they lack the necessities of life[3] they are constantly at work in the fields, and do not covet the possessions of others. They find more satisfaction in working on the land than in ruling and in engaging in public affairs, so long as there are no great gains to be made out of holding office; for the many are more interested in making a profit than in winning honour. An indication of this is to be found in the fact that they put up with tyrannies in the old days and

1. IV, iv, vi, xi, all useful preliminary reading for this chapter.
2. I.e. as well as other constitutions.
3. I.e. they have to work to get them.

oligarchies at the present time, so long as work is not denied them and nothing is taken from them. Some of them quickly acquire wealth; the rest are at any rate not destitute. Moreover, to have the sovereign power to vote at elections and to scrutinize outgoing officials makes up any deficiency which those who have ambitions may feel. For in certain democracies, where the many have sovereign power to deliberate but do not participate in elections to office (electors being selected from all by turns, as at Mantinea), even then they are content enough; and this arrangement too, which once existed at Mantinea, is to be regarded as a form of democracy.

1318b27   Hence for this other kind of democracy[4] which we have mentioned, it is advantageous as well as customary that all should elect to offices, call to scrutiny, and sit as jurymen; *but* that persons to fill the most important offices should be selected from among those possessing a certain amount of property (the greater the office, the higher the property-qualification) – or even not on the basis of property at all, but ability. Running affairs of state on this basis will be bound to be successful, because the offices will always be in the hands of the best persons, in accordance with the wishes of the people and without their being jealous of the respectable men. Moreover, this form of administration will satisfy the notables and the respectable sort, who will not find themselves ruled by their inferiors; and their own ruling will be just, because others will have the sovereign power to call them to scrutiny. For this dependence, and not allowing a man to follow all his own decisions, are beneficial. (Freedom to do exactly what one likes cannot do anything to keep in check that element of badness which exists in each and all of us.) The inevitable result is this most valuable of principles in a constitution: ruling by respectable men of blameless conduct, and without detriment to the populace at large.

4. Evidently that described in the preceding paragraph, without the Mantinean modification.

1319a4 It is clear then that this is the best of the democracies, and the reason also is clear, namely that the people is of the kind it is. In considering next the means whereby a people may be made an agrarian one we find that some of the laws which the ancients adopted in many places are exceedingly useful, such as absolutely to prohibit the acquisition of land above a certain amount, or at any rate to permit it only beyond a certain distance from the central citadel and city. And in many states in early times it was laid down by law that the original estates might not even be sold. A somewhat similar effect is produced by the law ascribed to Oxylus,[5] which prohibits a man from raising a loan on more than a certain proportion of his land. In present-day conditions matters should also be put right by means of the law of the Aphytaeans, which is very useful for the purpose which we have under discussion. For the Aphytaeans, though their numbers are large and their land small, are all tillers of the soil: assessments are not based on whole properties but on portions of them so small that even the poor easily exceed the property-qualification.

1319a19 Next to an agrarian population the best is a pastoral people, which earns a livelihood from cattle. There are many points of resemblance to agriculture proper; indeed, when it comes to the operations of war they are in a particularly well-trained condition, physically fit, and capable of living in the open.

1319a24 Virtually all the other populations that make up the other democracies are greatly inferior to these two. Their lives are inferior, and none of the work they do has the quality of virtue, a mass of mechanics and marketfellows and hirelings as they are. Also this class of person, which is constantly milling around the city and the market-place, can all too easily attend the assembly. An agrarian populace on the other hand is dispersed over the countryside; its members neither appear at meetings

5. An ancient king of Elis, in the Peloponnese.

nor feel the need of such gatherings to the same extent.
And where in addition the countryside is so situated as to
extend a long way from the city, it is easy to make a good
democracy or polity: the populace are then compelled to
make their homes far away, on the land; and so even if
there is a market-place crowd, it should not be allowed in
democracies to hold assemblies in the absence of the
country-dwellers. So much then for the first and best
democracy and how it should be composed. What we have
said will throw light also on the composition of the
others: they must deviate in order and at each stage
exclude the next inferior multitude lower down the list.[6]
1319b1 The most extreme democracy, in which all share,
is something which not every state can tolerate; and it
is not likely to last unless it is well held together by its
laws and customs. (I need hardly add more to what I have
said earlier[7] about the factors by which this and the other
constitutions may be destroyed.) As to the setting up of
this democracy and the establishment of the power of the
people, the leaders habitually add in as many men as
possible and make them all citizens, both the illegitimate
and those born in wedlock, and those also who are of
citizen stock on only one side, the mother's or the father's.
This whole policy is particularly characteristic of such a
democracy. Popular leaders regularly resort to such
measures; but the addition of new members ought to
continue only until the multitude just outnumbers the
notables and middle people, and no further. To go
beyond this point makes for disorganization in the constitution, and irritates the notables to such an extent that
they barely tolerate the existence of the democracy (it
was precisely this that caused the faction at Cyrene).[8] A

6. I.e. when citizenship is extended to a lower group, the *next*
lower group, which is inferior, should be excluded. Aristotle
makes the point in a curiously negative way; a democrat would
have said, positively, '*include* the next lower class at each stage'.

7. In Book V.

8. Possibly in 401.

371

small admixture of inferiority is disregarded, but a large one is all too obvious.

1319b19   There are other steps also which may be usefully taken in promoting this kind of democracy, such as those used by Cleisthenes[9] when he wanted to strengthen the democracy at Athens, and by the promoters of democracy at Cyrene. I mean that new tribes and brotherhoods should be established, more numerous than the old, and ceremonies held at private shrines should be concentrated on a few public ones; and in general one must fix things so that there is as much social intercourse as possible and a break-up of the former associations.

1319b27   Moreover there is evidently something characteristic of democracy in all the typical measures of tyranny – lack of control over slaves (which may be expedient up to a point), and over women and children, and disregard of everyone living as they please. There is a lot of support for this kind of constitution; most people prefer to live undisciplined lives, for they find that more enjoyable than restraint.

VI v

(1319b33–1320b17)

HOW DEMOCRACIES MAY BE PRESERVED

Aristotle opens the chapter by arguing that policies for securing the stability of a constitution may be drawn from observing and avoiding all those that make for instability. Already (V xi) he had suggested that the best way to preserve a tyranny is to make it as little like a tyranny as possible. Here, in this chapter and the next, the same is said of democracy and oligarchy: whatever is untypical is a source of strength, because too strict an adherence to doctrine is likely to undermine the regime. These two chapters present another aspect of Aristotle's desire for a

9. See III ii.

mixed constitution, which he generally calls a 'polity', in preference to a 'pure' one. See e.g. II vi (ad fin.), II ix (introduction), IV ix, and Kurt von Fritz, The Theory of the Mixed Constitution in Antiquity (New York, 1954), pp. 81–2.

The policy of 'welfare relief' recommended in the final three paragraphs is remarkable, but not new: Peisistratus had paved the way (see Aristotle's Constitution of Athens, ch. 16), and Aristotle cites a couple of precedents at Carthage and Tarentum. Two points may be made. (1) The policy is prudential rather than philanthropic or humanitarian: it is in the interests of the rich themselves to finance it. (2) Aristotle realizes that it is of limited use merely to hand out money for the destitute to live on: the money should be applied positively, to enable them to become independent for the future.

1319b33　The task confronting the lawgiver, and all who seek to set up a constitution of such a kind, is not only, or even mainly, to establish it, but rather to ensure that it is preserved intact. (Any constitution can be made to last for a day or two.) We should therefore turn back to our previous inquiries[1] into the factors which make for the continued preservation of a constitution and those which make for its dissolution. On this basis we shall try to provide for stability; we shall be on our guard against those features which we find to be destructive, and we shall lay down those laws, written and unwritten, which shall embrace the greatest number of features that preserve constitutions. We shall know not to regard as a democratic (or oligarchic) measure any measure which will make the whole as democratic (or oligarchic) as it is possible to be, but only that measure which will make it *last* as a democracy (or oligarchy) for as long as possible.

1320a4　Present-day popular leaders, in their endeavour to win the favour of their peoples, make use of the lawcourts for frequent confiscations.[2] Those who have the

1. In Book V.　　2. Of the property of the rich.

interests of the constitution at heart ought to resist these activities, by passing a law that everything taken from those found guilty should be used for sacred purposes and not be confiscated for the public exchequer. This will not make wrongdoers any less careful (the fines will be exacted just the same); but the common crowd will be less prone to condemn a man on trial if they are not going to get anything out of it. Besides, the number of public[3] cases that happen ought always to be reduced to a minimum, ill-considered litigation being restrained by high penalties.[4] For it is not their fellow-democrats that they are accustomed to bring into court, but the notables. The constitution ought, if possible, to command the support of all citizens; short of that, at least those who exercise sovereign power should not be regarded as enemies by them.

1320a17 In the extreme democracies populations are large and attendance at meetings of the assembly is difficult unless one is paid; and this, if money is not forthcoming from the revenues, militates against the notables, for the money has then to be raised by taxation and confiscation and depraved courts – things which before now have caused many democracies to fall. Whenever therefore the necessary revenue is not to be had, the number of meetings of the assembly must be few, and the courts, though consisting of many persons, should meet on few days. This helps to make the rich unafraid of the expenses which they have to meet if the wealthy receive no fee for attendance at court, but the poor do. It also helps to improve the trials of suits at law, through the presence of the wealthy, who are willing to spend a short time, but not long periods, away from their own affairs. On the other hand if revenues are available, one should not do what popular leaders today do – make a free distribution of the surplus. (When people get it, they want the same again: this sort of assistance to the poor is like the pro-

3. I.e. involving the public interest, not a private one.
4. Inflicted on unsuccessful prosecutors.

verbial jug with a hole in it.)[5] For the duty of the true democrat is to see that the population is not destitute; for destitution is a cause of a corrupt democracy.

1320a35   Every effort therefore must be made to perpetuate prosperity. And, since that is to the advantage of the rich as well as the poor, all that accrues from the revenues should be collected into a single fund and distributed in block grants to those in need, if possible in lump sums large enough for the acquisition of a small piece of land, but if not, enough to start a business, or work in agriculture. And if that cannot be done for all, the distribution might be by tribes or some other division each in turn. The rich meanwhile will contribute funds sufficient to provide pay for the necessary meetings, being themselves relieved of all frivolous public services.[6] It has been by running their constitution on some such lines that the Carthaginians have secured the goodwill of their people. From time to time they send some of them to live in the outlying districts and turn them into men of substance. When the notables are wise and considerate, they also split up the poor into groups and make it their business to provide them with a start in some occupation.

1320b9   What is done in Tarentum is also well worth copying; there they allow communal use of their property by those who have none of their own, thus ensuring the support of the populace. They also divide all the offices into two groups, filling one by election, the other by lot – the latter so that the people may participate in holding the offices, the former so that affairs of state are more efficiently administered. It is also possible to apply this to one and the same office, dividing it into two, so that some holders are appointed by lot, others by election. So much for the right way to organize a democracy.

5. Forty-nine daughters of Danaus murdered their husbands on their wedding-night, and were punished in Hades by being obliged to go on filling leaky jars for evermore.

6. See IV iv, n. 11.

THE PRESERVATION OF OLIGARCHIES (1)

*Aristotle embarks on his discussion of the preservation
of oligarchies by making about this form of constitution
essentially the same point as he made about democracy
in the preceding chapters, namely that an extreme oligarchy is less stable than a moderate one. Hence oligarchs
have an interest in being to some extent non-oligarchical:
they should allow fairly large numbers of the population
to 'share in the constitution', in order to ensure strong
enough support for the perpetuation of the regime.*

1320b18   How oligarchy should be handled is fairly clear
from the principles already stated. Working from opposites, we must draw up a list of oligarchies, working out
each in relation to the democracy opposite to it. We begin
with the first, which is also the best mixed and very near
to what we call polity. In it division of property-qualifications is necessary, so that some are low and some high,
and so that the qualification for holding essential offices
is low, but higher for the more sovereign ones. Anyone
who reaches the required assessment of property is entitled
to share in the constitution; by this means enough of the
people are brought in by the assessment to ensure that
they are stronger than the non-sharers. But these new
sharers must always be drawn from among the better sort
among the people. Similarly with the organization of the
next type of oligarchy, except that the reins are drawn a
little tighter.

1320b30   Finally, there is the oligarchy which corresponds to the extreme democracy, and is most like a power-
group and most like a tyranny; it is also the worst, and
there is proportionally greater need to watch it. For just
as our bodies, if they are in a healthy condition, or boats

if they are in proper trim for their crews to sail them, can tolerate errors without being destroyed by them (whereas bodies in a sickly condition and boats with loose timbers and incompetent crews are seriously affected by even minor mistakes), so it is with constitutions: the worst of them need most watching.

1321a1 Generally speaking, then, in democracies a large population[1] is a safeguard, just because weight in numbers is the counterpart of the principle of justice which allows weight to merit. But an oligarchy can on the contrary expect to secure its preservation only by enforcing good order.

VI vii

(*1321a5–1321b3*)

THE PRESERVATION OF OLIGARCHIES (2)

The mention of 'good order' at the end of VI vi apparently prompts Aristotle to consider the role of the military in an oligarchy: no doubt the narrower the oligarchy, the greater the need of a strong army. But just as the quality of democracy was related earlier in this book (especially in Chapter iv) to the kind of population and to geographical and economic conditions, so now these factors are shown to be important in determining the composition of the military forces too. Once again Aristotle stresses the notion of 'blending' – in this case by the enrolment, in the democratically inclined light infantry and naval troops, of a number of the sons of the oligarchs.

The second paragraph indicates briefly how an oligarchy may judiciously admit some of the populace to the politeuma, *the citizen-body, and so to the right to hold office. Aristotle's suggestion that the people may be led to acquiesce in exclusion from such privileges by displays*

---

1. *Poluanthrōpia*, evidently in the sense of 'a large citizen-body'.

of generosity financed by oligarchical office-bearers may strike us as cynical; it is at least a little naïve, for, as Newman notes (IV 546), there would be a temptation for them to 'recoup expenditure by illicit practices'.

1321a5 A population consists of roughly four main elements: the farmers, the mechanics, the traders, and those employed on hire by others. Personnel for use in war are likewise four: cavalry, heavy-armed infantry,[1] light-armed infantry, and naval forces. Wherever the territory happens to be suitable for deploying horses, the natural conditions are favourable for making the oligarchy strong. This is because the safety of the inhabitants of such a territory depends on the strength of the cavalry, and horse-breeding is an occupation confined to those who have large resources. The next form of oligarchy will flourish where the territory is suitable for heavy infantry, an arm of the service more within the means of the well-to-do than the poor. But the light-armed infantry force, and the naval, are essentially democratic. And so in practice, wherever these form a large population, the oligarchs, if there is faction, often fight at a disadvantage. To remedy this, one must follow the practice of the military commanders who to their force of cavalry and heavy-armed soldiers add the appropriate force of light-armed troops. It is by the use of light infantry in faction that peoples get the better of the rich: their light equipment gives them an advantage in fighting over cavalry and the heavy-armed. So to establish this force of these people is to establish a force against themselves.[2] But since there is already a difference of two age-groups (one older, the other younger), the oligarchs' own sons, while still in the younger, should be trained in light and unarmed infantry work and then, separated from the boys, themselves become fit for such service in the field.

1. Hoplites.
2. 'Themselves' = oligarchs who establish a light-armed force drawn from the poor.

1321a26 As to giving the populace a place in the citizen-body, this may be done (a), as previously stated,[3] in favour of those who possess a certain property-qualification, or (b) as at Thebes, after the lapse of a period of time spent away from mechanical occupations, or (c) as at Massalia, by making a selection of the most deserving both from those within the citizen-body and from those outside it. Again, the most supreme offices, which must be held by those who are members of the constitution, should have public services[4] associated with them. This will reconcile people to having no share in office, and make them think the more kindly of officials who pay heavily for their position. It is appropriate, too, that newcomers to office should offer magnificent sacrificial banquets and execute some public work. The object is that the people, when they share in the banquets and see their city being adorned with votive offerings and with buildings, may be satisfied to see the constitution continue. There is the further result that these will remain as memorials to the notables' expenditure. But nowadays those who are connected with an oligarchy do not do this, but rather the reverse, for it is the gains they are after, no less than the honour. Such oligarchies are well named 'democracies in miniature'.[5]

These then are the ways in which the various democracies and oligarchies ought to be constructed.

VI viii

(*1321b4–1323a10*)

A COMPREHENSIVE REVIEW OF OFFICIALDOM

After his fairly brief account in Chapters vi and vii of how oligarchy may be made to work best, we expect Aris-

3. VI vi.
4. See IV iv, n. 11.
5. Because to hold office for profit rather than honour is a characteristic of democracy.

totle to turn to other constitutions, as he promised in the third paragraph of Chapter i. Instead, we have a review of officials and procedures, which, like so much else in Book VI, looks back to Book IV; in particular, it supplements the discussion of IV xv and xvi.

The various headings under which the officials are grouped speak for themselves, but amid the welter of detail two points emerge as major preoccupations: (a) What offices must a state have, others being either unimportant, or important for one kind of state but not for another? (b) The difficulty Greek states had in enforcing the verdicts of their courts. Officials were essentially temporary part-timers, and in the course of their duties (for example in collecting a fine) could easily be caught up in embittered personal feelings, and (no doubt) be led into corrupt practices. Today we are able to avoid these predicaments at least partly because of a tradition of impersonal administration by a permanent full-time civil service. Impersonality and disinterestedness are what Aristotle is groping his way towards in the ingenious suggestions he makes for coping with the problem.

1321b4 Following upon what has been said comes the topic of the proper differentiation of offices – what offices and how many, and in what sphere each is to operate. This topic has been discussed already.[1] Without the essential offices there can be no state at all; without those concerned with good order and good conduct there can be no well-governed one. And in smaller states the offices will need to be fewer, but more numerous in the large, as has indeed been stated earlier.[2] We must therefore not neglect to consider which of them can appropriately be merged into one and which ought to be kept separate.
1321b12 The first essential responsibility is control of the market-place: there must be some official charged with the duty of seeing that honest dealing and good

1. IV xiv, xv, xvi.   2. IV xv.

order prevail. For one of the well-nigh essential activities of all states is the buying and selling of goods to meet their mutual basic needs; this is the quickest way to self-sufficiency, which seems to be what moves men to combine under a single constitution. Another and closely connected responsibility is for public and private properties within the town, the aim being to keep them in good shape; dilapidated streets and buildings have to be maintained and rebuilt, boundaries between properties fixed beyond dispute, and other matters of a like kind connected with this sphere of responsibility have to be seen to. Most people call this sort of office 'wardenship of the city', and it includes a number of branches. Where the number of inhabitants of the state is very large, the branches are administered separately, e.g. by Wall-Repairers, Harbour Guards and Superintendents of Springs. There is another essential and closely similar responsibility, with the same functions, but covering the countryside and the districts outside the town; the officials are called by some 'Country-Wardens', by others 'Foresters'. That makes three responsibilities so far.

1321b31 Next, that office which receives the revenues of public life, keeps them safe and distributes them to the various branches of the administration; names such as Receivers or Treasurers are given to these officials. Fifthly there is the office which keeps the records that have to be made of contracts made between private persons, and of law-court decisions; and this same office ought also to be the place for the lodging of prosecutions and for the introduction of suits. (Sometimes this office also is divided, and in some places a single supreme office covers them all.) The officials are called Keepers of Sacred Records, Controllers, Recorders, and other such names.

1321b40 Next, there is a connected office which is pretty well the most essential and the hardest of all, namely that of carrying out the sentences of the courts, of collecting moneys publicly declared to be due to the state, and of keeping prisoners in custody. This work is difficult, because it gives rise to much resentment. So, unless it is very profitable, people either refuse to undertake it, or if they do so, are reluctant to fulfil the demands of the laws. Yet it is essential: it is no good having trials on matters of justice if they are to have no effect. If it is impossible for men to live in a society in which there are no trials, it is also impossible where the verdicts are not carried out. It is therefore better that this work should not be assigned to a single official, but to various persons from the various courts; and an attempt should be made to distribute the work of publicly posting the fines to be paid. So too in the exaction of penalties: in some cases the officials should perform this duty, and in particular new officials should exact those imposed by their predecessors; and while they are in office the penalties should be exacted by a different official from the one who imposed them, the fines of Market-Officers being collected by the City-Wardens and theirs in turn by others. For the less resentment there is against the exactors, the better the chances of the exactions being paid in full. It doubles the resentment to have the same persons impose the penalties and exact them; when everything[3] is done by the same people, they are everyone's enemies.

1322a19 In many places the office of keeping custody of prisoners has been separated from that of exacting penalties, as at Athens in the case of the office of those called The Eleven. It is therefore better here also to separate the two, and to look for the best way of applying the same stratagem to the performance of this office[4] as well, which is just as essential as the one we have been

3. Probably 'every exaction' is meant.
4. I.e. custody of prisoners, to ensure their appearance at trial. (Imprisonment was not in use as a *punishment*.) 'The same stratagem' is presumably the separation of this custodial function from other functions. The example of The Eleven is odd, as in fact they performed a dual duty of custody and of executing certain sentences; but Aristotle probably thought of them as custodians first and foremost.

speaking of.[5] But respectable people try to avoid this office above all, and it is dangerous to commit it to the sovereign authority of the bad, who are themselves more in need of guarding than capable of guarding others. Therefore there ought not to be one specific single and perpetual office charged with the care of prisoners, but use should be made, where the system exists, of the young men doing military service and garrison duty in a particular year. And different sets of officials should undertake this responsibility in turn.

1322a29 The above-mentioned offices must be put first, as most essential; next, equally essential and of higher rank, as calling for much experience and great trustworthiness, are all those connected with the defence of the state, and those organized with a view to its needs in time of war. In war and peace alike there must be men charged with superintending the protection of walls and gates, and with inspecting and marshalling the citizens. In some states several separate offices look after all these matters, in others fewer; in small states, for instance, one office covers them all. Names given to the holders of such offices are General and War-Leader. If there are cavalry, light-armed troops, bowmen, and sailors, then for these too there are sometimes separate officials – called Commanders of Ships, of Cavalry, and of Battalions, and junior ranks in each case: Captains of Triremes, of Companies and of Tribes, and so on down to the smaller units. But they all belong to a single class discharging military responsibilities.

1322b6 There we leave this office. Now since some, if not all, of the offices handle great quantities of public property, it is essential to have yet another office, to receive accounts and carry out additional scrutinies; and it will have no function other than financial. Various names are given to these officials: Scrutineers, Accountants, Auditors, Advocates.

1322b12 As well as all the offices which we have men-

5. I.e. the exaction of penalties.

tioned there is the authority which is sovereign over all matters, in that often the same official (i) introduces business and brings it to completion, (ii) presides over the populace in places where the people is sovereign. The convening element is bound to be the sovereign element of the constitution.[6] This office is sometimes called the Pre-Council, because it deliberates beforehand, but in democracies[7] it is usually just called a Council.

1322b17 This pretty well covers the offices of the state, but there is another type[8] of responsibility, namely for religion. Here the officials are (for example) priests and supervisors of matters affecting the temples; and their task is to maintain buildings in good condition, repair dilapidated ones, and to take charge of whatever else is connected with the worship of the gods. Sometimes all this can be looked after by a single official, in small states for example. But sometimes we find, kept separate from the priesthood, a large number of other officials: Sacrificers, Temple-Guardians, Treasurers of Sacred Funds. Connected with this sphere of responsibility there is the special superintendence of all public sacrifices which by law are not entrusted to the priests but derive their prestige from the common hearth. The officials concerned are sometimes called Kings, sometimes Archons, sometimes Presidents.

1322b29 These then are the necessary responsibilities. We may recapitulate them as follows: religion, warfare, income and expenditure, the market, the town and its harbours, the countryside, the courts, registration of contracts, prisons, the exaction of penalties, computing and auditing of accounts, additional scrutinies of holders of office, and finally those concerned with the element that deliberates about public affairs.

---

6. Or, 'There must be an element to convene the sovereign element of the constitution'.

7. *Plēthos*.

8. Cf. IV xv (1299a18), VII xii. 'Offices of state' = *politikai* [*archai*].

1322b37 Some responsibilities are peculiar to states where leisure and prosperity are above the average and where attention is also paid to orderly behaviour. Such are control of women, control of children, guardianship of the laws, and management of gymnasia; and to these we should add the supervision of contests, both athletic and dramatic, and of any other similar public spectacles that there may be. Some of these offices are obviously not at all democratic, for example the control of women and children, because the poor, not having any slaves, are obliged to use their women and children as servants. Of the three offices (that of Guardians of the Laws, of Pre-Councillors and of Council), which some use to direct the election of sovereign officials, the Guardians of the Laws are aristocratic, the Pre-Councillors oligarchic, and a Council democratic. We have now sketched in outline pretty well all the offices.

BOOK VII

VII i

(1323a14–1324a4)

THE RELATION BETWEEN VIRTUE AND PROSPERITY

*The seventh and eighth books belong closely to each other
and stand somewhat apart from the preceding six. They
make an unfinished essay on a favourite theme of Greek
thinkers, 'What is the ideal form of state and constitution?' The first three chapters of VII form a philosophical
introduction: Aristotle debates, in the light of his own
teleological moral theory, the nature of that 'best life'
which the ideal state facilitates. The 'best life' is of course
a well-worn but inexhaustible subject: both the* Ethics
and the Politics *are full of it, and so are Aristotle's more
popular works and public lectures – if indeed either of
these are what he means by the 'external discourses' to
which he refers here and in III vi.*

*Although in VII and VIII Aristotle is seeking to define
the conditions of an ideal or perfect state, he still wants
it to be within the bounds of possibility (see iv, where he
begins to discuss practical details). His method and
approach are therefore far removed from those of
Plato's* Republic, *and much more like those of the*
Laws.

*The phrases used in the fourth paragraph of VII i
about the happiness of an individual or a state are impossible to translate effectively; yet they are important,
since Aristotle reinforces his argument by certain verbal
similarities, not to say ambiguities. Newman comments:[1]
'When Aristotle sought to show ... that the chief ingredient in eudaimonia [happiness] is virtue, his work was
half done for him by the ordinary use of the Greek
language.' Aristotle argues that a state cannot (a) be*

1. III 310.

'*happy*' *unless it (b) prospers (the common Greek expression* prattein kalōs, *literally 'do well, finely'); but it cannot prosper unless it (c) does good actions (*prattein kala, *literally 'do good things'); and it cannot do good things/actions unless it (d) has virtue (*aretē*). Requirement (c), particularly in view of its dependence on (d), seems to be a moral one; and its verbal resemblance to the prudential* prattein kalōs *facilitates Aristotle's argument that prosperity is dependent on virtue. And in so far as this argument applies to an individual also, it seems to follow that the same kind of activity — i.e. way of life — is required for the happiness both of the individual and of the state, which is, after all, individuals in the mass.*

*The connection between (a) and (b) is perhaps obvious, or at least plausible enough. But what are we to make of the rest of the argument? Aristotle can hardly be asserting, in the connection he makes between (b) and (c), that one cannot be prosperous unless one performs prosperous actions: that would seem sterile indeed. On the other hand an argument that 'moral' (*kala) *acts (i.e. acts which may be other than prudential), are needed for being prosperous (*prattein kalōs) *would hardly be supported by experience. The crucial connection for Aristotle is between (d) and (cb): the* kala, '*prosperous', deeds essential to* prattein kalōs, *prosperity, will not be done in the absence of virtue,* aretē, *which is a state of the soul which disposes and prompts the person to do them. The argument is therefore purely prudential: the expression* prattein kala *is a bridge between 'virtue' and prosperity, neatly calculated, by its similarity to* prattein kalōs, *to facilitate a connection between prosperity and mental or spiritual dispositions. In short, human happiness depends, in Aristotle's view, on 'virtue' (separated out in this chapter into the traditional four 'virtues') — a theme which is a fitting introduction to discussion of the 'best' state and, in Books VII xiii–xvii and VIII, its educational system, by which 'virtue' is fostered.*

The identity of the schools of thought reported in these

*first three chapters is not known for sure; for suggestions,
see the commentaries.*

1323a14 If we wish to investigate the best constitution
appropriately, we must first decide what is the most desirable life; for if we do not know that, the best constitution is also bound to elude us. For those who live
under the best-ordered constitution (so far as their circumstances allow) may be expected, barring accidents, to
be those whose affairs proceed best. We must therefore
first come to some agreement as to what is the most desirable life for all men, or nearly all, and then decide whether it is one and the same life that is most desirable for
them both as individuals and in the mass, or different ones.
1323a21 In the belief that the subject of the best life
has been fully and adequately discussed, even in the
external discourses,[2] I propose to make use of this material
now. Certainly nobody will dispute one division: that
there are three ingredients which must all be present to
make us blessed – our bodily existence, our intellectual
and moral qualities, and all that is external.[3] (No one
would call blessed a man who is entirely without courage
or self-control or practical wisdom or a sense of justice,
who is scared of flies buzzing past, who will stop at nothing to gratify his desire for eating or drinking, who will
ruin his closest friends for a paltry profit, and whose mind
also is as witless and deluded as a child's or a lunatic's.)
But while there is general agreement about these three,
there is much difference of opinion about their extent and
their order of superiority. Thus people suppose that it is
sufficient to have a certain amount of virtue, but they set
no limit to the pursuit of wealth, power, property, reputation, and the like.

   2. What these were, and whose, is not clear. Jaeger (276 ff.) believes
that in VII i–iii Aristotle is 'basing himself' on material in his own
early work, the *Protrepticus*, an exhortation to the philosophic life.
   3. Literally, 'things external, things in (of) the body, and things
in (of) the soul.' 'Things' are in effect 'goods', though *agatha* is not
in the Greek at this point.

1323a38 Our answer to such people will be twofold. First, it is easy to arrive at a firm conviction on these matters by simply observing the facts: it is not by means of external goods that men acquire and keep the virtues, but the other way round; and to live happily, whether men suppose it to consist in enjoyment or in virtue or in both, does in fact accrue more to those who are outstandingly well-equipped in character and intellect, and only moderately so in the possession of externally acquired goods – more, that is, than to those who have more goods than they need but are deficient in the other qualities. Yet the matter can be considered on the theoretical level too, and the same result will be seen easily enough. External goods, being like a collection of tools each useful for some purpose, have a limit: one can have too many of them, and that is bound to be of no benefit, or even a positive injury, to their possessors. It is quite otherwise with the goods of the soul: the more there is of each the more useful each will be (if indeed one ought to apply to these the term 'useful', as well as 'admirable'). So clearly, putting it in general terms, we shall maintain that the best condition of anything in relation to the best condition of[4] any other thing is commensurate in point of superiority with the relationship between the things themselves of which we say these conditions are conditions. Hence as the soul is a more precious thing (both absolutely and relatively to ourselves) than both property and the body, its best condition too will necessarily show a proportionate relationship to that of[4] each of the others. Moreover, it is for the sake of our souls that these things are to be desired, and all right-minded persons ought to desire them; it would be wrong to reverse this priority.

1323b21 Let this then be agreed upon at the start: to each man there comes just so much happiness as he has of virtue and of practical wisdom, and performs actions dependent thereon. God himself is an indication of the

4. These last four words slightly expand the Greek, in the interests of clarity.

truth of this. He is blessed and happy not on account of any of the external goods but because of himself and what he is by his own nature. And for these reasons good fortune must be something different from happiness; for the acquisition of goods external to the soul is due either to the coincidence of events[5] or to fortune, but no man is just or restrained as a result of, or because of, fortune. A connected point, depending on the same arguments, applies with equal force to the state: the best and well-doing[6] state is the happy state. But it is impossible for those who do not do good actions to do well,[6] and there is no such thing as a man's or a state's good action without virtue and practical wisdom. The courage of a state, or its sense of justice, or its practical wisdom, or its restraint have exactly the same effect and are manifested in the same form as the qualities which the individual has to share in if he is to be called courageous, just, wise[7] or restrained.

1323b36 These remarks must suffice to introduce the subject; it was impossible to start without saying something, equally impossible to try to develop every relevant argument, for that would be a task for another session. For the present let this be our fundamental basis: the life which is best for men, both separately, as individuals, and in the mass, as states, is the life which has virtue sufficiently supported by material resources to facilitate participation in the actions that virtue calls for. As for objectors,[8] if there is anyone who does not believe what has been said, we must pass them by for the purposes of our present inquiry and deal with them on some future occasion.

5. See *Physics* II iv–vi: *to automaton*: 'coincidence of events'; *tuchē*: 'fortune'.

6. *Kalōs prattein*. Some such slightly uncouth English is difficult to avoid here, if the verbal force of the Greek is to be conveyed. 'Do good actions' = *kala prattein*. See the introduction to the chapter.

7. *Phronimos*; 'practical wisdom' = *phronēsis*.

8. I.e. to 'the Platonic identification of virtue and happiness' (P. Shorey, *Classical Philology*, 26 (1931), p. 429).

VII ii

(1324a5–1325a15)

THE ACTIVE LIFE AND THE PHILOSOPHIC LIFE (1)

The question raised at the beginning of this book, 'Which is the most desirable kind of life?', has not yet been answered in detail: the preliminaries just referred to are still in progress and continue to the end of iii. So far, the 'happiness' (eudaimonia) of both state and individual has been shown to be inseparable from the 'good' life and therefore from virtue. On 'happiness' see the Nicomachean Ethics *I, where in Chapter xiii it is defined as 'an activity of the soul according to perfect virtue'.*

Aristotle now asks, is the happy life one that is busy and active in public affairs, or is it contemplative and philosophic? Little is said of the latter option; the main purpose of the chapter seems to rule out of consideration one view of the active life, namely that it should be directed towards enabling the state to aggrandize itself by conquest and mastery of neighbouring states. He lists some states which encourage military virtue above all (cf. Plato, Laws *init.), and in an anthropological spirit mentions some devices they use in order to do so. He then attacks such an attitude by a number of arguments of which perhaps the most interesting is from the 'ladder of nature': no doubt some animals are naturally intended for forcible exploitation by us, e.g. those we hunt for food – but not our fellow-men. War, he maintains, is a means of defending the good life; it is not the good life itself.*

1324a5 It remains to ask whether we are to say that happiness is the same for the individual human being and for the state, or not. The answer is again obvious: all would agree that it is the same. For those who hold the view that the good life of an individual depends on

wealth will likewise, if the whole state be wealthy, count
it blessed; and those who prize most highly the life of a
tyrant will deem most happy that state which rules over
the greatest number of people. So too one who commends
the single individual on the basis of his virtue will also
judge the more sound state to be the happier.

1324a13 But there are still these two questions needing
consideration: (a) Which life is more desirable, the life
of participation in the work of the state and constitution,
or one like a foreigner's, cut off from the association of
the state?[1] (b) What constitution are we to lay down
as best, and what is the best condition for the state to be
in (whether we assume that participation in the state is
desirable for all or only for the majority)? The first
question was a matter of what is desirable for an individual; the second belongs to political theory and insight,
and we have chosen to examine it now. The other question would be merely incidental, this second one is the
business of our inquiry.

1324a23 Obviously the best constitution must be one
which is so ordered that any person whatsoever may
prosper best and live blessedly; but it is disputed, even
by those who admit that the life of virtue is the most
desirable, whether the active life of a statesman[2] is preferable to one which is cut off from all external influences,
i.e. the contemplative life, which some say is the only life
for a philosopher. Both in earlier and in modern times
men most ambitious for virtue seem generally to have
preferred these two kinds of life, the statesman's or the
philosopher's. It makes a considerable difference which
of the two is correct, because we must, if we are right-
minded people, direct ourselves to the better of the two
aims, whichever it may be; and this equally as individuals
and collectively as members of a constitution. Some hold

1. *Politikē koinōnia*, 'the partnership that is the state (*polis*)';
see I i. Such partnership is enjoyed by the citizen (*politēs*), who
as 'statesman' (*politikos*) rules and is ruled by turn.
2. *Politikos bios*; cf. n. 1.

that to rule over one's neighbours in the manner of a slave-master involves the greatest injustice, but that to do so in a statesmanlike way[3] involves none, though it does mean making inroads on the comfort of the ruler. Others hold pretty well the opposite, namely that the life of active statesmanship is the only one worthy of a man, and activity springing from each of the individual virtues is just as much open to those who take part in public affairs under the constitution as to private persons. That is one view, but there is also a set of people who say that the only style of constitution that brings happiness is one modelled on tyranny and on mastery of slaves. And in some places the definitive purpose both of the laws and of the constitution is to facilitate mastery of the neighbouring peoples.

1324b5 Hence, even though in most places the legal provisions[4] have for the most part been established on virtually no fixed principle, yet if it is anywhere true that the laws have a single purpose, they all aim at domination. Thus in Sparta and Crete the educational system and the bulk of the laws are directed almost exclusively to purposes of war; and outside the Greek peoples all such nations as are strong enough to aggrandize themselves, like the Scythians, Persians, Thracians, and Celts, have always set great store by military power. In some places there are also laws designed to foster military virtue, as at Carthage, where men reputedly receive decorations in the form of armlets to the number of the campaigns in which they have served. There used also to be a law in Macedonia that a man had to be girdled with his halter until he had slain his first enemy; and at a certain Scythian feast when the cup was passed round only those were allowed to drink from it who had killed an enemy. Among the Iberians, a warlike race, the tombs of their warriors have little spikes stuck around them showing the number of

3. I.e. with the interests of the ruled in mind, presumably (who should be free, and equal in status to the ruler: cf. III iv).
4. *Nomima.*

enemy slain. There are many other such practices, some established by law and some by custom, among different peoples.

1324b22 Yet surely, if we are prepared to examine the point carefully, we shall see how completely unreasonable it would be if the work of a statesman were to be reduced to an ability to work out how to rule and be master over neighbouring peoples, with or without their consent. How could that be a part of statecraft or lawgiving, when it is not even lawful[5] in itself? To rule at all costs, not only justly but unjustly, is unlawful, and merely to have the upper hand is not necessarily to have a just title to it. Nor does one find this in the other fields of knowledge: it is not the job of a doctor or a ship's captain to persuade or to force patients or passengers. Certainly most people seem to think that mastery is statesmanship, and they have no compunction about inflicting upon others what in their own community they regard as neither just nor beneficial if applied to themselves. They themselves ask for just government among themselves; but in the treatment of others they do not worry at all about what measures are just. Of course we may be sure that nature has made some things fit to be ruled by a master and others not, and if this is so, we must try to exercise master-like rule not over all people but only over those fit for such treatment – just as we should not pursue human beings for food or sacrifice, but only such wild animals as are edible and so suitable to be hunted for this purpose.

1324b41 Surely too a single state could be happy even on its own (provided of course that its constitution runs well), since it is possible for a state to be administered in isolation in some place or other, following its own sound laws; the organization of its constitution will not be directed to war or the defeat of enemies, for the non-existence of these is postulated. The conclusion is

5. *Nomimon.*

obvious: we regard every provision made for war as admirable, not as a supreme end but only as serving the needs of that end. It is the task of a sound legislator to survey the state, the clan, and every other association and to see how they can be brought to share in the good life and in whatever degree of happiness is possible for them. There will of course be different rules[4] laid down in different places; if there are neighbouring peoples, it will be part of the legislative function to decide what sort of attitude is to be adopted to this sort and that sort, and how to employ towards each the proper rules for dealing with each. But this question, 'What end should the best constitution have in view?', will be properly examined at a later stage.[6]

VII iii

(1325a16–1325b32)

THE ACTIVE LIFE AND THE PHILOSOPHIC LIFE (2)

Aristotle now returns to the general theme of these three introductory chapters – the good life. Is the happy life for the individual one of philosophy and reflection, or one of action and contribution to public affairs? In effect, the chapter seeks to rid their respective partisans of certain misconceptions. A partisan of the philosophic life might object to the active life by arguing that since happiness (eudaimonia) *is prosperity or 'doing well'* (eu prattein), *unlimited power, used 'despotically' as a slave-master* (despotēs) *uses his over his slaves, is needed to ensure maximum prosperity. Aristotle points out in reply that a slave-master's rule is a fairly humdrum thing, and no model for a 'statesman' to emulate, whose ruling of his peers and being ruled by them in turn is just as effective in achieving prosperity. Besides, unlimited power*

6. VII xiii and xiv.

to do good is rarely used to do only good; it needs to be conjoined with virtue (aretē). On the other hand, Aristotle is anxious to assert, as against partisans of the active life who (pardonably, perhaps) suppose that the philosophic life is not active (and therefore presumably not happy either), that reflection can lead to action, and that (a very subtle argument this – see note 3) thought is 'active' in a special sense. The final paragraph argues that a state living an 'isolated' life need not be 'inactive', since its internal 'parts' may relate to each other in an active way (indeed how could they not?).

Underlying the entire argumentation of these first three chapters is Aristotle's fundamental teleological conviction that 'happiness' is a form of activity: activity is obviously what man, as an animal, is made for, and he cannot be happy if he is not active. Successful action depends on virtue (see introduction to VII i, and its fourth paragraph).

1325a16 We must now deal with those who, while agreeing that the life which is conjoined with virtue is the most desirable, differ as to how it is to be followed. Some reject altogether the holding of state-offices, regarding the life of a free man as different from that of a statesman, and as the most desirable of all lives. Others say that the statesman's life is best, on the grounds that a man who does nothing cannot be doing well, and happiness and doing well are the same thing.[1] To both parties we may say in reply, 'You are both of you partly right and partly wrong. Certainly it is true, as some of you maintain, that the life of a free man is better than the life like that of a master of slaves: there is no dignity in using a slave, *qua* slave, for issuing instructions to do this or that routine job is no part of noble activity. But not all rule is rule by a master, and those who think it is are mistaken. The

1. See introduction to VII i: presumably (a) and (b) are in question in this sentence; 'do well' renders *prattein eu, eupragia*, and *eupraxia*.

difference between ruling over free men and ruling over slaves is as great as the difference between the naturally free and the natural slave, a distinction which has been sufficiently defined in an earlier passage.[2] And we cannot agree that it is right to value doing nothing more than doing something. For happiness is action; and the actions of just and restrained men represent the consummation of many fine things.'

1325a34 But perhaps someone will suppose that if we define things in this way, it means that absolute sovereignty is best, because then one is in a sovereign position to perform the greatest number of fine actions; and so anyone who is in a position to rule ought not to yield that position to his neighbour, but take and keep it for himself without any regard for the claims of his parents or his children or friends in general, sacrificing everything to the principle that the best is most to be desired and nothing could be better than to do well.[1] Perhaps there is some truth in this, but only if we suppose that this most desirable of things is in fact going to accrue to those who use robbery and violence. But maybe this is impossible and the supposition is false. For a man who does not show as much superiority over his fellows as husband over wife, or father over children, or master over slave – how can his actions be fine actions? So he who departs from the path of virtue will never be able to go sufficiently straight to make up entirely for his previous errors. As between similar people, the fine and just thing is to take turns, which satisfies the demands of equality and similarity. Non-equality given to equals, dissimilar positions given to similar persons – these are contrary to nature and nothing that is contrary to nature is fine. Hence it is only when one man is superior in virtue, and in ability to perform the best actions, that it becomes fine to serve him and just to obey him. But it should be remembered that virtue in itself is not enough; there must also be the power to translate it into action.

2. I vii.

1325b14 If all this is true and if happiness is to be equated with doing well,[1] then the active life will be the best both for any state as a whole community and for the individual. But the active life need not, as some suppose, be always concerned with our relations with other people, nor is intelligence 'active' only when it is directed towards results that flow from action. On the contrary, thinking and speculation that are their own end and are done for their own sake are *more* 'active', because the aim in such thinking is to do well, and therefore also, in a sense, action.[3] Master-craftsmen in particular, even though the actions they direct by their intellect are external to them, are nevertheless said to 'act', in a sovereign sense.

1325b23 As for states that are set up away from others and have chosen to live thus in isolation, there is nothing in that to oblige them to lead a life of inaction. Activity too may take place as among parts: the parts of a state provide numerous associations that enter into relations with each other. The same is true of any individual person; for otherwise God himself and the whole universe would scarcely be in a fine condition, for they have no external activities, only those proper to themselves. It is therefore clear that the same life must inevitably be the best both for individuals and collectively for states and mankind.

VII iv

(*1325b33–1326b25*)

THE SIZE OF THE IDEAL STATE

The preliminary remarks are now complete, and it remains to discuss and describe the ideal state. In Book II,

3. That is to say, thought has an end or aim (*telos*), which is to 'do well' (eu*praxia*), which is thus action (*praxis*); when therefore thought is 'for its own sake', its end or aim (action) is thought; thought is therefore, *qua* aim, action; thought is therefore 'active' in a double sense, as both agent and aim.

where others' accounts of it were criticized, Plato's Laws
had been much less severely handled than his Republic,
*and less systematically. What now follows (chapters iv to
xii) is similar in method and principles, but not always
in detail, to the* Laws. *Aristotle treats first the materials
and the conditions of the ideal state, its population, size,
situation and climate (iv–vii); next its institutions, social,
political, and religious, especially as concerns citizenship,
ownership of land, and division into classes (viii–x); and
then the siting and layout of the ideal state itself (xi–xii).
All this is somewhat external; the account of the constitution as such begins at Chapter xiii with a discussion of
education, which is the main subject of the rest of Book
VII and all that remains of Book VIII. However, nowhere in the* Politics *is there an account of a constitutional framework such as Plato in his* Laws *described in
detail.*

*As for the size of the ideal state, Plato had advocated
(*Laws *737e ff.) the mathematically convenient number of
5,040 citizen farmers, plus their families and slaves, and
an admixture of resident aliens. Aristotle, however, does
not commit himself to a particular number: he is content
to suggest only empirical guidelines for determining the
maximum and minimum. True to his teleological principles, he argues that the population must be neither too
large nor too small to prevent the state from fulfilling its
function.*

1325b33 Now that our introduction to these matters is
finished, and since we have earlier discussed the other constitutions, the first part of what remains to be discussed
will deal with the question, 'What are the fundamental
postulates for a state which is to be constructed exactly
as one would wish, and provided with all the appropriate
material equipment, without which it could not be the
best state?' We must therefore postulate everything as
we would wish it to be, remembering however that nothing must be outside the bounds of possibility. I mean for

example with respect to a body of citizens, and territory.
Other craftsmen, say a weaver or a boatmaker, must have
a supply of their materials in a state suitable for the
exercise of their craft; and the better these materials are
prepared, the finer will inevitably be the result which the
craftsmen's skill will produce. So too a statesman or lawgiver must have the proper material in suitable condition.
1326a5 The first part of a state's equipment is a body
of men, and we must consider both how many they ought
to be and with what natural qualities. The second is territory; we shall need to determine both its extent and
its character. Most people think that if a state is to be
happy it has to be great. This may be true, but they
do not know how to judge greatness and smallness in a
state. They judge greatness by the number of people
living in it; but one ought to look not at numbers but
at capacity. A state too has a function to perform, and
the state which is most capable of discharging that function must be regarded as greatest, rather in the same way
that one might say that Hippocrates was 'bigger', not as
a man but as a physician, than one of greater bodily
size. However, even granting that we must have regard
to numbers, we must not do so without discrimination:
although we must allow for the necessary presence in
states of many slaves and foreigners (resident or visitors),
our real concern is only with those who form *part* of the
state, i.e. with those elements of which a state properly
consists. Pre-eminence in numbers of these is a mark of a
great state, but a state cannot possibly be great which
can put into the field only a handful of heavy-armed
soldiers[1] along with a large crowd of mechanics. A great
state and a populous one are not the same.
1326a25 Moreover, experience has also shown that it is
difficult, if not impossible, for a populous state to be run
by good laws; at any rate, we know of no state with a
reputation for a well-run constitution that does not re-

1. Hoplites, i.e. *citizen*-soldiers wealthy enough to possess heavy
armour.

strict its numbers. The language itself makes this certain. For law is itself a kind of order, and to live under good laws is necessarily to live in good order. But an excessively large number cannot take on any degree of order; that would require the operation of a divine power, such as actually holds together the universe. Moreover, *beauty* commonly arises in a context of size and number; so the state, too, will necessarily be most beautiful if, though large, it conforms to the limitation just mentioned.[2] But there must also be a norm for the size of a state, as there is a normal size for everything else – animals, plants, instruments, and so on. Each of these can only keep the power that belongs to it if it is neither too large nor too small; otherwise its essential nature will be either entirely lost or seriously impaired. Thus a boat a span long will not really be a boat at all, nor one that is two stades long.[3] There is a certain size at which it will become either too large or too small to be navigated well.

1326b2 It is just the same with a state: if it has too few people it cannot be self-sufficient, whereas a state *is* a self-sufficient thing. If it has too many people, it can certainly be self-sufficient in its basic requirements, but as a nation, not as a state, because it is difficult for a constitution to subsist in it. For who will be military commander of this excessive population? Who will be their crier unless he has the voice of a Stentor? Therefore, when the population first becomes large enough to be sufficient for itself in all that is needed for living the good life after the manner of an association which is a state, then that must be a state of a primitive kind.[4] It is possible to go on from there; a state greater in population than that will be a larger state, but as we have said, this process is not unlimited.

2. I.e. the limitation of being small enough to facilitate order, *taxis*, which is essential to beauty.

3. A span is a few inches, a stade about 202 yards.

4. Literally, 'a first state', one which just satisfies the minimum criteria of 'stateness'. Cf. I ii, about households and villages, and Plato, *Republic* II 367 ff.

1326b11 What the limit of the extra should be can easily be determined by an examination of the facts. The activities of a state are those of the rulers and those of the ruled, and the functions of the ruler are decision and direction. In order to give decisions on matters of justice, and for the purpose of distributing offices on merit, it is necessary that the citizens should know each other and know what kind of people they are. Where this condition does not exist, both decisions and appointments to office are bound to suffer, because it is not just in either of these matters to proceed haphazardly, which is clearly what does happen where the population is excessive. Another drawback is that it becomes easy for foreigners, and aliens resident in the country, to become possessed of citizenship,[5] because the excessive size of the population makes detection difficult. Here then we have ready to hand the best limit of a state: it must have the largest population consistent with catering for the needs of a self-sufficient life, but not so large that it cannot be easily surveyed. Let that be our way of describing the size of a state.

VII v

(*1326b26–1327a10*)

THE TERRITORY OF THE IDEAL STATE

For the Platonic background to this chapter and the next, see Laws *IV* init., *760a ff., 842b ff., 949e ff.*

1326b26 The case is similar when we turn our attention to the territory. As regards quality of land, everyone would be in favour of the most self-sufficient; that is to say, it must be the most universally productive, for to have everything on hand and nothing lacking is to be self-sufficient. As to size and extent, these should be such that the inhabitants can live a life that affords the leisure of a

5. Literally, 'get a share in the constitution'.

free man, but one lived in a spirit of moderation. Whether this definition is good or bad is a point into which we must later[1] go in greater detail, when we come to discuss the general question of property and abundance of possessions, and ask what procedures and arrangements ought to govern their use. It is a question with many points of dispute, because of those who pull to extremes, some to extravagance of life-style, others to niggardliness.

1326b39 The general configuration of the land is not difficult to state (though there are some points on which we must also take the opinion of those who have experience of conducting operations of war): it ought to be hard for a hostile force to invade, easy for an expeditionary force to depart from. Apart from that, just as we remarked that the population ought to be easily surveyed, so we say the same of the territory; in a country that can easily be surveyed it is easy to bring up assistance at any point. Next, the position of the state: if we are to put it exactly where we would like best, it should be conveniently situated for both sea and land. One definitive requirement, mentioned above, is that it should be well placed for sending assistance in all directions; a second is that it should form a centre for the easy receipt of crops as well as of timber, and of any other similar raw material for whatever manufacturing processes the land may possess.

VII vi

(*1327a11–1327b18*)

THE IMPORTANCE OF THE SEA

The advantages of a maritime situation are now argued in greater detail, perhaps partly in answer to Plato, who constantly expressed disapproval of sea-ports and navies,

1. No such discussion is to be found in the remainder of the *Politics*, but see II v and II vi, 5th paragraph.

foreign trade and travel (see e.g. Laws *IV* init., *and 949
ff.). Aristotle in this chapter gives first some positive
advantages, then some ways in which drawbacks can be
met; for he agreed with Plato in holding it to have been
a disastrous policy for Athens to extend citizenship to the
lower social groups, in deference to their position as
rowers in the navy, on which the Athenians relied for
their political hegemony in Greece and for their food-
supply. Aristotle, like Plato, regards such people, however important to a state, as not 'part' of it, i.e. as not
deserving citizenship; cf. VII viii.*

1327a11 There is a good deal of argument about communication with the sea and whether it is a help or a
hindrance to states governed by good laws. Some say that
to open one's state to foreigners, brought up in a different
legal code, is detrimental to government by good laws,
and so is the large population, which, they say, results
from the using of the sea to dispatch and receive large
numbers of traders, and is inimical to running a good
constitution. If these evil consequences can be avoided,
it is obviously better both for ensuring an abundance of
necessities and for defensive reasons that the state and its
territory should have access to the sea. To facilitate resistance to an enemy and ensure survival, the population
needs to be in a position to be readily defended both by
sea and by land, and even if they cannot strike a blow
against invaders on both elements, it will be easier to
strike on one, if they have access to both. So too people
must import the things which they do not themselves
produce, and export those of which they have a surplus.
For a state's trading must be in its own interest and not
in others'. Some throw their state open as a market for
all comers for the sake of the revenue they bring; but a
state in which such aggrandisement is illegitimate ought
not to possess that kind of trading-centre at all. We see
in modern times also many states and territories in possession of anchorages and harbours conveniently situated

for the city, not so near as to encroach and become part of the same town, but close enough to be controlled by walls and other such defence-works. It is therefore clear that if communication with those places is productive of good, then that good will accrue to the state; but if of evil, it is easy to guard against that by laying down laws to prescribe who are and who are not to be allowed to come into contact with each other.

1327a40 Then there is this matter of naval forces. Clearly it is excellent that there should be a certain quantity of these available, for it is important that by sea as well as by land a state should be formidable and able to render aid, not only internally but to certain of its neighbours. The number and size of the naval force will have to be decided in the light of the way of living of the state concerned. If it is to play an active role as a leading state,[1] it will need naval as well as land forces large enough for such activities. The large population associated with a mob of seamen need not swell the membership of the state, of which they should form no part. The troops that are carried on board are free men belonging to the infantry; they are in sovereign authority and have control over the crews. A plentiful supply of sailors is sure to exist wherever the outlying dwellers[2] and agricultural labourers are numerous. We can see examples of this even today: at Heraclea, though their city is of comparatively modest size, they find crews for many triremes. So much then for territory, harbours, cities, sea and naval forces; we pass now to the citizen population.

1. Literally, 'a leading life, as between states' (*politikos*), i.e. an *active* as distinct from the 'private' life discussed in VII ii and iii.
2. *Perioikoi*; see VII ix, VII x and the introduction to II ix. The 'troops' and 'free men' are citizens; the 'crews' and 'sailors' are not.

THE INFLUENCE OF CLIMATE

In this chapter Aristotle is probably indebted to the 'Airs, Waters, Places' of Hippocrates, a work dealing with the effect of the climate of a country on the health and character of the inhabitants (translated in Hippocratic Writings, *ed. G. E. R. Lloyd, Pelican Classics, 1978; cf. VII xi and Plato,* Laws *747de).*

It may seem unfortunate that Aristotle does not develop the theme, casually suggested in the first paragraph, of a unification of Hellas as a world-ruling power; but perhaps he intended it only as a formal and theoretical possibility, not to be taken seriously.

In the second paragraph Aristotle discusses one of the desirable qualities possessed by some Greeks: thumos, 'spirit', treated by Plato in the Republic *as the self-assertive part of the soul, the seat of ambition, enterprise and righteous indignation. Aristotle makes the interesting but (on the face of it) somewhat implausible suggestion that thumos must be responsible for friendly feelings, because we are more indignant when ill-treated by our friends than we are when ill-treated by others. And as in II i–vi, he is not at his best when commenting on Plato, who, while requiring a combination of friendliness and aggression in his Guardians, did not actually require them to be aggressive towards strangers as such, in spite of Aristotle's querulous suggestio falsi.*

1327b18 We have already spoken[1] about limiting the number of citizens; we must now ask what kind of natural qualities they should have. We could form a fair notion of the answer if we glanced first at the most famous Greek states, and then at the divisions between nations in the

1. VII iv.

whole inhabited world. The nations that live in cold regions and those of Europe are full of spirit, but somewhat lacking in skill and intellect; for this reason, while remaining relatively free, they lack political cohesion[2] and the ability to rule over their neighbours. On the other hand the Asiatic nations have in their souls both intellect and skill, but are lacking in spirit; so they remain enslaved and subject. The Hellenic race, occupying a midposition geographically, has a measure of both, being both spirited and intelligent. Hence it continues to be free, to live under the best constitutions, and, given a *single* constitution, to be capable of ruling all other people. But we observe the same differences among the Greek nations themselves when we compare one with another: some are by nature one-sided, in others both these natural faculties, of intellect and courage, are well combined. Clearly both are needed if men are to be easily guided by a lawgiver towards virtue.

1327b38 Some say that to feel friendly at the sight of familiar faces and fierce at the approach of strangers is a requirement for the Guardians.[3] Now friendliness springs from spirit, from the power in our souls whereby we love. We see this from the fact that our spirit is aroused more if it thinks that our intimates and friends neglect us than by the conduct of those whom we do not know. (Hence the lines of Archilochus, reproaching his friends but addressed to his own spirit, are aptly spoken: 'About your friends you choke.')[4] The urge we all have to be free and in command springs from this faculty, spirit, because spirit is something imperious and unsubdued. But what he says about harshness to strangers is, I think, quite wrong; one ought not to behave thus to anyone, and

2. *Apoliteuta*, i.e. they do not live in states, *poleis*.

3. See Plato, *Republic*, II–IV, esp. 375a ff.

4. Fr. 67 in J. M. Edmonds, *Elegy and Iambus, II* London and Cambridge, 1931, Loeb edition). Archilochus of Paros flourished about the middle of the 7th century; he wrote combative and passionate poetry on many topics, notably love.

fierceness is not a mark of natural greatness of mind except towards wrongdoers. As we have said, it is aroused the more strongly with respect to intimates, when we believe ourselves to be wrongly used by them. And this is understandable: where men expect to receive kindness as their due, they reckon that they are actually deprived of it, quite apart from the harm they suffer. Hence the proverbial sayings, 'Grievous is fraternal strife' and 'Excessive love turns to excessive hate'.[5]

1328a17 So much for the members of the state, their proper number and natural character, and so much for the right size and kind of territory; we need say no more, because one cannot expect the same attention to detail in theoretical discussions as one would in the case of data perceived by the senses.

VII viii

(*1328a21–1328b24*)

MEMBERSHIP AND ESSENTIAL FUNCTIONS OF THE STATE

Since this is a theoretical discussion and not an analysis of empirical data, Aristotle now leaves that part of the subject and turns to consider the ideal state itself. He opens with one of his now familiar generalizations, incidentally reminding us that a polis *is something in accordance with nature. He draws a distinction between a part of an organism and, as he puts it, a 'without which not', a 'sine qua non', which, though indispensable, need not be a part in the strict sense. The list of products and activities in the third and fourth paragraphs includes those both of the citizens (genuinely 'parts' of the state), and of slaves, craftsmen, foreigners etc. (mere 'sine qua nons').*

5. The first quotation is Euripides fr. 975 in A. Nauck, *Tragicorum Graecorum Fragmenta* (2nd ed., Leipzig, 1889); the second is ibid., *fr. adesp.* 78.

Once again we have it starkly brought home to us just how exclusive is Aristotle's view of membership of the state, and how his teleology colours his whole treatment of this question. The state is 'for' happiness and the good life, which is the full use of all our distinctively human capacities; some occupations – notably handicraft and trading – preclude such use; therefore traders and craftsmen, and a fortiori slaves, cannot be members ('parts') of the state: they are in the service of those who are (i.e. citizens). That craftsmen and traders are essential to the state does not affect the issue, as Aristotle is keen to point out. It is hardly enough to dismiss this doctrine as exploded metaphysics buttressing class-prejudice: Aristotle poses, in his own terms, problems that are still with us. For example, can a man with some menial and grindingly repetitive job lay claim to social and political wisdom entitling him to a say in public affairs? Aristotle would say 'no', but the answer 'yes' may on examination be found to depend on assumptions about merit, virtue, judgement, and the good life, which are just as arbitrary as his.

1328a21 Just as, in the case of any other compound object that exists in nature, those things without which the whole would not exist are not 'parts' of that compound, so too we must not list as parts of a state the indispensable conditions of its existence; nor must we treat in that manner any other form of community[1] that makes up something single in kind – because all the members,[1] irrespective of whether their degree of participation is equal or unequal, necessarily have some one single identical thing in common,[1] e.g. food-supply, an extent of territory, or the like. But whenever one thing is a means and another an end, there can be no other thing in common between them than this – that the one acts, the other is acted upon. Take any tool and consider it along with its users in relation to the work

1. *Koinōnia, koinōnos, koinos* respectively.

which they produce, for example a house and its builder. There is nothing in common between house and builder, but the builder's skill is a means towards building a house. *1328a33* Hence a state needs to own property, but the property is no part of the state, even though many parts of the property are living creatures.[2] A state is an association of similar persons whose aim is the best life possible. What is best is happiness, and to be happy is an active exercise of virtue and a complete employment of it. It so happens that some can get a share of happiness, while others can get little or none. Here then we clearly have the reason for the existence of different kinds and varieties of states and the plurality of constitutions. Different sets of people seek their happiness in different ways and by different means, and so make for themselves different lives and different constitutions.

1328b2 We must also ask how many are those things without which there can be no states. (We include what we call 'parts' of the state, because their presence too in the list[3] is essential.) Let us therefore make a count of all the functions, for that will show the answer. They concern (a) food, (b) skills (for life requires many tools), (c) arms. Arms are included because the members of the association must carry them even among themselves, both for internal government in the event of disobedience and to repel attempts at wrongdoing coming from outside. (d) A good supply of money, too, is required both for military and for internal needs. Then (e, though it might have been put first) religion, responsibility for which we call a priesthood; and, most essential of all, (f) a method of arriving at decisions about matters of expedience and justice as between one person and another.

1328b15 These then are the essential functions; every state, we may say, has need of them. For a state is not a chance agglomeration but, we repeat, a body of men

---

2. E.g. slaves; cf. I iv.

3. Because the 'parts' too are essential to the state (while not all 'essentials' are 'parts').

which is self-sufficient for the purposes of life; and if any of these six is lacking, it will be impossible for the association concerned to be thoroughly self-sufficient. It is therefore essential, in setting up a state, to make provision for all these operations. So a number of agricultural workers will be needed to supply food; and skilled workmen will be required, and fighting men, and wealthy men, and priests, and judges of what is necessary and expedient.

VII ix

(1328b24–1329a39)

CITIZENSHIP AND AGE-GROUPS

This chapter contains some of Aristotle's most characteristic observations on society. The governing element in the state, he maintains, must be the citizens, all of whom have by definition sufficient 'virtue' to enable them to make legal and political decisions, to bear arms, and to live a kind of gentleman's life. Now, however, Aristotle finds himself in some slight difficulty: if all citizens are to share in the central activities of the state – military, legal etc. – then we have the odd result that old men will have to be soldiers, and young men (who typically have an undeveloped judgement) will function as judges and 'statesmen'; and yet if these age-groups do not perform these functions they will not be doing what citizens should. He therefore prescribes, sensibly enough, that the citizens will, in their various 'primes of life' (the Greek for 'age-group', in effect), be successively (a) soldiers, (b) judges and statesmen, being finally pensioned off to (c) priesthoods – a provision which nicely reveals the non-professional nature of that office in ancient Greece.

1328b24 This enumeration being finished, it remains to consider whether they should all take part in all these activities, everybody being farmer and skilled workman and deliberator and judge (for this is not impossible) – or shall we postulate different persons for each task? Or again, are not some of the jobs necessarily confined to some people, while others may be thrown open to all? The situation is not the same in every constitution; for as we have said,[1] it is equally possible for all to share in everything and for some to share in some things. These features are what make the constitution different: in democracies all share in all things, in oligarchies the opposing practice prevails.

1328b33 But since our present inquiry is directed towards the best constitution, that is to say, the one which would make a state most happy, and since we have already said[2] that happiness cannot exist apart from virtue, it becomes clear that in the state with the finest constitution, which possesses just men who are just absolutely and not relatively to the assumed situation,[3] the citizens must not live a mechanical or commercial life. Such a life is not noble, and it militates against virtue. Nor must those who are to be citizens be agricultural workers, for they must have leisure to develop their virtue, and for the activities of a citizen.

1329a2 The state has within it one element concerned with defence, and another with deliberation about what policy is expedient and with deciding about questions of justice; and these elements are obviously to a special degree parts of it. And when we ask whether these roles are to be assigned to different persons or to be kept both together in the hands of the same people, our answer is clear here also: partly the one alternative and partly the other. In so far as the two tasks themselves differ in the prime of life best for their performance, one requiring practical wisdom, the other strength, they should be as-

1. E.g. IV xiv.
2. VII i.
3. *Hupothesis*, here the basic assumptions and demands of some constitution other than the best. Cf. III iv, IV vii, IV xi, n. 9, and V ix *init*.

signed to *different* people. But in so far as it is impossible to secure that those who are strong enough to resort to force or stand up to it shall tolerate being ruled by others for ever,[4] to that extent the tasks must be assigned to the *same* people. For those who are in sovereign control of arms are in a sovereign position to decide whether the constitution is to continue or not. So we are left with this conclusion: that the constitution should put both these tasks into the hands of the same persons, but not simultaneously.[5] Rather we should follow nature: the young have strength, the older have practical wisdom, so it seems both just and expedient that the distribution of tasks should be made on that basis, to both, because this is a division which takes into account fitness[6] for the work.

1329a17 Property too must belong to these people; it is essential that the citizens should have ample subsistence, and these are citizens. The mechanical element has no part in the state nor has any other class[7] that is not productive of virtue.[8] This is evident from our principle: for being happy must occur in conjunction with virtue, and in pronouncing a state happy we must have regard not to part of it but to all its citizens. It is also clear that property must belong to these, since the agricultural workers must be slaves, or non-Greeks dwelling in the country roundabout.[9]

1329a27 Of the list which we made earlier there remains the class[7] of priests. The arrangement here too is clear: no farmer or mechanic should be made a priest, since it is only right and proper that the gods should be worshipped

4. Throughout their lives, presumably.
5. I.e. neither young soldiers nor older men will both fight *and* deliberate.
6. *Axia*, 'desert, merit'.
7. *Genos*, 'type', 'sort'.
8. *Tēs aretēs dēmiourgos*, perhaps a reminiscence of Plato, *Republic* 500d.
9. *Perioikoi*, but here apparently not Greeks; cf. VII vi, VII x and introduction to II ix.

by the *citizens*. Now as we have divided the citizen element into two parts, the military[10] and the deliberative, and as it is right and proper that those who have thus spent themselves in long service should both serve the gods and enjoy their retirement, it is they who should be appointed to the priestly offices.

1329a34　We have now stated what the essential requirements of a state are, and how many parts it has. There must be farmers and skilled workers and hired labourers; but as to *parts* of the state, these are the military[10] and deliberative elements. Each is separated, either permanently or successively.[11]

VII x

(*1329a40–1330a33*)

THE FOOD-SUPPLY AND THE DIVISION
OF THE TERRITORY

The first two paragraphs of this chapter form a digression, perhaps inserted by an editor (there is no reason to suppose that Aristotle was not the author). It is partly an historical and geographical sketch of the early history of 'Italy' (i.e. what we would today call the 'toe' of Italy – see the map on p. 515 of Susemihl/Hicks), partly a brief defence of the value of studying antiquity and of the view that inventions are made independently and repeatedly in various places in the course of time, and are in general not traceable to a single source. As a whole, this half of the chapter is not concerned with the ideal state as such, but seems to occur here because it refers to social groups and common meals – just after Aristotle's discussion of

10. Literally, 'hoplite' (heavy armed).

11. I.e. the essentials (slaves, etc.) are *permanently* sundered from the parts (citizens); the parts are separated *from each other* by turns, in that a (young) soldier eventually becomes an (old) deliberator.

*the former and just before his recommendations for the
financing of the latter.*

*Many of the provisions of the second half of the chapter
are reminiscent of those in Plato's Laws (see especially
739a ff., 776b ff., 779d ff.); on the common meals see also
II ix and x.*

1329a40 That a division of the state into classes is necessary, and that the fighting class should be different from
the agricultural, seems not to be a modern or even a
recent discovery of political philosophers.[1] In Egypt this
pattern still exists today, and in Crete too; Sesostris is
said to have introduced laws in this sense for Egypt,
Minos for Crete. The system of communal feeding also
appears to be ancient, and to have been introduced in
Crete in the reign of Minos, but in Italy very much
earlier. For the chroniclers of the settlers there tell us of
a certain Italus who became king of Oenotria, after whom
the people of Oenotria changed their name to Italians,
and the name Italy was given to that part of the promon-
tory of Europe which lies within the Scylletic and Lam-
petic gulfs, where the distance across is half a day's
journey. This Italus, they tell us, transformed the
Oenotrians from a pastoral people into farmers, and in
addition to other laws which he laid down for them instituted the common meals. So even to this day some of his
successors keep up the common meals and follow some
of his laws. On the Tyrrhenian side dwelt the Opicians,
called Ausonians both in ancient and modern times; on
the other side, that of Iapygia and the Ionian Sea, there
was the land called Siritis; and the Chonians also were by
race Oenotrians. The system of common messing, then,
originated thence, whereas class-distinctions within the
population of the state originated in Egypt, for the kingship of Sesostris goes back very much farther than that of
Minos.

1. Literally, 'those who philosophize about constitutions'. 'Class'
in this chapter = *genos*, 'type', 'sort'.

1329b25 We must, I think, regard it as fairly certain
that the other institutions as well have been in the course
of the ages discovered many times over, or rather infinitely
often. In the first place there are things we cannot do
without, and need itself probably teaches us them.
Secondly, when once these are available, the process
presumably goes on tending towards more comfort and
greater abundance. So we should accept it as a fact that
the same process takes place in the case of constitutional
features too. That these are all ancient is shown by
Egyptian history: the Egyptians are reputed to be the
most ancient people, and they have always had laws and
a constitutional system. Thus we ought to make full use
of what has already been discovered, while endeavouring
to find what has not.

1329b36 We stated earlier[2] (a) that the land ought to be
possessed by those who have arms and participate in the
constitution, (b) why the cultivators should be different
from them, and (c) the nature and extent of the territory
required. We must speak first about the division of the
land and about those who cultivate it: who should they
be, and what kind of person? We do not agree with
those[3] who have said that property should be communally
owned, but we do believe that there should be a friendly
arrangement for its common use, and that none of the
citizens should be without means of support.

1330a3 Next as to communal meals: it is universally
agreed that this is a useful institution in a well-constructed
state, and why we too are of this opinion we will say
later.[4] All citizens should partake of them, though it is
not easy for those who are badly off to pay from their
private resources the contribution fixed and to keep a
household going at the same time. Another thing that
should be a common charge on the whole state is the

2. VII v and ix.
3. Probably Plato is meant: see e.g. *Republic* 416d ff., *Laws*
739b ff., and cf. II v.
4. In fact, no such passage is to be found in the *Politics*.

worship of the gods. Thus it becomes necessary to divide the land into two parts, one communally owned, the other privately. Each of these has to be further divided into two, and one part of the common land will support the public service of the gods, while the other will meet the expenses of the communal feeding.

1330a14 Of the privately owned land one part will be near the frontier, the other near the city, so that each man may have two estates and everyone may have a share of both localities. This is not only in accordance with justice and equality, but makes also for greater unity in the face of wars with bordering peoples. Without this dual arrangement, some underestimate the dangers of frontier quarrels, others regard them too cautiously, even sacrificing honour in order to avoid them.[5] Hence in some countries it is the law that when war against a neighbour is under consideration, those who live near the border should be excluded from the discussion as being too personally involved to be able to give advice honourably. It is therefore important that the territory should for the reasons given be divided in the manner stated.

1330a25 As for those who are to till the land, the best thing (if we are to describe the ideal) is that they should be slaves. They should not be all of one stock nor men of spirit; this will ensure that they will be useful workers and no danger as potential rebels. A second-best alternative to slaves is non-Greek 'peripheral'[6] people, men of the same nature as the slaves just mentioned. They fall into two groups according to whether they ought to work privately, as the private possessions of individual owners of property, or in communal ownership on the common land. I hope later on[4] to say how slaves ought to be treated, and why it is a good thing that all slaves should have before them the prospect of receiving their freedom as a reward.

5. Literally, '. . . too cautiously, even contrary to what is fine' (*to kalon*).
6. Cf. VII vi, VII ix, n. 9, and introduction to II ix.

(1330a34–1331a18)

THE SITING AND DEFENCE OF THE CITY

The chapter which follows is a good example of the way in which Aristotle resumes his earlier discussions (in this case VII, v, vi, and vii) in order to elaborate on them. However, the four things to be looked for in siting a city – good air, good water, administrative convenience, defensive possibilities (if these are indeed the 'four considerations' mentioned in the first paragraph) – are handled unevenly and unsystematically. Once again we note his probable debt to the 'Airs, Waters, Places' of Hippocrates; cf. VII vii. His grim remarks about contemporary advances in the precision of military 'hardware', and about 'escalation' in warfare, have a distinctly modern ring.

In this chapter (cf. VII vi) polis is usually translated as 'city', as distinct from surrounding territory; the combination of the two makes a 'state'.

1330a34 We have already noted[1] that so far as conditions allow a city should have equally easy communication with the sea, the mainland and the whole of its territory. We must hope, as an ideal, that the land upon which the city itself is to be sited will be sloping, and we should keep four considerations in mind. First, it is essential that the situation be a healthy one. A slope facing east, with winds blowing from the direction of sunrise, gives a healthier site, but second-best is one on the lee side of north, which gives more shelter in winter. One other point is that it should be well situated for carrying out all its civil and military activities. For the purposes of the latter, the site should be one from which

1. VII v.

the inhabitants can easily go out, but which attackers
will find difficult to approach and difficult to surround.
Water, and especially spring water, should be abundant
and if possible originate on site; alternatively, a way has
been discovered of catching rain water in large vessels
numerous enough to ensure a substitute supply whenever
fighting prevents the defenders from going out into their
territory.

1330b8 Since consideration must be given to the health
of the inhabitants, which is partly a matter of its site
being in the best place and facing the right way, partly
also dependent on a supply of pure water, this too must
receive careful attention – because those things that our
bodies use most frequently and in greatest quantity make
the greatest contribution to our health, and this is the
scale on which air and water have a natural capacity to
affect us. Hence, a state will be well advised to keep
water for human consumption separate from water for all
other uses, unless of course all the water is alike and there
are plenty of springs that are drinkable.

1330b17 In the matter of defensive positions, what is
advantageous for one constitution is not so good for
another. A lofty central citadel[2] suits both oligarchy and
monarchy, a level plain democracy; neither suits an aristocracy, which prefers a series of strongly held points. As
for the layout of private dwelling-houses, the modern or
Hippodamean[3] scheme of regularity is more attractive
and more useful for all activities except ensuring safety
in war, for which the old-fashioned layout was better,
being hard for foreign forces to get into and to penetrate
in their attack. It follows that both methods should be
used, and this is quite possible: arrange the buildings in
the same pattern as is used in fields for planting vines, in
what some people call clusters, and do not lay out the
whole city with geometric regularity but only certain

2. Literally, 'an acropolis'.   3. See II viii.

parts and localities.[4] This will meet the needs both of safety and of good appearance.

1330b32 As for walls, it is quite out of date to say, as some do,[5] that cities that lay claim to valour[6] should not have them; such people can after all see that cities which made that boast are condemned by events. Doubtless there is something dishonourable in seeking safety behind strong walls, at any rate against an enemy equal in number or only very slightly superior. But it can happen that the superiority of the attackers is too much for the valour[6] both of the average man and of a choice few. If then they are to save themselves and avoid misery and oppression, we must reckon that to secure the greatest degree of protection that strong walls can afford is also the best military measure. The truth of this is emphasized by all the modern improvements in the accuracy of missiles and artillery for attacking a besieged town. Deliberately to give cities no walls at all is like choosing an easily attacked territory and clearing away the surrounding high ground; it is as if we were to refrain from putting walls round private houses for fear of rendering the inhabitants unmanly. Another thing that should not be lost sight of is that those who have provided their city with a wall round it are in a position to regard that city in both ways, to treat it either as a fortified or as an unfortified city. Those who have no walls have no such choice. And if this is so, then it is a duty not only to build encircling walls but also to maintain them in a manner suitable both for the city's good appearance and for its military needs, particularly those which have come to light in modern times. For just as the attacking side is

---

4. To modify slightly Newman's explanation ad loc., 'Aristotle's plan will be to drive straight wide streets between rows of "clumps" or "clusters" of houses, but to leave the interior of each cluster a tangle of narrow lanes.'

5. Probably a reference to Plato, *Laws* 778d.

6. *Aretē*, 'virtue'.

always on the lookout for methods which will give them an advantage, so too the defenders must investigate and study[7] means of defence additional to those already discovered. An enemy will not even attempt an attack in the first place on those who are well prepared to meet it.

VII xii

(*1331a19–1331b23*)

THE SITING OF MARKETS,
TEMPLES AND COMMUNAL REFECTORIES

Aristotle now gives further details of the physical layout of the ideal state, before declining to go into further petty detail (cf. Plato's similar disdain for the niceties of administration, Republic *425c ff.). On the duties of officials in charge of markets, streets, countryside etc., see VI viii. The meeting-place or square (agora) for free men is known in Persia also; according to Xenophon,* Education of Cyrus, *I 2, iii, its main purpose was to keep them from acquiring a taste for the degrading practice of trade. This* agora *therefore reinforces, like numerous other physical and administrative details in Aristotle's 'utopia', the social and political structure of the state.*

1331a19 Since the body of citizens should be distributed over a number of feeding-centres, and the walls should be furnished at suitable points with towers and garrison-posts, it is obviously required that some of the feeding-centres should be located in these posts. So much for how one might arrange that. Buildings devoted to the service of the gods, and the chief feeding-places of members of committees, should have a suitable position on the same site, unless the law or some pronouncement of the Pythian oracle requires any of the sacred buildings to be erected

7. *Philosophein*, literally 'philosophize', 'be a lover of wisdom'.

somewhere apart. Our purpose would be well served by a site which provides a suitable balance between conspicuousness and excellence of location, and is at the same time comparatively easy to defend in relation to the neighbouring parts of the city.

1331a30 Just below this is the proper place to lay out a square[1] of the kind which in fact they keep up in Thessaly under the name of 'free' square. Here nothing may be bought or sold, and no mechanic or farmer or anyone else like that may be admitted unless summoned by the authorities. This area could be made attractive if the gymnasia of the older folk were also laid out there; for in this amenity also there should be separation of age-groups, the younger in one place, the older in another; the latter should follow this pursuit in the company of the officials, and some of the officials should mingle with the younger men, since the presence of authority's watchful eye instils genuine deference – dread as felt by a free man.[2] The market[1] proper, where buying and selling are done, must be a different one, in a separate place, conveniently situated for all goods sent up from the sea and brought in from the country.

1331b4 The government of the state being divided into officials and priests, it is right that the latter too should have their eating-places established round the sacred buildings. As for the boards concerned with contracts, with the entering of suits-at-law, with summonses, and with the ordering of such matters generally (also surveillance of markets[1] and what is called 'wardenship of the city') – these should all be located near a market and general meeting-place. This will, of course, be the area intended for the market it is essential to have – the one for the transaction of essential business; the upper one that we mentioned is intended for leisure. A similar arrangement should be applied to the country districts,

---

1. *Agora.*
2. For modesty/deference/respect (*aidōs*) as a 'good fear', cf. Plato, *Laws* 647a, 673c, 698b, 699c ff.

for there too the officials, Forest Wardens or Field-Wardens or whatever they may be called, must have eating-places and garrison-posts to enable them to carry out their work of protection; likewise shrines in honour of gods and heroes must be distributed over the country-side.

1331b18 But it is really not necessary now to go on describing all these matters in detail. It is not at all difficult to think what things are needed, though it is quite another matter to provide them. Our talk is the expression of our desires, but the outcome is in Fortune's hands. Therefore we will say no more about such matters now.

VII xiii

(*1331b24–1332b11*)

HAPPINESS AS THE AIM OF THE CONSTITUTION

Dismissing the rather humdrum matters of the preceding chapters, Aristotle deals next with what for him is clearly the most important part of the business – the politeia *and all that that untranslatable word stands for: the whole social, political, legal and economic structure of the state. At this point we should remember that a* politeia *is essentially a collection of* people. *Whether they be many or few, they are a body of 'sound' men, united in their acceptance of all the standards, moral and spiritual, intellectual and artistic, which belong to and are pre-scribed by the constitution by which they live. It follows that these standards will have to be learned by all the citizens; a man must know the* nomoi *(laws) of his* polis *(state), and he must start learning them when he is quite young. Hence the most important part of any constitu-tion is, as both Plato and Aristotle saw, the education of those who are going to be its members; and this is especially true when we are looking for the ideal state, for then we must also look for the ideal education. So all the rest of Aristotle's* Politics *as we have it, from here to the end of Book VIII, deals with education, its aims and its methods. But first Aristotle discusses happiness, since the aim of education is the good and happy life; and this is a point which Plato, according to Aristotle, had effectively neglected (see II v, at the end).*

Nicomachean Ethics *I vii ff. will be invaluable background reading for the philosophical argument of this chapter. Briefly stated, Aristotle's position is that happiness* (eudaimonia) *is the complete and perfect use of all our faculties under the guidance of* aretē *('virtue'); hence the best constitution, in order to produce happiness, must consist of and be operated by men who are 'utilizing virtue' and are therefore 'sound'* (spoudaioi). *In the final paragraph Aristotle swiftly enumerates the three factors which go to make the* spoudaios: *nature, habit and reason* (logos), *the last being a distinctively human faculty. All three are open to influence by the educational programme worked out by the legislator.*

1331b24 We must now discuss the constitution itself, and ask ourselves what people, and what kind of people, the state ought to be composed of if it is going to be blessed and have a well-run constitution. The well-being of all men depends on two things: one is the right choice of target, of the end to which actions should tend, the other lies in finding the actions that lead to that end. These two may just as easily conflict with each other as coincide. Sometimes, for example, the aim is well-chosen, but in action men fail to attain it. At other times they successfully perform everything that conduces to the end, but the end itself was badly chosen. Or they may fail in both, as sometimes happens in the practice of medicine, when doctors neither rightly discern what kind of condition a healthy body ought to be in, nor discover the means which will enable their goal to be attained. Wherever skill and knowledge come into play, these two must both be mastered: the end and the actions which are means to the end.

1331b39 It is clear then that all men aim at happiness and the good life,[1] but some men have an opportunity to get it, others have not. This may be due to their nature, or to some stroke of fortune, for the good life needs certain material resources (and when a man's disposition is comparatively good, the need is for a lesser amount of these, a greater amount when it is comparatively bad). Some indeed, who start with the opportunity, go wrong from the very beginning of the pursuit of happiness. But as our object is to find the *best* constitution, and that means the one whereby a state will be best ordered,[2] and since we call that state best ordered in which the possibilities of happiness are greatest, it is clear that we must keep constantly in mind what happiness is. *1332a7* We defined this in our *Ethics*[3] (if those discussions were worth anything), and we here state, again, that happiness is an activity and a complete utilization of virtue, not conditionally but absolutely. By 'conditionally' in this connection I refer to things that are necessary, and by 'absolutely' I mean moral.[4] For example, actions relating to justice, the infliction of just chastisements and punishments, spring from virtue; but they are 'necessary', and whatever good[4] is in them is there by necessity. (It is preferable to have a state of affairs in which such things would be *un*necessary both for state and for individual.) But actions directed towards honours and abun-

1. *To eu zēn*, 'to live well'. A few lines below, 'good life' = *to zēn kalōs*, 'to live finely'. See the introduction to VII i.

2. *Arista politeuesthai*, 'to be best run under a constitution, best governed, best administered', etc. Cf. *politeuesthai kalōs*, 'have a well-run constitution', in the first sentence of this chapter.

3. *Nichomachean Ethics*, I vii.

4. 'Moral' = *kalos, kalōs*, cf. nn. 1, 2 and 5. The word 'utilize' in these two paragraphs is *chrēsthai*, to 'use', 'employ', 'handle'. 'Conditionally' = *ex hupotheseōs*, 'in an assumed situation'; cf. references in VII ix, n. 3.

dant resources are noblest[5] actions, in an absolute sense.
For the former actions are but the removal of some evil,
the latter sort are not; they are on the contrary the creation and the begetting of positive goods.

1332a19 A sound man will nobly[4] utilize ill-health,
poverty and other misfortunes; but blessedness requires
the opposite of these. (This definition too was given in
our ethical discussions[6] – that the sound man is the sort
of man for whom things absolutely good are good, on
account of his own virtue; and clearly his utilization of
them must be sound and noble[4] absolutely.) Hence men
imagine that the causes of happiness lie in external goods.
This is as if they were to ascribe fine[7] and brilliant lyre-
playing to the quality of the instrument rather than to
the skill of the player.

1332a28 From what has been said it follows that, while
some things must be there from the start, others must be
provided by a lawgiver. Ideally, then, we wish for the
structure of our state all that Fortune has it in her sovereign power to bestow (that she *is* sovereign, we take for
granted). But it is not Fortune's business to make a state
sound; that is a task for knowledge and deliberate choice.
On the other hand, a state's being sound requires the
citizens who share in the constitution to be sound; and
for our purposes *all* the citizens share in the constitution.
The question then is, 'How does a man become sound?'
Of course, even if it is possible for all to be sound,[8] and
not just each citizen taken individually, the latter is
preferable, since each entails all.

1332a38 However, men become sound and good because
of three things. These are nature, habit, and reason. First,
nature: a man must be born, and he must be born a
man and not some other animal; so too he must have

5. *Kallistai* (superlative of *kalos*); cf. nn. 1, 2 and 4
6. E.g. *Nicomachean Ethics*, III iv; cf. Plato, *Laws* 661c.
7. *Kalōs*, obviously this time in a non-moral sense.
8. I.e. in the mass, collectively, with some individual exceptions.

body and soul with certain characteristics. It may be of no advantage to be born with some of these qualities, because habits cause changes; for there are some qualities which by nature have a dual possibility, in that subsequent habits will make them either better or worse. Other creatures live by nature only; some live by habit also to some extent. Man, however, lives by reason as well: he alone has reason, and so needs all three working concertedly. Reason causes men to do many things contrary to habit and to nature, whenever they are convinced that this is the better course. In an earlier place[9] we described what men's nature should be if they are to respond easily to handling by the legislator. After that it becomes a task of education, for men learn partly by habituation and partly by listening.

VII xiv

(*1332b12–1334a10*)

EDUCATION FOR CITIZENSHIP

Aristotle now seeks to relate his educational programme to the duties of citizenship. If the principle of continuous personal rule were to be accepted, and the conditions necessary for it were forthcoming, the education of the citizens would be quite different from that required in the kind of constitution favoured by Aristotle, under which they are expected to hold office by turns. In this consideration of the ideal state Aristotle does not altogether reject the former type of rule, any more than he did in III xvii–xviii, where he discussed absolute monarchical rule; but he lays it aside as not practicable. So he now asks how a man is to be educated for citizenship, i.e. how he is to be made morally and intellectually fit to hold office in his turn and to behave himself when it

9. VII vii.

*is not his turn. Such an alternation will satisfy the demand
for equality, which it is dangerous to leave unsatisfied,
and will at the same time do justice to merit and ability.
Within the citizen or governing class only a distinction
of age-group will operate, as in VII ix.*

*In the third paragraph Aristotle begins his description
of the educational process by linking it with the psychology on which it is based. The soul has two 'parts', the
rational and the irrational, and the aim of education
affects mainly the former. The aim is 'leisure', scholē, i.e.
not rest and recreation so much as the undistracted opportunity to devote oneself to something worth while:
the pursuits of citizenship and 'statesmanship' in time
of peace. Aristotle complains that these aims are not
always recognized. Spartan education in particular he
held at fault for being directed predominantly to the
waging of war. Spartan militarism he criticized towards
the end of II ix (cf. references there to Plato's Laws), and
he now renews the topic with more emphasis on the
founder of the system (here unnamed, but presumably
Lycurgus). However, the Spartan military supremacy had
come to an end by the time this chapter was written.*

1332b12 Since every association of persons forming a
state[1] consists of rulers and ruled, we must ask whether
those who rule and those who are ruled ought to be
different persons or the same throughout life; for the
education which will be needed will depend upon which
way we make this distinction.[2] If one group of persons
were as far superior to all the rest as we believe gods and
heroes to be superior to men, and if they had both bodies
and souls of such outstanding quality that the superiority
of the rulers were indisputable and evident to those
ruled by them, then it would obviously be better that
the same set of persons should always rule and the others
always be ruled, once and for all. But since this is not a

1. *Politikē koinōnia*, see I i.
2. I.e. between rulers and ruled.

condition that can easily be obtained, and since rulers are not so greatly superior to their subjects as Scylax[3] says the kings are in India, it is clear that, for a variety of reasons, all must share alike in the business of ruling and being ruled by turns. For equality means giving the same to those who are alike, and the established constitution can hardly be long maintained if it is contrary to justice. Otherwise everyone all over the country combines with the ruled in a desire to introduce innovations, and it is quite impossible for even a numerous citizen-body to be strong enough to withstand such a combination.

1332b32 Yet it cannot be disputed that rulers have to be superior to those who are ruled. It therefore becomes the duty of the lawgiver to consider how this is to be brought about and how they shall do the sharing. We noted earlier[4] that nature herself has provided one way to choose: that very element which in respect of birth is all the same she has divided into older and younger, the former being fit for ruling, the latter for being ruled. No one objects to being thus ruled on grounds of age, or thinks himself too good for it; after all, once he reaches the required age, he will get back his contribution to the pool.[5] There is then a sense in which we must say the 'same' persons rule and are ruled, and a sense in which we must say that they are 'different' persons. So their education too must be in one sense the same, in another different; for, as is often said, one who is to become a good ruler must first himself be ruled. (Rule, as was said in our first discussions,[6] is of two kinds, according as it is exercised for the sake of the ruler, which we say is master-like rule, or for the sake of the ruled, which we say is rule over free men; and some instructions that are given

3. Scylax travelled to India in the late sixth or early fifth century: see Herodotus, IV 44.
4. VII ix.
5. I.e. 'being ruled' is his contribution, and the privilege of ruling will be the 'return' he gets in due course.
6. III iv and vi.

differ not in the actual tasks to be performed, but in their purpose,[7] which is why many jobs generally considered servile may be honourably[8] performed even by free men, by the younger among them. For the question whether a job is honourable[8] or not is to be decided less with reference to the actions themselves than in the light of their end and purpose.)[7] But since we hold that the virtue of citizen and ruler is the same as that of the best man, and that the same man should be first ruled and later ruler, it immediately becomes an essential task of the lawgiver to ensure that they both may become *good* men, and to consider what practices will make them so, and what is the aim of the best life.

1333a16 Two parts of the soul are distinguished, one intrinsically possessing reason, the other not possessing reason intrinsically but capable of listening to it. To these belong, we think, the virtues which qualify a man to be called in some sense 'good'. To those who accept our division of the soul there is no difficulty in answering the question 'In which of the two parts, more than in the other, does the *end* lie?' For what is inferior is always for the sake of what is superior; this is equally clear both in matters of skill and in those of nature; and the superior is that which is possessed of reason. There is a further two-fold division, which follows from our custom of making a distinction between practical reason and theoretical reason; so clearly we must divide this part[9] similarly. Actions, we shall say, follow suit: those of that which is by nature better[9] must be regarded as preferable by those who are in a position to attain all three[10] or two of

7. Or, 'for whose sake', *tinos heneka* being ambiguous as between 'for the sake of what' and 'for the sake of whom'.

8. *Kalon*.

9. I.e. the intrinsically rational part of the soul.

10. That is, all three (kinds of action) or the two (kinds of action), the three being those (a) of theoretical reason, (b) of practical reason, and (c) of the second of the two parts of the soul, i.e. of the part which 'listens to' reason. 'The two' are presumably (b) and (c).

them. For each man, that which is the very highest that he can attain is the thing most to be preferred.

1333a30 Again, all of life can be divided into work and leisure, war and peace, and some things done have moral worth,[11] while others are merely necessary and useful. In this connection the same principle of choice must be applied, both to the parts of the soul and to their respective actions – that is to say, we should choose war for the sake of peace, work for the sake of leisure, necessary and useful things for the sake of the noble.[11] The statesman must therefore take into consideration the parts of the soul and their respective actions, and in making laws must have an eye to all those things,[12] but more especially to the better ones and to the ends in view; and he must regard men's lives and their choice of what they do in the same light. For one must be able to work and to fight, but even more to be at peace and have leisure; to do the necessary and the useful things, yes, but still more those of moral worth.[11] These then are the targets at which education should be aimed, whether children's education or that of such later age-groups as require it.

1333b5 It is obvious however that those Greeks who have today a reputation for running the best constitutions, and the lawgivers who drew up those constitutions, did not in fact construct their constitutional plans with the best possible aim, and did not direct their laws and education towards producing all the virtues; but instead, following the vulgar way of thinking, they turned aside to pursue virtues that appeared to be useful and more lucrative. And in a similar manner to these some more recent writers have voiced the same opinion: they express their approval of the Lacedaemonians' constitution and admire the aim of their lawgiver, because he ordered all his legislation with a view to war and conquest. This is a view which can easily be refuted by reasoning, and already in our own day has been refuted by the facts. Just

11. *Kala*; cf. VII xiii, esp. nn. 1, 2, 4 and 5, VIII iv, n. 2.
12. War, peace, etc.

as most men crave to be master of many others, because
success in this brings an abundance of worldly goods, so
the writer Thibron[13] is clearly an admirer of the Laconian
lawgiver, and so too is each of the others who, writing
about the Spartan constitution, have stated that thanks
to their being trained to face dangers they came to rule
over many others. But since today the Spartan rule is no
more, it is clear that they are not happy and their lawgiver was not a good one. There is also something laugh-
able in the fact that, for all their keeping to his laws, and
with no one to stop them from using those laws, they
have lost the good life.[14]

1333b26 They are also wrong in their notion of the
kind of rule for which a lawgiver ought to display admiration; for rule over free men is nobler[15] than master-like
rule, and more connected with virtue. To say that a state
has trained itself in the acquisition of power with a view
to ruling its neighbours – that is no ground for calling it
happy or applauding its lawgiver. Such an argument may
have dangerous consequences: its acceptance obviously
requires any citizen who can to make it his ambition to
be able to rule in his own city – the very thing that the
Lacedaemonians accuse King Pausanias of seeking, and
that too though he was already in a position of such high
honour. So none of these theories or laws is of any value
for a statesman, and they are neither useful nor true. The
same things are best for a community and for individuals,
and it is these that a lawgiver must instil into the souls
of men.

1333b37 And as for military training, the object in
practising it regularly is not to bring into subjection those
not deserving of such treatment, but to enable men (a)
to save themselves from becoming subject to others, (b) to
win a position of leadership, exercised for the benefit
of the ruled, not with a view to being the master of all,

13. Not otherwise known.
14. *To zēn kalōs*: cf. n. 11 and references.
15. *Kalliōn*, comparative of *kalos*.

and (c) to exercise the rule of a master over those who deserve to be slaves. The lawgiver should make particularly sure that his aim both in his military legislation and in his legislation in general is to provide peace and leisure. And facts support theory here, for though most military states survive while they are fighting wars, they fall when they have established their rule. Like steel, they lose their fine temper when they are at peace; and the lawgiver who has not educated them to be able to employ their leisure is to blame.

VII xv

(*1334a11–1334b28*)

THE PROPER EDUCATION FOR CULTURED LEISURE

Aristotle has one more chapter of preliminary discussion before coming to detailed recommendations for the educational programme of the ideal state. He discusses first the virtues required for the procuring and employment of leisure (scholē), and then, in a careful paragraph of teleological and empirical argument, concludes that the education of the body and of the appetitive element of the soul must precede that of the soul's rational part. The aim of the educational programme as a whole is to inculcate the virtues needed for the proper employment of leisure in cultural, intellectual and 'political' activities.

A modern educationist may not wish to criticize Aristotle's recommendations about the chronological priority of the education of the body and the emotions over that of the intellect; but he will almost certainly object to Aristotle's teleological mode of reasoning. No doubt in natural processes earlier stages lead up to and are in some sense 'for' the later; but that does not entail that since intellectual training is a late stage in the educational process, the other and earlier stages are 'for its sake', as something grander and better and the real natural 'aim' of the whole sequence. Put differently, Aristotle's view of the development of human faculties is reasonable enough, though the distinction between appetite/emotion and reason may seem over-simple; subject to the same caveat, his recommended sequence in education is similarly reasonable; but his imposition on all this of a value judgement about the natural superiority *of reason and the intellect is perhaps to be resisted. The cultured leisure of an educated man – perhaps the 'gentleman scholar' of a later age – is as an aspiration civilized and superb; but are Aristotle's arguments for it good enough? If they are, do we have to conclude that those who do not attain to it are morally inferior?*

1334a11 Since it seems that men have the same ends whether they are acting as individuals or as a community, and that the best man and the best constitution must have the same definitive purpose, it becomes evident that there must be present the virtues needed for leisure; for, as has often been said,[1] the end of war is peace and leisure is the end of work. Of the virtues useful for leisure and civilized pursuits, some function in a period of leisure, others in a period of work – because a lot of essential things need to be provided before leisure can become possible. Hence a state must be self-restrained, courageous and steadfast; for as the proverb says, 'no leisure for slaves', and those who cannot bravely face danger are the slaves of their attackers. We need courage and steadfastness for our work, philosophy[2] for leisure, and restraint and a sense of justice in both contexts, but particularly in times of leisure and peace. For war *forces* men to be just and restrained, but the enjoyment of prosperity, and leisure in peacetime, are apt rather to make them arrogant. Therefore a great sense of justice and much self-restraint are demanded of those who are

1. VII xiv.
2. *Philosophia*, not in the strong academic sense but roughly 'cultural and intellectual activity'.

thought to be successful and to enjoy everything the world regards as a blessing, men such as might be living, in the poets' phrase, in the Isles of the Blest.[3] For these especially will need philosophy,[2] restraint, and a sense of justice; and the greater the leisure that flows from an abundance of such blessings, the greater that need will be. Clearly then the state, too, if it is to be sound and happy, must have a share in these virtues. For if it is a mark of disgrace not to be able to use advantages, it is especially so in a period of leisure – to display good qualities when working or on military service, but in leisure and peace to be no better than slaves.

1334a40 Training in virtue, therefore, should not follow the Lacedaemonian model. The difference between them and other nations lies not in any disagreement about what are the greatest goods but in their view that there is a certain[4] virtue which will produce them with particular effectiveness. Since they value good things and their enjoyment more than the ... of the virtues, ... and that ... for its own sake, is clear from these things; and we have to consider how and by what means.[5]

1334b6 We have already[6] distinguished three essentials – nature, habit, and reason. Of these we have already dealt with the first,[7] determining the qualities we should have by natural endowment; next we must ask whether education should first proceed by means of reason or by the formation of habits. Certainly these must chime in perfect unison; for it is possible to make an error of reason about the best principle, and to find oneself equally led astray by one's habits.

3. See Hesiod, *Works and Days*, 170–4 and Pindar, *Olympians* II, 70 ff.; and compare Homer, *Odyssey* IV, 561 ff.

4. I.e. courage.

5. There is something missing from the Greek, probably the end of one sentence and the beginning of the next. Apart from 'they value', I have refrained from conjectural supplementation; see Newman ad loc.

6. VII xiii.

7. VII vii.

1334b12 One thing is clear from the start: just as in everything else, so here too coming into being originates in a beginning, and the end which originates in some beginning is itself the beginning of another end;[8] and for us, reason and intelligence are the end to which our nature tends. Thus it is to these that the training of our habits, as well as our coming into being, must be directed. Next, as soul and body are two, so also we note two parts of the soul, the reasoning and the unreasoning; and each of these has its own condition, of intelligence[9] in the former case, of appetition[10] in the latter. And just as the body comes into being earlier than the soul, so also the unreasoning is prior to that which possesses reason. This is shown by the fact that, while passion and will as well as desire are to be found in children even right from birth, reasoning and intelligence come into their possession as they grow older. Therefore the care of the body must begin before the care of the soul, then the training of the appetitive element,[10] but this latter for the sake of the intelligence, and the body's training for the sake of the soul.

VII xvi

(1334b29–1336a2)

SEX, MARRIAGE AND EUGENICS

The general conditions of life, climate, race, etc., in which it is desirable to be born were stated in Chapters iv–vii and x–xii of this book. Now, dealing with the upbringing of children from the very start, Aristotle gives advice on birth itself, marriage, parenthood, and procreation. In

---

8. In less austere language, in any sequence (here the birth and growth of a human being) the completion of one stage is itself the beginning of a further stage.

9. *Nous*, and so for the remainder of the chapter.

10. *Orexis*, and so for the remainder of the chapter.

ancient Greece when a child was born, it was a matter for the father's decision whether it was to be reared or left to die in an exposed place. This practice must have come under criticism by the fourth century, for Aristotle makes it clear that there was a body of opinion opposed to using exposure of healthy infants merely for the purpose of keeping down the population. But in spite of the textual difficulties in this part of the chapter, it is beyond doubt that Aristotle was prepared to countenance (a) exposure of deformed births, and (b) abortion of the embryo before it acquires sensation and life, as a measure of population control, at least in certain circumstances. Tantalizingly, he does not say when he supposes the embryo to reach this crucial stage.

1334b29 Now as it is a lawgiver's duty to start from the very beginning in looking for ways to secure the best possible physique for the young who are reared, he must consider first the union of their parents, and ask what kind of people should come together in marriage, and when. In making regulations about this partnership he should have regard both to the spouses themselves and to their length of life, in order that they may arrive at the right ages together at the same time, and so that the period of the father's ability to beget and that of the mother's to bear children may coincide. A period when one of the two is capable and the other not leads to mutual strife and quarrels. Next, as regards the timing of the children's succession,[1] there should not be too great a gap in age between father and children; for then there is no good that the young can do by showing gratitude to elderly parents, and their fathers are of no help to them. Nor should they be too close in age, for this causes the relationship to be strained: like contemporaries, people in such a position feel less respect, and the nearness in age

1. I.e., at their parents' death, to their estate – the culmination of a period of mutual service as between them and the children, facilitated by an age-gap neither too wide nor too narrow.

leads to bickering in household affairs. And further, to go back to the point we started from, one should ensure that the physique of the children that are produced[2] shall be in accordance with the wishes of the legislator.

1335a6 All these purposes can be fulfilled, or nearly so, if we pay sufficient attention to one thing. Since, generally speaking, the upper limit of age for the begetting of children is for men seventy years and for women fifty, the beginning of their union should be at ages such that they will arrive at this stage of life simultaneously. But the intercourse of a very young couple is not good for child-bearing. In all animals the offspring of early unions are defective, inclined to produce females, and diminutive; so the same kind of results are bound to follow in human beings too. And there is evidence that this is so: in states where early unions are the rule, the people are small in stature and defective. A further objection is that young women have greater difficulty in giving birth and more of them die. (Some say that here we have also the reason for the oracle given to the people of Troezen:[3] there is no reference to the harvesting of crops, but to the fact that the marrying of girls at too young an age was causing many deaths.) It is also more conducive to restraint that daughters should be no longer young when their fathers bestow them in marriage, because it seems that women who have sexual intercourse at an early age are more likely to be dissolute. On the male side too it is held that if they have intercourse while the seed is just growing, it interferes with their bodily growth; for the seed is subject to a fixed limit of time, after which it ceases to be replenished except on a small scale. Accordingly we conclude that the appropriate age for the union is about the eighteenth year for girls and for men the

---

2. *Ta gennōmena*, 'the children being produced'. In the first paragraph, probably of both born and unborn children; in the third, probably of born children only; in the fourth, of the unborn only (cf. Plato, *Laws* 788c ff.).

3. 'Do not cut (i.e. plough) a new (i.e. young) furrow.'

thirty-seventh. With such timing, their union will take place when they are physically in their prime, and it will bring them down together to the end of procreation at exactly the right moment for both. And the children's succession,[1] if births take place promptly at the expected time, will occur when they are at the beginning of their prime and their parents are past their peak, the father now approaching his seventieth year.

1335a35 We have spoken now about the time when the union should take place, but not about the seasons of the year best suited for establishing this form[4] of living together. However, the common practice of choosing winter is satisfactory. The spouses too should study for themselves, in good time, the advice of doctors and natural scientists to assist them in bearing children; the former give suitable information about crucial stages in the life of the body, the latter about the winds (they recommend the northerly ones rather than the southerly). To the question of what kind of physique is most advantageous for the offspring that are produced,[2] we must give closer attention in the works[5] on the training of children; for our present purpose the following outline will suffice. The condition of an athlete does not make for the physical fitness needed by a citizen, nor for health and the production of offspring. A condition of much coddling and of unfitness for hard work is equally undesirable. Something between the two is needed, a condition of one inured to hard but not violently hard toil, directed not all in one direction as an athlete's, but towards the various activities typical of men who are free. These requirements are applicable to men and women alike.

1335b12 Further, it is important that women should look after their bodies during pregnancy. They must not relax unduly, or go on a meagre diet. It is easy for a legislator to ensure this by making it a rule that they shall each day take a walk, the object of which is to wor-

4. I.e. in marriage.   5. If written, not now extant.

ship regularly the gods whose office is to look after child-birth. But while the body should be exercised, the intellect should follow a more relaxed regime, for the unborn infant[2] appears to be influenced by her who is carrying it as plants are by the earth.

1335b19 With regard to the choice between abandoning an infant or rearing it, let there be a law that no cripple child be reared. But since the ordinance of custom forbids the exposure of infants on account of their numbers, there must be a limit to the production of children. If contrary to these arrangements copulation does take place and a child is conceived, abortion should be procured before the embryo has acquired life and sensation; the presence of life and sensation will be the mark of division between right and wrong[6] here.

1335b26 Since we have already decided the beginning of the period of life at which male and female should enter on their union, we must also decide upon the length of time during which it is proper that they should render the service[7] of producing children. The offspring of elderly people, like the offspring of the unduly young, are imperfect both in intellect and in body; and those of the aged are feeble. We should therefore be guided by the highest point of intellectual development, and this in most cases is the age mentioned by certain poets[8] who measure life by periods of seven years, that is to say about the fiftieth year of life.[9] Thus anyone who has passed this age by four or five years ought to give up bringing children into the world. But provided it is clearly for the sake of health or other such reason intercourse may continue.

1335b38 As for extra-marital intercourse, it should, in

6. *To hosion kai to mē*, literally 'that which is holy/lawful/permitted, and that which is not'.

7. *Leitourgein*, on which see IV iv, n. 11.

8. E.g. Solon, fr. 27 in J. M. Edmonds, *Elegy and Iambus*, I (Loeb edition, London and Cambridge, 1931).

9. I.e. the husband's.

general, be a disgrace[10] to be detected in intimacy of any kind whatever, so long as one is a husband and so addressed. If anyone is found to be acting thus during the period of his begetting of children, let him be punished by such measure of disgrace as is appropriate to his misdemeanour.

VII xvii

(1336a3–1337a7)

THE MAIN PERIODS OF EDUCATION; CENSORSHIP

'Aristotle in this chapter', remarks Newman (III 478), 'says little which has not already been said by Plato' (chiefly in the seventh book of the Laws*). Education up to five years of age needs no formal teaching; from five to seven visual methods may be used. The main periods are the next two, seven to fourteen and fourteen to twenty-one. The digression on censorship interrupts the sequence, and deals with the young in general, especially adolescents. The final paragraph sketches a programme of inquiry for the next (and last) book.*

There is one important feature of Plato's educational proposals in the Laws *that is conspicuously missing from Aristotle's in this chapter: the polemic against change. Plato wished to preserve the same educational programme in perpetuity, even down to small details like the children's games (*Laws *797a ff.), on the grounds that novelty makes for social instability. To that extent, Aristotle is a less 'utopian' thinker than Plato: he shows no desire to 'freeze' society permanently into one particular form. Perhaps his detailed study of the various constitutions had left him too impressed by their mutability to think it realistic to seek any kind of permanence as an ideal.*

10. *Mē kalon*, 'not fine, not admirable'; for some idea of the range of *kalon*, cf. VII xiv (esp. references in n. 11).

1336a3 Once he is born, the quality of the nourishment given to a child must be reckoned to make a big difference to the strength of his body. It is clear, from an examination both of other animals and of those nations that make a point of rearing their young to be in a condition ready for war, that an abundant milk diet is very suitable for their bodies; so too one that includes comparatively little wine, because of the illnesses wine produces. Next, it is good for them to make all the bodily movements that they are capable of at that age. (To prevent the still soft limbs from becoming bent, some nations still make use of mechanical devices which keep the children's bodies straight.) From earliest infancy, it is good for them to be used to cold also; to be thus habituated is most useful for health and for the activities of warfare. Hence among many non-Greek peoples it is the custom to dip newly born infants in cold river-water; many others, for example the Celts, put on them very little clothing. It is certainly better to start very young in accustoming children to such things as it is possible to accustom them to, but the process must be gradual; and the warmth of the young body gives it a condition well-suited for training to resist cold. In these and similar ways, then, it is advantageous to care for children in infancy.

1336a23 The next stage is up to five years of age. During this period it is not a good plan to try to teach them anything, or make them do demanding tasks that would interfere with their growth. At the same time they must have sufficient exercise, through play in particular and other activities also, to prevent their bodies from getting slack. Their games, like everything else, should be worthy of free men and neither laborious nor undemanding. The officials known as Trainers of Children ought to pay attention to deciding what kind of stories and legends children of this age are to hear; for all that kind of thing should be preparation for their subsequent occupations. Hence their games ought to consist largely in imitating what they will later be doing in earnest. It is wrong to forbid small children to cry and dilate their lungs, a prohibition found in the *Laws*;[1] it is in effect gymnastic training for the body, which is beneficial for its growth, because holding one's breath gives extra strength in exertion, and this is the effect on children too when they dilate their lungs.

1336a39 In keeping an eye on the children's way of life in general, the Trainers of Children should particularly see that as little time as possible is spent in the company of slaves, because children of this age and up to seven must unavoidably be brought up at home, when even as young as that they presumably pick up behaviour unworthy of a free man, either by eye or by ear.

1336b3 The legislator ought to banish utterly from the state, as he would any other evil, all unseemly talk; for the unseemly remark lightly dropped results in conduct of a like kind. Especially, therefore, must it be kept away from youth; let them not hear or see anything of that kind. If anyone is found doing or saying any of the forbidden things, he shall, if he is of free birth but not yet entitled to recline at the common tables, be punished by measures of dishonour and a whipping; while anyone who is rather older shall be punished by measures of dishonour not normally visited on free men, precisely because his conduct has been that of a slave. And since we exclude all unseemly talk, we must also forbid gazing at debased paintings or stories.[2] Let it therefore be a duty of the rulers to see that there shall be nothing at all, statue or painting, that is a representation of unseemly actions, except in the shrines of certain gods[3] whose province is such that the law does actually permit scurrility. The law further allows men who have reached the appropriate age to pay honour to these gods on behalf of their wives,

1. Plato, *Laws* 792a – if indeed it is Plato who is referred to: the Greek says merely 'those who prohibit in the(ir) laws'.
2. Enacted on stage, I take it.
3. Notably Dionysus; see e.g. Aristotle, *Poetics* IV.

their children and themselves. But it should be laid down that younger persons shall not be spectators at comedies or recitals of iambics,[4] not, that is to say, until they have reached the age at which they come to recline at banquets with others and share in the drinking; by this time their education will have rendered them completely immune to any harm that might come from such spectacles.

1336b24 What we have just been saying has been said only incidentally; we must later[5] think hard about the question and decide it in greater detail, debating first whether or not they ought to watch, and, if so, under what conditions. We have only said as much as would serve the present occasion. Theodorus the tragic actor used to make what is perhaps an apt remark. He never allowed any other actor, even quite an inferior one, to appear on the stage before him – because, he said, an audience always takes kindly to the first voice that meets their ears. The same thing is true of men's relations both with each other and the things they encounter: we always delight more in what comes first. Therefore we must keep all that is of inferior quality unfamiliar to the young, particularly things with an ingredient of wickedness or hostility.

1336b35 When they have completed their fifth year, they should for the next two years observe lessons[6] in whatever they will be required to learn. Education after that must be divided into two stages – from the seventh year to puberty, and from puberty to the completion of twenty-one years. For those who divide life into periods of seven years[7] are not far wrong, and we ought to keep to the divisions that nature makes. For all skill and education aim at filling the gaps that nature leaves. It therefore becomes our business to inquire whether we ought to set up some organization to deal with children,

4. The iambic metre was often used for scurrilous purposes.
5. No such discussion survives.
6. Cf. Plato, *Republic* 466e ff., *Laws* 643b ff.
7. Cf. VII xvi, n. 8.

then whether it is advisable to make the responsibility for them a public one, or leave it in private hands (as is the usual practice in states even at the present time), and thirdly to discuss the proper form of this responsibility.

BOOK VIII

VIII i

(1337a11–1337a32)

EDUCATION AS A PUBLIC CONCERN

This chapter addresses itself to the first two of the three questions asked at the end of Book VII: (a) Should we have some system of education? And (b), should responsibility for education be public or private? The first hardly needs answering, and the second too is soon disposed of. The rearing and education of the children of citizens should indeed be a matter of public concern, since they are the future citizens, the future rulers of the state, and one needs to learn to be a citizen, just as a craftsman needs to be trained in his particular skill. Moreover, the education of the potential citizen will depend largely on the type of state and on the kind of life which it is desired to lead; Aristotle himself has in mind especially the intellectual, artistic, cultivated life which the Greeks called scholē, *usually translated 'leisure'. No citizen, therefore, 'belongs to himself': he is part of the state, and is not entitled to be educated privately in private tastes and standards. All these remarks Aristotle makes very swiftly, and naturally does not pause over certain questions a modern critic may wish to ask: (i) Is the doctrine totalitarian, allowing nothing to private discretion? (ii) Does it allow for anything approaching a 'mixed' society? (iii) Is there to be no debate about the ends of education?*

It is not until the second chapter that Aristotle turns to the actual subject-matter of education; and a great deal of the rest of this final book is concerned with no more than music and singing. But we do not know how much of the book is lost; it certainly now appears to be unfinished, as the thirteenth-century translator William of Moerbeke saw.

451

1337a11 No one would dispute the fact that it is a lawgiver's prime duty to arrange for the education of the young. In states where this is not done the quality of the constitution suffers. Education must be related to the particular constitution in each case, for it is the special character[1] appropriate to each constitution that set it up at the start and commonly maintains it, e.g. the democratic character preserves a democracy, the oligarchic an oligarchy. And in all circumstances the better character is a cause of a better constitution. And just as there must also be preparatory training for all skills and capacities, and a process of preliminary habituation to the work of each profession, it is obvious that there must also be training for the activities of virtue. But since there is but one aim for the entire state, it follows that education must be one and the same for all, and that the responsibility for it must be a public one, not the private affair which it now is, each man looking after his own children and teaching them privately whatever private curriculum he thinks they ought to study. In matters that belong to the public, training for them must be the public's concern. And it is not right either that any of the citizens should think that he belongs just to himself; he must regard all citizens as belonging to the state, for each is a *part* of the state; and the responsibility for each part naturally has regard to the responsibility for the whole. In this respect the Lacedaemonians will earn our approval: the greatest possible attention is given to youth in Sparta, and all on a public basis.

1. I.e. of the persons living under the constitution in question.

VIII ii

(1337ᵃ33–1337ᵇ23)

CONTROVERSY ABOUT THE AIMS OF EDUCATION

*In this chapter Aristotle first describes briefly the variety
of assumptions about the purpose of education that prevailed in his day. One view, then as now, is that education should be utilitarian; and so in the second paragraph he indicates how far free men should engage in
'useful' activities. If his requirements seem unrealistic,
we should remind ourselves that he is thinking of the
education of a 'free' man, who will in due course become
a citizen and 'statesman', living among a non-citizen population of artisans and slaves. We may find Aristotle's
views prejudiced and objectionable, but unrealistic they
are not: they reflect views common among the ancient
Greeks, and certain economic features of Greek states.
Interestingly, he believes that even 'liberal' activities can,
if pursued too zealously, do harm similar to that done
by mechanical and menial work. He has something of the
feeling for the gentleman-amateur which is still detectable
in our own society, particularly (as is sometimes claimed)
in the higher grades of the British civil service.*

1337ᵃ33   It is clear then that there should be laws laid
down about education, and that education itself must be
made a public concern. But we must not forget the question of what that education is to be, and how one ought
to be educated. For in modern times there are opposing
views about the tasks to be set, for there are no generally
accepted assumptions about what the young should learn,
either for virtue or for the best life; nor yet is it clear
whether their education ought to be conducted with more
concern for the intellect than for the character of the soul.
The problem has been complicated by the education we see
actually given; and it is by no means certain whether

training should be directed at things useful in life, or at those conducive to virtue, or at exceptional accomplishments. (All these answers have been judged correct by somebody.) And there is no agreement as to what in fact does tend towards virtue. For a start, men do not all prize the same virtue, so naturally they differ also about the training for it.

1337b1 Then as to useful things: there are obviously certain essentials which the young must learn; but it is clear (a) that they must not learn *all* useful tasks, since we distinguish those that are proper for a free man and those that are not, and (b) that they must take part only in those useful occupations which will not turn the participant into a mechanic. We must reckon a task or skill or study as mechanical if it renders the body or intellect of free men unserviceable for the uses and activities of virtue. We therefore call mechanical those skills which have a deleterious effect on the body's condition, and all work that is paid for. For these make the mind preoccupied,[1] and unable to rise above lowly things. Even in some branches of knowledge worthy of free men, while there is a point up to which it does not demean a free man to go in for them, too great a concentration on them, too much mastering of detail – this is liable to lead to the same damaging effects that we have been speaking of. In this connection the purpose for which the action or the study is undertaken makes a big difference. It is not unworthy of a free man to do something for oneself or for one's friends or on account of virtue; but he that does the same action on others' account may often be regarded as doing something typical of a hireling or slave. The established subjects studied nowadays, as we have already noted,[2] have a double tendency.

1. *Ascholon*, 'without leisure'.
2. In the first paragraph.

VIII iii

(1337b23–1338b8)

*The chief aim of a gentleman's, that is, a citizen's educa-
tion is to enable him to employ his intellectual and
artistic faculties to the full, to live a life of 'virtue' and of
'leisure'. The following chapter is one of the best sources
for understanding what Aristotle meant by* scholē; *and
his discussion of* mousikē, *'music', makes it clear that the
good life should have a high cultural and artistic content.
Rather abruptly, the final paragraph then resumes a
theme broached in VII xv, and asserts the necessity of*
gymnastikē, *physical training, to which Chapter iv is then
devoted, the treatment of music being resumed at greater
length in VIII v. On the meaning of the term* mousikē,
see the introduction to that chapter.

1337b23 Roughly four things are generally taught to
children, (a) reading and writing, (b) physical training, (c)
music, and (d), not always included, drawing. Reading
and writing and drawing are included as useful in daily
life in a variety of ways, gymnastic as promoting courage.
But about music there could be an immediate doubt.
Most men nowadays take part in music for the sake of
the pleasure it gives; but originally it was included in
education on the ground that our own nature itself, as has
often been said,[1] wants to be able not merely to work
properly but also to be at leisure in the right way. And
leisure is the single fundamental principle of the whole
business, so let us discuss it again.

1337b33 If we need both work and leisure, but the latter
is preferable to the former and is its end, we must ask

1. Cf. II ix *ad fin.*, VII xiv–xv. '. . . our own nature itself':
literally, 'Nature herself', apparently quasi-personified.

ourselves what are the proper activities of leisure. Obviously not play; for that would inevitably be to make play our end in life, which is impossible. Play has its uses, but they belong rather to the sphere of work; for he who toils needs rest, and play is a way of resting, while work is inseparable from toil and strain. We must therefore admit play, but keeping it to its proper uses and occasions, and prescribing it as a cure; such movement of the soul is a relaxation, and, because we enjoy it, rest. But leisure seems in itself to contain pleasure, happiness and the blessed life. This is a state attained not by those at work but by those at leisure, because he that is working is working for some hitherto unattained end, and happiness is an end, happiness which is universally regarded as concomitant not with pain but with pleasure. Admittedly men do not agree as to what that pleasure is; each man decides for himself following his own disposition, the best man choosing the best kind of enjoyment from the finest sources. Thus it becomes clear that, in order to spend leisure in civilized pursuits, we do require a certain amount of learning and education, and that these branches of education and these subjects studied must have their own intrinsic purpose, as distinct from those necessary occupational subjects which are studied for reasons beyond themselves.

1338a13 Hence, in the past, men laid down music as part of education, not as being necessary, for it is not in that category, nor yet as being useful in the way that a knowledge of reading and writing is useful for business or household administration, for study, and for many of the activities of a citizen, nor as a knowledge of drawing seems useful for the better judging of the products of a skilled worker, nor again as gymnastic is useful for health and vigour – neither of which do we see gained as a result of music. There remains one purpose – for civilized pursuits during leisure; and that is clearly the reason why they do introduce it, for they give it a place in what they regard as the civilized pursuits of free men. Thus Homer's

line, 'to summon him alone to the rich banquet'; and
after these words he introduces certain other persons,
'who summon the bard whose singing shall delight them
all'. And elsewhere Odysseus says that the best civilized
pursuit is when men get together and 'sit in rows up and
down the hall feasting and listening to the bard'.[2]

1338a30   Clearly then there is a form of education which
we must provide for our sons, not as being useful or essential but as elevated and worthy of free men. We must on a
later occasion[3] discuss whether this education is one or
many, what subjects it embraces, and how they are to be
taught. But as it turns out, we have made some progress
in that direction: we have some evidence from the ancients too, derived from the subjects laid down by them –
as the case of music makes clear.

1338a37   It is also clear that there are some useful things,
too, in which the young must be educated, not only
because they are useful (for example they must learn
reading and writing), but also because they are often
the means to learning yet further subjects. Similarly they
must learn drawing, not for the sake of avoiding mistakes
in private purchases, and so that they may not be taken
in when buying and selling furniture, but rather because
it teaches one to be observant of physical beauty. But to
be constantly asking 'What is the use of it?' is unbecom-
ing to those of broad vision[4] and unworthy of free men.

1338b2   Since it is obvious that education by habit-
forming must precede education by reasoned instruction,
and that education of the body must precede that of the
intellect, it is clear that we must subject our children to
gymnastics and to physical training; the former produces
a certain condition of the body, the latter its actions.

2. The first line is not in Homer as we have him, but in view
of the similarity of the second quotation to *Odyssey*, XVII 385, it
may have belonged to that context. The third quotation is *Odyssey*,
IX 7 and part of 8.

3. There is no such discussion.

4. *Megalopsuchos*, 'great-souled', 'magnanimous'.

THE LIMITS OF PHYSICAL TRAINING

Physical training for military and athletic purposes was a prominent feature of Greek education, and criticisms of excessive enthusiasm for it, and of an extreme admiration for athletes, are fairly frequent in Greek literature, the most celebrated attack being Xenophanes' (sixth century or early fifth century). Aristotle links his own attack with a renewal of his oft-repeated criticism of Sparta for cultivating only one virtue, courage. His distinction between courage and mere ferocity is well taken, but we may wonder about his view that strenuous mental and strenuous physical exertion ought not to be combined in one and the same period of life (cf. Plato, Republic *537b): has it any real empirical or physiological basis? The critical and negative side of this chapter is stronger than the positive recommendations, which are very brief. His main point is that training should be kept within the natural capacity of the body: as a teleologist, he believes that the body has certain natural limits to its development and strength, and that attempts to exceed them can only harm it.*

1338b9 In our own day some of those states which have the greatest reputation for looking after their youth aim at producing an athlete's condition, to the detriment of both the appearance and the growth of the children's bodies; while the Spartans, who have avoided that error, nevertheless by severity of exercise render them like wild animals, under the impression that this is particularly conducive to courage. But, as has often been pointed out,[1] the care of the young must not be directed to producing one virtue only, nor this one more than the rest. And even

---

1. E.g. II ix *ad fin.*, VII xiv–xv.

if courage should be the aim, they do not manage to secure even that. For neither among animals nor among foreign races do we find courage to be a characteristic of the most fierce, but rather of the gentler and lion-like disposition. And there are many foreign races that enjoy slaughter and the consumption of human flesh, Achaeans and Heniochians among those around the Euxine Sea, and some other mainland races equally or in some cases even more prone to it. Raiders they may be, but they are not endowed with courage.

1338b24 And of the Lacedaemonians themselves too we know that so long as they alone went in for strenuous exercises, they were superior to the rest, but nowadays they fall short of others in the struggles of war and of athletics. For their former superiority was due not to their drilling of their young in this way, but to the fact that they alone trained and their opponents did not. The first place, therefore, must be taken not by any animal quality but by nobility.[2] One cannot imagine a wolf or any other wild animal engaging in a struggle against noble[2] danger; but that is what a good man will do. Those who permit their young to indulge in excessive physical training, leaving them without education in essentials, are effectively turning them into mechanics,[3] making them useful for one function only[4] of statesmanship, and even for that, as our argument shows, less useful than others. We should judge the Spartans by their present-day performance, not by what they used to do. They now have rivals in the field of education, which formerly they did not have.

2. *Kalon*; cf. VII xvi, n. 10.

3. Cf. Aristotle's remarks on the narrowing and degrading results of excessive concentration on reaching a high standard of performance in music in VIII v and vi, and cf. VIII ii. A man trained only to fight is as much a 'mechanic' in the use of his body (and weapons) as a highly trained musician, or any other skilled worker, is in the use of instruments and tools.

4. I.e. warfare: *hē polemikē*, the skill of fighting, is a part of *hē politikē*, the skill of statesmanship, of being a statesman, *politikos*.

1338b38 There is, then, general agreement about the need to employ gymnastic training, and about the methods to be used. Up to puberty the exercises prescribed should be on the light side; nothing should be done that would interfere with the body's growth, no hard dieting or punishing exertion; for these have just that ill-effect, as is shown by the fact that it is rare to find the same people successful in the Olympic games both as boys and as men: their severe gymnastic training as boys has caused them to lose their strength. But when for the three years after puberty they have been engaged in learning other things, then the subsequent period of life may properly be devoted to strenuous exercise and compulsory hard dieting. Vigorous exercise of intellect and body must not be combined; each naturally works in the opposite direction from the other, bodily toil interfering with the mind, intellectual toil with the body.

VIII v

(1339a11–1340b19)

EDUCATION IN MUSIC (2)

While the needs of the body are straightforward, the needs of the mind are not; and so Aristotle returns again to music. It was shown in VIII iii that learning music was not an essential in the same way as learning to read and write, but that it was traditionally a subject of a liberal education. But to learn the rudiments of music in childhood is one thing; it is quite another in manhood to cultivate, understand and perform. A gentleman should enjoy and appreciate music, but not become a mere mechanic by devoting time and effort to reaching a high standard of performance (cf. VIII vi, and introduction to VIII ii, on gentlemen-amateurs).

Music, Aristotle argues, is something more than amusement; yet one of its great merits is that it gives pleasure,

*so that it is a powerful instrument of moral formation:
by learning to associate the admirable and virtuous
characters depicted in music with the pleasure given by
its performance, the audience is encouraged to imitate
what it sees and hears, and so become virtuous itself.
Aristotle's view of the matter is thus substantially that of
Plato in Book III of the* Republic *and Book II of the*
Laws; *and common to them both is the belief that since
mankind is essentially imitative, particularly in childhood, the arts are not merely 'entertainment' but exercise
a crucial influence in education, and need therefore to be
controlled by what we should call 'censorship'. In brief,
a man's taste in music (or dress or anything else) is worth
training; for it is part of his character.*

I have allowed 'music' as a translation of (hē) mousikē
(technē), *'the skill presided over by the muses', though
it is not entirely satisfactory, as the meaning of the Greek
term varies somewhat. Aristotle uses it chiefly in a fairly
restricted sense, to describe performances which make
their primary appeal to the ear, and which are given on
musical instruments, with or without sung words.
'Mousikē' covered also performances which included
dancing, and it could be used in the even wider sense of
'the arts' in general; indeed, it is noticeable how towards
the end of this chapter Aristotle broadens his discussion of*
mousikē *so as to include painting and sculpture, arts
whose appeal is visual. For a summary of the meanings of*
mousikē, *see* S. Michaelides, The Music of Ancient
Greece, An Encyclopaedia *(London, 1978), pp. 213–16;
Aristotle's views on music in general are discussed in* W.
D. Anderson, Ethos and Education in Greek Music *(Cambridge, Mass., 1966), ch. IV.*

In this chapter the concept of diagōgē *becomes prominent. Translation is very difficult: what English word
conveys 'that special way of life appropriate to a leisured
and cultivated citizen-gentleman-statesman'? I have opted
for 'civilized pursuits'.*

461

1339a11 We have already discussed[1] some of the questions that arose about music, but we should do well to resume the subject and carry it further, so as to provide a sort of keynote to any future discussions about it. To begin with, it is not easy to define either what the effect of music is or what our object should be in engaging in it. Is it for our amusement and refreshment, like taking a nap or having a drink? These things are not in themselves of serious importance, though they are pleasant and help us to forget our worries, as Euripides says.[2] (This is in fact what causes some people to put all three on the same level, sleep, drink, and music, and to use them all in the same way; and dancing is also added.) Must we not rather regard music as a stimulus to virtue, capable of making a certain kind of character (in just the same way as gymnastic training produces a body of a certain type), by accustoming men to be able to enjoy themselves in the right way? Third on this list of possibilities must be that it has a contribution to make to civilized pursuits and practical wisdom.

1339a26 It is clear then that we are not to educate the young with a view to their amusement. Learning brings pain, and while children are learning they are not playing. Nor yet are children of such age-groups fit to be assigned civilized pursuits, because what is complete[3] does not belong to the incomplete. Still, one might perhaps suppose that serious activity in childhood may have for its aim the amusement of the complete and adult man. But if this is so, what need is there for them themselves to learn music? Why not do as kings of Persians and Medes do, have others to make music for them, so that they may learn and enjoy it in *that* way? For surely those who have perfected their skill in the job of making music will give better performances than those who have devoted to music only such time as will enable them to

1. VIII iii.
2. *Bacchae* 381. 'Of serious importance' = *spoudaia*.
3. *Telos*, 'an end'; 'incomplete' here means 'not yet adult'.

learn it. But if we must ourselves work hard at such
things, does it follow that we must also busy ourselves
with preparing high-class meals? Certainly not.

1339a41 The same question arises when we ask whether
music has the power to improve the character. Why
learn these things oneself and not rather do as the Lacedaemonians do – learn to judge and to be able to enjoy
oneself in the right way through listening to others?
Without actually learning music, they are capable, they
say, of distinguishing correctly wholesome tunes from
unwholesome. The same argument applies again, when
we ask whether music ought to be performed as a contribution to the cheerful and civilized pursuits worthy of
free men. Why must they learn to perform themselves,
instead of simply enjoying the performances of others?
We may in this connection refer to our conception of the
gods; the poets do not depict Zeus as playing the lyre
and singing in person. In fact we call the performers
'mechanics' and think that a man should not perform
except for his own amusement or when he has had a good
deal to drink.

1339b10 Perhaps this question should be postponed till
later;[4] our chief inquiry now is whether or not music is to
be included in education, and what it can achieve. To
take the three things we have canvassed, does music
promote education, or amusement, or civilized pursuits?
It is reasonable to reply that it is grouped with, and
apparently forms part of, all three. Amusement is for the
purpose of relaxation, and relaxation must necessarily
be pleasant, since it is a kind of cure for the ills we suffer
in working hard. As to civilized pursuits, there must, as is
universally agreed, be present pleasure as well as nobility,[5]
for happiness consists of both these. Now we all agree
that music is among the most pleasant things, whether
instrumental or accompanied by singing (at any rate the

4. See VIII vi.
5. *To kalon*; cf. e.g. V x, n. 9, VII xiv, n. 11, VII xvi, n. 10, and
VIII iv.

poet Musaeus[6] says 'singing is man's greatest joy', so because it can make men feel happy, it is properly included in social intercourse and civilized pursuits) – so that one might from that fact too infer that the young should be taught it. For things that are pleasant and harmless as well rightly belong not only to the end in view but also to relaxation by the way. But since it rarely happens that men attain their goal, and they frequently rest and indulge in amusements with no other thought than the pleasure of them, there is surely a useful purpose in periodic refreshment in the pleasures derived from music.

1339b31 On the other hand, men have come to make amusements an end in themselves. No doubt there is something pleasant about the end too, but it is a very special kind of pleasure, and men in seeking pleasure mistake the one kind for the other. For there is indeed a resemblance to the end of their actions: for the end is not to be chosen for the sake of anything that may accrue thereafter, and similarly these pleasures of recreation are not for purposes in the future but arise from what is past, e.g. labour and pain. This would seem to be a reasonable explanation of why men try to get happiness through these pleasures. But men take up music not for this reason alone, but also, it seems, because it is useful in providing relaxation.

1339b42 Nevertheless we must ask whether, though this has been the incidental result, the true nature of music is not something of greater value than filling the need we have described. Music certainly gives a certain natural pleasure: all ages and all types of character like to engage in it. But we must do more than merely share in the general pleasure which all men feel in it; we must consider whether music has also some effect on the character and the soul. We could answer this question if we could say that we become of such and such a character through

6. A mythical singer.

music. And surely it is obvious from many examples that
we do, not least from the tunes composed by Olympus.[7]
These are well known to put souls into a frenzy of excitement – an excitement which is an affection of the character of the soul. Again, when listening to imitative performances all men are affected in a manner in keeping
with the performance, even apart from the tunes and
rhythms employed. And since it so happens that music
belongs to the class of things pleasant, and since virtue
has to do with enjoying oneself in the right way, with
liking and hating the right things, clearly there is no
more important lesson to be learned or habit to be
formed than that of right judgement and of delighting
in good characters and noble[5] actions.

1340a18 Now in rhythm and in tunes there is the closest
resemblance to the real natures of anger and gentleness,
also of courage and self-control, and of the opposites of
these, indeed of all the other kinds of character; and the
fact that hearing such sounds does indeed cause changes
in our souls is an indication of this. To have the habit of
feeling delight (or distress) in things that are *like* reality
is near to having the same disposition towards reality
itself. I mean if a man enjoys looking at a likeness of
someone for no other reason than the actual shape of it,
then inevitably he will enjoy looking at its original too,
whose likeness he is at the moment contemplating. Now
it so happens that other objects perceived by the senses,
e.g. those touched or tasted, do not present any similarity
to characters – except that perhaps objects seen present
a faint similarity, since postures suggest character, but
only to a small extent; and not all people are sensitive
enough to notice. Moreover the postures and colours that
are produced are not strictly representations of character
but indications rather, and these indications are par-

7. A Phrygian composer for the pipes, perhaps mythical; if historical, of the seventh century.

ticularly conspicuous when emotion is felt.[8] It does, however, even here, make some difference what it is we look at; and the young ought not to contemplate the works of Pauson but rather those of Polygnotus[9] and of other painters and sculptors who have a concern for character. In music, however, character *is* present, imitated in the very tunes we hear. This is obvious, for to begin with there is the natural distinction between the modes, which cause different reactions in the hearers, who are not all moved in the same way with respect to each. For example, men are inclined to be mournful and solemn when they listen to that which is called Mixo-Lydian; but they are in a more relaxed frame of mind when they listen to others, for example the looser modes. A particularly equable feeling, midway between these, is produced, I think, only by the Dorian mode, while the Phrygian puts men into a frenzy of excitement. These are the excellent results of work which has been done[10] on this aspect of education; the investigators have drawn evidence from the sheer facts, and have based their conclusions on them. The same is true also of the different types of rhythm: some have a steadying character, others an unsettling, and of these latter some give rise to vulgar movements, some to those more worthy of free men.

1340b10 It follows from all this that music has indeed the power to induce a certain character of soul, and if it can do that, then clearly it must be applied to education, and the young must be educated in it. And the teaching of music is particularly apt for the nature of the young;

8. The drift of these last nine words is not very clear. I take Aristotle to mean that indications of character can be most effectively conveyed by a sculpture or painting when it is a representation of someone under the influence of emotion.

9. Artists of the fifth century, of whom Aristotle remarks in the *Poetics* (1448a5) that Polygnotus portrayed men as better than they are, whereas Pauson portrayed them as worse.

10. Literally, 'excellent statements of those who have philosophized on . . .': cf. VII xi, n. 7. On the 'modes' (*harmoniai*), see introduction to VIII vii.

for because of their youth they do not willingly tolerate
anything that is not made pleasant for them, and music
is one of those things that by nature give spice to life.
Moreover there seems to be a certain affinity between us
and music's harmonies and rhythms; so that many experts[11] say that the soul *is* a harmony, others that it *has*
harmony.[12]

VIII vi

(1340b20–1341b18)

GENTLEMEN VERSUS PLAYERS

*Aristotle postpones consideration of the more technical
side of music until Chapter vii, and digresses to discuss
more fully how far free men, eleutheroi, should themselves learn to play musical instruments. He takes the
view that in the interests of acquiring 'correct' musical
taste and judgement, such skills should certainly be
learned; but they must not be studied to a very high level
of competence, which requires excessive application making the performer into a mere 'mechanic' (banausos), and
so injuring his ability to attain a citizen's 'virtue' (aretē).
With the polemic against 'low' or 'popular' music in the
final paragraph, compare Plato, Laws II in general, and
III 700a ff. The chapter contains also a brief but interesting history of the chief Greek wind instrument, the auloi,
the twin pipes; see S. Michaelides, The Music of Ancient
Greece, An Encyclopaedia (London, 1978), pp. 42–6.
(Note that the common translation of aulos, 'flute', is
incorrect.)*

1340b20 We must now return to a question raised

11. E.g. the Pythagoreans.
12. Apparently a glancing reference to Plato, *Phaedo* 93c. On
harmonia (roughly 'ordered construction') see introduction to VIII
vii.

earlier:[1] must they learn music by singing themselves and playing instruments with their own hands, or not? Clearly, personal participation in playing is going to make a big difference to the quality of the person that will be produced, because it is impossible, or at any rate difficult, to produce sound judges of musical performances out of those who have never themselves played. (At the same time learning an instrument will provide children with a needed occupation. Archytas'[2] rattle must be reckoned an excellent invention, for children cannot remain still, and they are given this toy to play with, so that they may be kept from smashing things about the house. Of course it is only suitable for the very young: for older children education is their rattle.) Such considerations thus make it clear that musical education must include participation in actual playing.

1340b33 It is not difficult to decide what is appropriate and what is not for different ages, or to find an answer to those who assert that to perform is the concern of a mechanic. First, since to join in the playing is needed to make a good judge, they should play the instruments while young, and later, when they are older, give them up; they will then, thanks to what they have learned in their youth, be able to judge fine music and enjoy it in the right way. As for the objection, brought by some, that music makes them into mechanics, this can easily be answered if we consider to what extent persons who are being educated to exercise the virtue of a citizen ought to take part in the playing, what tunes and with what rhythms they are to play, and on what instruments they are to learn, for that too will probably make a difference. On the answers to these questions will depend the answer

1. VIII v, 2nd and 3rd paragraphs.
2. Presumably the Sicilian mathematician of the early fourth century, who carried out research into mechanics and acoustics. The final sentence of the parenthesis seems to be a piece of waggish cynicism: education keeps older children out of mischief, just as rattles did when they were younger.

to the objection, since it is by no means impossible that certain styles of music do have the effect mentioned.[3]

1341a5   It is clear, then, that learning music must not be allowed to have any adverse effect on later activities, nor to turn the body into that of a mechanic, ill-fitted for the training of citizen or soldier – ill-fitted, that is, both for the lessons in youth and for the application of them in later years. Such a result can be avoided if the pupil does not struggle to acquire the degree of skill that is needed for professional competitions, or to perform those peculiar and sensational pieces of music which have penetrated the competitions and thence education. Musical exercises should not be of this kind, and should be pursued only up to the point at which the pupil becomes capable of enjoying fine melodies and rhythms, and not just the feature[4] common to all music, which appeals even to some animals, and also to a great many slaves and children.

1341a17   From these considerations we can also see what kinds of musical instruments ought to be employed. We must not permit the introduction of pipes into education, or of any other instrument that requires the skill of a professional, the lyre and such-like, but only such as will make good students, whether in their musical education or in their education in general. Furthermore, the pipes are not an instrument of ethical but rather of orgiastic[5] effect, so their use should be confined to those occasions on which the effect produced by the show is not so much instruction as a way of working off the emotions.[6] We may add to the educational objections the fact that playing on the pipes prevents one from employing speech.

1341a26   For these reasons our predecessors were right in

3. I.e. of making men 'mechanics' (*banausos*).
4. I.e. the pleasure music gives, presumably.
5. In the technical sense of 'arousing excitement of the kind associated with the frenzied celebration of *orgia*' (the rites of certain ecstatic religions, notably the Dionysiac).
6. 'Way . . . emotions' translates *katharsis*; cf. VIII vii.

prohibiting the use of the pipes by the young and by free men, though at an earlier period it was permitted. This is what took place: as resources increased, men had more leisure and acquired a loftier pride[7] in standards of virtue; and both before and after the Persian wars, in which their success had increased their self-confidence, they fastened eagerly upon learning of every kind, pursuing all without distinction; and hence even playing on the pipes was introduced into education. At Sparta there was a chorus-leader[8] who himself piped for his chorus to dance to, and at Athens playing the pipes took such firm root that many, perhaps the majority, of the free men took part in it. Thrasippus, who acted as chorus-trainer for Ecphantides, dedicated a tablet[9] which makes that clear. But at a later date, as a result of actual experience, the playing of pipes went out of favour, as men became better able to discern what tends to promote virtue and what does not. Many of the older instruments were similarly rejected, for example the plucker, the barbitos, and those which merely titillate the ear, the heptagon, triangle, sambuca, and all those that require manual dexterity.[10] There is sound sense too in the story told by the ancients about the pipes – that Athena invented them and then threw them away. It may well be, as the story adds, that the goddess did this because she disliked the facial distortion which their playing caused. But a far more likely reason is that an education in playing upon the pipes contributes nothing to the intellect; to Athena, after all, we ascribe knowledge and skill.

7. *Megalopsuchos*: cf. VIII iii, n. 4.
8. *Chorēgos*: cf. IV xv, n. 2. The point is that the accompaniment on the pipes would normally have been delegated to someone of humble status.
9. Presumably one recording a victory in a competition, and the fact that Thrasippus played the pipes in it. Ecphantides was an Athenian comic playwright of the fifth century.
10. *Epistēmē*, usually 'knowledge'.

1341b8 We reject then a professional[11] education in the instruments and their performance – professional in the sense of competitive, for in this kind of education the performer does not perform in order to improve his own virtue, but to give pleasure to the listeners, and vulgar pleasure at that. We do not, therefore, regard such performing as a proper occupation for free men; it is rather that of a hireling. The consequences are to degrade the players into mechanics, since the end towards which the performance is directed is a low one. The listener is a common person and usually influences the music accordingly, so that he has an effect both on the personality of the professionals themselves who perform for him, and, because of the motions which they make, on their bodies too.

VIII vii

(*1341b19–1342b34*)

MELODIES AND MODES IN EDUCATION

The effects of listening to the various kinds of music were touched on in Chapter v, but not specifically in relation to education. Melē, melodies or tunes, are of three kinds: (A) ethical, i.e. expressive of ēthos, character; (B) active, praktika, encouraging us to perform certain actions; (C) producing in us certain powerful excitements, emotions or inspirations (enthousiasmos). Music can confer three benefits; (a) to promote education; (b) to 'purify' or 'purge' emotion; (c) to provide relaxation in leisure.

Kind (A) is obviously linked to (a), and (C) to (b); but (B) and (c), which seem not to be connected, are not discussed at any length. The differences between (A), (B) and (C) are perhaps less sharp than may appear at first

11. In this chapter 'professional' = *technikos* (adjective), *technitēs* (noun); cf. third paragraph.

sight: in (A), the characters portrayed by the music affect our own, and so indirectly and ultimately affect our actions; in (B), we are presumably likewise stimulated to action, but immediately *(e.g. to march, by a marching tune); and in (C) the emotions aroused in us can lead to movements and actions of the body, as in 'orgiastic' ritual dancing. In fact, all three kinds of tune lead or can lead to action.*

The final paragraph, rather unexpectedly, introduces the further consideration that different age-groups require different harmoniai, *modes. A harmonia is a 'way of fitting together', an 'ordered combination or construction of notes', in effect a particular 'style' or 'mode' of music (see S. Michaelides,* The Music of Ancient Greece, An Encyclopaedia, London, 1978, pp. 127–9). *Since Aristotle's remarks on the modes in this paragraph are not entirely easy to square with what he has said earlier in this chapter and in others, this paragraph has sometimes been suspected of being by another hand (see C. Lord, 'On Damon and music education',* Hermes, 106 (1978), pp. 32–43, esp. 38ff.). *However that may be, it is here that his discussion of education tails off, leaving a great many topics unexamined. On this ragged ending of the* Politics, *E. Barker well remarks (*The Politics of Aristotle, Oxford 1946, p. 352), *'Aristotle's notes stopped at this point. This is just what happens to a set of notes or a course of lectures, as many lecturers can testify; and there is no more to be said. We cannot apply the standards of a printed book to the manuscript of a set of notes.'*

1341b19 That being so, we must investigate further this matter of modes and rhythms. Are we, for educational purposes, to make use of *all* the modes and rhythms or should we make distinctions? And will the same basis of classification serve for those who work at music for educational purposes, or must we lay down some other? Certainly music is, as we know, divided into melody-making and rhythm, and we must not omit to consider what effect each of these has on education, and whether we are to rate more highly music with a good melody, or music with a good rhythm. We believe that these topics are well and fully dealt with both by some modern musicians, and by others whose approach is philosophical but who have actual experience of musical education; so we shall leave those who want detailed treatment of the several questions to seek advice in that quarter. Here let us give a generalized[1] account and simply refer to the usual typology.

1341b32 We accept the classification of melodies as given by some philosophers: ethical, active, and exciting; and they regard the modes as being by nature[2] appropriate to each of these – one to one melody, one to another. But we say that music ought to be used to confer not one benefit only but many: (i) to assist education, (ii) for cathartic[3] purposes (here I use the term *cathartic* without further qualifications; I will treat it more fully in my work on *Poetics*),[4] and (iii) to promote civilized pursuits, by way of relaxation and relief after tension. Clearly, then, we must make use of all the modes, but we are not to use them all in the same manner: for education we should use those which are most ethical, whereas for listening to others performing we should accept also the most active and the most emotion-stirring. Any feeling which comes strongly to some souls exists in all others to a greater or less degree – pity and fear, for example, but also excitement. This is a kind of agitation by which some people are liable to be possessed; it may arise out of religious melodies, and in this case it is observable that when they have been listening to melodies that have an

1. Literally 'law-like', i.e. by stating broad principles, without regard to the details of particular cases.

2. I omit Ross's conjectural τὴν in 1341b35.

3. *Katharsis*, 'purification', 'purgation'; cf. VIII vi, n. 6.

4. Apparently a reference to a part of the *Poetics* not now extant (or indeed never written), since in the celebrated sixth chapter the term *katharsis* is taken for granted, without discussion.

orgiastic[5] effect on the soul they are restored as if they had undergone a curative and purifying[3] treatment. Those who are given to feeling pity or fear or any other emotion must be affected in precisely this way, and so must other people too, to the extent that some such emotion comes upon each. To them all inevitably comes a sort of pleasant purgation[3] and relief. In the same way 'active' melodies bring men an elation which is not at all harmful.

1342a16 Hence these are the modes and melodies whose use ought to be permitted to those who enter contests in music for the theatre. Now in the theatre there are two types of audience, the one consisting of educated free men, the other of common persons, drawn from the mechanics, hired workers and such-like. For the relaxation of this latter class also competitions and spectacles must be provided. But as their souls have become distorted, removed from the condition of nature, so also some modes are deviations from the norm, and some melodies have high pitch and irregular colouring.[6] Each group finds pleasure in that which is akin to its nature. Therefore permission must be given to competitors before this class of audience to use the type of music that appeals to it.

1342a28 But for educational purposes, as we have said, we must use tunes, and modes too which have *ethical* value. The Dorian mode, as we mentioned earlier,[7] is in that category, but we must also admit other modes if they have passed the scrutiny of those who combine the pursuit of philosophy with a musical education. It is to be regretted that Socrates in the *Republic*[8] singled out the Phrygian mode to be added to the Dorian – and this in

5. Cf. VIII vi, n. 5.
6. A technical term, indicating broadly extreme elaboration. See Anderson (VIII v, introduction), pp. 139, 144–5 (with notes), and for Greek music in general the detailed account in the *Oxford Classical Dictionary* (2nd ed.), s.v. 'Music'.
7. VIII v.
8. 399a ff.

spite of having rejected altogether, from among the instruments, the use of the pipes. Yet among the modes the Phrygian has exactly the same effect as the pipes among instruments: both are orgiastic[5] and emotional, for all Bacchic frenzy and all similar agitation are associated with the pipes more than with other instruments, and such conduct finds its appropriate expression in tunes composed in the Phrygian mode more than in those composed in other modes. (This is shown by poetry: the dithyramb, for example, is universally regarded as Phrygian. Experts in this field point to numerous examples, notably that of Philoxenus,[9] who tried to compose *The Mysians* in the Dorian mode, but could not do so: the very nature of his material forced him back into the Phrygian, the proper mode.) But about the Dorian mode all are agreed that it is the steadiest, and that its ethical character is particularly that of courage. Further, since we approve of that which is midway between extremes and assert that that is something to be aimed at, and since the Dorian, in relation to the other modes, does by nature possess this characteristic, it is clear that Dorian tunes are more suitable than the others for the education of the young.

1342b17 Two things we keep constantly in view – what is possible and what is appropriate; and it is possible and appropriate action that every set of men must undertake. But these two categories of things also are different for different ages. For instance, those who go through age have grown weary do not find it easy to sing in the high-pitched modes; but for such men nature offers the low-pitched ones. Hence once again some of the musical experts rightly take Socrates to task because he rejected the low-pitched modes as useless for education; he regarded them as having the same effect as drink, not as intoxicating them but as lacking energy. (Intoxication produces,

9. A dithyrambic poet, 436–380. Dithyrambs were choral songs which, at least in the early history of the genre, had special connections with the god Dionysus.

rather, a Bacchic frenzy.) So looking to future years too, when we are older, we must go in for that kind of mode and that kind of melody – as well as any other mode of a type which, because of its power to combine orderliness with educative influence, is suitable for the age of child-hood (the Lydian would seem to be a case in point). It is clear, then, that we have these three goals to aim at in education – the happy mean, the possible, and the appropriate.

SELECT BIBLIOGRAPHIES

There is a huge quantity of modern literature on the *Politics*, but as yet no comprehensive and systematic bibliography has been published. However, most of the books and articles listed below provide at least some references to other work, and rich seams of bibliographical information may be mined in:

I. DÜRING, *Aristoteles, Darstellung und Interpretation seines Denkens* (Heidelberg, 1966), pp. 623–40, esp. pp. 637–8

G. BIEN, *Die Grundlegung der politischen Philosophie bei Aristoteles* (München, 1973), pp. 369–94

Up-to-date information is to be found in the latest edition of *L'Année Philologique*, and in *Polis*, the periodical of the Society for Greek Political Thought (note in particular vol. I, 2 (April 1978), pp. 19–22). There is also a good bibliography in the third collection of essays below which also gives (pp. 219–20) further bibliographical sources.

COMPOSITION, TRANSMISSION AND ESTABLISHMENT OF THE TEXT

W. JAEGER, *Aristotle: Fundamentals of the History of his Development* (2nd ed., Oxford, 1948), esp. pp. 259–92. (A translation by Richard Robinson of *Aristoteles, Grundlegung einer Geschichte seiner Entwicklung*, Berlin, 1923)

H. VON ARNIM, 'Zur Entstehungsgeschichte der aristotelischen Politik', *Sitzungsberichte der Akademie der Wissenschaften in Wien*, philos.-hist. Kl., 200.1 (1924), pp. 1–130

I. DÜRING, 'Notes on the history of the transmission of Aristotle's writings', *Symbolae Philologicae Gotoburgenses*, 56.3 (1950), pp. 35–70, esp. pp. 57 ff., 64 ff.

W. THEILER, 'Bau und Zeit der aristotelischen Politik', *Museum Helveticum*, 9 (1952), pp. 65–78. (Reprinted in F. P. Hager (ed.), *Ethik und Politik des Aristoteles*, Darmstadt, 1972, pp. 253–74 (Wege der Forschung 208))

R. WEIL, see under 'History and Historiography' below, pp. 25–84

A. DREIZEHNTER, *Untersuchungen zur Textgeschichte der*

aristotelischen Politik (Leiden, 1962) (Philosophia Antiqua 10)

A. H. CHROUST, 'The first thirty years of modern Aristotelian scholarship', *Classica et Mediaevalia*, 24 (1963), pp. 27–57, esp. pp. 46–9

J. DUNBABIN, 'The Reception and Interpretation of Aristotle's *Politics*', in *The Cambridge History of Later Medieval Philosophy*, ed. N. Kretzmann, A. Kenny and J. Pinborg (Cambridge, 1982), pp. 723–37

Note also certain essays in the first two collections below.

TEXTS WITH COMMENTARY

Vastly learned and on a princely scale, with an abundance of explanatory and supplementary material:

W. L. NEWMAN, *The Politics of Aristotle, with an Introduction, Two Prefatory Essays and Notes Critical and Explanatory*, 4 vols. (Oxford, 1887–1902)

Less comprehensive but still spacious:

F. SUSEMIHL and R. D. HICKS, *The Politics of Aristotle, A Revised Text with Introduction, Analysis and Commentary, Books I–V* (London and New York, 1894)

In both these editions Books VII and VIII in the customary order are renumbered IV and V; hence 'I–V' in Susemihl and Hicks' title are I–III plus VII–VIII, and Newman's 'VI–VIII' are IV–VI thus displaced to the end of the sequence. See pp. 33ff. above.

TEXTS

W. D. ROSS, *Aristotelis Politica* (Oxford, 1957) (Oxford Classical Text)

A. DREIZEHNTER, *Aristoteles Politik, eingeleitet, kritisch herausgegeben und mit Indices versehen* (München, 1970) (Studia et Testimonia Antiqua 7)

TRANSLATIONS

The Works of Aristotle, translated into English under the editorship of W. D. Ross, vol. X: *Politica*, by B. Jowett, rev. W. D. Ross (Oxford, 1921). (Contains also *Oeconomica*,

SELECT BIBLIOGRAPHIES

trans. E. S. Forster, and *Atheniensium Respublica*, trans. F. G. Kenyon)

H. RACKHAM, *Aristotle*, vol. XXI (London and Cambridge, Mass., 1932; corrected ed. 1944) (Loeb Classical Library; Greek and English on facing pages)

E. BARKER, *The Politics of Aristotle, Translated with an Introduction, Notes and Appendices* (Oxford, 1946; corrected ed. 1948)

EDITIONS OF ONE OR TWO BOOKS

R. ROBINSON, *Aristotle's Politics, Books III and IV*, translated with introduction and comments (Oxford, 1962) (Clarendon Aristotle Series)

E. BRAUN, 'Das dritte Buch der aristotelischen "Politik": Interpretation', *Sitzungsberichte der Österreichischen Akademie der Wissenschaften*, philos.-hist. Kl., 247.4 (Wien, 1965)

GENERAL AND COMPREHENSIVE ACCOUNTS

E. BARKER, *The Political Thought of Plato and Aristotle* (London, 1906, repr. New York, 1959), pp. 208–524

W. D. ROSS, *Aristotle* (Oxford, 1923; 5th ed. 1949), pp. 235–69

M. DEFOURNY, *Aristote: Études sur la 'Politique'* (Paris, 1932)

T. A. SINCLAIR, *A History of Greek Political Thought* (London, 1951, 2nd ed. 1967), pp. 209–38

D. J. ALLAN, *The Philosophy of Aristotle* (Oxford, 1952), pp. 191–200

J. H. RANDALL, *Aristotle* (New York, 1960), pp. 243–71

G. H. SABINE, *A History of Political Theory* (3rd ed., London, 1963), pp. 88–105

D. KAGAN, *The Great Dialogue: History of Greek Political Thought from Homer to Polybius* (New York and London, 1965), pp. 195–230

I. DÜRING, *See above*, pp. 474–505

G. E. R. LLOYD, *Aristotle, the Growth and Structure of His Thought* (Cambridge, 1968), pp. 246–71

G. BIEN, *see above*

J. B. MORRALL, *Aristotle* (London, 1977) (Political Thinkers 7)

R. G. MULGAN, *Aristotle's Political Theory* (Oxford, 1977)

COLLECTIONS OF ESSAYS

Five very useful collections of essays have appeared:

(1) *La Politique d'Aristote* (Geneva, 1965) (Foundation Hardt, Entretiens sur l'antiquité classique XI; each paper is followed by a discussion; two indexes):

R. STARK, 'Der Gesamtaufbau der aristotelischen *Politik*'

D. J. ALLAN, 'Individual and state in the *Ethics* and *Politics*' (Reprinted in German translation in F.-P. Hager, *Ethik und Politik des Aristoteles*, Darmstadt, 1972, pp. 403–32 (Wege der Forschung 208)

P. AUBENQUE, 'Théorie et pratique politiques chez Aristote'

P. MORAUX, 'Quelques Apories de la politique et leur arrière-plan historique'

R. WEIL, 'Philosophie et histoire. La Vision de l'histoire chez Aristote' (reprinted in translation in collection (3) below)

G. J. D. AALDERS H. Wzn., 'Die Mischverfassung und ihre historische Dokumentation in den *Politica* des Aristoteles'

O. GIGON, 'Die Sklaverei bei Aristoteles'

(2) *Schriften zu den Politika des Aristoteles*, herausgegeben von P. Steinmetz (Hildesheim and New York, 1973) (Olms Studien 6; photographic reprints):

J. MESK, 'Die Buchfolge in der aristotelischen *Politik*' (= *Wiener Studien*, 38 (1916), pp. 250–69)

J. L. STOCKS, 'The composition of Aristotle's *Politics*' (= *Classical Quarterly*, 21 (1927), pp. 177–87)

E. BARKER, 'The life of Aristotle and the composition and structure of the *Politics*' (= *Classical Review*, 45 (1931), pp. 162–72)

A. ROSENBERG, 'Aristoteles über Diktatur und Demokratie (*Politik* Buch III)' (= *Rheinisches Museum für Philologie*, 82 (1933), pp. 339–61)

W. SIEGFRIED, 'Zur Entstehungsgeschichte von Aristoteles' *Politik*' (= *Philologus*, 88 (1933), pp. 363–91)

D. WILLERS, 'Aufbau der aristotelischen *Politik*' (= *Neue Jahrbücher für Wissenschaft und Jugendbildung*, 9 (1933), pp. 127–32)

K. KAHLENBERG, 'Beitrag zur Interpretation des III. Buch der aristotelischen *Politik*' (= Inaugural dissertation, Friedrich-Wilhelms Universität zu Berlin, 1934)

O. GIGON, 'Einleitung zu einer Übersetzung der *Politik* des Aristoteles' (= Aristoteles, *Politik und Staat der Athener, eingeleitet und übertragen von O. G.*, Zürich, 1955, pp. 7–51)

O. LENDLE, 'Die Einleitung des dritten Buches der aristotelischen *Politika*'

W. SIEGFRIED, 'Untersuchungen zur Staatslehre des Aristoteles' (Zürich, 1942)

P. CLOCHÉ, 'Aristote et les institutions de Sparte' (= *Les Études classiques*, 11 (1942), pp. 289–313)

M. WHEELER, 'Aristotle's analysis of the nature of political struggle' (= *American Journal of Philology*, 72 (1951), pp. 145–61)

G. R. MORROW, 'Aristotle's comments on Plato's *Laws*' (= I. Düring and G. E. L. Owen (eds.), *Aristotle and Plato in the mid-fourth century*, Göteburg, 1960, pp. 145–62 (Studia Graeca et Latina Gothoburgensia XI, Proceedings of Symposium Aristotelicum, Oxford, 1957)

E. BRAUN, 'Die Summierungstheorie des Aristoteles' (= *Jahreshefte des Österreichischen Archäologischen Instituts*, 44 (1959), pp. 157–84)

E. BRAUN, 'Eine Maxime der Staatskunst in der *Politik* des Aristoteles' (= *Jahreshefte des Österreichischen Archäologischen Instituts*, 44 (1959), pp. 385–98)

E. BRAUN, 'Die Ursache der Pluralität von Verfassungsformen nach Aristoteles' (= *Wissenschaftliche Arbeiten aus dem Burgenland*, 35 (1966), pp. 57–65)

(3) *Articles on Aristotle: 2, Ethics and Politics*, ed. J. Barnes, M. Schofield and R. Sorabji (London, 1977) (invaluable annotated bibliography, with two indexes; the articles relating to the *Politics* are with one exception reprints, translated into English when necessary, and with minor changes of format; there are ten other essays, on Aristotle's ethics):

K. VON FRITZ and E. KAPP, 'The development of Aristotle's political philosophy and the concept of nature' (= the authors' *Aristotle's Constitution of Athens and Related Texts*, New York, 1950, pp. 39–66 (retitled))

W. W. FORTENBAUGH, 'Aristotle on slaves and women' (not previously published)

M. I. FINLEY, 'Aristotle and economic analysis' (= *Past and Present*, 47 (1970), pp. 3–25; repr. also in *Studies in Ancient*

Society, ed. M. I. Finley, London, 1974, and in German translation in *Jahrbuch für Wirtschaftsgeschichte*, 2 (1971), pp. 87–105)

M. WHEELER, 'Aristotle's analysis of the nature of political struggle' (= *American Journal of Philology*, 72 (1951), pp. 145–61)

H. KELSEN, 'Aristotle and Hellenic-Macedonian policy' (= pp. 16–51 (with n. 39 printed at the end as an 'additional note') of 'The philosophy of Aristotle and the Hellenic-Macedonian policy', *International Journal of Ethics*, 48 (1937–8), pp. 1–64; the article was reprinted in W. Ebenstein (ed.), *Political Thought in Perspective*, New York, 1957, pp. 56–86; full references to other appearances in G. Bien (*see above*), p. 381)

M. DEFOURNY, 'The aim of the state: peace' (= translation of id., *Aristote: Études sur la 'Politique'*, Paris, 1932, pp. 475–89)

R. WEIL, 'Aristotle's view of history' (= translation of Weil's article in the Fondation Hardt volume above)

The remaining two collections are on specialized topics:

(4) *Marxism and the Classics* (= *Arethusa*, 8.1 (1975)). (Not primarily devoted to the *Politics* or even to Aristotle, but with much relevant material and an extensive annotated bibliography)

(5) *Population Policy in Plato and Aristotle* (= *Arethusa*, 8.2 (1975))

The following sections are confined to material not contained in the five volumes listed above.

POLITICAL PHILOSOPHY

J. LAIRD, 'Hobbes on Aristotle's *Politics*', *Proceedings of the Aristotelian Society*, 43 (1942–3), pp. 1–20

G. BOAS, 'A basic conflict in Aristotle's philosophy', *American Journal of Philology*, 64 (1943), pp. 172–93

K. R. POPPER, *The Open Society and Its Enemies* (London, 1945; 5th ed. 1966), esp. II, pp. 1–26 (and notes, pp. 281ff.)

F. KORT, 'The quantification of Aristotle's theory of revolution', *The American Political Science Review*, 46 (1952), pp. 486–93

K. VON FRITZ, *The Mixed Constitution in Antiquity* (New York, 1954)

E. A. HAVELOCK, *The Liberal Temper in Greek Politics* (London, 1957), pp. 339–75

J. DE ROMILLEY, 'Le classement des constitutions d'Hérodote à Aristote', *Revue des Études Grecques*, 72 (1959), pp. 81–99

E. BRAUN, 'Aristoteles über Bürger- und Menschentugend: zu *Politica* III, 4 und 5', *Sitzungsberichte der Österreichischen Akademie der Wissenschaften*, philos.-hist. Kl., 236.2 (Wien, 1961)

M. CHAMBERS, 'Aristotle's "Forms of democracy"', *Transactions of the American Philological Association*, 92 (1961), pp. 20–36

J. BLUHM, 'The place of the "polity" in Aristotle's theory of the ideal state', *Journal of Politics*, 24 (1962), pp. 743–53

L. STRAUSS, *The City and Man* (Chicago, 1964), pp. 13–49

H. C. BALDRY, *The Unity of Mankind in Greek Thought* (Cambridge, 1965), pp. 88–101

F. D. HARVEY, 'Two kinds of equality', *Classica et Mediaevalia*, 26 (1965), pp. 101–46 (esp. p. 113 ff.), and 27 (1966), pp. 99–100

J. HINTIKKA, 'Some conceptual presuppositions of Greek political theory', *Scandinavian Political Studies*, 2 (1967), pp. 11–25

C. MOSSÉ, 'La conception du citoyen dans la *Politique* d'Aristote', *Eirene*, 6 (1967), pp. 17–21

J. PEČIRKA, 'A note on Aristotle's definition of citizenship and the role of foreigners in fourth century Athens', *Eirene*, 6 (1967), pp. 23–6

T. J. TRACY, *Physiological Theory and the Doctrine of the Mean in Plato and Aristotle* (The Hague and Paris, 1969), esp. pp. 311–26 (Studies in Philosophy 17)

R. G. MULGAN, 'Aristotle and the democratic conception of freedom', in B. F. Harris (ed.), *Auckland Classical Studies Presented to E. M. Blaiklock* (Auckland and Oxford, 1970), pp. 95–111

R. G. MULGAN, 'Aristotle's sovereign', *Political Studies*, 18 (1970), pp. 518–22

G. DOWNEY, 'Aristotle as an expert on urban problems', *Talanta*, 3 (1971), pp. 56–73

H. FLASHAR, 'Ethik und Politik in der Philosophie des Aristoteles', *Gymnasium*, 78 (1971), pp. 278–93

G. HUXLEY, 'Crete in Aristotle's Politics', *Greek, Roman and Byzantine Studies*, 12 (1971), pp. 505–15

S. CLARK, 'The use of "man's function" in Aristotle', *Ethics*, 82 (1971–2), pp. 269–83

S. CASHDOLLAR, 'Aristotle's politics of morals', *Journal of the History of Philosophy*, 11 (1973), pp. 145–60

R. DEVELIN, 'The good man and the good citizen in Aristotle's *Politics*', *Phronesis*, 18 (1973), pp. 71–9

R. A. DE LAIX, 'Aristotle's conception of the Spartan constitution', *Journal of the History of Philosophy*, 12 (1974), pp. 21–30

R. BRANDT, 'Untersuchung zur politischen Philosophie des Aristoteles', *Hermes*, 102 (1974), pp. 191–200

R. G. MULGAN, 'Aristotle's doctrine that man is a political animal', *Hermes*, 102 (1974), pp. 438–45

R. G. MULGAN, 'A note on Aristotle's absolute ruler', *Phronesis*, 19 (1974), pp. 66–9

R. G. MULGAN, 'Aristotle and absolute rule', *Antichthon*, 8 (1974), pp. 21–8

R. ZOEPFFEL, 'Aristoteles und die Demagogen', *Chiron*, 4 (1974), pp. 69–90

J. M. RIST, 'Aristotle: the value of man and the origin of morality', *Canadian Journal of Philosophy*, 4 (1974–5), pp. 1–21

F. ROSEN, 'The political context of Aristotle's categories of justice', *Phronesis*, 20 (1975), pp. 228–40.

W. MATHIE, 'Justice and the question of regimes in ancient and modern political philosophy: Aristotle and Hobbes', *Canadian Journal of Political Science*, 9 (1976), pp. 449–63

E. SCHÜTRUMPF, 'Probleme der aristotelischen Verfassungstheorie in Politik Γ', *Hermes*, 104 (1976), pp. 308–31

E. F. MILLER, 'Primary questions in political inquiry', *Review of Politics*, 39 (1977), pp. 298–331

C. J. ROWE, 'Aims and methods in Aristotle's *Politics*', *Classical Quarterly*, 27 (1977), pp. 159–72

R. MCKEON, 'Person and community: metaphysical and ethical', *Ethics*, 88 (1977–8), pp. 207–17

E. M. WOOD and N. WOOD, *Class Ideology and Ancient Political Theory: Socrates, Plato and Aristotle in Social Context* (Oxford, 1978), esp. pp. 209–57

C. LORD, 'Politics and philosophy in Aristotle's *Politics*', *Hermes*, 106 (1978), pp. 336–57

G. HUXLEY, *On Aristotle and Greek Society* (Belfast, 1979)

S. M. OKIN, *Women in Western Political Thought* (Princeton, 1979, London, 1980), pp. 73–96

E. SCHÜTRUMPF, *Die Analyse der Polis durch Aristoteles* (Amsterdam, 1980)

ECONOMICS; ARISTOTLE AND MARXISM

K. MARX, *Capital* (3rd German edition, 1883, and in various English translations), chs. I, sect. 3A3, II *ad init.*, IV *ad fin.*, V *ad fin.*

A. A. TREVER, *A History of Greek Economic Thought* (Chicago, 1916), pp. 81–124.

R. SCHLAIFER, 'Greek theories of slavery from Homer to Aristotle', *Harvard Studies in Classical Philology*, 47 (1936), pp. 165–204. (Reprinted in M. I. Finley (ed.), *Slavery in Classical Antiquity*, Cambridge and New York, 1960)

V. JOHNSON, 'Aristotle's theory of value', *American Journal of Philology*, 60 (1939), pp. 445–51

J. SOUDEK, 'Aristotle's theory of exchange', *Proceedings of the American Philosophical Society*, 96 (1952), pp. 45–75

E. KAUDER, 'Genesis of the marginal utility theory, from Aristotle to the end of the eighteenth century', *Economic Journal*, 63 (1953), pp. 638–50

J. A. SCHUMPETER, *History of Economic Analysis* (New York, 1954), pp. 57–65

J. J. SPENGLER, 'Aristotle on economic imputation and related matters', *Southern Economic Journal*, 21 (1955), pp. 371–89

K. POLANYI, 'Aristotle discovers the economy', in K. Polanyi, C. M. Arensberg and H. W. Pearson (eds.), *Trade and Market in the Early Empires* (Glencoe, Ill., 1957), pp. 69–94. (Reprinted in G. Dalton (ed.), *Primitive, Archaic and Modern Economies*, New York, 1968)

E. C. WELSKOPF, *Die Produktionsverhältnisse im alten Orient und in der griechischen-römischen Antike* (Berlin, 1957), pp. 336–46

B. J. GORDON, 'Aristotle and the development of value theory', *Quarterly Journal of Economics*, 78 (1964), pp. 115–28

W. F. R. HARDIE, *Aristotle's Ethical Theory* (Oxford, 1968; 2nd ed. 1980), pp. 195–201

E. C. WELSKOPF, 'Marx und Aristoteles', in J. Burian and L. Vidman (eds.), *Antiquitas graeco-romana et tempora nostra* (Prague, 1968), pp. 231–40

S. T. LOWRY, 'Aristotle's "natural limit" and the economics of price regulation', *Greek, Roman and Byzantine Studies*, 15 (1974), pp. 57–63

G. E. M. DE STE CROIX, 'Early Christian attitudes to property and slavery', *Studies in Church History*, 12 (1975), pp. 1–38

T. J. LEWIS, 'Aquisition and anxiety: Aristotle's case against the market', *Canadian Journal of Economics*, 11 (1978), pp. 69–90

S. MEIKLE, 'Aristotle and the political economy of the *polis*', *Journal of Hellenic Studies*, 99 (1979), pp. 57–73

G. E. M. DE STE CROIX, *The Class Struggle in the Ancient Greek World* (London, 1981), esp. chs. II iv, VII ii, iii

LAW

F. D. WORMUTH, 'Aristotle on law', in M. R. Konvitz and A. E. Murphy (eds.), *Essays in Political Theory Presented to George H. Sabine* (Cornell, 1948), pp. 45–61

M. HAMBURGER, *Morals and Law: The Growth of Aristotle's Legal Theory* (new ed. New York, 1965)

W. VON LEYDEN, 'Aristotle and the concept of law', *Philosophy*, 42 (1967), pp. 1–19

D. N. SCHROEDER, 'Aristotle on Law', *Polis*, 4 (1981), pp. 17–31

HISTORY AND HISTORIOGRAPHY

K. VON FRITZ, 'Die Bedeutung des Aristoteles für die Geschichtsschreibung' in *Histoire et historiens dans l'antiquité classique* (Geneva, 1956), pp. 83–145 (Fondation Hardt, Entretiens sur l'antiquité classique IV). (Reprinted in F.-P. Hager (ed.), *Ethik und Politik des Aristoteles*, Darmstadt, 1972, pp. 313–67 (Wege der Forschung 208))

K. VON FRITZ, 'Aristotle's contribution to the practice and theory of historiography', *University of California Publications in Philosophy*, 28 (1958), pp. 113–37

R. WEIL, *Aristote et l'histoire: essai sur la 'Politique'* (Paris, 1960) (Études et Commentaires 36)

J. DAY and M. CHAMBERS, *Aristotle's History of Athenian Democracy* (Berkeley and Los Angeles, 1962) (University of California Publications in History 73)

G. HUXLEY, 'On Aristotle's historical methods', *Greek, Roman and Byzantine Studies*, 13 (1972), pp. 157–69

G. E. M. DE STE CROIX, 'Aristotle on history and poetry (Poetics 9, 1451a36–b11)', in B. Levick (ed.), *The Ancient Historian and His Materials: Essays in Honour of C. E. Stevens on His 70th Birthday* (Farnborough, 1975), pp. 45–58

F. E. ROMER, 'The Aisymnēteia: A problem in Aristotle's historic method', *American Journal of Philology*, 103 (1982), pp. 25–46

ARISTOTLE AND MACEDONIA

V. EHRENBERG, *Alexander and the Greeks* (Oxford, 1938), 62–102

A. H. CHROUST, *Aristotle: New Light on His Life and on Some of His Lost Works*, I (Notre Dame and London, 1973), pp. 125–76. (Chapters X–XIII, versions of earlier articles, as follows: X, *Classical Folia*, I (1966), pp. 26–33; XI, *Laval théologique et philosophique*, 23 (1967), pp. 244–54; XII, *Historia*, 15 (1966), pp. 185–91; XIII, *Laval Théologique et Philosophique*, 22 (1966), pp. 186–96)

THE 'POLITICS' AND PLATO'S 'LAWS'

E. BORNEMANN, 'Aristoteles' Urteil über Platons politische Theorie', *Philologus*, 79 (1923), pp. 70–111, 113–58, 234–57

EDUCATION, THE ARTS

A. BUSSE, 'Zur Musikästhetik des Aristoteles', *Rheinisches Museum*, 77 (1928), pp. 34–50

J. L. STOCKS, 'ΣΧΟΛΗ' [Leisure], *Classical Quarterly*, 30 (1936), pp. 177–87

E. KOLLER, 'Musse und musische paideia: über die Musikaporetik in der aristotelischen *Politik*', *Museum Helveticum*, 13 (1956), pp. 1–37, 94–124

F. SOLMSEN, 'Leisure and play in Aristotle's ideal state', *Rheinisches Museum*, 107 (1964), pp. 193–220

W. D. ANDERSON, *Ethos and Education in Greek Music: The Evidence of Poetry and Philosophy* (Cambridge, Mass., 1966), pp. 111–46

C. LORD, *Education and Culture in the Political Thought of Aristotle* (Ithaca and London, 1982)

THEOLOGY AND RELIGION

W. J. VERDENIUS, 'Traditional and personal elements in Aristotle's religion', *Phronesis*, 5 (1960), pp. 56–70

GLOSSARIES

NOTES ON SCOPE AND USE

These glossaries offer not a guarantee but only a strong *likelihood* that in any passage of the *Politics* a given Greek term will have been rendered by one of the English words shown in the Greek–English list, and that conversely a given English word is the translation of the Greek terms indicated in the English–Greek list.

The glossaries are not exhaustive: in particular, (i) they concentrate on the more common terms of political, constitutional, legal, economic and social importance, with much lighter coverage of terms ethical, logical, metaphysical, psychological, artistic, epistemological and methodological; (ii) no attempt has been made to cover certain common and general notions for which Aristotle uses a wide range of apparent synonyms, e.g. the various words for 'rich', 'poor', 'type', 'necessary'.

Some terms listed are exclusively technical, but most have a wide range of ordinary non-technical usages also, which are *not* listed. E.g. *archē*: technical meanings 'rule', 'official', etc., non-technical 'beginning'; *gnōrimos*: non-technical adjective 'familiar', but also in a technical sense, 'a notable', to denote a member of a particular social and political group.

Generally, only one word from a 'set' is given, when the various forms and renderings of the rest may easily be inferred. E.g. the entry *archē*, 'rule', etc. suffices for *archein* 'to rule' and *archōn* 'ruler'; but the rendering of *archeion* as 'board' or 'committee' could not be inferred, and is therefore listed. Comparatives and superlatives of adjectives and adverbs, and passive forms of verbs, are similarly omitted.

Some of the more important departures from the equivalents shown are noted in footnotes or in the introductions to the chapters.

GREEK–ENGLISH

adikos unjust
   adikein to treat unjustly, to wrong, to do wrong, to commit crime, to be criminal

adikia   injustice, crime
agathos   good
allagē   exchange
andreia   courage
anisos   unequal
aoristos   unlimited
archē   (i) authority, rule; (ii) office, officer, official
  archeion   board, committee
aretē   virtue
aristokratia   aristocracy
aristos   best
autarkēs   self-sufficient
axia   desert, merit, value

banausos   mechanic(al)
barbaros   non-Greek
basileus   king
  basileuein   to reign
  basilikos   royal
boulē   council
  bouleuesthai   to deliberate
  bouleutikos   deliberative

chrēmata   goods, money
  chrēmatismos   business
  chrēmatistikē   acquisition of goods or wealth, money-making
  chrēmatizesthai   to acquire goods or wealth, to make money

dēmagōgos   demagogue, popular leader
dēmiourgos   workman
dēmokratia   democracy
dēmos   (i) people; (ii) democracy; (iii) deme
  dēmosios   public (*adj.*), cf. *koinos*
despotēs   master
diagōgē   civilized pursuits
dianoia   intellect, intelligence
dikaios   just, fair
  to dikaion   justice
  dikaiosunē   justice; sense of justice
  dikē   case, justice, lawsuit, penalty, trial
dikastēs   juryman, judge
doulos   slave

dunamis   capacity, faculty, function
dunasteia   power-group

ekklēsia   assembly
eleutheros   free, free man
  eleutherios   of *or* worthy of a free man, liberal
epieikēs   reasonable, respectable
epimeleia   care, concern, duty, responsibility, superintendence, supervision
ergon   function, purpose
ethnos   nation, *usually with the adjective* 'foreign'
eudaimonia   happiness
eugenēs   well- *or* nobly born
  eugeneia   good *or* noble birth
eunomia   life under, *or* government by, good laws
euthuna   account, scrutiny

genos   birth, family, race
gnōrimos   notable
grammata   written rules

hairetos   chosen by election, elected, elective
harmonia   mode (in music)
hippeis   cavalry
homoios   (a)like, similar
hoplitēs   heavy-infantryman
hubris   arrogance, arrogant ill-treatment *or simply* ill-treatment
hupothesis   assumption, principle, assumed *or* given situation

isos   equal

kalos   *a fairly wide range of commendatory words, commonly*
  fine, noble, good (*overlaps inevitably with agathos*)
kapēleia   trade
kataphronēsis   contempt
  eukataphronētos   easily despised
kerdos   profit
klēros   (i) lot; (ii) estate
koinos   common, communal, public, social, shared
  koinōnein   to associate, to participate in, to share, to be a
  member of

koinōnia association, participation, community
krisis case, choice, decision, judgement, verdict
ktēma piece *or* article of property
  ktēsis property, *in concrete sense, but esp. of its* acquisition *or* possession
kurios binding, decisive, sovereign, supreme

leitourgia public service
logos (i) reason, reasoning; (ii) ratio

menein to endure, last long, survive, be stable *or* permanent
meros part, section
  kata meros by turns
mesos middle, intermediate
  to meson the mean
metabolē change, *esp. of constitutions*
  metablētikē exchange (*of goods*)
metechein to share
monarchos monarch, single *or* sole ruler
mousikē music

nomisma coin(age), currency; money
nomos convention, enactment, law, legislation, regulation
  kata nomon legally; according to, *or* subject to, law
nomothetēs lawgiver, legislator
nous mind

oikonomia household-management
oligoi few
oligarchia oligarchy
orthos right, correct
ousia possessions

paideia education
pambasileia absolute kingship
parekbasis deviation
penesteia serfs
perioikoi peripheral population
philia affection, friendship, goodwill
  philein to be well disposed towards
philotimia ambition
phronēsis practical wisdom

phthora   destruction, dissolution
phulē   tribe
phusis   nature
plēthos   multitude, populace; bulk *or* mass (of citizens, people, population, etc., according to context)
polis   state
   politeia   (i) constitution; (ii) polity; (iii) *Republic* (Plato's)
   politēs   citizen
   politeuesthai   *expressions such as* to administer, operate *or* live under, a constitution; to engage in politics *or* affairs of state; to live, *or* function as a citizen *or* statesman, in a state
   politeuma   citizen-body
   politikē   statesmanship
   politikos   (i) statesman; (ii) to do with, affecting, appropriate in, a citizen, state, statesman, constitution, polity; political
polloi   many, masses
praxis   act, action, activity, deed, practice
proboulos   pre-councillor
prostatēs   champion
prutanis   president
psēphisma   decree
psuchē   soul

scholē   leisure, time off
sōphrosunē   restraint, self-control
sōtēria   maintaining, preservation, safety, stability
spoudaios   sound, worthy
stasis   faction
stratēgos   general (n.)
sussitia   common meals, refectories

technē   skills, technique
   technitēs   skilled worker
telos   end
thēs   hired worker, hireling
timē   esteem, distinction, honour, value
timēma   property-class, -assessment, -qualification
turannos   tyrant

ENGLISH–GREEK

account   *euthuna*
act, action, activity   *praxis*
affection   *philia*
(a)like   *homoios*
ambition   *philotimia*
aristocracy   *aristokratia*
arrogance, arrogant ill-treatment   *hubris*
assembly   *ekklēsia*
association   see *koin-* set
assumption, assumed situation   *hupothesis*
authority   *archē*

best   *aristos*
binding   *kurios*
birth   *genos*
board   *archeion*
bulk (of the people, etc.)   *plēthos*
business   *chrēmatismos*

capacity   *dunamis*
care   *epimeleia*
case (legal)   *dikē, krisis*
cavalry   *hippeis*
champion   *prostatēs*
change (n.), esp, of constitutions   *metabolē*
choice   *krisis*
citizen   *politēs*
citizen-body   *politeuma*
civilized pursuits   *diagōgē*
coin(age)   *nomisma*
committee   *archeion*
common   see *koin-* set
common meals   *sussitia*
communal, community   see *koin-* set
concern   *epimeleia*
constitution   *politeia*
contempt   *kataphronēsis*
convention   *nomos*
correct   *orthos*

courage   *andreia*
crime   *adikia*
criminal (be), commit crimes   *adikein*
currency   *nomisma*

decision   *krisis*
decisive   *kurios*
decree   *psēphisma*
deed   *praxis*
deliberate (v.)   *bouleuesthai*
  deliberative   *bouleutikos*
demagogue   *dēmagōgos*
deme   *dēmos*
democracy   *dēmokratia, dēmos*
desert   *axia*
despised, easily   *eukataphronētos*
destruction   *phthora*
deviation   *parekbasis*
dissolution   *phthora*
distinction (*i.e.* honour, *etc.*)   *timē*
duty   *epimeleia*

education   *paideia*
elected, elective, chosen by election   *hairetos*
enactment   *nomos*
end   *telos*
endure   *menein*
equal   *isos*
estate   *klēros*
esteem   *timē*
exchange   *allagē, metablētikē*

faction   *stasis*
faculty   *dunamis*
fair   *dikaios*
family   *genos*
few   *oligoi*
fine   *kalos*
free, free man   *eleutheros*
  of *or* worthy of a free man   *eleutherios*
friendship   *philia*
function   *dunamis, ergon*

495

general (n.) *stratēgos*
given situation *hupothesis*
good *agathos* (usually, but see also *kalos*)
good *or* noble birth *eugeneia*
good laws: government by *or* life under *eunomia*
goods *chrēmata*
  acquisition of goods *chrēmatistikē*
  to acquire goods *chrēmatizesthai*
goodwill *philia*

happiness *eudaimonia*
heavy-infantryman *hoplitēs*
hired worker, hireling *thēs*
household-management *oikonomia*

ill-treatment, arrogant ill-treatment *hubris*
injustice *adikia*
intellect, intelligence *dianoia*
intermediate *mesos*

judge, juryman *dikastēs*
judgement *krisis*
just *dikaios*
justice *to dikaion, dikē*
  sense of justice *dikaiosunē*

king *basileus*
kingship, absolute *pambasileia*

last long *menein*
law *nomos*
lawgiver *nomothetēs*
lawsuit *dikē*
legally *kata nomon*
legislation *nomos*
legislator *nomothetēs*
leisure *scholē*
liberal *eleutherios*
lot *klēros*
  selected *or* chosen *or* appointed *or* filled, by lot *klērōtos*

maintaining (n.) *sōtēria*
many *polloi*
mass (of the people, *etc.*) *plēthos*
master (of slaves) *despotēs*
mean, the *to meson*
mechanic(al) *banausos*
member see *koin-* set
merit *axia*
middle *mesos*
mind *nous*
mode (in music) *harmonia*
monarch *monarchos*
money *chrēmata*; *nomisma* (esp. coinage)
  money-making (n.) *chrēmatistikē*
    to make money *chrēmatizesthai*
multitude *plēthos*
music *mousikē*

nation, foreign nation *ethnos*
nature *phusis*
noble *kalos*
nobly born *eugenēs*
non-Greek *barbaros*
notable *gnōrimos*

office, officer, official *archē*
oligarchy *oligarchia*

part *meros*
participation see *koin-* set
penalty *dikē*
people *dēmos*
peripheral population *perioikoi*
permanent, be *menein*
political *politikos*
polity *politeia*
populace *plēthos*
popular leader *dēmagōgos*
possessions *ousia*
power-group *dunasteia*
practical wisdom *phronēsis*
practice *praxis*

497

pre-councillor *proboulos*
preservation *sōtēria*
president *prutanis*
principle *hupothesis*
profit *kerdos*
property *ktēsis*
  piece *or* article of property *ktēma*
property-class, -assessment, -qualification *timēma*
public *dēmosios,* and see *koin-* set
public service *leitourgia*
purpose *ergon*

race *genos*
ratio *logos*
reason, reasoning *logos*
reasonable *epieikēs*
refectories *sussitia*
regulation *nomos*
reign (v.) *basileuein*
Republic (Plato's) *politeia*
respectable *epieikēs*
responsibility *epimeleia*
restraint *sōphrosunē*
right (adj.) *orthos*
royal *basilikos*
rule(n.) *archē*

safety *sōtēria*
scrutiny *euthuna*
section *meros*
self-control *sōphrosunē*
self-sufficient *autarkēs*
serfs *penesteia*
share (v.) *metechein*
shared see *koin-* set
similar *homoios*
single *or* sole ruler *monarchos*
situation (assumed or given) *hupothesis*
skill *technē*
  skilled worker *technitēs*
slave *doulos*
social see *koin-* set

soul   *psuchē*
sound   *spoudaios*
sovereign   *kurios*
stability   *sōtēria*
stable, be   *menein*
state   *polis*
    statesman   *politikos*
    statesmanship   *politikē*
superintendence   *epimeleia*
supervision   *epimeleia*
supreme   *kurios*
survive   *menein*

technique   *technē*
time off   *scholē*
trade   *kapēleia*
treat unjustly   *adikein*
trial   *dikē*
tribe   *phulē*
turns, by   *kata meros*
tyrant   *turannos*

unequal   *anisos*
unjust   *adikos*
unlimited   *aoristos*

value   *axia*
verdict   *krisis*
virtue   *aretē*

wealth, acquisition of   *chrēmatistikē*
  to acquire wealth   *chrēmatizesthai*
well-born   *eugenēs*
well disposed (be) towards   *philein*
workman   *dēmiourgos*
worthy   *spoudaios*
written rules   *grammata*
wrong (v.), do wrong   *adikein*

INDEX OF NAMES

This index covers the translation and the Greek names in the footnotes and in the italicized prefaces to the chapters; it does *not* cover the two Introductions. References to Aristotle's works, other than the *Politics*, are included; but Aristotle himself, who occurs *passim*, is not; nor, for the same reason, are 'Greece' and 'Greek', except when the 'Greeks' collectively are contrasted with 'non-Greeks'.

MORE ABOUT PENGUINS, PELICANS
AND PUFFINS

For further information about books available from Penguins please write to Dept EP, Penguin Books Ltd, Harmondsworth, Middlesex UB7 0DA.

In the U.S.A.: For a complete list of books available from Penguins in the United States write to Dept DG, Penguin Books, 299 Murray Hill Parkway, East Rutherford, New Jersey 07073.

In Canada: For a complete list of books available from Penguins in Canada write to Penguin Books Canada Ltd, 2801 John Street, Markham, Ontario L3R 1B4.

In Australia: For a complete list of books available from Penguins in Australia write to the Marketing Department, Penguin Books Australia Ltd, P.O. Box 257, Ringwood, Victoria 3134.

In New Zealand: For a complete list of books available from Penguins in New Zealand write to the Marketing Department, Penguin Books (N.Z.) Ltd, P.O. Box 4019, Auckland 10.

In India: For a complete list of books available from Penguins in India write to Penguin Overseas Ltd, 706 Eros Apartments, 56 Nehru Place, New Delhi 110019.

Aristotle in Penguin Classics

ETHICS

Translated by J. A. K. Thomson

Aristotle (384–322 B.C.), probably the greatest teacher who ever lived, surveyed in his *Ethics* the ends to which conduct should be directed. The importance of this work to a modern reader lies in Aristotle's boldness in introducing psychology into his study of human behaviour. He extended the frontiers of philosophy to include universal science, by converting ethics from a theoretical to a practical science, based on a careful observation of life and a genuine understanding of human nature.

and

ARISTOTLE HORACE LONGINUS
Classical Literary Criticism

Translated by T. S. Dorsch

The power of poets has always been recognized – and often feared. Plato would have banned them from his ideal republic; other thinkers, fascinated by poetic genius, have tried to understand it. This volume contains three famous classical discussions of creative writing: Aristotle's *Poetics*, the *Ars Poetica* of Horace, and the treatise *On the Sublime* (long, though falsely, attributed to Longinus). These 'sacred books' of literary criticism have been the source of much subsequent appreciation of literature.

Plato in Penguin Classics

THE REPUBLIC

Translated by Desmond Lee

Here Plato attempts to apply the principles of his philosophy to political affairs. Ostensibly a discussion on the nature of Justice, *The Republic* lays before us Plato's vision of the ideal state, and includes some of his most important writing on the nature of reality and the theory of the 'forms'.

THE LAWS

Translated by T. J. Saunders

The rigours of life in Plato's utopian Republic are not much tempered here, but *The Laws*, depicting a society permeated by the rule of law, is a much more practical approach to Plato's ideal.

THE SYMPOSIUM

Translated by Walter Hamilton

This masterpiece of dramatic dialogue is set at a dinner party to which are invited several of the literary celebrities of Athenian society. After dinner, it is proposed that each member of the company should make a speech in praise of love.

GORGIAS

Translated by Walter Hamilton

Although Gorgias was a Sicilian teacher of oratory, the dialogue is more concerned with ethics than with the art of public speaking. Its chief interest lies less in Gorgias' courteous outline of his art than in the clash between Socrates, the true philosopher, and Callicles, a young Athenian of the stamp of Alcibiades, who brashly maintains that might is right.

Plato in Penguin Classics

TIMAEUS AND CRITIAS
Translated by Desmond Lee

In the *Timaeus*, and its unfinished sequel the *Critias*,
Plato attempted a scientific explanation of the universe's origin. The two works form the earliest Greek
account of a divine creation, and they have latterly
attracted considerable attention as the source of the
Atlantis legend.

THE LAST DAYS OF SOCRATES
Translated by Hugh Tredennick

The trial and condemnation of Socrates, on charges of
heresy and corrupting the minds of the young, forms
one of the most tragic episodes in the history of Athens
in decline. In the four works which form this volume –
Euthyphro, The Apology, Crito and *Phaedo* – Plato, his
most devoted disciple, has preserved for us the essence
of his teaching.

PROTAGORAS AND MENO
Translated by W. K. C. Guthrie

Protagoras, possibly Plato's dramatic masterpiece of dialogue, deals, like *Meno*, with the problem of teaching
the art of successful living and good citizenship. While
Protagoras keeps to the level of practical commonsense,
Meno leads on into the heart of Plato's philosophy, the
immortality of the soul and the doctrine that learning
is knowledge acquired before birth.

PHAEDRUS & LETTERS VII AND VIII
Translated by Walter Hamilton

In *Phaedrus*, Plato attempts to establish the principles
of rhetoric, arguing that rhetoric is only acceptable as
an art when it is firmly based on the truth inspired by
love. The two letters included in this volume offer a
fascinating glimpse into the contemporary power
struggle in Sicily, and evidence Plato's failure to put
into practice his theory of the philospher king.